The Reluctant Film Art of

WOODY ALLEN

Peter J. Bailey

THE UNIVERSITY PRESS OF KENTUCKY

Publication of this volume was made possible in part by a grant from the National Endowment for the Humanities.

Editorial and Sales Offices: The University Press of Kentucky
663 South Limestone Street, Lexington, Kentucky 40508–4008

07 06 05 04 03   5 4 3 2 1

Library of Congress Cataloging-in-Publication Data
Bailey, Peter J., 1946-
   The reluctant film art of Woody Allen / Peter J. Bailey.
   p. cm.
   Includes index.
   ISBN 0-8131-9041-X (pbk.: alk. paper)
   1. Allen, Woody–Criticism and interpretation. I. Title.

PN1998.3.A45 B35 2000
791.43'092–dc21   00-028308

For Frances Weller Bailey,

the constancy and magnitude of whose loyalty to me and to the completion of *The Reluctant Film Art* is so lacking in the depictions of wives and husbands in Woody Allen's films as to account almost singlehandedly for so many of these movies culminating in such disheartening resolutions.

Contents

Acknowledgments

Photofest provided the stills used in this book; Ron Mandelbaum was very helpful in making Photofest's trove of Woodiana available to me. Thanks to St. Lawrence University for providing support for this project in the form of sabbatical leave and research grants. It has been my privilege to teach at St. Lawrence for two decades, and I owe the college administration, my faculty colleagues, and my students a debt of gratitude for jointly providing me with such a richly satisfying academic career. The manuscript for *The Reluctant Film Art* benefited from critiques generously provided by friends, colleagues, and relatives: Thomas L. Berger, Shakespearean bibliographer and owner/player/manager of the English Department football team; Jackson Cope, mentor, *amico,* and intellectual inspiration; David Shields, novelist, pop culturist, former running companion, and continuing editor and literary confidant; and Lucretia B. Yaghjian, professor of theological writing and lifelong practitioner of "acceptance, forgiveness, and love." Frances Weller Bailey brought substantial knowledge of film technique and history to her extended critiques of the manuscript, benevolently excusing my penchant for reading the history of film as if it reached its culmination in Woody Allen movies.

The Reluctant
Film Art of

WOODY
ALLEN

That Old Black Magic

Woody Allen's Ambivalent Artistry

Deconstructing Harry opens with what is probably the raunchiest joke Woody Allen has committed to film. Ken (Richard Benjamin) and his sister-in-law, Leslie (Julia Louis-Dreyfus) are having an affair; while their respective families are down by the lake enjoying a picnic, the lovers are inside his house, copulating. Enter Leslie's blind grandmother. "Come," she bids Leslie, "lead me down to the lake." Having no idea what the couple is doing, Grandma cheerfully engages Ken in a discussion of the merits of martini garnishes. He eventually achieves a clamorous orgasm, prompting Grandma to comment, "Boy, you must *really* love onions!"

The most significant element of this visual joke is that the viewer only gradually realizes that the scene is not Woody Allen's one-liner but Harry Block's—that it's a visualization of a scene from his recent novel. As so often happens in Allen's films, this projection of the protagonist's art provokes laughs while epitomizing its maker's personality: Harry, we will find, is as willing to sacrifice the people in his life for a laugh as he is to sacrifice his characters. In addition to exposing the character of Harry's art (which might be described as a darkly eroticized, cynical exaggeration of Allen's), this dramatized excerpt of Harry's novel creates an aura of self-consciousness about the making of art, a sort of teasing artistic self-referentiality never completely absent from Allen's films. The likelihood that this mediation effectively absolves Allen of the gag's crudity by transferring culpability to a fictional novelist is small: so unrelenting is *Deconstructing Harry*'s indictment of artists that Allen can't help tarring himself with his film's unsparing brush. *Deconstructing Harry*, he told John Lahr while shooting the film, is "about a nasty, shallow, superficial, sexually obsessed guy. I'm sure that everybody will think—I know this going in—that it's me."[1] Allen's purpose was to insist that Harry is not him, but as the film's incriminations accumulate against this artist who, by his own admission, doesn't "care about the real world" but cares "only about the world of fiction," the viewer's confidence in the absolute distinction between screenwriter/director Allen and his novelist/protagonist precipitously declines. A film about an author who literally cannibalizes his life and heedlessly exploits his friends and lovers for material for fiction constitutes dubious testimony for the incommensurability of life and art.

The earliest of the movie's many accusations of literary exploitation against Harry is delivered by Lucy (Judy Davis), a former sister-in-law of Harry's upon whom he has modeled Leslie and with whom he's had a now-terminated lusty affair. Brandishing Harry's just-published novel, Lucy arrives at his apartment in a rage. "You're so self-engrossed, you don't give a shit who you destroy," she rants at him. "You didn't care enough to disguise anything."

"It was loosely based on us," Harry objects, sounding remarkably like Allen defending his screenplay for *Husbands and Wives,*[2] but Lucy won't be mollified: "I was there—I know how loosely based it was . . . And now, two years [after our affair's ending], your latest magnum opus emerges from this sewer of an apartment where you take everyone's suffering and turn it into gold, into literary gold. You take everyone's misery—you even cause them misery—and mix your fucking alchemy and turn it into gold, like some sort of black magician."[3]

Lucy's denunciation has two things in common with the numerous other impeachments of art and artists pervading Allen's films. Her description of his art as a form of black magic aligns her critique with the numerous Allen movies—*Shadows and Fog* being the most obvious—in which art is allegorically configured as a form of magic act. Additionally, her charge that Harry's fiction "spins gold out of human misery" invokes the necessary parasitism of art upon life, the quality of aesthetic vampirism dramatized in the fictional authorial self-incriminations of Philip Roth (*The Counterlife* and *Operation Shylock*)[4] and in Raymond Carver's "Intimacy."[5] *Deconstructing Harry* intentionally inflates the corruptness of artist Harry Block for comic effect; nonetheless, the film constitutes a fully appropriate coda for Allen's career precisely because of its extravagantly exaggerated censure of a life dedicated to and obsessed with art. The most unequivocally peevish of Allen's depictions of artists, *Deconstructing Harry* represents less a new direction for Allen than a concentrated dramatic reprisal of his previous films' indictments against them.

In *Stardust Memories,* Allen's sourest portrait of the artist before *Harry,* one of those attending a screening of Sandy Bates's film-in-progress articulates a particularly cynical view of cinematic art in dismissing the work of Bates and other filmmakers: "His insights are shallow and morbid," Bates's producer, Walsh (Laraine Newman) insists, employing terms Allen not infrequently applies to himself, "I've seen it all before. They try to document their private suffering and fob it off as art."[6] The fact that Walsh, like all the figures in this most surreal of Allen's films, often seems less a distinct individual than a projection of Bates's personal self-incriminations effectively reinforces the charge of solipsism with which Bates, the unstably demoralized artist, indicts himself throughout the film. Nonetheless, the possibility that artists are merely "documenting their personal suffering and fobbing it off as art" appears sufficiently often in Allen's films to seem an issue he hasn't resolved for himself, one which is at least in part responsible for his intransigently skeptical, highly conflictual attitude toward his own art. That ambivalence, so repeatedly dramatized in the content of his films and so often contested by their visual calculation, their formal balance and symmetry, is the central tension of Allen's cinematic art, one obliquely summarized by a psychoanalyst in one of Harry Block's stories. Assessing the fiction of her former patient and current husband, Helen Epstein (Demi Moore) explains that "What one comes away with is your total isolation, your fear of people, your panic over closeness, and that's why your real life is so chaotic and your writing is so much more controlled and stable." Although it may be risky to identify Allen too closely with the psyche of an artist fabricated by Harry Block, a fictional character in one of Allen's films, this much can be asserted: each Woody Allen film from *Play It Again, Sam* onward constitutes the director's highly self-conscious reconfiguring of the relationship between the chaos of experience and the stabilizing, controlling capacities of aesthetic rendering. Delineating and illuminating the evolution of that tension through Allen's movies is the primary objective of this study. Accordingly, the Woody Allen who emerges from it is a devotedly Modernist filmmaker, whose movies gravitate incessantly—if reluctantly—toward the interrogation of their own conditions of postmodernist skepticism, disillusionment, and narcissistic self-reflexivity.

In *Manhattan,* the first of Allen's films to dramatize the cultural decline from Modernist ideality to postmodernist circumscription, Isaac Davis's ex-wife offers a denigratory take on the artistic enterprise similar to Walsh's. Her book documenting the collapse of their marriage punctures her ex-husband's artistic pretensions by revealing that Isaac "longed to be an artist but balked at the necessary sacrifices. In his most private moments, he spoke of his fear of death, which he elevated to tragic heights when, in fact, it was mere narcissism."[7]

The artistic impulse among Allen's creators is never undefiled by narcissism, the most extreme exemplar of this attribute being Cheech, the mob hit man/dramatist of *Bullets Over Broadway.* Because he's convinced that she's "a horrible actress" who is butchering the lines of dialogue he contributes to David Shayne's play, Cheech executes Olive, thereby pushing his refusal to compromise his artistic principles to a homicidal extreme which none of this film's—or any other Allen film's—artists can approach. Although less murderous, Harry Block is little more sympathetic, his fiction constituting nothing but exploitations of and predations upon those he is supposed to love, the art he produces representing his primary means of feeding his rapacious ego. As his analyst, echoing Epstein's analyst, summarizes Harry's work, "You expect the world to adjust to the distortion you've become."

Over the course of Allen's thirty years in filmmaking, art and its valorization as a source of meaning to justify human existence have come progressively under assault on both thematic and formal levels. His movies constitute a veritable population explosion of artists and artists *manqué:* filmmakers, novelists, playwrights, an interior decorator, musicians, magicians and other circus performers, memoirists, poets, literary and art critics, screenwriters, and television producers proliferate throughout his oeuvre; their preponderance attests to Allen's preoccupation with human lives, like his own, dedicated to the production of art. As if in corroboration of the line he borrows from Groucho Marx for the opening of *Annie Hall*—"I would never wanna belong to any club that would have someone like me for a member"[8]—the artists in Allen's movies are consistently depicted as self-obsessed individuals whose ultimate commitment to their art is indistinguishable from neurosis and whose obsession with gaining an audience is frequently attended by an utter indifference to the effect their work might have on the lives of the audience they attract. Accordingly, the art they create often constitutes a sentimental falsification of actuality or a repudiation of the very thing it was created to chronicle—life. At his most forgiving, Allen portrays art as an all-too-human means of imbuing existence's random succession with the consolation of beginning-middle-end sequentiality and purposefulness. In more skeptical moods, he depicts it as the projection of the maker's narcissism, or—most critically— as a medium the pursuit of and devotion to which becomes a high-minded excuse for the withdrawal from human contact and responsibility. Harry Block's sister, Doris, could be characterizing a number of Allen's artists in her indictment of her brother: "You have no values—your whole life is nihilism, it's cynicism, it's sarcasm and orgasm."

At the opposite end of Allen's artist spectrum are those protagonists who desperately seek but fail to locate any artistic capacity in themselves. They are victims of the American cultural privileging of the artistic, characters who, like Frederick Exley's eponymous protagonist, could acknowledge that "Whether or not I am a writer, I have—and this is my curse and my virtue— cultivated the instinct of one . . . without, in my unhappy case, [possessing] the ability to harness and articulate" that instinct.[9] Joey in *Interiors,* Lane in *September* and the title protagonist of *Alice* are the most obvious of Allen's characters who perceive their artistic deficiency as a deficiency of self, as evidence of interior emptiness. The most fortunate of the three, Alice Tate, ultimately repudiates her artistic ambitions in favor of "raising my children with the right values . . . exposing them to the things that matter most."[10] Those things clearly don't include the corruptions to which artistic ambition is vulnerable. Choosing life over art is a constant temptation not only for Allen's artistically challenged protagonists but for his most successful artists as well, his later films coming increasingly to affirm the art of life over the life of art. "I'll never be the artist you are," Harry's Luciferian alter-ego, Larry (Billy Crystal) tells him after marrying Fay (Elisabeth Shue), Harry's former lover, in *Deconstructing Harry:* "You put your life into your work; I put it into my life. I can make her happier."

Those Allen protagonists who manage to move successfully from expressive paralysis to artistic creation consistently create human difficulties for themselves in the process. In *Hannah and Her Sisters,* the first script Holly writes once she's abandoned her abortive acting career reflects self-indulgent exploitation of others similar to that with which Walsh impugns Bates's film and which characterizes Harry Block's "art." The play she "writes" is basically an elaborate appropriation of intimate family history: Holly defends as "a made-up story" derived from the "essence" of Hannah's marriage "blown up into drama,"[11] her narrative constructed largely out of Lee's knowledge of the marriage gained through the affair she's having with Elliot. Repeatedly in Allen's films, artistic impulse and human relations are set at odds with one another, the devotion to art either disrupting existing relations, as in *Hannah and Her Sisters,* or preventing the formation of families. Alice Tate is not the only would-be artist in Allen's films to renounce art in the name of family: "A family," affirms Paul, the circus artist of *Shadows and Fog,* "is death to an artist."[12] Like David Shayne in *Bullets,* Paul commits himself to marriage and children only after he has forsworn his artistic ambitions. Clearly, for someone who has devotedly turned out on average a film a year since 1970, Allen has used that work to articulate and dramatize a remarkably skeptical attitude toward the value of art to human beings. A scene in *Play It Again, Sam* nicely epitomizes this dismissive attitude: Linda Christie's response to the art museum she and Alan Felix are walking through is "Do you realize we're in a room that holds some of the highest achievements of Western Civilization?" Felix replies, "There's no girls."[13] Much of Allen's work evokes a similarly derisive perception of art's deficient relationship to life, the critique of *vissi d'arte* having become progressively pervasive in his movies. From *Play It Again, Sam* forward, Allen's films often constitute a personal debate he's waging with himself about the premises, promises, and capacities of art, and about the price exacted upon the artist and those around her/him for the commitment to it.

Lest that personal debate seem a purely intellectual or artistic contention, this book demonstrates that the crisis of attitude toward aesthetics consistently played out in Allen's films has serious implications in terms of the evolution of his own career. It's a testament to his honesty and integrity as an artist (and to the turmoil of his not-so-private life in the early 1990s) that Allen has painted himself into the aesthetic corner he has. His films have expressed such growing skepticism toward the possibilities of art as to make its creation increasingly problematic for him, so intently and single-mindedly has he narrowed the values of the artistic enterprise to which he enacts annual allegiance. In thematic terms, he has repeatedly dramatized artists as egotists whose products, at best, provide audiences either with images of impossible glamour to which they become addicted (*The Purple Rose of Cairo*) or an illusory solace about existence (*Shadows and Fog*). At worst, their creative spark is—according to the testimony of the doctor in *Shadows and Fog* and the example of hit-man-turned-playwright Cheech—indistinguishable from that impulse which prompts a psychopath to commit murder.

Nor is the impulse to create art in Allen's films free of even more demeaning associations. "You can't control life—it doesn't wind up perfectly," Sandy Bates proclaims in *Stardust Memories.* "Only art you can control—art and masturbation, two areas in which I am an absolute expert" (p. 335). The price of control in both art and masturbation, Bates's comparison implies, is the diminution of life. Bates's likening of art to onanism is reinforced by his mother's forthright acknowledgment that when "The Great Sandy" as a boy practiced his art of magic alone in his room, his "paraphernalia" included photos of naked women. "It causes him great guilt," Bates's analyst abruptly responds to The Great Sandy's mother's admission, the shrink never quite clarifying whether magic tricks—Allen's favorite shorthand for artworks— or his solitary pleasures are the source of this guilt. "I don't know if I can cure him," the analyst complains, "I've been treating him for years already" (p. 303)—the same years in which Bates has been practicing the therapy of artistic creation.

In Allen's films, the magic of art is indicted not only for its confluences with self-abuse, but also for what it fails to achieve. Harry Block's analyst responds to one of Harry's patient's confessions by asking, "So writing saved your life?"—a question which *Deconstructing Harry* answers with a broad, equivocal irony. In fact, Allen's films consistently oppose the Modernist conception of the existence-redeeming capacities of art. A nurse in the closing fantasia of *Stardust Memories* articulates Bates's consummate artistic self-reproach: "All those silly magic tricks you do couldn't help your friend Nat Bernstein" (p. 364) who died suddenly of Lou Gehrig's disease. As the failure of Irmstedt's magic in *Shadows and Fog* demonstrates, art is helpless before the power of death. For Allen, as for many of his disaffected Modernist artist-personas, it is art's specific impotency in the face of death which constitutes art's irremediable and unforgivable insufficiency.

As if concurring in Bates's analyst's implication that artistic creation is indistinguishable from neurosis, David Shayne, in the concluding scene of *Bullets Over Broadway,* repudiates his playwright's vocation with the enthusiasm of someone cured of delusions. No Allen film, in fact, projects a positive conciliation of the conflict which the characters in *Bullets* repeatedly invoke in debating whether a woman loves "the artist or the man," the meeting ground between the two being consistently dramatized as a site of corruption for both.

Significantly, the farther the Woody Allen protagonist is from being an artist, the more likely is his narrative to result in a happy ending. Filmmaker Clifford Stern of *Crimes and Misdemeanors,* novelists Gabe Roth of *Husbands and Wives* and Harry Block of *Deconstructing Harry,* screenwriter Lee Simon of *Celebrity,* and jazz guitarist Emmet Ray of *Sweet and Lowdown* wind up desolate and solitary, largely because of the egocentric, elitist, and exploitative attitudes embedded in their art and the effects of those attitudes on those around them. On the other hand, unpretentious, thoroughly inartistic Leonard Zelig dies an untroubled, even happy death only slightly compromised by his failure to finish reading *Moby-Dick,* while the extravagantly unaesthetic Danny Rose—primarily as a result of his altruistic devotion to his utterly artless night-club acts—is the beneficiary of the most gratifying resolution Allen has scripted. Arguably, Alice Tate, Leonard Zelig, and Danny Rose comprise the one club Allen would like to join, but he's too much the artist to be admitted.

In *Shadows and Fog,* a roustabout who works in the circus for which a magician is the featured act effusively extols the prestidigitory abilities of "The Great Irmstedt": "Oh yes," he exults, "*everyone* loves his illusions!" The career-spanning debate Allen conducts with himself in his films over the effects, upon audience and artist alike, of the aesthetic illusions he has created and projected upon movie screens leaves real questions as to whether he loves the illusions he has created, or whether he thinks his audience should feel grati-tude toward him for conjuring them. By and large, however, Allen's continu-ing film-by-film interrogation of the value of the cinematic illusions he projects and upon which his professional reputation rests constitutes the basis of his status as a major American filmmaker—and artist.

That debate Allen is conducting with himself does not take place solely on the plot level of his films. As he has become increasingly skilled in the art of filmmaking, Allen has become progressively aware of his movies as synthetic visions, as fictions of affirmation or negation, as cinematic projections which embrace and/or celebrate a cheerful unreality *(A Midsummer Night's Sex Com-edy, Alice, Everyone Says I Love You)* or which present grimly naturalistic depic-tions of actuality *(Interiors, Another Woman, September),* or—most commonly—as filmic narratives that constitute an offbeat commingling of the two. Sandy Bates insists in *Stardust Memories* that he doesn't "want to make funny movies anymore . . . you know, I don't feel funny. I-I look around the world and all I see is human suffering" (p. 286). Although several of Allen's own films are reflective of such a determination, he has never settled there for long; the relentlessly somber *Interiors* was followed up by the mixed modali-ties of *Manhattan,* while the prevailing bleak introspectiveness of *Stardust Memories* seemed to spawn the fluffy pastoral romp of *A Midsummer Night's Sex Comedy* as a cinematic rejoinder. It can be argued that the most effective of Allen's movies are those that explore a middle ground between unrelenting dramatic gravity and comedy: films which enact a dramatic cinematic com-promise between fantasy and reality, between—to cite the central tension of *Shadows and Fog*—the magic of the circus and the existential necessities of the town, between comic affirmation and pessimistic negation. Danny Rose's philosophy of life is essentially indistinguishable from Allen's post-*Bananas* philosophy of filmmaking: "It's important to have some laughs, no question about it, but you got to suffer a little, too. Because otherwise, you miss the whole point of life."[14]

A corollary antinomy pervading Allen's filmmaking career involves the identification of his movies as comic inconsequentialities vs. the recognition of Allen as a creator of serious cinematic art. The substantial amount of criticism published on Allen's work has, of course, established the deliberately self-conscious and complexly self-reflective quality of his literary texts and films. Examples abound: *Play It Again, Sam* (in which a movie character named Allan Felix emulates the style of another movie character, Rick Blaine of *Casablanca*); "The Kugelmass Episode" (in which the protagonist has an affair with Emma Bovary in the pages of Flaubert's novel); *The Purple Rose of Cairo* (in which a movie matinee idol emerges from the silver screen to court a moviegoer in Depression America); *Mighty Aphrodite* (in which a chorus leader from Greek tragedy becomes a convert to the belief that "life is unbelievable, miraculous, sad, wonderful"[15]). Allen's most and least serious work has reveled in transgressing the boundaries between literature and life, in problematizing the distinction between fiction and fact, in complicating definitions of image and self. Allen critics such as Diane Jacobs, Nancy Pogel, Graham McCann, Sam B. Girgus, and others have clearly established how appropriate it is to consider Allen's work in the context of self-reflexive artists such as dramatists Chekhov, Pirandello, or Tennessee Williams, or filmmakers Godard, Fellini, Bunuel, or Bergman. Thanks to the work of these critics, it is no longer necessary for later Allen critics to justify his films as being completely deserving of serious, detailed critical examination. What their studies have succeeded more equivocally in accomplishing is delineating the points in his movies when serious artistic purpose is clearly distinguishable from Woody Allen *shtick*. Consequently, Sandy Bates isn't the only person whose attempt to distinguish between art and life results inevitably in self-consciousness and a self-mocking confession of self-abuse: it seems an inescapable experience of Woody Allen critics that our attempts to illuminate his films leave us occasionally making so much of a one-liner that the joke seems to be on us.[16]

The prevalence in Allen's movies of one-liners like Bates's convergence of art with masturbation invokes another tradition into which Allen's work fits even more comfortably than it does among canonical works of drama and film: the American comedic tradition, exemplified for him principally by the films of Charlie Chaplin, Buster Keaton, the Marx Brothers, and Bob Hope. That Allen's work is animated by a tension between high-culture sophistication and low-culture comedy explains, for one thing, why so many of his jokes—Bates's included—are predicated upon the prototypical Jewish American humor ploy of deflating profundity through puncturing it with the incongruously trivial. (A classic example is "'God is silent,' [Needleman] was fond of saying, 'now if we can only get Man to shut up'"[17]; another is Mickey Sachs's refusal in *Hannah* to embrace the Nietzschean notion of the eternal return because it would commit him to attending the Ice Capades again.) This crucial conflict accounts as well for the oddly hybrid, or in-between, quality of so many of his later films spanning seriousness and humor. Given the characteristic generic intermediacy of so many of his films, it's only appropriate that middle grounds turn out to be a place in which Allen's protagonists often find themselves.

The narrator of the comic essay, "My Apology," imagines himself as Socrates but finally has to admit, "I'm not a coward, and I'm not a hero. I'm somewhere in the middle."[18] Alfred Miller, the blacklisted writer for whom Howard Prince (Allen) is fronting in *The Front*, tells Prince, "You're always looking for a middle you can dance around in."[19] Isaac Davis tells Tracy in *Manhattan* that she's of the drugs-and-television generation, while he's World War II; when she objects that he was eight during the war, he acknowledges that "I wasn't in the trenches, I was caught in the middle. It was a very tough position."[20] In *Shadows and Fog*, Kleinman is asked by one of those who have devised a plan to trap the killer terrorizing the town, "Are you with us or against us?" Kleinman, who characterizes himself as the only person in town without a plan, replies, "I don't know—because I don't have enough information." "You have to choose," is his townsman's Kafkaesque admonition.

In characterizing Jewish humor, Stephen J. Whitfield found it to have at its heart a similar quality of in-betweenness:

> Heinrich Heine, along with Ludwig Boerne, is credited with the invention of the German feuilleton, the casual humorous monologue in which Jews have excelled, from the Viennese café wits to S.J. Perelman and Woody Allen. Heine helped to transmit to Jews who came after him the pertinence of irony, the prism of double and multiple meanings simultaneously held and accepted. It is the natural response of a people poised between two worlds: one, the matrix of ghetto and *shtetl*— to which they can no longer return; the other, the civil society of the West—in which they could not be fully at ease.[21]

That Allen's films repeatedly depict someone "not fully at ease" is clear enough; whether his life or films evoke someone "not fully at ease" in the "civil society of the West" depends on the perceiver's assumptions about cultural assimilation, its advantages and deficits, or on the extent to which we find in Jewish comedic *kvetching* veiled objections to and critiques of the culture into which the *kvetcher* is assimilating. (One way to summarize the complex issue of Allen's assimilation to mainstream American culture is to suggest that Jewish American culture's most significant influence on him has come through George Gershwin and Groucho Marx.[22]) For his part, Allen described his sense of his own in-betweenness in terms not completely different from Whitfield's: in invoking the significance of his evolution from stand-up comedy to comedic filmmaking and beyond, Allen described the public's—and his own—contradictory perception of him:

> There's a problem of self-perception and public perception of me. I'm an art film maker, but not really. I had years of doing commercial comedies, although they were never really commercial. Pictures like *Take the Money and Run* and *Bananas* were forerunners of movies like *Airplane*—although they didn't make a fiftieth of what *Airplane* made. First there was a perception of me as a comedian doing those comic films, and then it changed to someone making upgraded commercial films like *Annie Hall* and *Manhattan*. And as I've tried to branch off and make more offbeat films, I've put myself in the area of kind of doing art films— but they're not perceived as art films because I'm a local person. . . . What I should be doing is either just funny commercial films, comedies and political satires that everybody looks forward to and loves and laughs at, or art films. But I'm sort of in the middle. *Purple Rose of Cairo* and *Zelig* and *Radio Days* are examples of films that are not popular yet they're not so esoteric that they're art films exactly. They just fall into an odd category. If they're art films, they should be made for very little money and shown in 12 cities. But mine are shown in a hundred, or however many.[23]

It's been more than twenty years since he last produced what might be termed a "funny commercial film," and yet Allen continues to be associated primarily with comedy, partly because even "serious" films such as *Shadows and Fog* and *Husbands and Wives* contain moments of broad comedy which seem recognizably Woody Allen *shtick*.[24] Because of its lack of a sustained dramatic plot, *Radio Days* is sometimes perceived as the film in which Allen began deliberately to indulge a penchant for mixing mood and genre textures in his films; the resulting movie with its dramatization of old-time radio as a source of both the audience's giddiest fantasies and of news of human tragedies at the front and at home left a number of reviewers with conflicted responses. But *Manhattan* is an often uneasy blend of drama and humor, *Zelig* and *The Purple Rose of Cairo* are as difficult to categorize generically as Allen suggests, and the two murders in *Bullets Over Broadway* clearly complicate the viewer's reaction to what otherwise seems a light and highly likable comedy. "This is what I've been fooling with for a while now," Allen told Bjorkman in the early 1990s, "the attempt to try and make comedies that have a serious or tragic dimension to them."[25] Allen's ability to effectively intermingle the serious with the comic in film is one of the ways in which his craft as a screenwriter and director has grown considerably, but it's won him no points with those who insist that comedy is comedy and drama is drama—viewers for whom the interstices between the two, where Allen's movies tend to position themselves, are sites of emotional indeterminacy and artistic incoherence. Making a case for the affective and artistic effectiveness of Allen comedic/dramatic hybrids such as *Broadway Danny Rose, Radio Days, Crimes and Misdemeanors, Shadows and Fog, Bullets Over Broadway, Mighty Aphrodite, Deconstructing Harry,* and *Sweet and Lowdown* is another central critical task of *The Reluctant Film Art of Woody Allen.*

Arguably, the trick in successfully discussing Allen's collection of films involves sustaining the consciousness of its self-reflexive artistic context while simultaneously recognizing the comedic cultural context that is so central to Allen's background and influences. The critic who loses sight of the importance of the comedic context runs the risk of emulating the insufferably pompous intellectual posturings of the Columbia professor at the New Yorker theater in *Annie Hall* or, perhaps worse, of sounding like Alvy Singer ("The medium enters in as a condition of the art form itself") when he's trying to snow Annie with an expertise about photography he doesn't possess. (The critic too enamored of the comedic context of Allen's films, on the other hand, risks coming on like a stand-up comedian regurgitating Allen's zingiest one-liners, a critical strategy not lacking among the books published on Allen's films.) One of Danny Rose's aunts, counseling against adultery, admonishes him that "You can't ride two horses with one behind"[26]; it is a central objective of this study of Allen's movies to demonstrate that one of the major achievements of his filmmaking career has been to effectively straddle the two horses of comedy and art with one behind, becoming in the process neither a comedian nor an artist but something in between: a comic auteur.

In managing this trick, Allen is enacting another tendency attributed to the Jewish American artist: "The urban self-consciousness for which Jewish writers just now are the leading spokesmen is a sensibility which, for all its ideological origins, withholds commitments," Mark Shechner has argued.

> The impurity of its origins and the indeterminacy of its allegiances, however, constitute its strength: it is ideally suited to the expression of extremes of thought as well as extremes of doubt, that is, to modern states of informed confusion. Psychologically, this sensibility stands at the boundary between outer and inner worlds, just

as it seems, stylistically, to accommodate both realism and interior monologue, as though in acknowledgment that to be both Jewish and modern—in America, at any rate—is to be a bridge between worlds and to be required, above all else, to keep the traffic flowing.[27]

Shechner's suggestion that the Jewish American artist typically "withholds commitments" and hedges allegiances invokes a final manifestation of Allen's ambivalence toward art—in this case, his own. This equivocal attitude is exemplified most clearly by the methodicalness of his film production practices.

During a period in which the filmmakers with whom he is routinely compared as America's preeminent directors—Stanley Kubrick, Martin Scorsese, Oliver Stone, George Lucas, Spike Lee, Steven Spielberg—have released on average ten to fifteen films, Allen has completed twenty-nine, not counting the three (*Play It Again, Sam, The Front,* and *Scenes from a Mall*) in which he appeared but did not direct. To achieve this remarkable feat, Allen has had to commit himself to the production of films that, by Hollywood's standards, are extremely modest in scope. (To date, his most expensive production has been *Bullets Over Broadway,* which cost $20 million, approximately one-fifth of the Hollywood average.[28]) Allen's films generally take only three to four months to shoot from the day on which he finishes scripting them, their production schedules continuing to replicate those of Allen's earliest films: "I'm for turning out a comedy every year," he told Lee Guthrie in the middle 1970s, "I wish we could just keep turning them out."[29] Allen's gradual shift toward the creation of more serious films did not, in his mind, necessitate revised production schedules, in part because his filmmaking practices were inspired by one of the world's most serious filmmakers.

In his 1988 review of Ingmar Bergman's autobiography, *The Magic Lantern,* Allen offered a substantial argument for Bergman's illumination of his characters' interior lives through imagery, and then proceeded to celebrate a few of the Swedish filmmaker's other film-production virtues. "All this, ladies and gentlemen," Allen exulted, "and he works cheaply. He's fast; the films cost very little, and his tiny band of regulars can slap together a major work of art in half the time and for half the price that most take to mount some glitzy piece of celluloid. Plus he writes the scripts himself. What else could you ask for?"[30] Delete the honorific clause "major work of art" from this passage and what you might well be asking for—or getting—is a Woody Allen movie. From location selection through the employment of a fairly constant film crew to decisions about cutting techniques, Allen's films, like Bergman's, are conceived to be produced as quickly and cheaply as possible.

Between *Love and Death* (shot in Hungary and Paris) and *Mighty Aphrodite* (which contains brief scenes shot in Taormina, Sicily) and *Everyone Says I Love You* (with location shoots in Paris and Venice), Allen's films were

exclusively shot within an hour of New York City, the director having determined during the shooting of *Love and Death* that one sacrifice he was unwilling to make for his art was being unable to return to his apartment at the end
of the day. "I'm completely aware," he once told an interviewer, "that I'm
shooting in New York because it's easy."[31] Making a career of producing films
in New York City, of course, has confronted Allen and his production staff
with considerable artistic and logistical challenges. Nonetheless, it's probably
not unfair to say this: Fitzcarraldo Woody Allen isn't.

Further facilitating the expeditious production of Allen's films is the
crew he assembled which stayed with him from movie to movie and thus has
had years of training in the efficient creation of films.[32] Allen's preference for
master shots over the intercutting of scenes is another factor, the omission of
the step of reshooting scenes from numerous angles and then intercutting
them saving significant production time. That this cinematographic strategy
limits the visual variety and innovativeness of Allen's films is a price he's been
thoroughly willing to pay, one which has included his being largely disre-
garded by critics and moviegoers devoted to cinematic experimentation. The
fact that he has used three of film's finest cinematographers—Gordon Willis,
Carlo Di Palma, Sven Nykvist, and Zhao Fei—to shoot movies which are
predominantly script-driven and often visually conventional exemplifies simultaneously Allen's reverence for cinematic art and the modesty of his own
films' cinematic ambitions.

Such cinematographic modesty notwithstanding, the substantial criticism of Allen's work has well established what this book at length reaffirms:
that there is little uncalculated about the making of his films. There *is*, however, a certain offhandedness about their release. "I also wanted to go against
making it a special event when my films came out," Allen told Stig Bjorkman.
"I just want to make a lot of films and keep putting them out. And I don't
want it to be, 'Oh, it's the new Woody Allen film! Two years we've waited for
it!' I just want to turn them out and that's it. I like to work a lot, and I've made
a deal with the film company so that the minute I pull out the script from the
typewriter, the next day I'm in production. . . . For me it's like stamping out
cookies. I finish a film and move on to the next one."[33]

Coming from a filmmaker who speaks with such awe of the work of
Bergman and Fellini, Allen's industrious baker's model of film production is
disconcerting, prompting one to wonder whether a few of the cookies wouldn't
have been more delectable had they been given more time to bake. Nonetheless, Allen remains remarkably consistent in his workmanlike impiety toward
his own processes of aesthetic creation. "I make so many films," he has pointed
out, "that I don't care about individual successes and failures. . . . I hope I'll
have a long and healthy life," he continued in his conversation with Bjorkman,
"that I can keep working all the time, and that I can look back in old age and

say, 'I made fifty movies, and some of them were excellent and some of them were not so good, and some of them were funny.'"[34]

Allen's production strategy has generated a stunningly generous output of films, and it is a credit to the systematization of that filmmaking process that he was able to produce in periods of less than twelve months films as ambitious as *Zelig, Purple Rose of Cairo, Hannah and Her Sisters, Crimes and Misdemeanors,* and *Bullets Over Broadway.* It's tempting to wonder, however, whether the production limits imposed on each film don't reflect a deliberate refusal on Allen's part to invest himself overmuch in any project, an oblique means of expressing his disavowal of the masterpiece-aspiring objectives of serious art. Which returns us to the ambivalence toward art which is at the heart of Allen's artistic achievement. "I'm trying to make as wonderful a film as I can," he told William Geist in 1987, "But my priorities are always in order, and they're never artistic. Artistic accomplishment is always third or fourth."[35]

"I'm one of those people that believes there's no social value in art," he explained to Lee Guthrie in the 1970s, "not just comedy, but no social value in art at all, anyplace, anytime. To me, all [art]—opera, painting, anything— is a diversion, an entertainment. So I view my own work in that same way that there is no social value. . . . In the end, [serious drama or a symphony are] all entertainment. I don't believe in art as a social force."[36] Although these comments predate the production of the films on which Allen's reputation as a significant filmmaker rests, the incredulity he articulates here toward the grander claims made for art remains a consistent theme throughout his career, one only occasionally contested by his generous celebrations of other serious filmmakers and artists. Allen's production methods, then, contain embedded within them the assumption that there is no essential difference between comic and serious films; in his view, neither genre has any significant social impact on human values or behavior, and both of them constitute nothing more, finally, than entertainment. It is impossible to perceive Allen's films adequately without paying substantial attention to those movies' pervasive skepticism toward the very art of which they are a product. Although Harry Block's attitude toward art is demonstrably more cynical than Allen's, we will nonetheless encounter in these pages many temptations to recall Harry's concluding repudiation of the human capacity to misconstrue and misrepresent our experience: "Our life," he asserts, "consists of how we choose to distort it." Like Harry's, Woody Allen's distortion of choice is called art.

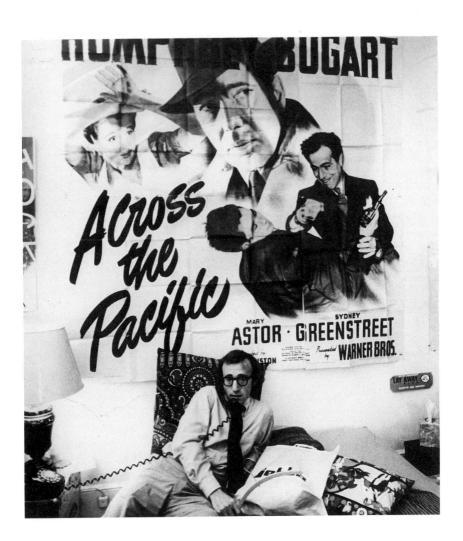

2

Strictly the Movies

Play It Again, Sam

TRACY: So what happens to us?
ISAAC: Well, you know, we'll always have Paris.

—Isaac Davis in *Manhattan* telling Tracy that their relationship has no future

All it would have taken was a single moviegoer. It's 1972, and that lone film enthusiast enters a theater hardly a minute after the feature's published starting time. Although he's read nothing about it, he is looking forward to watching *Play It Again, Sam*. Instead of the new Woody Allen-scripted film, however, he's confronted with the ending of *Casablanca*, awash in a strange shade of blue. Bewildered, the filmgoer heads off to the box office to ask whether the theater has without notice been transformed into a rerun house. He's directed back to his seat, assured that it is *Play It Again, Sam* that's being shown. As he reenters the theater, he sees on the screen Woody Allen's face in close-up, slack-jawed with wonder; it becomes clear that Allen's character is watching Bogart's "the problems of three little people don't amount to a hill of beans in this crazy world" monologue. The moviegoer settles comfortably into his seat, relieved to know that he's arrived at the film he'd intended to see. But afterwards, whenever he thinks of *Play It Again, Sam,* he'll never completely shake the uneasy impression that *Casablanca* had somehow displaced Allen's movie: that Michael Curtiz's film had overwhelmed—even usurped—Allen's.

Although that moviegoer's response is the result of a misconception, it is completely appropriate to the film he was beginning to watch. There may be no better emblem anywhere in Allen's canon for the power of film to overwhelm and overpower competing realities than *Play It Again, Sam*'s opening displacement by *Casablanca,* and it's to an analogous effacement of himself by cinema which Allan Felix refers in voice-over as he leaves the movie house following Bogart's chipper assurance to Captain Louis Renault that "I think this is the beginning of a beautiful friendship." "Who am I kidding?" Felix asks himself, introducing the negative comparison of himself to Bogart's Rick Blaine persona which will pervade the film. "I'm not like that. I never was, and I never will be. It's strictly the movies."

As the first chapter established, the disparity between fantasy and reality, art and life, is a particular preoccupation of Allen's literary and film work;

however, the dichotomy between cinematic reality and actuality is of such intense importance to his sense of his filmmaking career to demand an introductory chapter of its own. Two of the films generally acknowledged as being among Allen's best—*Stardust Memories* and *The Purple Rose of Cairo*—deal specifically with this disparity as a primary theme, while two others—*Hannah and Her Sisters* and *Manhattan Murder Mystery*—are indebted to the movies of other filmmakers for their thematic resolutions. Most of Allen's other films contain blatant echoes of other movies or—to some critics, more unforgivably—seem patently derivative of the films of masters of European cinema. *Radio Days,* the imitative argument maintains, is inspired by Fellini's *Amarcord; Interiors* owes its gravid mood and close-up intensity to Bergman's *Persona,* while *Midsummer Night's Sex Comedy* is an excessively reverential homage to *Smiles of a Summer Night; Stardust Memories* is an Americanization and Woody Allenization of *8½,* while *Alice* mimics *Juliet of the Spirits; Another Woman* borrows liberally from the plot and dream imagery of *Wild Strawberries,* which also figures substantially in Harry Block's journey to receive an honorary degree in *Deconstructing Harry; Shadows and Fog* is a pastiche of German Expressionist film styles blended with Bergman's *Sawdust and Tinsel;* and *Manhattan Murder Mystery* seeks to resurrect the Nick and Nora Charles mode of 1940s film mystery/comedy. Admittedly, Allen's cinematic debt to these films, filmmaking styles, and filmmakers cannot be denied, but it can be argued that Allen is every bit as aware of his influences as are the critics who with such patronizing glee catalogue imitative moments in his films. More than that, Allan Felix's ongoing attempt to escape the anxiety of cinematic influences is very much what *Play It Again, Sam* dramatizes and is a central dynamic tension pervading Allen's film career as well. To understand how this is true, we need to go to the movies with young Allan Stewart Konigsberg.

In Eric Lax's biography, Allen recalls the pleasures he experienced as a child going to Brooklyn's Midwood Theater on Saturdays. "I remember being the first person in line many times on a Saturday morning," he reminisced:

> I would be there at eleven o'clock and the theater would open at twelve. The theater would be lit up and it was amazing because in those days the theater was just beautiful—the carpets and brass and everything. . . . There was always a white-haired matron in a white costume with a flashlight who tended the children's section, so your mother could bring you, put you in your seat, and go. Then four hours later you'd feel a tap on your shoulder and she'd be picking you up. And you'd say, "I don't want to go! I don't want to go!"

Allen evoked the wonder of 1940s movie palaces in the Radio City Music Hall scene of *Radio Days;* the human wonderment at what appears on the screen is visualized in the enchanted expressions of Allan Felix in *Play It Again, Sam* as he watches Rick and Ilsa, and in Cecilia's rapturously adoring attention in *The Purple Rose of Cairo* to Fred and Ginger's *Top Hat* choreography. That "your mother" will arrive to pull you out of such grand illusions is ever the irresolvable problem not only of Allan Stewart Konigsberg but also of many of Allen's protagonists and may suggest why mothers generally come off so badly in Allen's films. "The sense of dread in facing reality after hours of pleasurable escape," Lax cites Allen as suggesting,

> is the worst experience in the world. . . . You'd go into the theater at noon on a hot summer day, and you'd sit through *The Scarlet Pimpernel* and *The Return of The Scarlet Pimpernel,* and it would be nothing but sheer magical joy, eating chocolate-covered raisins for three or four hours. Then you would come out at three in the afternoon and leave the world of beautiful women and music, and, you know, bravery or penthouses or things like that. And suddenly you would be out on Coney Island Avenue in Brooklyn and the trolleys would be passing and the sun would be blinding and there was no more air conditioning. I remember that sense of coming out into the ugly light when I walked out of *Always Leave Them Laughing* with Milton Berle and after *The Secret Life of Walter Mitty.*[1]

That Allen should choose for his two examples of movie magic culminating in disenchantment via reality's "ugly light" these two films—a movie about the vicissitudes of a comedian and the film version of James Thurber's story about a man incapacitated by daydreams—seems highly significant: laughter and indulgence in fantasy are what happens in movie theaters, and many of Allen's own films are devoted to eliciting laughter or exploiting the fantasies of their audiences. These films, in effect, combine to provide the means through which Allan Stewart Konigsberg could stay inside the theater for good—by becoming a comic filmmaker. But then, even young Konigsberg may have intuited that living in the movie theater might not be an unequivocally good thing.

In *Play It Again, Sam,* Allan Felix's wife files for divorce expressly because of her husband's preoccupation with movies. She wants "to do things, to be a participant in life," but "All we ever do is see movies. You like movies because you're one of life's great watchers." Another of Allen's "great watchers" is Alvy Singer of *Annie Hall,* who indulges his morbid streak by repeatedly going to see *The Sorrow and the Pity. Stardust Memories* is unquestionably Allen's most dyspeptic assessment of the interaction between human beings and movies; *The Purple Rose of Cairo* is his most ambivalent depiction of the audience's fervent imaginative dependency on cinematic illusion; *Crimes and Misdemeanors* seems to cast a dubious eye upon Clifford Stern's "playing hooky" by going to movies in the afternoon with his niece, the film's ending equating Hollywood movies with perversely embraced delusions. Larry, the oddly phlegmatic protagonist of *Manhattan Murder Mystery*, seems to work up excitement only for the prospect of watching old Bob Hope films on cable television. Once Allan Felix finally gets a date in *Play It Again, Sam*, he attempts to lure her to an "Erich Von Stroheim Film Festival" before she drags him off to a biker bar. "Movies," Felix's wife, speaking as well for other Allen protagonists, complains about her soon-to-be ex-husband: "that's his whole life."

This book's later chapter on *Radio Days* offers a somewhat standard New Critical admonition against the necessary reductionism implicit in confusing Allen's protagonists with Allen; at this point it can be suggested that Nancy Felix's charge really is applicable to Woody Allen. Support for that claim can be found in Allen's numerous, highly enthusiastic acknowledgments of the importance of movies in his childhood, the prevalence of movie-within-movie structures in his films, and his extensive knowledge of American and European film modes. More tellingly, there's also the factor we've already considered: in producing twenty-nine movies over the past thirty years, Allen has hardly experienced as much as a three-month period in which he wasn't either writing, shooting, or cutting a film. As *Husbands and Wives* was widely interpreted as obliquely dramatizing, Allen finds time while scripting and directing movies to pack in a good deal of personal experience; nonetheless, a life so completely dominated by filmmaking can provide just so much material for the development of new screenplays. Therefore, it seems reasonable that for Allen, even more than for the other movie-fixated directors of his generation (Scorsese, Levinson, Lucas, Coppola, Kubrick, and Spielberg), movies constitute source material which other artists find in lived experience. Nothing typifies better Allen's ambivalence toward the power of his cinematic inheritance than that his own movies project this central influence in his work as both virtue and flaw, as source of energy and experiential deficiency.

Push the argument that Allen's oeuvre is remarkably possessed by the spirit and substance of other films far enough, and we have another neat allegory to put beside the *Play It Again, Sam* movies-and-life dramatic antinomy: if Leonard Zelig derives his personality from the behavior and characteristics of others, Woody Allen's films can be construed as being similarly imitative, a noticeable portion of their content being derived from other makers' films. The elucidation of this Zelig/Allen parallel later in this book will demonstrate that Allen's peculiar form of intertextuality reflects not, as many reviewers self-congratulatorily maintain, his greatest limitation as a filmmaker, but his unremitting recognition of our late twentieth century, mass media-inspired self-consciousness about other plots, other narratives, other movies, and the role they play in our construction of selves. Just as *Zelig* problematizes the existence of the individual, integral, uncontingent self,[2] Allen's movies assume that film narratives are similarly and inescapably mediated by previously existing film narratives. The ways of seeing which are Bergman's and Fellini's movies, his screenplays suggest, inflect the ways of seeing which are Allen's movies, which have, in turn, inflected the ways of seeing of films by Albert Brooks, Kenneth Branagh, Nora Ephron, Spike Lee, Rob Reiner, and Billy Crystal, among others. The Woody Allen constructed in this text, then, is a distinctly postmodernist filmmaker who—except in the title of *Deconstructing Harry*—devotedly eschews the lexicon of post-structuralism, but whose films nonetheless repeatedly address and enact many of the issues debated within that critical field. The primary question his film career has dedicated itself to posing—and which is, thus, a crucial question of this study of his films—can be stated in remarkably untheoretical terms: Is our preoccupation with films a psychologically healthful indulgence in bracing, reassuring illusions, or is it instead a means of artificially mediating, distorting, or protecting us against lived experience? To put the question differently, is Bogart an ideal that Felix must emulate if he is to be successful with women, or is he a fraudulent compendium of gender fictions which can only feed actual human beings' feelings of inadequacy and insufficiency? For one of Allen's many cinematic responses to that question, we need to return to *Play It Again, Sam*.[3]

The Humphrey Bogart incarnation (Jerry Lacy) who appears intermittently in *Play It Again, Sam* to counsel Felix in how to imitate him is such a naturally comical invention that it's easy to overlook how completely self-conscious a device it is. Allen's films proliferate with such contrivances—imaginary characters who reflect projections of the protagonist's inner life or scenes that dramatize conflicts through anachronism or imaginary confrontations. At one end of the spectrum are the relatively congruent and less self-conscious scenes in which Annie and Alvy amusingly visit Alvy's Brooklyn childhood in *Annie Hall* and the more sober attendance of Judah Rosenthal at his father's yesteryear seder in *Crimes and Misdemeanors* in order to have his father pass judgment on his conspiracy in murder. At the other end of the spectrum are the more extravagant devices of Tom Baxter abandoning the screen to inhabit Cecilia's Depression-era reality in *The Purple Rose of Cairo* and Alice's airborne date with a deceased lover in *Alice*. In short, Allen's films consistently manifest their unwillingness to remain within the boundaries of cinematic realism and probability. Like the best of these devices in *Annie Hall*—Marshall McLuhan's appearance to repudiate a pompous Columbia professor's interpretation of his work, or the subtitles reflecting the sexual subtext of Annie and Alvy's debate about the aesthetics of photography—the Bogart figure, rather than invoking the artifice of the film medium by puncturing its realistic illusion, hilariously directs the audience's attention to the protagonist's conflict. That conflict in *Play It Again, Sam* has been described most often, and quite justifiably so, as existing between Felix's insecurity about his masculinity and the confident, charismatic manliness of which Bogart is Felix's psychic projection. Without completely sacrificing that reading of the interaction between Felix and Bogart, we should also recognize Bogart's inescapably cinematic character, and notice how Felix's exchanges with him embody Allen's ambivalence about his own—and our—psychic dependence upon the movies.[4]

Evidence for that interpretation is provided not only by Nancy's indictment but also by the fact that Felix writes for a film magazine and that his apartment is wall-to-wall movie posters; if there's anywhere a shade of Bogart should feel comfortable, it's at Felix's place. As the movie proceeds, references to the disparity between actuality and silver screen images escalate: when Felix describes how thoroughly Bogart represents a role model for him, Linda Christie (Diane Keaton) lectures him, "Allan, that's not real life. I mean you set too high a standard."[5] He holds himself up to the same standard, invariably finding himself wanting: "It's like Fred Astaire looks good in tails, and I look lousy," he complains at one point, never quite registering that he has no occasion to wear tails.[6] Felix's self-recriminations culminate in a fantasy in which he imagines his ex-wife, Nancy (Susan Anspach), summarizing his character: "You're a dreamer. You're awkward. You're clumsy. [Women] could see how desperate you are. . . . You may be very sweet, but you're not sexy."

That Felix's self-assessment is delivered by a phantasm of his gorgeous ex-wife establishes an antinomy for which Bogart provides the opposition. (The contention between them for ascendancy in Felix's soul is signaled by the one scene in which the two phantoms appear together: re-enacting a scene from *They Drive by Night*, Nancy shoots Bogart.) In another fantasy of his wife's post-divorce freedom from him, Felix imagines her making love to a biker: "It's been so long," she rapturously moans, "since I've been made love to by a tall, strong, handsome, blue-eyed blond man." Felix has attributed to this imagined biker all the qualities he so conspicuously lacks; thus, his fantasy Nancy expresses his inner voice of self-denigration, articulating his perception of himself as urban neurotic, hypochondriac, self-consciously Jewish, irredeemably uncool, and hopelessly unsexy. In short, she tactlessly invokes the negative/comic pole of the Woody Allen protagonist. It is in response to internal proddings of the self-doubts she embodies that Felix, anticipating Leonard Zelig's chameleon tendencies, decides he should leave books open around his apartment for dates to see because "it creates an image" and because "carefully placed objects will create the proper impression." It is the Bogart projection's function in Felix's psychic economy to offer him encouragement, to coach him in the virtues of self-assertiveness and masculine self-reliance, the *Casablanca* fugitive constituting a counterargument to the self-vilification which Felix's Nancy projection consistently expresses. As we'll see, however, Bogart often seems as much a symptom of Felix's psychic conflict as a means to its remediation.

Nancy's consummate indictment—"You may be very sweet, but you're not sexy"—prompts the Bogart projection to materialize for damage control; he coaches Felix through an erotic encounter with Linda, encouraging him to disregard feelings of guilt over his friendship with her husband, Dick (Tony Roberts), by repeatedly urging him to abandon his equivocations and "Go ahead and kiss her." Felix finally complies, but his erotic foray sends Linda fleeing from his apartment. Recalling the impassioned declaration of love in which his romantic advances culminated, however, Linda quickly returns, and the kisses they share at his front door are intercut with *Casablanca* images of Rick and Ilsa kissing. It's difficult not to notice that Rick and Ilsa do it better, that there's something clumsy and unattractive about Felix and Linda's very mouthy kisses, but the point of the intercutting seems less to contrast osculatory techniques than to suggest that even in moments of deepest passionate gratification, Felix's pleasure is irremediably mediated by film. In other words, even when he gets what the movies have taught him to desire and to fantasize about attaining, the movie version in his head remains more compelling.

The brief affair generated by these kisses precipitates the usual marital and extramarital tensions, circumstances replicating the plot of an Ida Lupino film, *They Drive By Night,* which Linda wants to watch on the late movie. It's "the one where she's happily married and suddenly becomes involved with her husband's best friend," Linda explains. In a film so centrally concerned with the intercession of film narratives within our emotional lives, it is only appropriate that Felix's anxieties about informing Dick of the affair get configured as movie scenes: Felix and Dick become stuffy Brits amicably resolving their romantic conflict without ever removing their pipes from their mouths; then Felix imaginatively transforms them into characters in a Vittorio deSica movie in which bakery workers Felix and Dick scream at each other through thick Italian accents. All of this is preparing for the climactic airport scene in which Felix will have the opportunity to play out Rick's romantic love-renunciation scene, delivering a speech which, he forthrightly admits, is "from *Casablanca.* I've waited my whole life to say it."

"That's beautiful," is Linda's response to Felix's thoroughly practiced "you'll regret it—maybe not today, maybe not tomorrow" recitation, insisting that "the most wonderful thing in the world has happened" because Felix seduced her without leaving "open books lying around" and he didn't have to "put on the proper mood music." In effect, he had "scored" without resorting to all the self-conscious stratagems he used previously in his hapless attempts to "make an impression" on women. He had managed, Linda is suggesting, to overcome his film-inspired self-consciousness and act forthrightly upon his desire. Bogart adds his own commendation of Felix's closing monologue: "That was great," Bogart tells him after Linda and Dick have deplaned for Cleveland, "you've really developed yourself a little style."

"I do have a certain amount of style, don't I?" Felix responds in wonderment. This realization achieved, Felix's phantasmagoric model of unself-conscious masculine artlessness has become dispensable. Accordingly, Bogart tells him, "Well, I guess you won't be needing me anymore," paying his protégé the ultimate male compliment by acknowledging, "There's nothing I can tell you now that you don't already know." Significantly, Bogart never mentions that it's Linda, not Felix, who renounces their affair in order to return to her marriage by flying off to Cleveland with Dick. This deviation from the *Casablanca* paradigm notwithstanding, Felix is clearly poised on the very brink of epiphany, one that builds upon his admission that he has "a certain amount of style." "The secret's not being you," he boasts at last, "it's being me. What the hell—I'm short enough and ugly enough to succeed on my own."

Untold thousands of moviegoers have been charmed by Felix's self-liberating declaration and by the salute Bogart offers him in response to it: reprising the affectionate appellation he has used with Felix throughout the film, Bogart smiles broadly at him, saying "Here's looking at you, kid." It's a lovely moment of closure, the echo of Rick's final words to Ilsa seeming to translate that scene's sad farewell into *Play It Again, Sam*'s affirmation of Felix's achievement of freedom from Bogart's oppressive influence. It's evident that what we are watching is the end of a beautiful split-protagonist friendship. But then, "Here's looking at you, kid," was the toast Rick and Ilsa shared in avowal of their love, a sentimental formula for the idea that "we'll always have Paris." Rick never says their obsession with each other will cease simply because "the problems of two little people don't amount to a hill of beans in a crazy world like this"; if the most famous scene in American movie history works, the film's dramatic evocation of the emotional cost of that renunciation is the reason. Rather than merely being a shorthand good-bye, Rick's "Here's looking at you, kid," is a way of recalling Paris, of asserting that memory's potency, and of affirming that Rick and Ilsa's separation will be geographical, not emotional or spiritual.

When Bogart salutes Felix with the same expression, he is implicitly commending him for so impressively reenacting the role which Bogart initiated, acknowledging the psychic progress that Felix's playing out of the climactic scene constitutes, and perhaps saying as well that Felix too "will always have Paris"—that he hasn't completely escaped the mental thrall in which he's held by Hollywood-inspired romance, by Bogart's bravura masculinity, by the movies. In other words, Felix's mind may be forswearing its dependency upon the romantic ethos of *Casablanca* but his heart is wailing, "I don't want to go! I don't want to go!" The "little style" Felix has developed is utterly mediated by *Casablanca,* and despite his putative declaration of independence from Bogart and from the desire to reenact the *Casablanca* plot, the only way he has contrived to assert his independence from that narrative has been through plagiarizing it. As Douglas Brode pointed out in discussing the "South American Way" scene in *Radio Days,* "As the men in Joe's family slip into the mood by lip-synching the male chorus's song lines, they too briefly turn their lives into 'art.' The desire to do that—to become one, if only for a second, with either popular or classic art—has been at the root of Allen's characters since his very first film."[7]

As Felix confidently walks off across the airport tarmac, alone, embraced by his newly discovered insularity and self-reliance, the soundtrack undercuts the ending's determinacy and sense of felicitous closure: Sam is playing it again—playing "As Time Goes By," the song which Rick forbade him to perform at Rick's Place in *Casablanca* because it was too potent a reminder of Ilsa and Paris. The "fundamental things apply as time goes by," Dooley Wilson croons as Felix vanishes into airport fog, and we know that those fundamental things include the fact that "when two lovers woo, they still say 'I love you.'" *Play It Again, Sam* is the first of many Allen films which consistently and deliberately merges the "fundamental things" of human romance with their idealized representations on movie screens, the film depicting simultaneously Allan Felix's self-liberation from the *Casablanca* mythos and his continuing obsession with it.

In *The Purple Rose of Cairo,* a Hollywood actor offers Cecilia a sentiment invoking the same basic paradox depicted in *Play It Again, Sam*'s ending: "Look, I-I love you. I know that o-only happens in movies, but . . . I do." When D.J. of *Everyone Says I Love You* explains how the film of her family's crazy year evolved, she recalls her half-sister, Skylar, suggesting that it must be "a musical or no one will believe it"; as a result, the characters constantly and highly self-consciously burst into song to express the status of their current relationship to Eros. Allen's translation of the old bromide that people might never have fallen in love if they'd never heard it talked about would be that few people would fall in love were they not acting out the plots of movies or the lyrics of popular songs. There *are* Woody Allen films in which human love is affirmed as real and redemptive—*Midsummer Night's Sex Comedy, Hannah and Her Sisters, Manhattan Murder Mystery,* and *Mighty Aphrodite* can all be construed in these terms—but his most substantial films more typically depict the human erotic tropism as being irremediably inbred with media-inspired illusions; the "same old story, the fight for love and glory" often gets configured somewhat jadedly as just "the same old story" recycled endlessly through movie vehicles like *Casablanca.*

Lee Guthrie's 1978 biography quotes Allen's characterization of the original theatrical version of *Play It Again, Sam,* which opened on Broadway in 1969. It's "an autobiographical story about a highly neurotic lover, an accumulation of themes which interest me: sex, adultery, extreme neuroses in romance, insecurity. It's strictly a comedy. There's nothing remotely non-comic about it."[8] The equivocation perceivable here between Allen's acknowledgment of the autobiographical nature of the play with its dramatic themes and his insistence upon its "strictly comic" character is typical of Allen's assessment of his early work, though the tendency to minimize the serious ambitions of his films, as we'll see, continues down through his comments on *Deconstructing Harry.* Julian Fox cites the comments of Allen friends of the period who located the inspiration for the play in Allen's recent divorce from Louise Lasser, the plot exploiting his friends' not-always-felicitous attempts to fix him up with dates; additionally, Fox registers those Allen associates' view that *Play It Again, Sam* represented the first time that Allen's dramatic work had "engineered a more than passing connection between his on-screen and off-screen identities." Allen's disclaimers notwithstanding, Fox argues, "the one autobiographical element which he could never be able to deny is the way he has exploited his lifelong addiction to cinema."[9] Many of the parodies of *film noir* scenes which proliferate in the movie are absent from the theatrical version, but Allen's satirical piece about his recently-opened play in *Life Magazine* gave readers an introduction to the Bogart-fixation those parodies would amplify cinematically in the movie. Allen—who seems as intent upon blurring the distinction between himself and Allan Felix in the article as he was in eliminating the distinction between himself and his comic persona in his stand-up act— claims to have fallen in love with a woman named Lou Ann Monad, who breaks his heart by leaving him for the drummer of a rock group called Concluding Scientific Postscript. "Clearly," Allen contends, it was time to fall back on the unassailable strength and wisdom of Humphrey Bogart. I curled my lip and told her that she was a dame and weak and quoted a passage of hard-line Bogey from *Key Largo*. When that didn't work, I resorted to an emotional plea culled from the high points of *Casablanca*. Then I tried something from *The Big Sleep* and then *Sahara*. . . When it still left her unmoved, I fell back on *The Petrified Forest* and then *Sabrina*. Panicky now, I switched to a grubby Fred C. Dobbs in *The Treasure of the Sierra Madre* and asserted myself with the same petty ego he used on Tim Holt, to no avail. She laughed derisively, and moments later I found myself clicking two steel balls together and begging her not to leave me as I muttered something about the strawberries. I was given the gate.[10]

Arguably, "[t]here's nothing remotely non-comic about" this classic bit of Woody Allen *shtick*—nothing, that is, except the understanding of human insecurity required to imagine a character so lacking in self as to so desperately seek to fill the gap with this succession of Humphrey Bogart movies. Allen would, of course, suggest a decade later that there is nothing non-comic about Leonard Zelig, either.

"Apart from its commercial success, [*Play It Again, Sam*] also offered Woody a brand new perspective and maturity for his future career," Fox contended; "starting with *Sam,* a popular image of [Allen] had begun to appear which, for movie audiences at least, was taken to be both a reflection of themselves and all the things they assumed that Woody was about."[11] Fox is right about this and it is also true that it's impossible to completely separate Allan Felix's self-affirmation that "I'm short and ugly enough to succeed on my own" from Woody Allen's own gradual, hard-won transformation of himself from reluctant stand-up comedian to playwright and lead Broadway actor of *Play It Again, Sam,* to screenwriter, lead actor, and director of *Sleeper, Love and Death, Annie Hall,* and so on. By the time he had completed the play script of *Play It Again, Sam,* it was clearly obvious to Allen that, given all the project ideas he had to shelve to appear in the Broadway play,[12] "I guess I do have a little style, don't I?" The film version—facilitated by the remarkably unobtrusive directorial efforts of Herbert Ross—allowed Allen/Allan Felix the perfect personal apotheosis of making that declaration in the medium in which the "little style" he'd discovered in himself would express itself most emphatically over the ensuing three decades.

Play It Again, Sam is undeniably a watershed work in Allen's career, one which obliquely celebrates his transcendence of the intimidations of the cinematic models whose grandeur inspired and inhibited his own creativity much as Bogart inhibits/inspires Felix's efforts with women. However, as the Bergman-haunted, Fellini-inflected films that followed *Play It Again, Sam* suggest, that transcendence was tentative and partial; Woody Allen, filmmaker, is still subject to bouts of the extreme anxiety of influence, vulnerable to acquiescing to the strategy of "when in creative doubt, invoke the masters." This characteristic is less a failing than Allen's acknowledgment of the sometimes dominating affect of other filmmakers' visions upon his own, his way of dramatizing the idea that the existence of an unadulterated, unmediated plot is no more conceivable than a completely original, uncontingent self. However much style we generate, in other words, we're still haunted by the distinctive styles of other films, other selves, and Woody Allen's films are honest enough repeatedly to acknowledge that omnipresence of influence. "I said I would never leave you," Ilsa tells Rick in the concluding scene of *Casablanca,* and his response predicts the trajectory of Allen's film career in terms of its sustained permeation by filmic precedents and influences: "And you never will." To understand what can be construed as a fundamental antinomy of Woody Allen's filmmaking career, one must appreciate how completely conflictual in Allen's mind is Rick's most affecting reassurance to Ilsa: "We'll *always* have Paris."

Ascribing such self-conscious aesthetic purposes to a Woody Allen film is, of course, a highly chancy business, not least because of the filmmaker's impatience with excessively cerebral analyses of his work. "It astonishes me what a lot of intellectualizing goes on over my films," Allen, rehearsing the attitude of dismissive skepticism we've previously seen him adopting in response to what he considers excessively ingenious readings of his work, objected. "They're just films. Yet they treat me like a genius at times, at other times like a criminal. Because I've produced 'bad art.'"[13] The inconsistency of critical responses to his work probably does give Allen cause for complaint. And yet, Allen—whose films are so often *about* tensions between art and entertainment—is sometimes less willing than he might be to acknowledge how the character of his films and career have precipitated such contradictory responses.

Possibly *Take the Money and Run, Bananas,* and *Sleeper can* be designated "just films," if what that means is that the fulfillment of their comic designs exhausts their aesthetic purposes—which would seem to limit criticism of these movies to the distinguishing between which scenes are funny and which aren't. (That criticism is *never* limited to affect clearly dictates that—to film critics, at any rate—there are no such things as "just films," no movies that *don't* invoke meanings beyond their own adherence to generic templates.) Because he didn't actually direct *Play It Again, Sam,* by Allen's own estimation, and by nearly unanimous critical consent, *Annie Hall* represented the beginning of Allen's serious filmmaking career. That means, assumedly, that the analysis of *Annie Hall* rewards critical scrutiny by revealing subtextual synapses and less-than-explicit thematic convergences which gradually accumulate to comprise an ideational/artistic coherence distinguishable from plot, a thematic intentionality apparently absent from the gag-to-gag structure of *Take the Money and Run* and *Sleeper*. Thus dawns, consequently, the descent into complexity, the beginning of the critical tendency to read Allen's work as more than "just films." What makes *Annie Hall* a text-to-be-interpreted while *Sleeper* and *Love and Death* remained "just films" unrewarding of critical scrutiny?

In addition to the *Annie Hall* screenplay's greater depth of characterization and its effective convergence of setting with plot and theme, Allen and Marshall Brickman introduced into the film too many sophisticated rhetorical devices derived from film and drama for the movie to be perceived as pure comedy, for it to be understood solely in terms of its pervasive comic dynamics. Never completely distinguishable from gags, these devices reflect a self-consciousness about film craft categorically different from the parodic moments in Allen's "earlier, funny movies." It is these devices that will be the focus of our examination of *Annie Hall*.

3

Getting Serious

The Antimimetic Emblems of *Annie Hall*

Boy, if life could only be like this!

—Alvy Singer, after producing Marshall McLuhan from behind a coming
attractions billboard to defend his point of view against a boorish
professor pontificating in a movie theater lobby in *Annie Hall*

From its opening sample of Rick and Ilsa's farewell scene to its closing comic
revision of Michael Curtiz's famous denouement, *Play It Again, Sam* is thoroughly preoccupied with *Casablanca;* what Allen's film isn't, as previously indicated, is a parody of *Casablanca.* Rather than merely exaggerating the
melodrama of *Casablanca* for the purposes of satire, *Play It Again, Sam* critiques and reinterprets the medium it has appropriated, creating a dynamic
tension between *Casablanca*'s primary projection, Bogart, and Allan Felix, an
art/life tension which eventually produces the protagonist's fully traditional
reversal and recognition. Like the metafictional explorations of fairy tales,
folk tales, and popular culture narratives conducted in the late '60s by writers
such as John Barth, Donald Barthelme, and Robert Coover, Allen's *Play It
Again, Sam* enriches the viewer's response to *Casablanca* rather than merely
deflating the original through caricature: it simultaneously exposes the ado-
lescent thought-modes underlying *Casablanca* while dramatizing the tremendous hold they exert on the American male imagination.

   Sleeper and *Love and Death,* Allen's films between *Play It* and *Annie Hall,*
are parodies which only inconstantly delineate a coherent position on the
protagonist's relationship to the medium being parodied. If *Love and Death* is
the more memorable of the two, it's because of Allen's greater affection for the
material he's spoofing there; the same brooding Russian literary spiritual introspectiveness which—as Douglas Brode noticed—will pervade *Interiors* and
September inspires moments of brilliant parody in *Love and Death.*[1] In other
words, futuristic films and Russian literature provide Allen with numerous
sources of gags in *Sleeper* and in *Love and Death,* but neither film adds much
to the exploration of the interpenetrations of fiction and actuality he had
begun with *Play It Again, Sam.*

   In *Annie Hall,* of course, Allen returns to this project, transforming the
discrepancy between aesthetic artifice and actuality from a wellspring of ex-

tended gags to a source of thematic unity. With *Annie Hall,* then, Allen takes full advantage of his status as screenwriter/director, revisiting the argument with artistic representation which he had begun waging in *Play It Again, Sam.* *Annie Hall* resumes Allen's debate with himself over the possibility that art is synonymous with illusion-mongering and sentimental fraudulence. That skepticism is frequently expressed in Allen's films through his characters' offhand disparagements of aesthetic contrivance. "That's movie talk, that's not real," Cecilia says in *The Purple Rose of Cairo;* "If you want a happy ending," Judah tells Cliff in *Crimes and Misdemeanors,* "you should see a Hollywood movie"; for Rain in *Husbands and Wives,* writing fiction is "just a trick . . . When I was ten I wrote this whole story on Paris. It's just a trick"; "I know, you're an artist," David Shayne's agent fulminates at him in *Bullets Over Broadway,* "Now let me tell you something, kid—that's a real world out there, and it's a lot tougher than you think." The inception of this debate, however, is located in *Annie Hall's* Alvy Singer, who quite appropriately introduces himself as someone who has "a little trouble between fantasy and reality."[2]

In the play Alvy (Allen) writes, which is inspired by his relationship with Annie (Diane Keaton), the couple has a fractious confrontation in a Los Angeles health food restaurant, one culminating—as it never does in the film framing the play—in an utterly unmotivated reconciliation providing Alvy's drama with a happy ending. The female lead of Alvy's play, Sunny, delivers verbatim the lines that Annie uses in terminating her relationship with Alvy, accusing Alvy's aptly named dramatic surrogate, Arty, "You're like New York. You're an island." Arty responds with a melodramatic line which Alvy had the tact to suppress ("it all ends here, in a health food restaurant on Sunset Boulevard") before taking leave of Sunny. "Wait, I'm going with you," Sunny unexpectedly replies, bestowing on Arty the happy ending which Alvy is denied because of Annie's silence as she and Alvy enter their cars in the health food restaurant parking lot. Apologizing for the sentimentality of his resolution, Alvy asks the movie audience, "Tsch, whatta you want? It was my first play. You know, you know how you're always tryin' t' get things to come out perfect in art because it's real difficult in life" (p. 102). The great boon of art is that it is easier to resolve than life, which is also the incontestable proof of its innate capacity for falsification.

Alvy's genial denigration of art as aesthetically ameliorated life is a pervasive postulate of Allen's films, a theme evident in movies as early as *Play It Again, Sam* (Allan Felix ultimately resolving that he's "short and ugly enough to make it on my own,"[3] thus relinquishing his *Casablanca*-inspired mentor and alter ego) to one as late as *Bullets Over Broadway* (David Shayne declaring that "I'm an artist, . . . but first I'm a human being"[4]). As in those films, however, *Annie Hall's* critique of the contrivances of art contains a significant equivocation. For many in the film's audience, it was common knowledge that the Sunny/Arty couple bears an intriguingly similar relationship to Annie/ Alvy as Annie/Alvy does to Diane Keaton/Woody Allen, whose romance and breakup the film was widely recognized as fictionalizing. The *roman a clef* aspect of *Annie Hall* adds yet another layer of art/life ambiguity to the movie, reminding the attentive viewer that, for all its pretensions to documentary veracity, *Annie Hall* too is aesthetic artifice, another creator's deliberately fabricated effort to "get things to come out perfect in art."

Alvy's delivery of this line directly to the camera is what makes the scene so likable; clearly, the film's repeated pattern of such spontaneous soliloquies accounts for the fact that *Annie Hall* remains for many viewers Allen's most appealing film. Alvy, this self-deprecating assessment of his art invites viewers to believe, is leveling with us, and when he isn't actually addressing the audience, the film contains other devices (the subtitles which reveal what Annie and Alvy are actually thinking while they're engaging in seductive getting-to-know-you small talk, for instance, or the split-screen projection of the two discussing their divergent perceptions of their relationship with their analysts) which extend and reinforce *Annie Hall's* winsome ethos of plain-dealing and ingenuousness. The paradox of *Annie Hall,* of course, is that the devices that allow the audience access to the reality underlying appearances in the film are themselves highly self-conscious artifices, artistic contrivances masquerading as vehicles of representational authenticity and veracity.

In his review of Ingmar Bergman's autobiography, *The Magic Lantern,* Allen suggests one possible source for the self- conscious cinematic devices of *Annie Hall:* in the *Passion of Anna,* Allen wrote, Bergman "had the chutzpah to stop the engrossing story at intervals and let the actors explain to the audience what they are trying to do with their portrayals," such moments constituting for him "showmanship at its best."[5] Whether Allen derived *Annie Hall's* illusion-dispersing devices from Bergman's film, from Theater of the Absurd dramatists such as Pirandello or Ionesco, from Brechtian theatrical alienation techniques, or from Groucho Marx's mischievous addressing of the film audience throughout *Horse Feathers* matters less than their effect. That effect is to undermine the film's representationality while establishing a visual approximation of Alvy's subjective reality, which is, contradictorily, more "real" than the one it displaces. Because these devices partake of and embody Allen's ambivalence toward artistic representation, constituting cinematic convergences of verisimilitude with falsification, they will be the focus in this chapter's discussion of *Annie Hall.*

Peter Cowie characterizes these devices as "visual inventions"[6] and Annette Wernblad describes them as "unusual technical and narrative devices"[7]; because of their mimesis-suspending tendencies and illustrative nature, they can be designated antimimetic emblems. Some of these devices are admittedly—and very significantly—indistinguishable from jokes, and might, conse-

quently, be perceived as the earliest moments in Allen's career in which comedian and artist converge. When Alvy Singer, age forty plus, appears in a second grade classroom among his classmates, defending his lack of a latency period in childhood and inviting them to describe for the movie audience their adult occupations (e.g., "I used to be a heroin addict," one boy explains, "Now I'm a methadone addict") and interests ("I'm into leather," another confesses [p. 8]), the comic effect is immediate and relatively uncomplicated.[8] The conventions of cinematic realism have been suspended here not only for the straightforward purposes of humor, but also to emblematize visually the point Alvy's mother will make about him in the scene's concluding line: "You never could get along with anyone at school. You were always outta step with the world" (p. 9).

Equally funny is Alvy's producing Marshall McLuhan from behind a billboard at the New Yorker theater to refute a pompous Columbia professor's self-congratulatory disquisition upon McLuhan's work, but the scene's culminating line—Alvy's apostrophe to the audience, "Boy, if life could only be like this!"—also introduces a subtextual theme that *Annie Hall* consistently elaborates. It begins with Alvy's oblique explanation for the non-linear structure of *Annie Hall* in his admission that "I have a hyperactive imagination. My mind tends to jump around a little, and I have some trouble between fantasy and reality" (p. 6). The theme culminates in his apology for the disjunction between reality and art in his play, which serves as prelude to his closing one-liner suggesting that we keep pursuing romantic relationships because of our need for the illusory eggs they provide. The connection is clear: only in artistic wish-fulfillment is Marshall McLuhan available to serve our yearnings for revenge against the outrages reality inflicts; only in fantasy do relationships provide the eggs we crave. The disparity between mental projections of reality and actuality is the pedal chord of *Annie Hall,* and its antimimetic emblems are the notes comprising that chord.

Annie Hall is, of course, permeated with antimimetic emblems like McLuhan's magical appearance, scenes in which realistic cinematic rendering is sacrificed to the expression of a different sort of truth. Alvy's recurrent addressing of the camera/audience is another such device, as is the cartoon in which Annie is depicted as the wicked witch from *Snow White,* her evil nature exacerbated by the onset of PMS. Alvy's amusing conversations on the street with complete strangers knowledgeable about his personal problems, his metamorphosis into a Hassidic rabbi at Annie's family's Easter dinner, the Hall and Singer families conversing over their Easter dinners across a split screen are further examples of these emblems. Such self-reflexive cinematic devices in *Annie Hall* constitute ingenious filmic means of dramatizing the difference between surface and substance, visual emblems incessantly distilling the distinction between the world mentally constructed and reality. As Graham McCann has argued, these devices reflect Allen's desire to "capture in images the variety of impressions and subjectivity of interpretations one experiences in the mind."[9] The irony of such scenes is that they distort the surface cinematic reality of a situation (Alvy and Annie's conversational sparring over the aesthetics of photography) in order to express its underlying reality (the subtitles manifesting the truth that they're scrutinizing each other as prospective sexual partners). Although the evolution of *Annie Hall* is too complicated to be understood in such neatly linear terms, these antimimetic emblems can be seen as the transitional tools of Allen's transformation of himself into a serious filmmaker, allowing him to transcend the movie and literary parodies of *Sleeper* and *Love and Death* with a form of comedic satire that explores the psychic and emotional sources of film and novelistic illusions.

Allen's ability to address with dramatic effectiveness the disparity between human perception or desire and reality is, more than anything else, the element of his work responsible for its having become more substantial than— to choose the most obvious and oft-cited contrast—the films of Mel Brooks, which generally settle for the parodying of literary and cinematic forms without exploring the psychic needs served by the forms being parodied. Brilliant as it is as film satire, Brooks's *Young Frankenstein*—probably his best film— seeks to displace *Frankenstein* through humor rather than seeking to illuminate the human desire that the original horror film addressed; it's Allen's examination of the needs that art is fulfilling for its audience which most emphatically differentiates his films from Brooks's.[10] Comedy, it can be argued, is *always* about the difference between what we think the world is and its actuality; what distinguishes *Annie Hall* from Allen's earlier comic films as well as from Brooks's is that its visual emblems evoke not only the difference between fantasy and reality, but they also dramatize the emotional cost to the perceiver of the awareness of that disparity. Rather than—as Brooks characteristically does—objectifying his protagonist in order to make him an easy target for laughter, these devices draw the viewer inside Alvy so that his emotional landscape becomes the viewer's as well. Cinematic correlatives of the theatrical soliloquy, the antimimetic emblems of *Annie Hall* simultaneously provide Allen's film with a quirky mode of humor, heighten the movie's aura of plain-dealing candor through their incessant transgression of cinematic conventions of representation, and entertainingly project the subjective reality of Alvy Singer. In their contradictory repudiation and enactment of artistic contrivance, they are the perfect artifices to inaugurate the serious filmmaking career of an artist irremediably suspicious of art.[11]

It's amusing, for example, that at the end of the film, Alvy's complaint about missing Annie elicits from a random pedestrian the fact that she is living with Tony Lacey (Paul Simon) in L.A., but underlying its humor is an effective dramatization of a preoccupation with Annie so overwhelming that Alvy imagines everyone on the streets of New York is acquainted with the details of their relationship.[12] Still more humorously affecting is the dramatization of Alvy's irrepressible need to articulate his problems with women as being so acute that he must unburden himself of them to a horse on which a mounted policeman sits. Even when his spirits are up, as they are when he and Annie have briefly reunited, Alvy's interior landscape gravitates toward admonitions and dire predictions anticipating the Cassandrean anxieties incessantly expressed by the chorus in *Mighty Aphrodite*. The visit to Alvy's Brooklyn childhood by Annie, Alvy, and Rob (Tony Roberts) culminates in Alvy's Aunt Tessie's assurances that she was a "great beauty," Alvy's mother affirming, "When she was younger, they all wanted to marry Tessie" (p. 74). That Tessie is no "great beauty" at this moment in Alvy's childhood is what Alvy is reminding himself of in revisiting the scene, the time having come for her (as it will for him) when "they" all no longer want to marry her. In the debate he is conducting with himself, which is the scene's subtext and stimulus, Alvy is worrying that if he doesn't marry Annie while she is pressuring him to make the commitment, before he knows it he'll be talking about his attractiveness to women in the past tense.

These privileged glimpses into Alvy's subjectivity don't convey truths solely about him. When, during the Easter dinner at Annie's, Alvy assures the film audience how different his family was from hers, the abruptly emerging split-screen dramatization of his point comically visualizes the contrast between them. The Halls' well-bred, WASPishly disinterested conversation about "swap meets and boat basins" contends with the antagonistic, emotionally intense dinner talk of the Singers, their conversation endlessly preoccupied with illnesses and other familial examples of human frailty and extremity. The Halls seem to prevail in the first round of the debate between families, which ensues when their dialogue between them across the split screen prompts Alvy's father (Mordecai Lawner) to admit to Mom Hall (Colleen Dewhurst) that he doesn't know what sins his family is seeking to atone for in fasting on the Easter holiday. However, there is another round.

After dinner, Annie's brother, Duane (Christopher Walken), invites Alvy into his room and confesses the morbidly masochistic fantasies he experiences while driving, his desire to precipitate an apocalyptic crash causing his own and others' annihilation. The pan shot through the windshield of Duane's MG which follows—Duane intently driving, Annie complacently watching the road, Alvy's face frozen in abject terror—is one of Allen's great comic triumphs; it tacitly represents a triumph for Alvy's family as well. If the Halls' dinner conversation weren't quite so bloodlessly civilized or were concerned with issues more substantial than swap meets and boat basins—if it acknowledged some of the darker realities of existence on which the Singers' communication seems so extravagantly fixated—Duane might be less subject to the development of a symptomatic neurosis spawned in part by his admission of such actualities to consciousness only in the privacy of his fantasies. (Had Alvy's family not been quite so combative over dinner, of course, his personality, "which is a little nervous, I think" [p. 6], would probably have benefitted as well.) The visual joke created by the pan across Duane's windshield isn't completely dependent upon the contextualizing effect of the split-screen device, but the laugh goes deeper if the viewer recognizes the extent to which this vignette cleverly reconfigures the film's thematic organizing conflict of fantasy and reality, the Halls' utter repudiation of actuality compensatorily tempting Duane to transform the oppressively civilized ordinary into the shape of his morbid fantasies. Alvy's father can't think of what sins his family is attempting to atone for by fasting; the Halls' Easter dinner scene dramatizes the familial sin for which Duane is unconsciously atoning: the denial of reality.

Of course, the denial of reality is also what Alvy's play is about. His acknowledgment of the desire to create art which deliberately attempts to improve aesthetically on the material that actuality has offered him introduces a conflict that pervades numerous Allen films, one reflected both in the choices his artist characters make and in the range of movies he has himself produced. Although *Annie Hall* does not end on the note of romantic reconciliation which is Alvy's play's resolution, the film's evolution reflects that it underwent a not dissimilar redemption by imposition of aesthetic form. "The whole conception of the picture changed as we were cutting it," Allen has explained. "It was originally a picture about me exclusively, not about a relationship. It was about me, my life, my thoughts, my ideas, my background, and the relationship was one major part of it. But sometimes it's hard to see at the outset what's going to be the most interesting drift."[13] The foregrounding of the Alvy/Annie relationship necessitated the elimination of nearly all of the original script's most surreal comic flights, which, as Ralph Rosenblum describes them, pushed well past the self-reflexivity of the antimimetic emblems discussed here into bizarre and surreal fantasia. In one deleted scene, Annie, Alvy, and Rob go to Hell, noting its various circles ("Layer Five: organized crime, fascist dictators, and people who don't appreciate oral sex") as they descend[14]; in another, Alvy and the *Rolling Stone* reporter (Shelley Duvall) visit the Garden of Eden and discuss the female orgasm with God; Alvy plays basketball against the New York Knicks on a team comprised of Kafka, Kierkegaard, Nietszche, and other literary giants[15]; Alvy and Annie reenact *The Night of the Living Dead* with a podded Rob in Beverly Hills.[16]

The disparity between the script which contained all these comedic excesses and the relatively tempered and coherent screenplay printed in *Four Films of Woody Allen* is both huge and hugely instructive. That disjunction becomes more striking when we consider another of Allen's characterizations of *Annie Hall's* evolution: "I said to myself," Allen recalled to Stig Bjorkman, "'I think I will try and make some deeper film and not be as funny in the same way [as in *Sleeper* and *Love* and *Death*]. And maybe there will be other values that will emerge, that will be interesting or nourishing for the audience'."[17] The transformation of this project from a comic script which would accommodate every kind of extravagant *shtick* Allen and Marshall Brickman could devise to the comparatively restrained and orderly retrospective narrative of *Annie Hall* contains within it the first stage of the transformation of Woody Allen from comic to serious film director.[18] Those antimimetic emblems considered insufficiently extreme to tear the film's realistic surface apart remain in the text and constitute the initial effective convergences of comedian and artist, exemplifying the first fully effective cinematic conciliations of Allen's conflicting desires to entertain and illuminate which continue to animate his movies. What that script also contains in the two endings projected by Arty and Alvy is the expression of a related ambivalence which has similarly pervaded Allen's entire filmmaking career: his conflict between "tryin' to get things to come out perfect in art" by making movies which reach gratifying resolutions, and making movies which close in the ungratifying but realistic irresolution of the ending of *Annie Hall.*

The anticlimax of that ending is tempered somewhat by the dramatization of the last meeting between Annie and Alvy in which they indulge themselves in the pleasure of "kicking around old times," and through which Allen offers the affirmation he has ready when his narrative leaves him with nothing else to affirm: memories. The soundtrack reprises Annie's/Keaton's lovely rendition of "Seems Like Old Times," the performance exemplifying the growth in artistic self-confidence that Annie has achieved, at least in part, as a consequence of her relationship with Alvy. (Inherent in the sophistication of the song's performance, ironically, is the inevitability of their relationship's termination, one provoked by Annie's desire to seriously pursue the singing career Alvy has encouraged her to believe she can have.) Then the screen fills with a montage of the couple's—and the audience's—favorite moments of their past together: of Alvy and Annie contesting live lobsters' resistance to becoming their dinner, of the two buying books which have "death" in their titles, of Annie withdrawing the negligee he bought for her birthday from its gift box,[19] of the two kissing on FDR Drive silhouetted against the New York skyline, and so on. Alvy, in voice-over, sums it all up by explaining, "After that it got pretty late. And we both hadda go. But it was great seeing Annie again, right? I realized what a terrific person she was and-and how much fun it was just knowing her, and I-I thought of that old joke, you know." (p. 105). The one-liner about the crazy brother who thinks he's a chicken follows, its conclusion suggesting that his brother would have him institutionalized but "we need the eggs."

Framed by the café table and chairs they sat in for their reunion lunch, their used plates and cups evoking an aura of pleasure spent and things used up, Annie and Alvy part on a Manhattan street, awkwardly shaking hands and then kissing, as the published script describes it, "friendly like" (p. 105). The protagonist who acknowledges having "some trouble between fantasy and reality" is left having to embrace fantasy in the form of romantic memories of Annie; given the highly sentimental "Seems Like Old Times" finale of *Annie Hall* to which we will return in the *Stardust Memories* chapter, Allen's distinctly hedged affirmation closing the film suggests that nostalgically projected imaginary eggs are better than never having had any eggs at all.

However, even that equivocal affirmation of the human capacity for nostalgia and the affectingly bittersweet close it undergirds, are problematized by the resonating overtones of Alvy's concession, "You know how you're always tryin' t' get things to come out perfect in art because it's real difficult in life." Perhaps appropriately, few viewers or critics applied Alvy's judgment to Allen's film, declining to perceive *Annie Hall* as, in its own way, an attempt to "get things to come out perfect in art," and therefore to be mistrusted as an aesthetically compromised vision of life. (Only Allen and Keaton, after all, know exactly how much *Annie Hall* constitutes an effort to "get things to come out perfect in art" which ended unhappily in life, and their perceptions probably differ as much as do Alvy's and Annie's as they analyze their relationship for their analysts.) Far from being received as a self-conscious artifice decrying its own artificiality, of course, *Annie Hall* was critically celebrated as a particularly inspired convergence of cinematic realism and artistic calculation, and it's probably advisable not to insist too vehemently on the presence of a dynamic of critical self-referentiality in the film. Alvy's comical effort to impress Annie with his ability to wield analytical jargon in their discussion of photography —"the medium enters in as a condition of the art form itself" (p. 40)—contains an admonition to critical restraint which is probably best to heed in this most transitional of serious Allen films. In the end, *Annie Hall* is at least as much about the disintegration of a romantic relationship as it is about art's capacity to distort reality, the film's hearteningly nostalgic ending discouraging viewers from applying Alvy's suspiciousness about artistic contrivance to the Woody Allen film they've just seen.

In *Annie Hall*, Allen had not yet resolved to make Alvy's—or his own—skepticism about his art and the subjective needs it fulfills for the artist a critical template according to which this film must, in turn, be evaluated. Nor—because Alvy's play is only viewed in rehearsal—had he begun to consider the affect of art upon its audience in his films. But four years later, in *Stardust Memories,* Allen forthrightly reconfronted that issue of artistic self-referentiality, making the romantic reconstruction of actuality which is artistic rendering precisely what his movie was about. Sandy Bates—a much more jaded and conflicted artist than neophyte dramatist Alvy—spends much of *Stardust Memories* trying to devise an appropriate ending for the film he's soon to release, his difficulty reproducing a recurrent dilemma of Allen's own scriptwriting and filmmaking career obliquely signaled in *Annie Hall's* alternative resolutions.[20]

Bates is subjected to endless pressures by Hollywood studio executives to create an upbeat commercial ending: they want him to revise the garbage dump wasteland that is the destination of the protagonist and other train passengers in Bates's original Bunuelian resolution into a sprightly "Jazz Heaven" close. Bates balks at this improbable ending, insisting that such a conclusion is a romantic distortion of the realities of human existence. In an ending-within-an-ending recalling *Annie Hall's*, and anticipating the thematic resolution of *Purple Rose of Cairo*, Bates settles for closing his film with the romantic reconciliation of the Bates character and Isobel. Isobel is clearly a traditionally maternal woman whose solidity counterpoints "the dark women (Dorrie and Daisy) with all their problems" to whom Bates is masochistically attracted throughout the film. Accordingly, a "big, big kiss" between Bates's protagonist and Isobel is the final image in Bates's movie, the scene paralleling the happy ending of Alvy's play, exemplifying Bates's attempt to "get things to come out perfect in art." Their ramifications differ, but the endings of Bates's film and Alvy's play converge in this: they constitute artistic resolutions dictated by what the heart hopes rather than by what the head knows.

Stardust Memories doesn't end with the ending of Bates's film, of course, but extends beyond dramatizing the need the movie has served its creator to the depiction of the audience's response to it. One viewer judges the movie "heavy," another pedantically scrutinizes the symbolic significance of the Bates character's Rolls Royce, the actresses who played Isobel and Daisy deplore Bates's French kissing techniques, and an elderly Jewish viewer expresses his preference for "melodrama, a musical comedy with a plot" (p. 378). Once the audience has left the auditorium, Bates enters, stares disconsolately up at the screen on which his film avatar's felicitous fate has recently played itself out, retrieves his sunglasses from a seat, and leaves the building, alone. It's obvious that Bates's downbeat exit is the scene *Annie Hall* omits, the one which necessitates that the audience of *Stardust Memories* compare the resolution of the protagonist's movie with the resolution of the Woody Allen film they are watching.

We return to *Stardust Memories* in a later chapter to consider the effect of its film-within-film complexities on Allen's conceptualization of the value of art to human lives; for the moment, only the alternative endings of *Annie Hall* and the disjunction between the conclusions of Bates's film and that of *Stardust Memories* will be compared. Allen's film never accounts for Bates's capitulation to a happy ending for his movie—perhaps the contrasting bleakness of *Stardust Memories'* close provides rationale enough. Nancy Pogel's reading of *Stardust Memories* emphasizes its debt to *8½,* tracing Bates's sunglasses to Fellini's movie and suggesting that Allen's placement of them among the seats in which the audience sat conveys the idea that, unlike Fellini's artist, whose superiority of aesthetic sensibility is never really challenged, Bates has been director *and* audience member, Allen's film making no claim for the supremacy of or distance between artist and audience.[21] *Stardust Memories* clearly *does* dramatize how much the audience wants Bates to be different from them, an artist to admire if not worship. However, the final scene introduces a point Allen's films repeatedly make about the artist: s/he's one of them, an individual no more capable of imagining a way out of the human dilemma than are they.

Similarly, the variety of the audience's responses to Bates's film reprises the multiplicity of personal obsessions which the attendees of the Sandy Bates Film Festival have psychically invested in him and importuned the director with throughout the weekend. The possibility of any narrative conclusion—to say nothing of an entire narrative—speaking to all of their lives, to their conditions, their circumstances, and their preoccupations, is minuscule. The only difference between them and Bates is that he's gained access to the media machinery enabling him to project his fantasies on movie screens. Produced nearly contemporaneously with the publication of sociological critiques of the American fixation upon the self such as *The Fall of Public Man* and *The Culture of Narcissism, Stardust Memories* suggests that the world is too multifarious and much too comprised of self-willed individualists driven by not-completely-sane obsessions for a film resolution dramatizing a conventionally romantic conjunction of man and woman to be anything more than an irrelevant oversimplification of life's dilemmas and complexities, a pretty lie predicated on an obsolescent aesthetic. In *Annie Hall,* Alvy's play indulges his own and his audience's desire for romantic closure in art; *Stardust Memories* dramatizes how inefficacious that act of artistic indulgence is for both audience and filmmaker.

Consequently, the sampling of the film's audience's response which is *Stardust Memories'* closing scene reflects no hint of audience gratitude for the romantic leap of faith in Bates's ending, nor is there any indication that the movie has managed even slightly to dislodge its viewers (or its actresses) from their professional complaints and personal anxieties or given them new ways of thinking about their everyday realities. Instead, the audience's response to Bates's film dramatizes Allen's earlier-cited contention that "there's no social value in art,"[22] the viewers displaying complete obliviousness to the film's idealistic conclusion. In terms of affect, the "big finish" of Bates's film is utterly ineffective, its generically romantic close exhilarating only Bates's most enthusiastic fan, whose verdict—"heavy!"—reflects nothing more than his subjective predisposition to adore anything Bates projects on the screen. This is certainly not Bates's first film, but the rest of Alvy's apology for his "Sunny" play seems completely applicable: "You know how you're always tryin' t' get things to come out perfect in art because it's real difficult in life." Few scenes in Allen's films dramatize art's perfection and the imperfectness of life more clearly than the image of Sandy Bates staring up disconsolately at the blank screen upon which his fictional persona's happy ending has moments before so purposelessly visualized itself.

For Bates, far more than for Alvy, the impulse to create art is inextricable from the human desire to locate in human existence the principles of order, coherence, aesthetic beauty, meaning, and the possibility for happiness. Bates derives his darker portion of this knowledge from 1981 Woody Allen, whose films had begun consistently to dramatize this desire and the inevitability of its disappointment. In *Stardust Memories,* Allen revisits and revises the sentimentally uncritical resolution of *Annie Hall,* finding little solace in the capacity of the mind to spin cheering illusions from the material of the past. From *Annie Hall* onward, Allen's film canon progressively constitutes a protracted debate between projections of the human imagination summarized by scenes from *Annie Hall* and *Stardust Memories:* Alvy Singer's effusion in the New Yorker theater lobby, "Boy, if life could only be like that," and Sandy Bates's wordless exit from a movie theater in which all images signifying erotic reconciliation and felicitous resolution of existential narrative have been erased from the screen.

4

Art and Idealization

I'll Fake *Manhattan*

People are always telling me that they don't know the New York I write about, that they don't know that it really ever existed. It may have only existed in movies, I don't know.

—Allen interview with Anthony DeCurtis in Rolling Stone

The idea that, as Garp phrases it in John Irving's *The World According to Garp,* "Fiction"—and thus, art in general—"has to be better made than life,"[1] is one of the central tenets of Modernism, a concept which, in a round-about way, assumes the compensatory capacity of aesthetic creation and the superiority of crafted art to gratuitous, inchoate existence. It is a notion to which Allen adheres in his own filmmaking practice, but one which provides his artist-characters with remarkably little compensatory solace for their sufferings.

Alvy Singer's play is, presumably, "better made than life," but it doesn't alter the actual circumstances it distorts; it's just a play, human existence manipulated into the patterns and rhetorical expectations of theatrical literature, a well-intended but disingenuous artifice. In *Bullets Over Broadway,* Cheech articulates a similarly irreverent attitude toward art, agreeing to a revision in his and David Shayne's play by replying, "Sure, why not? It's a play anyhow, but it'll be stronger." Whether the film for which Sandy Bates is seeking an ending in *Stardust Memories* is particularly "well-made" is difficult to determine given the brief scenes we see; what is certain is that this is an artwork which, once it has run its onscreen course, definitely seems to have a negligible effect on the lives of those who have watched it and apparently even less upon the life of its creator.

For Eve of *Interiors,* the pursuit of art's superiority to life culminates in complete alienation from life. The disparity between the disorderliness of human life and the "well-madeness of art" also provides a central dramatic tension in Allen's *Manhattan,* though in that film Allen has absorbed the aesthetic artifice so effectively into the film's narrative—which is to say into the consciousness of the movie's protagonist—that the tension between them becomes largely indistinguishable from the movie's plot. The exquisite craft of the film, which conjures up a city of Gershwinian sublimity, is contravened by the interior lives of its characters; in a significant sense, *Manhattan* is about its own cinematic "faking" of Manhattan.

The film opens with a series of images of New York—the skyline at dawn, the Empire State Building silhouetted against the sun, the neon lights of Broadway, Park Avenue on a snowy morning—cinematically framed in anamorphic long shot evoking a romantically inflationary distance, Gordon Willis's visualization of the ideal city synchronized with the soaring magnificence of Gershwin's "Rhapsody in Blue" on the soundtrack. The scale of these images and of Gershwin's composition complement each other perfectly, sight and sound culminating in a Central Park fireworks display which is this effusion of urban grandeur's apotheosis. Should the viewer wonder whose extraordinarily idealistic vision of the city this is, Isaac Davis's voice-over quickly resolves the mystery: "Chapter One," is his highly literary way of introducing himself. "He adored New York City. He idolized it all out of proportion. Uh, no, make that, he—he . . . he romanticized it all out of proportion." The opening three minutes of the film have dramatically visualized Isaac's romanticization of Manhattan, his perception of it as "a town that existed in black-and-white and pulsated to the great tunes of George Gershwin." As anyone who has watched *Hannah and Her Sisters, Another Woman, Alice, Manhattan Murder Mystery,* or *Everyone Says I Love You* can attest, romanticizing New York City "all out of proportion" is a proclivity Allen shares with his *Manhattan* protagonist. One distinguishing feature of his more substantial films is that they do what *Manhattan* does: they deliberately place under ironic scrutiny their own tropism toward idealizing New York. That self-critical attitude manifests itself in *Manhattan* through the juxtaposition of the city's magnificently visualized surfaces with what Isaac characterizes as its human substance and heart: "the decay of contemporary culture." To configure the central antinomy of the film differently, the cinematic art which makes *Manhattan* such a sumptuously gratifying visual experience finds nothing resembling an answering moral perfection in its characters, the film's repeatedly invoked disparity between surface and subject, form and content, generating its major thematic dynamic. To demonstrate that point, we need to move from the prologue's inspiring images of the New York cityscape to the tawdry domestic melodramas for which they provide an incongruously romantic backdrop.

In *Manhattan* we meet a number of characters who are, narrator Isaac Davis (Allen) posits in writing a short story, creating emotional and almost exclusively erotic difficulties for themselves—"unnecessary neurotic problems" which distract them from having to confront "more unsolvable, terrifying problems about . . . the universe" (p. 267). Yale Pollock (Michael Murphy) is having an affair with Mary Wilke (Diane Keaton) of which his wife, Emily (Anne Byrne), may be aware but refrains from confronting him about it. Yale's best friend, Isaac (whose ex-wife, Jill [Meryl Streep], publishes a tell-all book about their marriage and thoroughly acrimonious divorce), is seeing seventeen-year-old Tracy (Mariel Hemingway), a girl he knows he's using but with whom he can't break off until he has the opportunity to replace Yale as Mary's lover, the warm friendship between the two men shattered by Yale's subsequent, covert, and successful attempt to win Mary back from Isaac.[2]

The film abounds with scenes evocative of human duplicity and betrayal, but one of the most striking is that in which artistic perfection is contrasted with human perfidy and deceit. Isaac and Mary, who have become a couple following the breakup of her affair with Yale, attend a concert with Yale and Emily. Allen's framing of the scene juxtaposes the knowledge of the three against the ignorance of the one, the situation causing Isaac, Mary, and Yale to squirm with awkwardness and embarrassment through the performance of the *Jupiter* Symphony while Emily listens intently to a concert evoking an order and harmony utterly absent from these audience members' lives. (Emily, we subsequently learn, knows about Yale's affairs, but remains silent about them out of a conviction that they are testimony to her inadequacy as a wife, her self-destructive marital strategy replicating Mary's in a former marriage.) "Not everybody gets corrupted," Tracy tells Isaac at the end of the film when he makes a last-ditch effort to revive his love affair with the film's single embodiment of human innocence: "Look, you have to have a little faith in people" (p. 270). As the image of Isaac's skewed smile on which *Manhattan* affectingly closes clearly communicates, he can think of not a single reason provided in the last hour and a half's narrative for "having a little faith in people," everyone in the movie—himself included—having acted out ethics ranging from the unapologetically narcissistic to the helplessly neurotic.[3]

The jaded egotism of the characters in *Manhattan* is so deliberately combined throughout the film with aesthetically stunning images of New York that a substantial dramatic tension establishes itself between the morally tangled interior realms of the characters and the lush exterior urban landscape luxuriantly imaged up throughout the film, the soundtrack complementing the images with stunning Gershwin melodies such as "'SWonderful," "Embraceable You," and "Someone to Watch Over Me."[4] "Visually, and with glorious help from an often ironically used Gershwin score," Richard Schickel argued in his review of the film, Allen "has turned Manhattan, which is one of Allen's passions, into a dream city, deliberately contrasting the awesome aspirations implicit in its construction with the distracted lives he sees taking place in it."[5] In addition to being masterful artistic compositions evoking the musical craftsmanship of a past era, these "great tunes of George Gershwin" conjure up relationships of greater stability and permanence than the self-indulgent, emotionally tenuous, and largely temporary erotic liaisons depicted in the film.[6] (Tracy's suggestion that "maybe people weren't meant to have one deep relationship. Maybe we're meant to have a series of relationships of different lengths" [p. 197] is both naively formulated and contrary to the emotional and thematic trajectory of the film, her view of human commitment intersecting with Mary's inability to plan ahead as far as four weeks.[7]) The prominence of Gershwin's songs in *Manhattan* is partly a function of the film's having been inspired by Allen's listening to them one day,[8] and it reflects an even more intense attention to musical detail than Allen—who takes complete responsibility for the soundtracks of his films—regularly exercises. The perfect architectures of these melodies project a conception of musical affect approximating that described by Stanley Elkin in *The Living End*. "He had forgotten about music," Elkin wrote of a character who, being dead, hasn't heard any for a while: he had "forgotten harmony, the grand actuality of the reconciled. Forgotten accord and congruence—all the snug coups of correspondence. He did not remember balance. Proportion had slipped his mind and he'd forgotten that here was where world dovetailed with self, where self tallied with sympathy and distraction alike."[9]

The "grand actuality of the reconciled," the creation of which constitutes art's primary beneficence for Elkin, is something *Manhattan*'s characters never experience. These selves with their "unnecessary neurotic problems" and erotic distractions from existential anxieties are too fragmented, too tenuously constructed, and too self-absorbed to dovetail with exterior reality. This point is perfectly visualized by Willis's image of the shadows of Isaac and Mary framed against a planetarium backdrop of deep, star-studded space as she laments the frustrations of "having an affair with a married man" (p. 222). So it's entirely appropriate that the movie opens with Isaac's attempt to craft the first paragraph of the autobiographical novel on Manhattan he's trying to write. In seeking that beginning, Isaac is searching, as Sam B. Girgus noticed, for "an adequate single voice and identity for himself"[10] among his perceptions of the place. Consequently, the prologue's positioning of the completely achieved musical authority of "Rhapsody in Blue" with Isaac's halting, improvisatory attempts to identify with his melodramatic projections of Manhattan introduces the film's central conflict between the wholeness of art and the inescapable fragmentariness and indeterminacy of life unmediated by it. Isaac's self-revelatory and self-reconstituting efforts to make self dovetail with the world of New York City continue:

> "To him, New York meant beautiful women and street-smart guys who seemed to know all the angles." Nah, too corny . . . for . . . my taste. I mean, let me try and make it more profound. "Chapter One: He adored New York City. To him, it was a metaphor for the decay of contemporary culture. The same lack of individual integrity to cause people to take the easy way out was rapidly turning the town of his dreams into—" No, it's gonna be too preachy. I

mean, you know . . . let's face it, I wanna sell some books here . . . "Chapter One. He was as tough and romantic as the city he loved. Behind his black-rimmed glasses was the coiled sexual power of a jungle cat." I love this. "New York was his town, and it always would be" (pp. 181–82).

Like *Annie Hall,* then, *Manhattan* opens with a Woody Allenesque monologue. However, the differences between Isaac's monologue and Alvy Singer's are instructive not only for the disparate tones they establish for the films they introduce, but also for the disparate levels of sympathy they elicit in the two films' audiences for their narrators/protagonists. Alvy addresses the movie audience directly, offering us jokes tinged with self-parody and the confession that he "can't get his mind around" losing Annie. The primary impression his monologue conveys is that of sincerity: through humor and self-revelation, he is honestly expressing his basic human vulnerability.[11] (The film's antimimetic emblems tend to reinforce its overall aura of genuineness, the instant empathy viewers experience with Alvy making colder and more cryptic subsequent Allen films such as *Interiors* and *Stardust Memories* seem, to *Annie Hall* devotees, a particularly unforgivable betrayal.) Although *Annie Hall's* dramatization of the evolution of Alvy's relationship with Annie exposes less than ideal character traits in him (condescension toward her want of intellect inspiring his project of reshaping her in his own image, for starters), Alvy remains merely humanly flawed, a protagonist whose predominantly sympathetic nature is never seriously questioned.[12]

In contrast, the more emphatically judgmental disposition of *Manhattan* is signaled by an opening monologue characterized by markedly greater rhetorical equivocation than is Alvy's. Rather than a forthright address to the audience, Isaac's monologue is, quite appropriately, internal, and its honesty derives not from a desire to deal plainly about himself with others but from his rapt attentiveness to his own personal agendas. Anyone who has ever tried to write seriously can empathize with Isaac's incessant revising of his book's beginning; what makes his restarts troubling is how completely they dramatize his self-consciousness about his task, the extent to which they are dictated by the response he expects others to have to them. As Isaac circulates through a *film noir* narrator's hard-bitten self-romanticizing to the diction of a moralizing cultural critic to an admission of his desire "to sell some books" and then on to his successful—in fantasy, at any rate—identification of himself with the city's sexual energy, it becomes patently evident that what he seeks is a construction of Manhattan which expresses him—the self, as Elkin suggests, seeking to dovetail with the world in a thoroughly narcissistic and fraudulent way. What's distinctly lacking from Alvy's monologue in Isaac's continual self-reconceptualizations is the sincerity manifested by Alvy's consistency of self-presentation, and if Isaac's rewrites fall well short of Leonard Zelig's chameleon-like responsiveness to and mimicry of others, they're nonetheless gravitating in that direction. What Isaac is doing, which Alvy never does, is trying to be someone he's not, and the Manhattan of the film which is his projection (or self-projection) can be said to manifest the same tendency: fictionalized inflation.[13]

In case we've failed to notice the moral critique implicit in Isaac's literary self-reconfigurings, the film's first dramatic scene portrays the protagonist even more dubiously than does the prologue. The "Rhapsody in Blue" fireworks extravaganza opening the film dwindles to a scene in Elaine's, where Yale and Emily are insisting that Isaac is in a condition nearly unprecedented for protagonists Allen plays: "You're drunk. You know you should never drink."[14] His attempt at hypercorrect diction ("I-I'm dating a girl wherein I can beat up her father" [p. 184]) confirms their perception. Like Isaac's opening monologue, the Elaine's scene dramatizes a discontinuity between Isaac's professed and actual selves, his mock explanation that he's smoking only because "I look so incredibly handsome with a cigarette" seeming narcissistic in a way more irritating than amusing. Subsequently, his assertion that "the most important thing in life is courage" is immediately trivialized by his self-proclaimed exemption from the moral test he has himself posited: if the four of them saw someone drowning in the icy waters on their way home, Isaac would "never have to face" the challenge to his courage the situation embodies because he can't swim.[15] Despite the moralistic poses he occasionally strikes in the film,[16] Isaac *does* perceive himself as being exempt from moral norms; that fact makes *Manhattan* the first of Allen's films in which the character of the protagonist he is playing is configured in such a way as to continually invite the viewer's ethical scrutiny and evaluation.[17]

Although he experiences temporary success in imbuing himself with the city's sexiest virtues, throughout the rest of the film the Manhattan in Isaac's mind remains an ideal, unchanging metropolis completely irreconcilable with the emotional inconstancy, faithlessness, and *ex tempore* egocentrism of its actual inhabitants. Isaac's tendency to disregard substance in favor of romantic surface also characterizes his perception of Tracy and of his relationship with her. He allegorizes her great beauty as "God's answer to Job," attributing to her a loveliness so cosmically significant that He could use it to justify His ways to humanity. "I do a lot of terrible things," Isaac's God acknowledges as Isaac gestures toward Tracy, "but I can also make one of *these*." Isaac's God's Exhibit A leaves Job with no response except, "Eh, okay—well, you win" (p. 227). Tracy's physical beauty is unquestionably the solitary grounds for Job's conceding God's case.[18] Isaac spends much of the movie denying any future for his relationship with Tracy, insisting that she is emotionally too young for him to take seriously. It follows that in a relative way, Isaac is able to dismiss the emotional devastation he visits upon Tracy in rejecting her in favor of

Mary ("You really hurt me," she acknowledges to him at film's end) as "just the way I was looking at things then" (p. 271). His justification constitutes nothing resembling the ethical stance of someone who is, in Yale's character-ization, so moral, so "perfect,"[19] and so "self-righteous" that "You think you're God" (p. 265). If Isaac thinks he's God, it's one who insists that physical beauty—surface appearance—is creation's best argument. When his ex-wife, Jill, reminds him that he knew her bisexual history when he married her, Isaac responds, "Yeah, I know. My analyst warned me, but you were so beautiful that I—I got another analyst" (p. 217).

Two other comments from Isaac epitomize his penchant for valuing surface and superficialities over substance, appearance over interiority. At a Museum of Modern Art reception, a discussion of orgasms prompts Isaac to acknowledge that even the worst ones he's had have been "right on the money" (p. 205), his assertion implicitly dismissing the claims of a partner to self-gratification. He articulates a similarly absolute preference for the purely physi-cal in repudiating reason to Mary Wilke: "Nothing worth knowing can be understood with the mind," he tells her. "E-e-everything really valuable has to enter you through a different opening . . . if you'll forgive the disgusting imagery." For someone putatively writing a book excoriating "decaying val-ues," Isaac situates himself in anything but an elevated vantage point from which to deliver moral maxims. "No, no . . . you rely too much on your brain," he concludes in his antirationalist sermon to Mary: "The brain is the most overrated organ, I think" (p. 223).

Perhaps the central emblem of the film's thematic surface/substance antinomy is the one visual gag Allen allowed himself to leave in the movie as it evolved from what producer Charles Joffe described as "a drama with comedy rather than a comedy with drama."[20] Isaac and Mary are rowing across the placid surface of a lovely Central Park lake; languorously trolling his wrist beneath the water's surface, Isaac withdraws a handful of mud. "Isn't it beautiful, Ike?" Mary asks him earlier in the film as they watch the dawn illuminating the 59th Street Bridge while a lushly orchestral "Someone to Watch Over Me" plays on the soundtrack. "Yeah, it's really—really so pretty when the light starts to come up," he answers, "This is really a great city . . . it's . . . really a knockout," (p. 212). The deeply poignant moment they've shared is abruptly annulled by Mary's announcement that she has to get home—she's meeting her lover, Yale, for an intimate lunch later that day. Nowhere in Allen's films is there a more compelling symbol of the idea that the human capacity to perceive—or create—beauty is not necessarily accompanied by a corollary moral capacity; in contravention of Keats's poetic equation, *Manhattan,* like Allen's other movies, suggests that beauty is beauty, and truth—if it exists at all—is something else.

What Allen crafts in *Manhattan* is a drama forged out of the disparity between his own romantic, nostalgic conception of New York ("I had a real urge to show New York as a wonderland," he told Eric Lax, "and I completely exorcised that feeling in *Manhattan*"[21]) and his opposed conviction of the debased, neurotic souls of late-twentieth-century New Yorkers whom Isaac characterizes as reflective of "the decay of contemporary culture." (*Manhattan,* Julian Fox quotes Allen as saying, sets the "romantic vision of New York against the mess that people make out of their lives."[22]) Until the very last images of the film, the only thing in *Manhattan* that survives corruption is the aesthetically perfect conception of New York which Isaac carries in his head and which Allen—in concert with Gordon Willis and George Gershwin—projects cinematically on the screen. That this conception of "New York as a wonderland" was intended to have a corresponding repository of images in the film is suggested by the major reservations Allen has, in retrospect, expressed about this movie.

Allen's two complaints about *Manhattan* seem to exist in inverse relation to each other: he had trouble finding sites to photograph beautiful enough to match the ideal image of New York in his mind, and he failed to capture on film the real magnitude of Mariel Hemingway's beauty. In the one instance, reality failed to live up to the filmmaker's imagination; in the other, an imaginative cinematic projection failed to do justice to the human reality. *Manhattan's* reviewers' unanimous acclamation for the film's complete success at "romanticizing New York out of all proportion" suggests that others saw no disparity between intention and achievement in the film's deliberate cinematic idealization of the city. Allen's second self-critique is more intriguing.

Shortly after hearing that Allen felt Mariel Hemingway's beauty had been shortchanged by the film, Pauline Kael told Allen that Hemingway looked perfectly lovely in it. Subsequently, Kael saw the actress in a restaurant. Declaring the young woman "a goddess," she confirmed Allen's conviction that *Manhattan* falls short of conveying the young actress's beauty. But perhaps even Kael couldn't imagine what the magnitude of that beauty was in Allen's eyes. Having seen pictures of Hemingway in *Interview*, Allen acknowledged, "I thought—and still do think—that she's probably the most beautiful woman the world has ever seen." If convincing the viewer of that perception was what Allen's film had to achieve in order to work, *Manhattan* seems to have been doomed to failure.[23]

Allen's ambitions for Tracy's visual presence in the film may suggest that Tracy and the Manhattan of George Gershwin were intended to correspond to each other more compellingly, to function more nearly as equivalents— Tracy representing in visual terms as much as the idealized city does an exception to and antidote for the corruption Isaac finds at the city's heart. That such a conception exists in the film is reflected in Tracy's association with the beautiful face of New York—particularly through the museums which she and Isaac frequent and through the Central Park hansom cab ride she insists they take together—and in Allen's comment that New York City "is sort of one of the characters in the film."[24] If one can imagine a character carrying the symbolic weight equal to a place Isaac and the Gershwin soundtrack have "romanticized out of all proportion," it becomes clear what is at stake in the final scene of *Manhattan.* Isaac not only fears losing Tracy while she's studying at the Academy of Music and Dramatic Arts in London: "You'll be with actors and directors," he tells her, "You'll eat lunch a lot. . . and, and well, you know, attachments form." He also dreads losing that element of Tracy which is as precious to him as his Gershwin-embellished conception of New York and which, in the film's symbolic economy, is indistinguishable from it.

If she carries through her plan to go to England for six months, he tells Tracy, "I mean, you-you'll change . . . in six months you'll be a completely different person. . . . I-I just don't want that thing I like about you to change" (p. 271). In *Shadows and Fog*, Max Kleinman responds to the assertion by Irmy that the sky is beautiful when the fog clears and the stars shine through, "Yes, but it passes so quickly . . . even now the fog is starting to go back in . . . everything's always moving all the time, everything's constantly in motion— no wonder I'm nauseous." In *Husbands and Wives*, Judy dismisses the assertion of her husband, Gabe, equating change with death as a "bullshit line" which would convince only his impressionable twenty-year-old students. In

Mighty Aphrodite, Amanda accuses her husband, Lenny, of being "opposed to change in any form." That Allen attributes to four different characters he portrays a fear of change is certainly not an insignificant fact. Having rejected Mary in favor of his marriage before reversing himself again, Isaac's former best friend, Yale, is *Manhattan's* central embodiment of inconstancy, Isaac telling his friend sarcastically that he can "change his mind" about Mary and Emily "one more time before dinner" if he likes (p. 264). Earlier in *Manhattan,* Isaac and Mary stop in front of a construction site, Isaac dismally reflecting that "The city's really changing" (p. 252). Ironically, the other agent in which Isaac has invested his preoccupation with fixity and permanence is the one in whom change is even more inevitable than it is in a major metropolis: a seventeen-year-old girl.

As Isaac confronts Tracy in the lobby of her apartment building in an effort to dissuade her from departing for London, the change he dreads is already noticeable in her response to him. For one thing, she's turned eighteen and is, as she points out, "legal." Isaac's attempt at a joke that "in some countries [at eighteen], you'd be . . ." fails to generate a punch line, assumedly because he doesn't relish pondering what she'd be eligible to do in other countries at eighteen. Discomfited by this thought, he shifts to more familiar, comfortable ground: "Hey, you look good." (When interiority unnerves you, Isaac believes, resort to appearances.) Isaac finds her response to his reappearance equally disconcerting. When he breaks off their relationship earlier in the film, she accuses him of making the severance sound "like it's to my advantage when it's you that wants to get out of it" (p. 245). What she intuits and rebukes there is Isaac's penchant for rhetorical indirection and prevarication, the nearly complete antithesis of the innocent ingenuousness he has so valued in her. Her reaction to his attempt to coerce her into staying in New York is to remind him of the arguments he previously offered her in support of her studying in England. The effect of her response demonstrates how closely Isaac has replicated Mary's incapacity to plan four weeks ahead, since it seems little longer ago than that that Isaac was urging Tracy to go to London, precipitating the breakup he's seeking to repair now. The film's central antagonist against impermanence is being given a lesson in his own inconstancy and changeability, one he ignores because of his intentness upon preventing Tracy from walking out the door to the limousine awaiting her. "We've gone this long," she replies, "What's six months if we still love each other?" Tracy's response to Isaac conveys dissimulation more than love, enacting her newly developed ability to turn Isaac's own choices and arguments against him. "Hey," Isaac responds irritably, exposing the *idée fixe* she represents for him, "don't be so mature, okay?" Ultimately, he resorts to pleading: "Oh, come on . . . you don't have to go."

"Six months isn't so long," she repeats before delivering the prevarication which reinforces that untruth: "Not everybody gets corrupted." It's not merely that the characters of Allen's movie provide no supporting evidence for Tracy's resonant declaration, thus invalidating it. Her subsequent admonition that "you have to have a little faith in people" (p. 271) is precisely what Isaac a few weeks before proved to her she couldn't have. His recognition of the disparity between what she knows and what she says in order to get away from him to the airport elicits the sadly bemused smile on Isaac's face in the film's final dramatic frames: in telling him disingenuously that not everybody gets corrupted, she's proving that she has been. Isaac's pained, crooked smirk silently registers his realization that "that thing I like about you" he feared would change over six months in London has changed already.[25]

As if in corroboration of the link between the now-tainted Tracy and the Gershwinized New York, *Manhattan* ends with "Rhapsody in Blue" swelling up once again, providing soundtrack for three concluding images: the city skyline in dazzling morning sunlight, the skyline shrinking into the distance as ponderous clouds descend upon it, and the city barely visible beneath a dense, dark overcast. That this closing montage is intended to evoke the lyrics ("With love to show the way, I've found more clouds of gray/ than any Russian play could guarantee") of Gershwin's "But Not for Me," which played underneath Isaac and Tracy's closing encounter, is highly probable; that the movie's last five minutes have all but simultaneously dulled the glow of Tracy and the romanticized New York seems incontestable. The teenager whom Isaac credited with being God's answer to Job seems to have descended just far enough into adult erotic legerdemain to no longer represent the ground on which God could justify the mysteriousness of His ways to humanity. She has fallen sufficiently in Isaac's estimation no longer to constitute the saving exception to the "decay of contemporary culture" epitomized by himself and his friends, his single extant proof that the creation is good having undergone the ultimate betrayal: change.

As for the film's idealized New York, its visualization culminates not in a repetition of the fireworks that close the stunning opening montage but fades into distance and obscurity despite the reprise of "Rhapsody in Blue," the musical artifice alone sustaining the emotional exaltation associated with the city throughout the film. The Manhattan of *Manhattan* turns out to be a fantasy projection so narcissistically magnificent and pure that it can live on only in art. Ironically, the capacity for which Allen is indicting art in *Manhattan* is its ability to transform reality into something more morally coherent, harmonious, and beautiful than it actually is. ("Beauty is untruth," might be the film's rewriting of Keats.) New York remains Isaac Davis's town at the end of *Manhattan,* and it probably always will be his town. But it's a much smaller, much bleaker, and much less romantic city than the one Tracy and George Gershwin—and Gordon Willis—illuminated for him. And for us.

5

Strictly the Movies II

How *Radio Days* Generated Nights at the Movies

It's me thinly disguised. I don't think I should disguise it any more—it's me.

—Harry Block acknowledging the autobiographical basis
of his fiction in *Deconstructing Harry*

In *Manhattan,* Isaac Davis is, as was Allen at the time, in the process of creating an artistic document culturally anatomizing Manhattan, one deliberately romanticizing its subject. The similarity of the artistic projects of Isaac and Allen—"Chapter One," Isaac/Allen opens the film without identifying himself—tends to blur the boundary separating protagonist from screenwriter, this elision having become one of the primary devices Allen's films employ to further complicate their exploration of the relationship between art and life. Since Charlie Chaplin, no other film actor has been more popularly and consistently conflated with his on-screen persona than Allen, who dresses his part every day on the set whether he's appearing in the film he's shooting at the moment or is only directing it. As a result, few moviegoers who have seen any of the films in which Allen appears would be confused by the term "Woody Allen protagonist." Even when Allen plays characters bearing personal histories divergent from his own in films set in other lands or eras (*Love and Death, Midsummer Night's Sex Comedy, Broadway Danny Rose, Shadows and Fog*), the small, Jewish, self-doubting, God-seeking, death-fixated egocentric who stutters when threatened and unaccountably attracts the screen's most beautiful women ultimately emerges, becoming the figure we conceptualize as that aggregate cinematic fabrication, "Woody Allen."

As Allen's biographers have clearly established, the "Woody Allen" persona was largely formed by the time television gag writer Allan Konigsberg changed his name to Woody Allen in the mentally trying process of transforming himself into a stand-up comedian,[1] his then agent Jack Rollins suggesting that "Woody's material was always about the person behind it."[2] Allen later cinematically confirmed the autobiographical connection between himself and this "Woody Allen" self-projection by incorporating into *Annie Hall* three different flashbacks: two in which Alvy Singer delivers jokes Allen used in his own stand-up routine in the 1960s,[3] and another in which a clip of Allen's appearance on *The Dick Cavett Show* impersonates a guest appearance by Alvy Singer.

Partly because of deliberate cinematic choices like these that Allen has made, the filmgoing public's identification of him with the protagonists he portrays in movies is so automatic as to seem transparent. What makes this issue worth delving into is Allen's awareness of that identification and his calculated exploitation of the relationship for rhetorical purposes in films such as *Radio Days* and *Deconstructing Harry*. That Allen's films to some degree reconfigure his personal experiences *is* self-evident,[4] a fact no more startling than that Truffaut's or Fellini's movies construct aesthetic artifices out of the raw material of these auteurs' lives; what Allen manages to do in *Radio Days* and *Deconstructing Harry* is to manipulate the audience's assumptions of the autobiographical nature of his work to generate subtextual tensions reinforcing the dynamics of his plots. Consequently, for the viewer, speculating about where actuality recedes and fabrication begins is one of the central interpretive pleasures of *Radio Days* and *Deconstructing Harry*, one only slightly less central to the rhetorical designs of *Annie Hall, Manhattan, Stardust Memories, Hannah and Her Sisters, Crimes and Misdemeanors,* and *Husbands and Wives.* Because so many of his major films deliberately exploit the ambiguous relationship between Allen's life and art, it seems necessary to briefly summarize what Allen's biographers delineate in much greater detail: the convergences and divergences between Allen's biography and how he fictionalizes it in movies.

Most significantly, perhaps, Alvy Singer's and Isaac Davis's pilgrimages from popular entertainment (stand-up comedy and scripting a television variety show) to play and novel writing roughly approximate the trajectory of Allen's own career. His professional transmutation from comedy writing and comic performance to the production of comic and then serious films is one also reenacted in truncated form in *Hannah and Her Sisters* by Mickey Sachs, who follows Isaac's lead in repudiating television by quitting his lucrative producer's job. In a more oblique parallel, Clifford Stern of *Crimes and Misdemeanors* rebels against his glitzy showbiz brother-in-law, Lester, by producing a PBS documentary on him so venomously satirical that Lester refuses to approve its airing and fires him from the project. Cliff's expulsion places him in the same circumstance his fellow protagonists have more consciously chosen: he has exiled himself from the world of television. We never see the ramifications of Cliff's self-exile from television, but it is obvious that Allen's own similar move away from pop culture to serious art carried a significant personal cost.

Of course, Allen himself abandoned television scriptwriting for stand-up comedy and, ultimately, serious filmmaking. However, it's difficult not to see in the defections of Bates, Sachs, and Stern allegory as opposed to autobiography: Allen is figuring another conversion from pop culture for serious art in those films. The preponderance of negative responses of film critics and reviewers to *Interiors* and to Allen's overall defection from comedy in the late

1970s figures centrally in the repeated admonitions of attendees at the Sandy Bates Film Festival in *Stardust Memories* that he should return to making his "early, funny movies," the existential preoccupations of Bates which incited the change clearly reproducing Allen's own frequently acknowledged depressive tendencies. Allen is never more autobiographical than when his films debate the virtues of entertainment vs. the culturally superior claims of serious art.

More personal details from life emerge in Allen's films as well. Allen experienced the loss of hearing in one ear, which Isaac briefly complains of in *Manhattan* and which Mickey Sachs undergoes a battery of tests to diagnose, both *Hannah* protagonist and his creator fearing that they had a brain tumor.[5] Allen's relationship with Diane Keaton (born Diane Hall) inspired *Annie Hall;* commentators and gossip columnists differ on which scenes and how much. Isaac's relationship with Tracy in *Manhattan* has its antecedent in Allen's late-1970s relationship with a seventeen-year-old actress named Stacey Nelkin, who saw little similarity between Tracy and Isaac's affair and hers and Allen's.[6] Nonetheless, one Allen associate found that film most closely approaching an autobiographical version of Allen's life: "Maybe he was most like himself in *Manhattan,*" Allen's longtime producer, Rollins, told Julian Fox, "I can't be specific but in my mind it's the closest to what he actually is."[7] Allen is right to object that critics identified him excessively with Sandy Bates in *Stardust Memories* and with Harry Block as well, but in doing so he often minimized the inducements those films offered to make them "think it's me."

That Allen's films—like Harry Block's fiction—appropriate lives other than his own for artistic purposes is easy to substantiate. Eve of *Interiors* was partly inspired by Louise Lasser's mother,[8] Mia Farrow has acknowledged that her parents and sisters provided the model for Hannah's family,[9] and *Alice* is interpretable as the narrative of a pampered, wealthy New York woman possessed of Farrow's Catholic girlhood who, through the magic realism intervention of Dr. Yang, gradually acquires Farrow's widely acknowledged virtues of maternal devotion and social conscience. *Husbands and Wives* draws at the very least its aura of fractiousness and acrimony from the emotions resulting from the disintegration of the Allen/Farrow relationship, from which *Manhattan Murder Mystery* seems in a highly self-conscious way to offer light comedic distraction. Diane Keaton's replacement of Farrow in the female lead of *Mystery* created a palely nostalgic resurrection of the Alvy/Annie pairing in the marriage of Larry (Allen) and Carol, Carol's adventurous pursuit of a neighbor's murder being repeatedly counterpoised with her husband's largely unexplained passivity and reclusiveness.[10] And then there is *Deconstructing Harry,* a film inconceivable—and unintelligible—without the background of the Allen/Farrow public melodrama which transformed Allen into a tabloid villain. As this brief survey suggests, autobiography figures significantly in Allen's scripts, a fact he has infrequently acknowledged. One such instance: "Maybe it's because I'm depressed so often that I'm drawn to writers like Kafka and Dostoevsky and a filmmaker like Bergman. I think I have all the symptoms and problems that their characters are occupied with: an obsession with death, an obsession with God or the lack of God, the question of why are we here. Almost all of my work is autobiographical—exaggerated but true."[11]

Much more typical of Allen, however, is to contest the assertion that his films are autobiographical, the filmmaker often patiently outlining differences between himself and his protagonists to substantiate the distinction. "I was not born under a roller coaster on Coney Island," he told the *Daily News* in response to a reporter's insistence that Alvy Singer *is* Woody Allen, "nor was my first wife politically active, nor was my second wife a member of the literary set, nor did Diane leave me for a rock star, or to live in California."[12] Similarly, Allen has argued, *Stardust Memories* was not about him but about "a filmmaker on the verge of a nervous breakdown who saw the world in a distorted way,"[13] the film visualizing Sandy Bates's distorted perspective rather than Allen's own.

Beyond the obvious fact that human beings and film characters aren't identical, there are other clear and significant differences between Allen and his aggregate screen persona. Few of his protagonists betray the shyness, reclusiveness, and preference for solitude which his biographers—and Allen himself—generally agree upon as his central personal traits. More importantly, none of them displays Allen's capacity to immerse himself in work, the dedication to screenwriting and filmmaking which has allowed him to produce a movie a year for nearly thirty years, nor has he granted them the musical ability documented throughout *Wild Man Blues* or his authority as a director. Because the Woody Allen persona was initially conceived as a comic construct, a character developed to elicit laughter from audiences, he must remain—even in his less comic incarnations in later films such as *Crimes and Misdemeanors, Shadows and Fog,* and *Everyone Says I Love You*—in some measure a failure in the world, a fictional distillation of Allen's feelings of human inadequacy largely omitting characteristics reflective of Allen's very real professional and artistic success.[14]

Tellingly, the protagonists of his with whom Allen most readily identifies aren't "Woody Allen" protagonists at all. Eve of *Interiors* and Marion Post of *Another Woman* are two of these, workaholic women whose cerebralism and personal austerity cripples their relationships with others; the third is *The Purple Rose of Cairo*'s Cecilia, whose wide-eyed adoration of the romantic illusions woven by Hollywood reflects the same vulnerability and personal emotional deprivation Eve and Marion have constructed elaborate defense mechanisms against having to acknowledge.[15] That the characters least resembling him are those with whom Allen most identifies seems an irresolvable contradiction of his work, one paralleling that which he invoked in yet another comment on *Annie Hall* which must serve as a coda for this tangled critical issue. "I was playing myself," Allen explained, "but not in autobiographical situations for the most part."[16]

Although the ambiguity of the relationship between Allen and his comic persona colors our experience of and significantly influences our interpretations of many of his films, it's in *Radio Days* that Allen most deliberately exploits that ambiguity to provide his film with a dramatic substructure. Reprising a device he used to great effect in *Annie Hall* and *Manhattan*, Allen delivers the opening monologue of *Radio Days* without introducing himself, his voice-over apologizing for the dramatic imagery appearing on the screen: "Forgive me if I tend to romanticize the past. [Rockaway] wasn't always as stormy and windswept as this, but I remember it that way because that was it at its most beautiful."[17]

Even as this monologue alerts viewers that the images they are about to see are intentionally romanticized versions of someone's past, the absence of any introduction of the speaker tacitly invites the audience to infer that the film is autobiography, to believe that in *Radio Days* the by-now highly familiar Woody Allen voice is presenting his own childhood in relatively unmediated terms. Not surprisingly, reviewers assumed that the film *was* Allen's personal memoir, disregarding Richard Schickel's admonition that because the movie's central family "lives near Allen's old neighborhood and includes a shy, slender, red-haired boy, the unwary may conclude that Allen is being autobiographical."[18] *Radio Days*, of course, *is* patently autobiographical: the Konigsbergs *did* live with relatives, they *did* have Communist neighbors, young Allan *was* an indifferent student more interested in radio programs than school, and he *did* use his mother's new coat for a chemistry experiment.[19] For all of its sources in Allen's childhood experiences and circumstances, however, and for all its painstakingly precise recreation of 1940s America through Santo Loquasto's stunning sets and Carlo Di Palma's honey-tinged cinematography, *Radio Days* remains an aesthetic artifice, an artistic distillation of life rather than a slavish naturalistic replication of it. "I think of *Radio Days* basically as a cartoon," Allen told Stig Bjorkman. "If you look at my mother, my Uncle Abe, my schoolteacher, my grandparents, they were supposed to be cartoon exaggerations of what my real-life people were like."[20]

So while there exists a strongly implied sense of autobiography, the memoir which is *Radio Days* is distinctly fictionalized. Although his name is used only once—and then nearly inaudibly—in *Radio Days* before its appearance in the closing credits, the red-haired boy (Seth Green) who plays the film's narrator as a child was referred to not as Allan but as "Little Joe" throughout the shooting of the film.[21] As Thierry Navacelle's diary of the film's shooting, *Woody Allen on Location*, illustrates in great detail, the process of script development and the production of the film differed little from the process of endless revision and reconceptualization involved in the making of Allen's more patently fictional movies.[22] The retention of no line or scene was ever justified on the grounds that it actually happened in Allen's childhood experience and had to be retained for that reason. It follows that the radio programs the film's characters listen to teasingly approximate actual titles and performers: *The Masked Avenger* with his admonition "Beware all evildoers, wherever you are!" recalls *The Shadow* and his trademark question, "Who knows what evil lurks in the hearts of men?"; *Guess that Tune* is modeled on 1940s radio's *Name that Tune;* Mr. Abercrombie's marriage counseling hour recalls a similar show hosted by Mr. Anthony; Irene and Roger's breakfast show resembles Pegreen and Ed Fitzgerald's; *Whiz Kids* changes only two letters of *Quiz Kids.*

The fictionality of *Radio Days* is worth insisting upon because, like Allen's other films, *Radio Days* uses dramatic manipulation of its materials to present an argument about its subject—in this case, radio's relationship to Allen's filmmaking career, and its relation to real life as well. What needs to be illuminated here is the way in which the movie exploits the ambiguity of the relationship between filmmaker and protagonist to close that argument and give it dramatic immediacy. Throughout the film, Little Joe's parents complain incessantly about their son's lackluster performance at school, which they ascribe to the distraction of radio programs. When Joe responds to an angry lecture from his Hebrew School rabbi (Kenneth Mars), "You speak the truth, my faithful Indian companion," the rabbi and his parents take turns slapping him around for being so influenced by radio shows. (That Little Joe in this scene enlists an icon from radio—the Lone Ranger—to buttress his rebellion against religious authority reflects a preference that Allen's protagonists consistently evince when obliged to choose between their ethnicity/religion and the popular culture so influential in their childhoods.) One day at the zoo, mother, father, and son meet a *Whiz Kids* contestant, who pointedly patronizes Little Joe. Impressed by this child's haughty brilliance, Joe's father (Michael Tucker) turns to his wife (Julie Kavner) and complains, "Why can't *he* [Joe] be a genius? Because he's too busy listening to the radio all the time!"

Probably the last appellation that Woody Allen is wont to apply to himself is "genius," but it's difficult not to notice that *Radio Days,* with its—for Allen—remarkably lush production values[23] and deliberate juxtaposition of the lovingly visualized realms of family and radio is, at the very least, dramatically manifesting the complete wrongheadedness of Little Joe's father's accusation. If genius is anywhere on display in this film, it's of a distinctly cinematic sort, the movie with extraordinary thoroughness evoking the physical reality of mid-1940s America on both sides of the radio receiver. Allen's craft as filmmaker creates the reality of the world within the radio which Little Joe's family and all other listeners never see other than through their imaginations; the movie suggests that the imaginative capacity making visualization possible owes a great deal to radio, to the Biff Baxters and Masked Avengers who Little Joe/Allan Konigsberg and other listeners had to picture in their minds to give them substance. During a broadcast, Biff Baxter encourages his young listeners to watch the ocean for Nazi submarines, which he describes for them in great detail; alone on Rockaway Beach one day, Little Joe thinks he's spotted one replicating precisely what Baxter depicted, but he keeps his sighting a secret "because I doubted my own experience" and knew that "no one would believe me . . . except Biff Baxter."[24]

That Biff Baxter enabled him to visualize in reality what doesn't exist and to understand the difference is the sincere compliment Allen pays to radio in *Radio Days,* one which an early version of the script had grown-up Joe's narration explicate. "[Y]ou couldn't just sit and watch passively like TV," he explains, "you had to participate as you listened and supply the images in your mind. . . . The involvement was very intense."[25] What Allen is able to do in *Radio Days* is to celebrate the imagination radio fostered in its listeners by depicting the worlds on both sides of the receiver, dramatizing not only Little Joe's family's ordinary life in Rockaway but also the lives of the radio personalities, including the social mobility of Sally White (Mia Farrow) moving from King Cole Room cigarette girl to hostess of her own Broadway interview show, "The Gay White Way." Early on in the film, the radio is associated with fiction and the fantasy gratifications embodied in the Masked Avenger, sentimental sports legends, and soap operas; gradually, however, radio transforms itself into a medium of real world bad news, becoming the family's source of information about the course of the war and leading them as well through the "sudden, unexpected human tragedy" of Polly Phelps. Allen's movie visualizes the scene at the Phelps farm in Stroudsberg, Pennsylvania, where little Polly Phelps, "despite all the efforts and prayers" of rescue workers and radio listeners all over the country, dies in the well she's fallen into as the nation listens in horror.[26] Certainly, part of the pleasure for Allen in making *Radio Days* lay in visualizing scenes on a movie screen which, as a boy, he'd been able to picture only in his imagination—not only the scene of the tragedy itself, but a number of the homes, taverns, and businesses around the country where people awaited word of Polly's fate.[27] Radio had its romance and fantasy programs, Allen seems to be suggesting through the Polly Phelps episode, which fails to resolve itself in the rescue and consequent answering of prayers the broadcaster is so clearly anticipating, but—as Judah's hard-bitten brother insists in *Crimes and Misdemeanors*—"Out there, in the real world, it's a whole different story."[28]

Radio Days, therefore, is not merely autobiographical, but can be perceived as the dramatization of the genesis of its maker's artistic life, the film, as Richard Combs's review recognized, fleshing out "its real subject—the show-biz biography of Woody Allen."[29] Rather than being merely a mildly diverting grab bag of reminiscences and radio anecdotes, *Radio Days* in its every scene visualizes the importance of radio to Allen's filmmaking, which is celebrated in the movie nearly as much as old-time radio is. The scene which most visibly establishes the connection between radio and filmmaking is one that seems only tenuously related to the film's procession of radio-related anecdotes: Aunt Bea (Dianne Wiest) and one of her many boyfriends (Joe Sabat, a member of Allen's film crew) take Little Joe to Radio City Music Hall, the 1979 restoration of which had returned to it the glamour Allan Konigsberg must have experienced there at Joe's age. "It was like entering heaven," Little Joe explains in voice-over: "I'd never seen anything so beautiful in my life." Nothing happens in the scene besides the presentation of a beautifully lit tracking shot by Carlo Di Palma visualizing the three characters walking, somewhat awestruck, through an amber-tinged world on their way to the theater's balcony—nothing, that is, except for the playing of Frank Sinatra's "If You Are But a Dream" on the soundtrack, the scene evoking Joe's "most vivid memory associated with an old radio song." "If you're a fantasy," Sinatra sings, "then I'm content to be in love with loving you and pray my dream comes true. . . . I'm so afraid that you may vanish in the air. So darling, if our romance should break up, I hope I'll never wake up, if you are but a dream."

Of course, Sinatra was portraying a lover singing to his beloved, but in the film's cinematic appropriation of the song, the singer's references seem to be to the lavishly plush, impossibly glamorous cathedral of American movies Joe has entered. Here "an old radio song" converges with Little Joe's encounter with "heaven" to create *Radio Days'* most ecstatic moment, Di Palma's cinematography providing compelling visual corroboration of the song's lyrical romanticism. This scene is probably as close as Allen has ever come to showing why he became a filmmaker. If the splendor of Radio City Music Hall, so utterly different from Little Joe's inglorious home circumstances, is a dream, it's one he doesn't want to wake up from. The song's phrase,"content to be in love with loving you," is as concise a summary of Allen's conflicted attitude toward the consolations of film's illusions as he's ever presented, distilling the close of his previous film, *The Purple Rose of Cairo,* in which Cecilia, who has personally experienced the fraudulence and duplicity that underlies the Hollywood romance fantasy, reembraces it nonetheless, "content to be in love with loving" it in spite of what she's seen. The Radio City Music Hall scene with its "If You Are But a Dream" soundtrack dramatizes a notion increasingly prevalent in Allen's most recent films—the affirmation of illusions embraced despite the knowledge that they are illusions. Our reward for embracing the illusion which is Allen's characters' pilgrimage through Radio City is another illusion: the Radio City scene culminates in what Sandy Bates calls "a big, big finish," the generic romantic consummation all moviegoers recognize in Katherine Hepburn's kissing James Stewart on the Music Hall screen.[30]

The so aptly named Radio City Music Hall partakes of the same illusion-imbued mystique attributed to radio by the film, radio's increasing tendency to become a repository less of imaginary wish-fulfillments than of dark truths reflective of Little Joe's maturation seeming—as it does so often in Allen's films—to generate, compensatorily, a greater need for the aural illusions of radio, the visual illusions of movies.

To see *Radio Days* as Allen's homage to the imaginative capacity engendered in him by the radio is to perceive as simple affirmation what is really a cinematic debate—a debate which had become a preoccupation of his films with *Purple Rose of Cairo*. To Little Joe and his family, the illusions of radio are relatively uncomplicated, pleasures of self-recognition which require more or less suspension of disbelief depending on their age and levels of sophistication. Little Joe's Aunt Ceil (Rene Lippin) enjoys a ventriloquist on the radio despite the insistence of her husband Abe (Josh Mostel) that the performance is invalidated if you can't see that the ventriloquist's lips don't move. Little Joe's experience of Radio City Music Hall is perfectly summarized for him in Frank Sinatra's "If You Are But a Dream," and Aunt Bea's intense longings for love find complete expression in the performance of "You'd Be So Nice to Come Home To" by a radio songstress (Diane Keaton) on New Year's Eve.[31] In general, the family members take on face value the reality the radio projects, believing, for instance, that Irene and Roger are "rich and famous" and that they move through a glamorous realm qualitatively different from the family's life in Rockaway. "There were two different worlds," adult Joe explains. "While my mother stood over the dirty plates in Rockaway, Irene and Roger ate their breakfast over the air from their chic Manhattan townhouse while they chatted charmingly about people and places we only dreamt of." But Allen's film also dramatizes what neither Little Joe nor his family could have known about: the actual lives of the radio performers, these scenes completely negating the performers' sophisticated and culturally elevated self-projections on the radio. Roger (David Warrilow) is erotically fixated upon proletarian Sally the cigarette girl at the King Cole Room, while his wife, Irene (Julie Kurnitz), is hotly pursuing "society's most interesting and exotic Latin playboy." Sally subsequently rises to have her own radio show, "Sally White's Great White Way," not by American hard work and initiative but through intervention of a mob hit man and the secrets she learns by sleeping with countless Broadway power brokers in her desperate social climbing. Allen's most honest films seldom settle for the conclusion, "I hope I never wake up"; they insist on dramatizing as well the waking reality, which is the inescapable knowledge that "you"—the reality projected on radio and embraced ecstatically by members of Little Joe's family—"are but a dream."

It is both entirely consistent with this equivocal construction of dreams and characteristic of Allen's films in general that the ending of *Radio Days* offers a markedly hedged conclusion regarding on which side of the receiver things are better.[32] Little Joe's family celebrates the New Year together, united by familial affection but envying the people on the radio greeting the New Year at the King Cole Room. "There are those who drink champagne at night-clubs," is Tess's social Darwinist summation, "and those who listen to them drink champagne on the radio." When her husband asks her, "What—you think they're happier than us?" Tess's sarcastic reply is "How long do I have to answer that question?" Through its protracted dramatizations of the sorrows and insufficiencies of the radio performers, however, *Radio Days* expresses Allen's far greater uncertainty that the answer to Martin's question is self-evident.

"[T]hose who drink champagne" on the roof of St. Regis Hotel which houses the King Cole Room prove incapable of replicating Little Joe's family's warm celebration. Instead of enjoying the moment ("It's okay—we're all to-gether, you know?" Martin affectionately assures Aunt Bea, dateless on New Year's Eve), the radio celebrities are agonizing over the mutability of their on-air fame. The Masked Avenger serves as their spokesman, boozily reflecting, "I wonder if future generations will ever even hear about us. It's not likely. After enough time, everything passes. I don't care how big we are, or how important in their lives." Deprived of any belief in the superiority of their condition because of their awareness of the radio illusion which is its source, the champagne drinkers must confront the same terrifying existential ques-tions that the characters in *Manhattan* seek to evade through entangling them-selves in the "unnecessary neurotic problems" created by their emotional/erotic engagements with other people. To be on the performers' side of the radio receiver is to understand the baselessness and insubstantiality of the reassurances their programs continually pump out to the audience; it is to know the fraudulence of radio's hourly consolation from the inside. No one could understand better than the diminutive actor who plays the Masked Avenger (Wallace Shawn), for instance, what a farce his "Beware all evildoers" threat is in a 1944 world so pervaded by palpable international evils; as this actor's last rendering of the canned admonition fades once the radio folk have left the roof, adult Joe's final lines in voice-over seem to confirm the Avenger's darkest fears of oblivion: "I never forgot that New Year's Eve when Aunt Bea awakened me to watch 1944 come in. And I've never forgotten any of those people, or any of the voices we used to hear on the radio. Although the truth is, with the passing of each New Year's Eve, those voices seem to grow dimmer and dimmer."

Perfection is not to be had on either side of radio's broadcast illusion for, as a press agent describes a similarly vexed antinomy in *The Purple Rose of Cairo*, "The real ones want their lives fiction, and the fiction ones want their lives real."[33] Nonetheless, *Radio Days* ultimately *does* celebrate the affect which radio's demand of imaginative involvement had on one listener—Little Joe/

Allan Konigsberg/Woody Allen, filmmaker—who has expressed his sincere gratitude by making a tenderly nostalgic movie insuring that those radio voices not dim out completely. The signature Woody Allen qualifier to this ostensibly Modernist affirmation of art's redemptive capacities is that *Radio Days* prevents from dimming out completely not the voices of Mr. Abercrombie or Pegreen and Ed Fitzgerald or the *Quiz Kids,* all of which have been stilled forever, but only the cinematic incarnations of them fabricated in Allen's film. For all their devious and ingenious blurring of life and art, Allen's films ultimately affirm one insuperable difference between the two, the disparity heralding bad news for the oblivious aesthete Harry Block: if you've been saved by art, Allen declares with cinematic indirection, it proves that you're nothing but a fictional character. "Woody Allen" may live on in the hearts of film viewers everywhere, but Woody Allen won't live on anywhere, and that discrepancy encapsulates Allen's primary gripe with art.

6
Life Stand Still Here

Interiors Dialogue

> Though his taste was described by many as lowbrow, it was his own.
>
> —Leonard Zelig, described by the narrator of *Zelig*

The art form celebrated in *Radio Days* is clearly a popular medium, and it is one of the significant characteristics of Allen's films that, as a component of their focus upon the life/art conflict, they consistently affirm popular culture over serious art. A major dramatic tension in *Stardust Memories* exists between Sandy Bates's desire to make socially significant movies and the groundswell of voices (a Martian named Og among them) encouraging him, "You want to do mankind a real service? Tell funnier jokes" (p. 367). In the same film, the one scene not permeated by Sandy Bates's anxieties and self-recriminations is the intensely lyrical "Stardust memory" in which the screen image of the beautiful Dorrie is imbued with Louis Armstrong's rendition of "Stardust," the conflation of human beauty with pop standard seeming to Bates to epitomize perfection. The list of "things to live for" Isaac Davis enumerates which inspires him to attempt a reconciliation with Tracy in *Manhattan* is dominated by popular culture icons—Louis Armstrong, Groucho Marx, Willie Mays, Frank Sinatra, and Marlon Brando—although such high-culture representatives as Flaubert, Cezanne, Swedish films, and the *Jupiter* Symphony (*Manhattan,* pp. 267–68) are also included in a roster Allen acknowledges as replicating his own personal list of favorites.[1] While institutionalized religions fail to provide the reasons to continue living that Mickey Sachs seeks in *Hannah and Her Sisters,* he locates such *raisons d'être* instead in a Marx Brothers movie:

> And I started to feel how can you even think of killing yourself? I mean, isn't it so stupid? I mean, I—look at all the people up on the screen. You know, they're real funny, and what if the worst is true? . . . What if there's no God and you only go around once and that's it? Well, you know, don't you want to be part of the experience? And I'm thinking to myself, geez, I should stop ruining my life . . . searching for answers I'm never gonna get, and just enjoy it while it lasts. . . . And then . . . I sat back and actually began to enjoy myself (p. 172).[2]

Of course, we will need to return to Mickey Sachs's pop culture epiphany, one which has become something of a rosetta stone in Woody Allen film criticism; for the moment it's sufficient to say that no matter how many serious films he produces, Allen's tendency to identify himself primarily in terms of entertainment has been fairly consistent throughout his career. "All I want is not to be taken seriously," he told Lee Guthrie shortly before shooting *Interiors:* "I have no great insight into poverty or integration or their relation to history, death, or God. I just want to tell jokes."[3]

It is probably not surprising that a filmmaker whose professional career was inaugurated through writing one-liners and doing stand-up comedy would celebrate popular forms in his art; it *is* remarkable, however, that a filmmaker whose work is so pervaded by issues relating to the sources of art and the psychology of the artist should find in the properties and potentials of aesthetic creation so little material for the dramatic resolution of his plots. Modernist literature proliferates with narratives which achieve the resolutions they do through the intercession of the artist's capacity to shape the ruins of contemporary reality into significant form. In Virginia Woolf's *To the Lighthouse,* for instance, art's saving function is characterized through the description of "Mrs. Ramsay making of the moment something permanent. . . . In the midst of chaos there was shape, this eternal passing and flowing . . . was struck into stability. Life stand still here, Mrs. Ramsay said,"[4] or the song sung by "the single artificer of the world" in Wallace Stevens's "The Idea of Order at Key West" who knows that "there never was a world for her/ Except the one she sang, and, singing, made."[5] "After one has abandoned a belief in God," Stevens wrote in a definitional articulation of the Modernist credo, "poetry is the essence which takes its place as life's redemption."[6] If, in high Modernism's formulation, art's preeminent benefit is lending coherence to lives otherwise contingent and random, one would expect at least a few of Allen's post-*Sleeper* films to achieve closure through the device of their artist/protagonists' completed artworks resolving the film's significant tensions in corroboration of Stevens's invocation of the saving powers of art.

As we've seen, *Radio Days* can be read as Allen's cinematic answer to the question, "What was the effect of radio on its listeners?" the film enacting visually the imaginative flights that popular medium fostered in him. The moral of that story, arguably, is that pop culture precipitated Allen's art. At the end of *Another Woman,* Marion Post's reading of Larry's treatment of their affair in his novel fills her with "a strange mixture of wistfulness and hope" such that "for the first time in a long time" she feels "at peace."[7] Her contentment with the transformation of her most intense emotional experience into art, however, leaves the viewer, as we'll see, with nagging questions about the authenticity of the conversion she undergoes from a bookish sublimator of feeling to someone who freely acknowledges and expresses her emotions. In other words, it's possible that reading a fictionalized version of herself as a "woman capable of great passion" is the only passionate experience of which Marion is capable.[8] Otherwise, we are left with the endings of *Play It Again, Sam* and *The Purple Rose of Cairo* as examples of resolution through artistic intercession, both protagonists remaining helplessly in the thrall of Hollywood illusions, or with Harry Block's closing affirmation that his art has saved his life once again, *Deconstructing Harry's* incessantly sour narrative prompting the viewer to ask what sort of art it is which could save someone so unworthy of salvation. For all their preoccupation with art and the artist, Allen's films are utterly lacking in conclusions affirming the redemption of high culture art, their endings most typically—as in *Another Woman* and *Deconstructing Harry*—simultaneously ironizing the putatively redemptive artwork and its artist as well.

The gratuitously happy ending of Sandy Bates's film leaves its filmmaker standing in the Stardust Hotel auditorium in an incongruously demoralized solitude; the second script Holly has written in *Hannah and Her Sisters* provides a pretext through which she and Mickey achieve a reunion culminating in marriage, but neither it nor her writing ambitions figures in the film's completely domestic resolution. The title character of *Alice* abandons completely her literary ambitions in favor of social activism without a hint of ambivalence or regret; nearly half of the characters in *September* are hopelessly frustrated artists, their expressive paralyses and attendant interpersonal estrangements remaining painfully unresolved at the film's close. In reconciling with his wife at the end of *Bullets Over Broadway,* playwright/director David Shayne could be expressing the unconscious desires of all these characters in affirming that, as a consequence of his experience producing his drama, *God of Our Fathers,* on Broadway, "I'm not an artist. There—I've said it, and I feel free. I'm not an artist."[9]

The notion of artist which Shayne repudiates here is very much a product of his era—the 1920s—in which Modernist art had already inaugurated its project of elevating the magnitude of the artist's cultural contribution, *Bullets Over Broadway* proliferating with pretentious discussions among artists of the superiority of art and artists to ordinary life. Although many aspects of the art/life tension are open to debate in Allen's films, the Modernist assumption of the artist's transcendent significance is a belief which is embraced by only his most unsympathetic or satirically conceived characters—Frederick in *Hannah and Her Sisters* being perhaps the most extreme example.[10]

"I don't believe that the artist is superior," Allen told Stig Bjorkman, "I'm not a believer in the specialness of the artist. I don't think to have a talent is an achievement. I think it's a gift from God, sort of. I do think that if you're lucky to have a talent, with that comes a certain responsibility."[11] It's the arrogant self-congratulation of the Modernist aesthetic, the extravagant claims made for art and artists, which Allen consistently rejects, his repudiation of its pseudoreligious aura and pretentions emerging repeatedly in interviews. "Art is like the intellectual's Catholicism, it's the promise of an afterlife," he contended in 1978, "but of course it's fake—you're only doing it because *you* want to do it."[12] "I hate when art becomes a religion," he explained to Michiko Kakutani eighteen years later. "I feel the opposite. When you start putting a higher value on works of art than on people, you're forfeiting your humanity. There's a tendency to feel that the artist has special privileges, and that anything's okay if it's in the service of art. I tried to get into that in *Interiors*. I always feel that the artist is much too revered: it's not fair and it's cruel."[13] Eve, the matriarch of *Interiors,* is Allen's most compelling avatar of the cultural overvaluation of art, his dramatic negation of the Modernist creed affirming art's transcendence of life. Ironically, she appears in the film of Allen's most markedly dedicated to emulating the canons of high Modernist art.

The near unanimity of Allen's films in their affirmation of popular culture over serious art and their skepticism about the value of art's contribution to human emotional well-being is complicated by the existence of a number of public comments Allen has made in apparent contradiction to these attitudes. Assessing his work to date in the late 1980s, Allen distinguished between his films and those of filmmakers he considered his superiors: "They're not A films, they're B films, though not in the way one usually talks about B films as second features; they're all solid pictures, they work in terms of what they set out to do, and there's inspiration in some of them. But I don't have a *Wild Strawberries* or a *Grand Illusion*. I'm going to try before my life is over to rise to the occasion and make one or two that would be considered great by any standard. . . . Maybe now that I've moved into my fifties and I am more confident, I can come up with a couple that are true literature."[14] The conclusion of *Stardust Memories*, with its exemplification of a cacophony of audience reactions to Bates's film, surely problematizes the idea expressed here of a film "great by any standard," but the sincerity of Allen's ambition to make films comparable to "true literature" is clear, even if it's an ambition about which he has elsewhere expressed ambivalence.

Allen's effort to "take a more profound path" in filmmaking began with the production of *Interiors* in 1977 and continued in *Another Woman* and *September,* films concentrating on an intensely sober analysis of the inward lives of their characters. If the influence of Bergman on these films wasn't largely self-evident, Allen's account of Bergman's major contribution to cinema confirms their shared purposes in art filmmaking. Bergman, Allen suggested, "evolved a style to deal with the human interior, and he alone among directors has explored the soul's battlefield to the fullest."[15] Allen's characterization of Bergman's work also delineates Allen's own objectives in his three "chamber movies." Admittedly, many critics judge *Interiors, Another Woman,* and *September* among Allen's least effective efforts. If these movies aren't completely successful, it's arguably not because Allen is too corrupted by comedic, pop culture impulses to make serious films, but because his major gifts as a filmmaker work against the creation of a *Wild Strawberries* or *Grand Illusion*, because the cultural circumstances and epistemologies necessary to the generation of such cinematic masterpieces have vanished, and because even when Allen tries to make such a film, the themes dramatized in it gravitate against the notion of art-as-transcendence inherent in his invocation of film's aspiration to "true literature." For all of its pretensions to Bergmanesque seriousness and its ambition to use drama "to rise to the occasion" of the creation of high art, the best of these films, *Interiors,* dramatizes nothing more eloquently than the aridity of lives aspiring to the condition of art. Because of Woody Allen's very real ambivalence about this issue, however, *Interiors* employs a self-conscious artistry unprecedented in his films to communicate the insufficiency of the aesthetic.

The opening images of *Interiors* seem an incarnation of Mrs. Ramsay's *To the Lighthouse* injunction "life stand still here": a starkly decorated living room, its window looking out on an ocean whose turbulence is imperceptible, dissolves to five vases aesthetically spaced on a mantle. The voice-over of Arthur (E.G. Marshall), the father of the film's unnamed protagonist family, implicitly ascribes the immobility of these analogues of the family members to the efforts of his wife, Eve (Geraldine Page). "By the time the girls were born . . . it was all so perfect, so ordered," Arthur explains. "The truth is, she'd created a world around us that we existed in . . . where everything had its place, where there always was a kind of harmony" (p. 114). Unlike the artistically coherent world Stevens's "single artificer . . . singing made," the harmony of Eve's projected cosmos is colorless and aesthetically oppressive. This harmony is expressed visually through Gordon Willis's cinematography and Mel Bourne's sets, which conspire to ensure that nothing in the frame—from the fine strawberry blond sheen of Mary Beth Hurt's hair to the predominant mauve caste of the family's wardrobe to the burnished gleam of their homes' hardwood floors—transgresses the "subtle statement of pale tones" which is Eve's signature color scheme. That the world she'd created for them to inhabit approximates an artwork is reinforced by the terms her husband uses to describe her, his diction continuing to invoke the terms formalist critics typically employed to compliment successfully executed aesthetic strategies. "She was very beautiful," Arthur explains, "Very pale and cool in her black dress . . . with never anything more than a single strand of pearls. And distant. Always poised and distant." The overall effect of the world she projected for them was one of "great dignity," Arthur concludes, "it was like an ice palace."

F. Scott Fitzgerald used the trauma Sally Carrol Happer experiences getting lost in a northwest ice palace to provoke her flight back to the South of her youth, away from the "Ibsenesque" Minnesotans who are "freezing up" into "righteous, narrow and cheerless" people "without infinite possibilities for great sorrow or joy."[16] It isn't physical chill but a grotesquely exaggerated attempt to transform the gross materials of human life into artistic perfection which has sunk Eve's family into their emotional deep freeze. When her daughter's lover moves a lamp which Eve bought to complement "what we were trying to do in the bedroom" into the dining room of his apartment so that he can work there, Eve aggressively returns it to the bedroom because "the shade is just wrong against all these slick surfaces" (p. 118). The scene epitomizes, in microcosm, Eve's chief blind spot, one that Allen invoked in arguing, "When you start putting a higher value on works of art than on people, you're forfeiting your humanity." It is the characters' conflicted attempts to deal with Eve's tyrannical, emotion-repressing privileging of the artistic which provides a primary dramatic trajectory for the first half of *Interiors*. That Eve's life-remediating project was impossible to begin with is conveyed by the emotional breakdown the effort has cost her before the film's opening: "An enormous abyss opened up beneath our feet," as Arthur recalls her mental collapse, "and I was staring into a face I didn't recognize" (p. 115). The episode of psychic dissociation has rendered Eve recuperative for life, her family seeking dutifully to foster her recovery by encouraging as therapy her rededication to the very source of her breakdown: a manic devotion to transforming human habitats into artworks through interior decoration.

As the film opens, Eve has been plying her craft in the apartment of her daughter, Joey (Mary Beth Hurt), and Joey's lover, Michael (Sam Waterston). She first appears with a vase which will complement the prevailing palette— "my beiges and my earth tones"—she has introduced in blatant disregard of Michael's obvious impatience with her foisting of expensive art objects upon him and Joey and his clearly expressed opposition to paying for endless renovations to the place in the name of nurturing Eve's aesthetic territoriality. Her daughters have responded to her with far greater ambivalence. All three of them regularly dress in "her beiges and her earth tones" while enacting their individual psychic strategies for winning her approbation at the same time that they're attempting to evade the emotional cost exacted for her approval.

The strategy of Renata (Diane Keaton) has, until recently, been the most successful: she's managed to become a widely published, prolific poet whose literary dedication justifies her withdrawal from the family's New York home to Connecticut on grounds of the artist's need for concentration and isolation, an argument her mother could contest only at the price of self-contradiction. The year-long writer's block Renata has experienced manifests her unconscious mind's refusal to play by her mother's rules any longer, her habitual artistic isolation beginning to extract its toll as she undergoes a terrible moment of complete estrangement between self and world: "It was like I . . .

was here, and the world was out there, and I couldn't bring us together" (p. 141).

The success of Flyn (Kristin Griffith) as an artist is considerably more equivocal, the acting career which has allowed her similarly to escape Eve's dominion having lately reduced her to roles in television movies which she is all-too-aware she has landed less for her acting prowess than for her physical beauty. "Form without content" is Renata's husband's assessment of his unsuccessful novels, and it's inevitable that he will take out his creative and sexual frustration on another artist—Flyn—whose art is characterized by the same deficiency and who therefore represents for him "a woman I [don't] feel inferior to" (p. 171).

Renata's and Flyn's defections in the name of art relegate the creatively infertile Joey to the role of Eve's caretaker, since, as she explains, "I feel a real need to express something, but I don't know what I want to express" (p. 125). Renata concurs in this assessment, avowing that Joey "has all the anguish . . . and the . . . anxiety, the artistic personality, without any of the talent" (p. 141). As a result, Joey and her mother have established a relationship in which Joey's tireless solicitousness to Eve's substantial needs is constantly shadowed by their mutual recognition of the artistic incapacity that leaves Joey time to play her mother's keeper. Add to these profiles the frustrations of Frederick (Richard Jordan), Renata's husband, in his failed attempt to live up to his promise as a novelist, and it's plain to see that the "artistic personality" consistently depicted in *Interiors* is a neurotically conflicted one, the film offering not a single example of artistic creation resulting in personal gratification. The closest the movie comes to the dramatization of artistic fulfillment is Renata's placing of a poem in *The New Yorker;* its publication, however, only serves to convince her the work is "too ambiguous" and must be completely revised.

The film's major embodiment of the artistic enterprise, of course, remains Eve, who spends the narrative seeking to resurrect her marriage with Arthur, a project which increasingly comes to seem a desperately nostalgic and ultimately futile effort to restore the lost "world she'd created around us." The forfeited humanity of that "world" is perhaps best symbolized by her desire to show Arthur a majestic Manhattan church she's discovered, insisting that they get there "before the place gets all cluttered up with people" (p. 157). Her suicide attempt immediately following one of the merely solicitous visits in which Arthur offers no promise for their reconciliation only exacerbates her family's penchant for perceiving Eve as—in Joey's characterization— "a sick woman"; as a result, her significance in the film begins to recede simultaneously with the emergence of her replacement and spiritual antithesis.

Allen has acknowledged that a structural weakness of *Interiors* was the belated introduction of Pearl (Maureen Stapleton), the woman whom Arthur obtains a divorce from Eve in order to marry. This highly demonstrative, utterly down-to-earth character who possesses "possibilities for great sorrow or joy" creates a counter-texture to the self-important gravity of the WASPish family in general and to Eve in particular, a contrary presence which, Allen conceded, would have been welcome earlier in the film.[17] Twice in *Interiors*, Eve closes windows because "street noises are just unnerving" (p. 117), and her first attempt at suicide by asphyxiation necessitates taping over the windows of her apartment. During the dinner party at which Arthur introduces Pearl to his family, Joey, claiming to be warm, opens a window, the conflation of these scenes suggesting that the "unnerving street noises" have entered with Pearl and that Joey, Eve's ever dutiful daughter, is seeking to force them back out.[18]

Pearl enters the film wearing a dress so jarringly red as to terminally disperse the earth tones color scheme Eve's aesthetic has imposed on her family and with which Gordon Willis's answering cinematography has saturated the movie's visual field. When asked what sites of cultural import she and Arthur visited while in Greece together, Pearl admits without apology that she'd seen enough "ruins" and was happy to lie on the beaches instead. At dinner, an off-Broadway play that everyone at the table has seen is debated, the family members offering interpretations of it spanning a spectrum of sophisticated ambiguities ("The writer argued both sides so brilliantly," is Joey's gloss, "you didn't know who is right") which Pearl missed completely. Not one to get becalmed at the center of irresolvable aesthetic paradoxes of the sort in which a number of Allen's own films—*Stardust Memories, Radio Days, Purple Rose of Cairo,* and *Crimes and Misdemeanors* among them—can be seen to conclude, Pearl locates an obvious moral contest in the play and casts her vote without experiencing a second's cognitive dissonance. "I didn't get that," she explains, "I mean, uh, to me it wasn't such a big deal. One guy was a squealer, the other guy wasn't. I liked that guy that wasn't" (p. 152).

It might be argued that it is only in the context of Eve's superesthete, hyperrefined family that Allen's work could seriously solicit sympathy for a character as forthrightly unreflective and blithely anti-intellectual as Pearl. In fact, his films contain a number of characters—Dulcy in *Midsummer Night's Sex Comedy,* Cecilia in *The Purple Rose of Cairo,* Cheech in *Bullets Over Broadway,* Linda Ash in *Mighty Aphrodite,* and Hattie in *Sweet and Lowdown*—whose virtues are inseparable from their want of cerebralism, though none of them save Hattie is expected to carry the burden of dramatic redemption assigned to Pearl. Delighting Frederick and Joey's husband, Mike, with a card trick after dinner, Pearl explains that she's "a gal that's been around. I've picked up a lot of useless information," including the ability to tell fortunes with cards. Frederick asks her if she also conducts séances, to which she responds, "Oooh, not me. I figure whatever's out there, it's their business. Besides, you—you think I want to bring back my ex-husbands?" (p. 154).

This is as close as the relentlessly somber script of *Interiors* ever comes to a joke, and it's significant that the congenial scene of Pearl with the family in-laws from which the one-liner emerges is juxtaposed against an excruciatingly tense confrontation occurring simultaneously in Renata's bedroom—a scene in which Arthur is demanding respectful treatment of his fiancée from Renata, who terms Pearl an "indiscreet" choice for him, and Joey, who dismisses her as a "vulgarian." Significantly, it is this vulgarian who restores Joey's capacity for self-expression to her, in addition to restoring her to life on the beach after her failed effort to avert Eve's second, successful, suicide attempt.

Despite their obvious differences, what Pearl and Joey have in common is epitomized in Pearl's one-liner and in much else that she says in the film: honesty. Pearl is willing to acknowledge to her fiancé's family the existence of her former, humanly imperfect husbands, one of whom was an orthodontist, she explains deadpan, the other an alcoholic. Joey analogously refuses to humor her mother's desperate need to believe in the imminence of her reconciliation with Arthur. While Renata and Flyn nurture Eve's self-delusory impossible dreams, Joey courts her mother's wrath by expressing the truth that Arthur has left Eve for good. The character in *Interiors* capable of performing magic tricks with cards (a capacity which in Allen's characterizational economy always confers a special, artist-approximating status) and who is responsible for the film's two moments of Allenesque Jewish humor converges with the non-artist whose name associates her with clowns and clowning[19] to compose an aggregate personification of candor, truthfulness, and tough-minded integrity. Joey's more dramatically named artist sisters consistently align themselves with deceptions and untruths associated with their aesthete mother: Renata hypocritically flatters Frederick's writing talents despite his deepening awareness of his literary limitations; Flyn uses her only artistic capacity to encourage physical intimacies with Frederick which result in his brutal, drunken attempt to rape her. In the film's dramatic climax, Joey alone of the sisters is present to attempt to prevent Eve's self-destruction, Gordon Willis's camera visualizing Renata and Flyn obliviously sleeping as Eve walks into the sea. Joey's attempted rescue of Eve necessitates Pearl's more efficacious rescue of her.

The disjunction between Eve's repressive aestheticism and Pearl's forthright unsophistication prompted many of the film's critics to posit an allegorical contrast between these alternative mother figures.[20] "In *Interiors*," David Edelstein suggested, "Allen had the wit to make his subject the war in his nature between the cold and cerebral (WASP) and the warm, materialistic, and embarrassingly vulgar (Jewish). Art leads to death, life to philistinism (and, by implication, comedy)."[21] Although perhaps excessively schematic, the antinomy Edelstein suggested in 1987 seems to have accurately characterized the film's central dualism while predicting the trajectory of Allen's subsequent films, an energetic philistinism being consistently preferred to life-denying aestheticism. Edelstein's formulation has two other virtues: first, it suggests how Pearl's arrival revitalizes the film—at the reception following her and Arthur's wedding, "Keepin' Out of Mischief Now" and "Wolverine Blues" suddenly burst through the Bergmanian silence which has pervaded this most musicless of Woody Allen films; second, it points up Allen's emotional investment in Eve. The *Radio Days* chapter of this book cites Allen's assertion that Eve is one of the three film protagonists with whom he most identifies, and it's clear that he was expressing through her the side of himself sympathetic to her comment about one of her interior decoration projects: "I'm not going to accept anything until I'm sure I can maintain the level I expect of myself" (p. 126). She is a projection of the relentlessly committed artist in Allen, the aesthete chronically dissatisfied with his cinematic achievements who routinely subordinates human relationships to that work; he might have been speaking in Eve's voice when he told an interviewer, "I'm not social. I don't get an enormous amount of input from the world. I wish I could get out but I can't."[22] A major difference between character and creator is that, through her, Allen is able to critique his own penchant for closing windows.

His ultimate disapproval of this self-projection is clearly represented in the fact that the film construes Eve's suicide as something which is, in its results, unequivocally positive. Her self-annihilation spurs the affectless Flyn to the single moment of authentic emotion—grief—she experiences in the film as she lays a white rose on her mother's casket. The suicide also unites Renata and Joey in a passionate embrace of shared sorrow, which dissolves the estrangement existing between them throughout the plot and liberates Joey to express on paper powerful memories of her childhood elicited by emotions stirred by her mother's absence.[23]

In order to perceive Eve's incontestably auspicious suicide as something other than an act of screenwriting cruelty, it's necessary—as Edelstein and others have recognized—to perceive *Interiors* as allegory rather than melodrama. Such a reading of the film is supported not only by Allen's comment that "I was more interested in the symbolic story. This is one of those things that takes place more metaphysically."[24] More evidence is provided by the undramatically explicatory nature of Joey's final speech to her mother, her dialogue in too obvious and calculated a way for a mimetic aesthetic tutoring the audience in how to interpret the cinematic narrative coming to a close. "I think you're uh, really too perfect . . . to live in this world," Joey tells Eve, who has somewhat improbably appeared at the family house in Southampton shortly after the celebration of Arthur's remarriage. "I mean all the beautifully furnished rooms, carefully designed interiors . . . everything so controlled. There wasn't any room for . . . any real feelings. None . . . between any of us" (p. 172). As the film's central embodiment of aesthetic standards which human beings are too flawed to achieve and of an utterly life-denying commitment to artistic creation, Eve must be sacrificed to the greater good of her family's spiritual and emotional liberation from her aesthete's perfectionist imperatives. Her life's quest, like that of Donald Barthelme's Dead Father—another incarnation of Modernist aesthetic imperatives[25]—must be repudiated because its effort to subject and subjugate reality to consciousness, to shape a disordered world according to the dictates of the human imagination, ultimately imprisons the self in its own projections, rendering the world outside it so alien and insufferably chaotic that the self's only recourse is to keep closing windows until *everything* is interior and there's no outside there anymore. The ultimate fulfillment of Eve's aesthetic—if it isn't her self-destruction—is the experience Renata suffers: "It was like I . . . was here, and the world was out there, and I couldn't bring us together."

Eve's chosen mode of suicide, losing herself in the ocean's violence, replicates Virginia Woolf's means of compelling life to stand still, the film's final scene visualizing Eve's daughters, united at last, looking out on the scene of her death and commenting on how tranquil the ocean has become. The film's more resonant affirmation of her act, however, is that its aftermath allows Pearl to save Joey's life. "In Europe they call mouth-to-mouth resuscitation the kiss of life," Allen told Diane Jacobs, "and that's what I wanted to convey—I wanted Pearl to breathe life into Joey."[26] Pearl is no human exemplar—she seems at points oblivious to the emotional dynamics of the family she's marrying into, symbolically enacting this failing by drinking excessively at the wedding and mindlessly smashing a vase holding a white rose which is all that remains of Eve in her former summer home. Her Manichean squealer/nonsquealer moral dichotomy isn't much help in sorting out the ethical conundrums posed by Allen's other films, either.[27] But this much Allen is willing to give her: she doesn't try to breathe art into a woman who's nearly stopped breathing. It's for her willful confusion of life and *vissi d'art* that neither Allen nor his movie can ever forgive Eve, or even work up much sympathy at the passing of this emblem of the complete inability of art to transcend life. In Eve, Allen created his most unambiguous and least compassionately drawn symbol of the inseparability of unconditional artistic commitment and self-delusion.

But—as Frederick comments about Pearl's reading of the off-Broadway play—"Well, it was a little more complex than that, don't you think?"

As numerous reviewers have noticed, *Interiors'* closing image of the three sisters gazing meditatively out the window at the ocean which took their mother's life self-consciously reprises the famous image of Bibi Andersson and Liv Ullman used as publicity stills for Bergman's *Persona*. The significance of this act of cinematic homage is complicated by the fact that Allen had reproduced the same image parodically toward the end of *Love and Death*.[28] "The water's so calm," Joey says as the window's light bathes the three women's faces. "Yes," Renata agrees, "it's very peaceful" (p. 175). This image undeni-

ably approximates the film's opening image, but with a highly significant difference: the five precisely spaced and perfectly framed vases evocative of Eve's aesthetically ordered familial cosmos which is that initial image have been replaced by three flesh-and-blood human beings. This image affirms that in the aftermath of the violence which took their mother, the sea is now calm and peaceful. In other words, Eve's self-sacrifice has been efficacious: there is sadness in the expressions of Joey, Flyn, and Renata, but there is an unprecedented resolution on their faces, too—one reflective, arguably, of their liberation from the art/life dichotomy their mother imposed upon them. For them this conflict seems to have been alleviated, but the Bergmanian saturation of the closing scene significantly problematizes the film's resolution of this thematic conflict. In *Play It Again, Sam,* Allan Felix attempted to throw off the yoke of Bogart's incapacitating influence on him by reenacting *Casablanca*'s most famous scene, his replication ironically reaffirming his thralldom. The ending of *Interiors* projects a similarly equivocal resolution. Whether Allen created this equivocal ending with the same purposefulness and deliberation is considerably less certain.

The plot of *Interiors* affirms the ascendancy of Pearl's vital philistinism over Eve's life-denying aestheticism but, as Pauline Kael pointed out, "After the life-affirming stepmother has come into the three daughters' lives and their mother is gone, they still, at the end, close ranks in a frieze-like formation. Their life-negating mother has got them forever."[29] As Kael implies, it is the film's style more than its plot which perpetuates Eve's dedication to the redemptions of formal symmetry, and it's difficult to separate the movie's final image from the filmmaker who so obviously inspired it. In *Interiors*, Allen was clearly attempting to create the sort of "poetic" film he perceived Bergman as making. Commenting on the unsurpassable effectiveness of Bergman's death metaphor in *The Seventh Seal*, Allen admitted that he'd "love to be able to transmit [his preoccupation with mortality] through poetry rather than through prose" as Bergman can. "On the screen one does poetry or one does prose. . . . *Persona* and *The Seventh Seal* are poetry, whereas a John Huston film is usually prose, of a wonderful sort . . . But Bergman works with poetry so frequently I have to think . . . which of his films are not poetic. If there are any that are not."[30] Allen has proven himself no more successful at creating Bergmanesque cinematic poems than Eve is at subjecting reality to her aesthetic imperialism, and it may be the "vulgarian" Pearl in Allen which has dictated that, his best poeticizing efforts to the contrary, he has continued throughout his career doing prose on screen. For all the sustained influence of Bergman's plots on Allen's films and their attempts—sometimes facilitated through the employment of Bergman's primary cinematographer, Sven Nykvist—to imitate the absolute visual purity of films such as *Autumn Sonata* and *Fanny and Alexander,* Allen's movies remain narratives, not poems. Rather than producing movies which dramatize the conclusion that so many of Bergman's films reach—as Renata phrases the idea, "it's hard to argue that in the face of death, life loses real meaning"—Allen's films tend to dramatize instead Pearl's interrogatory response to Renata: "It is?" (p. 151).

Interiors, therefore, is an extended homage to Ingmar Bergman which betrays great unease about its own indebtedness even as it unflaggingly invokes him as a major inspiration for techniques of serious filmmaking. The retreat from existence into art, which Eve epitomizes, is very much inflected by Allen's conception of Bergman, about whom he once commented, "All you ever heard of [Bergman] was how reclusive he was on his island, Faro."[31] In *Interiors*, Allen was incapable of completely repudiating the orderly consolations of aesthetic form encapsulated by Eve, for to do so would be to renounce his aspirations to the creation of serious art and to forswear the professional ambition that Bergman's artistic austerity epitomized for him. On the other hand, to repudiate Pearl would be to reject his own pop culture heritage and to contradict his fervently held idea of life's superiority to art. Consequently, Allen ended up making in *Interiors* a thoroughly honest and deeply conflicted film dramatizing, through its dichotomy between content and form, his own irresolvable ambivalence about life and art.

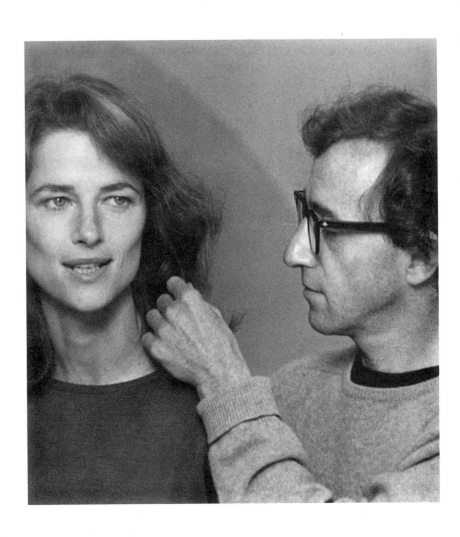

7

In the Stardust of a Song

Stardust Memories

KLEINMAN: Believe in God? I can't even make the leap of faith
    necessary to believe in my own existence.
JACK: That's fine, that's tricky—you keep making jokes until the
    moment when you have to face death.

—*Shadows and Fog*

Anyone who has heard a Woody Allen monologue or watched one of his films is familiar with Kleinman's rhetorical strategy, the same one employed by Sandy Bates in telling Isobel "You can't control life, it doesn't wind up perfectly. Only—only art you can control. Art and masturbation. Two areas in which I am an absolute expert" (p. 335). The difference in *Shadows and Fog* is that Jack, the philosophy student Kleinman befriends in Felice's brothel, challenges the maneuver so central to Allen's comedy. In both Bates's and Kleinman's one-liners, the speaker avoids committing himself to a position on a significant question by deflecting attention from the issue to himself and his own human inadequacies; thus, these jokes epitomize Allen's frequently invoked notion of comedy-as-evasion. "With comedy, you can buy yourself out of the problems of life and diffuse them," Allen told Frank Rich of *Time Magazine*, "In tragedy, you must confront them, and it is painful, but I'm a real sucker for it."[1] At the risk of reducing Allen's complex filmmaking career to a binary opposition, I'm contending that Jack's rebuke of Kleinman's comedic tactic for avoiding grave issues represents a summary explanation for Allen's evolution from making his "early, funny movies" in which the protagonist was a primary butt of jokes to the creation of his most thanatophobic movie, *Stardust Memories.*

    In the extended fantasia that closes out *Stardust Memories,* Sandy Bates imagines himself assassinated by a fan who tells him (in a chillingly exact anticipation of John Lennon's murder three months after the film's release), "You know you're my hero" before shooting him. At the memorial service, his analyst eulogizes the fallen Bates as someone "who saw reality too clearly. Faulty denial mechanism. Failed to block out the terrible truths of existence." (He failed, in other words, to produce one-liners capable of deflecting those truths.) "In the end his inability to push away the awful facts of being in the world rendered his life meaningless. . . . Sandy Bates suffered a depression common to many artists in middle age. In my latest paper for the *Psychoanalytic Journal,* I have named it Ozymandias Melancholia" (p. 370).

The analyst's invocation of Shelley's poetic incarnation of mutability ("'My name is Ozymandias, king of kings:/ Look on my works, ye Mighty, and despair'"[2]) wins the enthusiastic approval of his audience, their weirdly inappropriate applause for the analyst mocking the solemnity of his judgment, mediating the experience for the audience of Allen's film by reminding us that we're watching a projection of the narcissistic interior landscape of Sandy Bates.[3] The way in which this scene offers its content only to comically deflate it reflects how far Allen's rhetorical sophistication as a screenwriter had developed beyond the easy self-parodying jokes that represent in microcosm the structures of the early films. The fact that those self-deprecatory one-liners remain staples of his films down through *Deconstructing Harry* and *Celebrity* suggests the very real ambivalence Allen feels about his responsibility as a filmmaker to confront viewers with "the terrible truths of existence" or to distract them from these through comedy, which he once characterized as a means of "constantly drugging your sensibility so you can get by with less pain."[4] Years before producing *Manhattan Murder Mystery,* Allen addressed this issue from his side of the camera, explaining to Eric Lax his misgivings about undertaking that film project:

> I'm torn because I think I could be very funny in a comedy mystery and it would be enormously entertaining in a totally escapist way for an audience. But I can't bring myself to do that. This is part of my conflict. My conflict is between what I really am and what I really would like myself to be. I'm forever struggling to deepen myself and take a more profound path, but what comes easiest to me is light entertainment. I'm more comfortable with the shallower stuff. . . . I'm basically a shallow person.[5]

The ambivalence Allen expresses here about the production of comic as opposed to serious cinematic art has been one of the central preoccupations of his career, his debate with himself having manifested itself in two different forms early in his filmmaking work: in the scripting and production of *Interiors,* and, more self-consciously, in the creation of the film he considered his most aesthetically successful before *The Purple Rose of Cairo, Stardust Memories.*

"I don't want to make funny movies anymore," Sandy Bates complains in *Stardust Memories,* "They can't force me to. I—you know, I don't feel funny. I look around the world and all I see is human suffering" (p. 286). His preoccupation with humanity's pain is visualized by the infamous Song My assassination photo which seems to decorate his apartment wall just as images exteriorizing interior states appear on the fourth wall screen throughout Tennessee Williams' *The Glass Menagerie*.[6] Allen's own depressive tendencies notwithstanding, he has, quite properly, impatiently rejected the imputation that Sandy Bates *is* himself and that his perceptions are unmediated versions of Allen's values and feelings. Allen has indicated, among other differences, that he had himself never seriously considered ceasing to make comic films,[7] and that if he had as negative an attitude toward his own film audience as Bates seems to have, he is savvy enough not to dramatize the fact in a movie.[8] In addition, Allen often characterized Bates as a filmmaker on the verge of a nervous breakdown,[9] Allen's own production of a film a year over the past two decades offering little evidence of a director who ever faced psychic collapse. As I suggested in the *Radio Days* chapter, however, Allen's relationship to the protagonists he plays is nearly always a vexed conflation of fiction and autobiography; consequently, it seems self-evident that many of Bates's conflicts are exaggerated versions of conflicts that Allen has experienced. What those who criticize Allen for Bates's ideas and visions ignore is the divergence from cinematic realism *Stardust Memories* takes just before Bates heads off to the film festival being held in Connecticut in his honor.

Bates's housekeeper has prepared rabbit for his dinner, to which he responds vehemently, reminding her that he doesn't eat rodent. Allen's description of the remainder of this scene describes an intention not many viewers intuited: "He looks at this dead thing and it reminds him of his own mortality. And then the rest of the film takes place in his mind."[10] The film cuts to Bates's arrival at the film festival, Gordon Willis shooting the faces greeting him through a fisheye lens, which heightens the grotesquely predatory nature of their intense interest in Bates. The remainder of the film largely adheres to this surrealistic cinematic mode reflective of Bates's demoralized condition and utter disaffection with people; the nature of its perspectival aesthetic parallels that described by Tennessee Williams' explanation of his staging of *The Glass Menagerie*: "The scene is memory and is therefore nonrealistic. Memory takes a lot of poetic license. It omits some details; others are exaggerated, according to the emotional value of the articles it touches, for memory is seated predominantly in the heart."[11] *Stardust Memories* may also be "seated predominantly in the heart," but Bates's heart is one brimming not with nostalgia and longing but with repulsion and despair. That fact allows Allen's film to pose an inverted version of the question it is dramatizing through the tension between comic and serious art: if art has nothing to convey other than self-indulgent despair and hopelessness, the movie asks, is there any purpose in its creation? The first scene of *Stardust Memories* establishes this question as one of the film's central grounds of inquiry.

The opening scene is the one that Bates intends as the closing scene of his movie: the character Bates plays is on a train populated by passengers who

seem less human beings than Bergmanesque incarnations of human anguish and hopelessness. Outside the window he notices another train, this one carrying celebratory, beautiful passengers drinking champagne and exchanging Academy Awards. His efforts to convince the grim-visaged conductor on his train that he belongs on the other train are met with stony indifference.

Bates's desperate attempt to escape his train of misery and the grotesques who share it with him—his parents and sister included—is equally futile; the train deposits them at a beach-lot junkyard, a wasteland infested by scavenging seagulls, where they meet the passengers from the celebratory train approaching them from the opposite direction. "The whole point of the movie," Bates explains later in the film, "is that no one is saved" (p. 334), which is not what Bates's film's producer, Walsh (Laraine Newman), wants this film slated for an Easter release to express. On that account, funny movies with happy endings are presented as being what corporate America expects of Bates. One of the plot strands of *Stardust Memories* which carries through the Sandy Bates Film Festival weekend is Bates's attempt to exert control over the end of his movie and to fend off the studio heads' effort to transform the junkyard wasteland, which in Bates's imagination is the final destination of all passengers, into a musically redemptive "Jazz Heaven."

Like his creator, Bates refuses to be coerced into the mythology of art-as-salvation, into the Modernist notion of art as the conferrer of immortality.

"Oh, well . . . Sandy Bates's work will live on after him," Vivian Ornick (Helen Hanft), the festival director grandly declares after Bates's assassination, prompting him to reply, "But what good is it if I can't pinch any women or hear any music?" (p. 370). Allen's own attitude seems to be summed up by a nurse who watches Bates perform magic toward the end of the film. "All those silly magic tricks you do," the nurse, one of Bates's many self-projections who employs the same metaphoric elision of magic with art that Allen creates in *Shadows and Fog*, rebukes Bates, "couldn't help your friend Nat Bernstein" (p. 364), who died young of Lou Gehrig's disease.[12] Allen has, in fact, been quite explicit in acknowledging the rejection of the redemptive power of art which *Stardust Memories* dramatizes: "I didn't want [Bates] to be necessarily likable," he told Graham McCann, "I wanted him to be surly and upset: not a saint nor an angel, but a man with real problems who finds out that art doesn't save you."[13] Although the comic/serious art polarization continues to resonate throughout *Stardust Memories,* as the film proceeds, that issue is gradually subsumed into a larger accusation: that art not only fails to "save" its maker, but as Bates's producer, Walsh, contends early in the movie, artists merely "document their private suffering and fob it off as art" (p. 283). Among Allen's films, only *Interiors, Deconstructing Harry,* and *Celebrity* approach the negativity of *Stardust Memories'* exploration of the nature, uses, and value of art, the film finding in the inescapable subjectivity of artworks the principal source of their unreliability.

Before leaving New York for Connecticut and the Sandy Bates Film Festival, Bates's response to the idea of a festival of his old films is "it's absurd. It's . . . ridiculous," Allen's visual projection of the entire event through Bates's unremittingly subjective perspective providing consistent confirmation of that description. Like Guido Anselmi at the end of Fellini's *8½,* Bates is besieged by fans, filmmakers, actors, and would-be friends and lovers, all of whom perceive in his artistically inspired celebrity a means toward whatever form of happiness they imagine for themselves, and for many of whom his shift away from making his "early, funny movies" is understood as a betrayal. Their appeals range from the grotesque (one man has an idea for a comedy about the Guayana massacre/suicide, another a screenplay about jockeys) to the deadly serious (many want him to support charitable causes such as leukemia research, aid to the blind, and a global project seeking to free Soviet scientists incarcerated in insane asylums), the realms of the comic/pathetic and the tragic with which he's continually confronted proving postmodernly consecutive and impartible.

Bates's visit to his sister's Connecticut home is introduced by a declaration similar to that which prefaces his trip to his festival, Bates in a flashback responding to Dorrie's accusation that he had been flirting with her fourteen-year-old cousin at dinner, "You know how ridiculous that sounds? . . . I mean, doesn't that sound—it's, it's, it's absurd" (p. 231). Once again, Bates's recitation of the "ridiculous . . . absurd" formula seems to spawn a Eugene Ionesco reality. The film cuts to Debbie's apartment, where she and her sweatsuited friends (one of whom fled Manhattan out of fear for her personal safety, only to get raped in Connecticut) are doing yoga led by their Indian guru, where her husband is riding the exercise bicycle he apparently never gets off despite the fact that he's had as many heart attacks while using it as he'd had before he started, and where Debbie tells him of her worries about her runaway child who is selling stolen cameras in Texas. The scene culminates in the arrest of Bates's chauffeur, who is driving Bates and Isobel back to the Stardust Hotel, for mail fraud. Allen never dramatizes the reality of which these scenes are Bates's psyche's grotesque distortions. One cost of this decision was Allen's being branded an anti-Semite and worse by those who construed the film (and its admittedly unattractive depictions of Bates's Jewish admirers) as cinematic realism. Allen's intention seems to have been less to distinguish between actuality and Bates's perceptions of it than to use the film's immersion in Bates's point of view to intensify questions he is posing about movies and their relationship to life.[14]

In the film's most explicit articulation of Bates's condition, he complains, "I'm tired of everything. I'm tired of my lawyer and my accountant, and I'm-I'm-I can't help anybody. I can't help the Cancer Society and I can't help the blind people and the-the kidney victims. I can't help my sister." It's the disparity between his actual capacities as a human being and his fans' completely disproportionate adoration of him that prompts him to ask the interplanetary traveler Og, another self-projection he encounters at the flying saucer convention, "But shouldn't I stop making movies and do something that counts, like-like helping people or becoming a missionary or something?" (p. 366). Having read in the *Times* that matter is decaying and the universe is breaking down, Bates places the value of his own work and that of canonical art in that context of apocalyptic ultimacy: "There's not gonna to be anything left. . . . I'm not talking about my stupid little films here. I'm, uh—eventually there's not gonna be any more Beethoven or Shakespeare or—" (p. 286). Og's response—"You want to do mankind a favor? Tell funnier jokes"—prefigures Mickey Sachs's invocation in *Hannah and Her Sisters* of the possibility of watching Marx Brothers movies as reason enough to continue living. But *Stardust Memories* is a distinctly less sanguine film than *Hannah,* one in which, rather than representing film as a solution to human misery, the movie medium itself is implicated in the confusions that make answering ultimate existential questions so impossible. Rather than dramatizing art in high Modernism's terms as that which stabilizes and clarifies the vertiginous turmoil of life, *Stardust Memories* insists that art—film in particular—constitutes just one more projection of indeterminacy, of irresolvable enigmas, and of consequent human bewilderment. Actuating those enigmas and imposing that sense of bewilderment on his audience is Allen's primary objective in the last fifteen minutes of *Stardust Memories*.

Bates's complaint about his movies' affective uselessness continues, "and I don't wanna get married, Isobel. That's the last thing I need now, is a—is a family and commitment" (p. 369). Juxtaposed against *Stardust Memories'* dramatization of Sandy Bates's crisis of confidence in his artistic vocation are the erotic relationships Bates has with three women, his interactions with them constituting the primary plot this free associationally structured film can be said to have. Bates's romantic relationship with Dorrie (Charlotte Rampling) is strictly past tense, dramatized through Bates's mental flashbacks: the film suggests that her mental collapse terminated their relationship and that she's now recovered and living with her husband in Hawaii. She represents what Allen will characterize in *Husbands and Wives* as a "kamikaze woman," a lover who is "trouble" because her mental instability is inseparable from her erotic appeal. Allen's protagonists repeatedly involve themselves with kamikaze women out of the deluded belief—as Isaac Davis puts it in *Manhattan*—that he'll "be the one who makes 'em act different" (p. 261), whose love will be able to save them from the erratic impulses which make them so alluring. Isobel (Marie-Christine Barrault) is Dorrie's opposite, a practical-minded French mother of two children whom Bates associates with family and commitment and whose leaving of her husband raises the stakes of this weekend, pressuring Bates to make a choice concerning his relationship with her. Bates acknowledges that Daisy (Jessica Harper) reminds him of Dorrie: both come from the American upper middle class (unlike Isobel, who demonstrated her proletarian sympathies by joining the insurgent workers at the barricades in France in 1968); both are artistic (Dorrie is an actress, Daisy a concert violinist); and both are involved with drugs (Dorrie with lithium for her depression and speed for her figure, Daisy with recreational amphetamines) in a way which makes Bates (for whom drugs are "show business tranquilizers") highly uncomfortable. In telling Daisy at the UFO cultists' convention that he wants to run off with her, he's attempting to regenerate the absoluteness of his self-destructive emotional commitment to Dorrie. But before they can take off together, Isobel appears with the rest of the Sandy Bates Film Festival contingent, each of them rebuking him, raising questions, or making demands. He expresses his disenchantment with his career, his sense of the purposelessness of his art, and admits his reluctance to marry Isobel. He is then mercifully put out of the misery of all the choices these others are demanding of him by the fan (still another self-projection) who shoots him.

Given the risks to his emotional and psychological well-being embodied in the "kamikaze women," it's clear that Bates's reconciliation with Isobel represents the only happy ending possible for him, and so Bates rises from the dead to pursue that very conclusion.[15] The question that I posed in the *Annie Hall* chapter remains unanswered, however: Why does Bates choose to close his film, one originally intended to dramatize the idea that "nobody is saved," with a happy ending? The answer seems to be that the happy ending Allen has Bates create is far more ambiguous than it originally appears to be.

As we've seen, what viewers have to hold on to as ballast amid the erratic shifts between Bates's real world experiences and the fantasies into which those scenes of his life seamlessly blend, as well as the oscillations between Bates's films and his life, are the three women he has either romanced or is considering romancing. Each of them is introduced as being a participant in his real life, in other words, and if we're disoriented by the constant shifts of time, place, or mode of reality in the film, the appearance of one of the three women tends to relocate us in a largely accessible romantic plot. Consequently, we believe we know exactly where we are when we watch Bates waking from his fantasy assassination and following Isobel as she angrily hurries her children toward the Stardust Hotel train station. Inside a train car indistinguishable from the one that bore the Hogarthian inconsolables to the junkyard, Bates tells Isobel that as a result of the weekend, "I feel differently about a lot of things:

> I had a very, very remarkable idea for the ending of my movie—
> you know? We're-we're on a train, and there are many sad people
> on it, you know? And-and I have no idea where it's headin' . . .
> could be anywhere . . . could be the same junkyard . . . But it's not
> as terrible as I originally thought it was because-because, you know,
> we like each other, and . . . we have some laughs, and there's a lot
> of closeness, and the whole thing is a lot easier to take.

His teasing description of the train they're on and the experience they're undergoing charms her into a smile, and he then predicts that they're on the verge of a "big, big finish" which needs only a reconciliatory kiss to achieve consummation. "Here at last," Allen's audience might well think, "we're released from the spiraling, self-conscious obliquities of this movie by a generic boy-commits-himself-to-girl finish anyone can understand!" But then this kiss is greeted by applause from the Sandy Bates Film Festival audience, and as the film dissolves to the Stardust auditorium, we gradually come to understand that the scene constitutes the new ending of Bates's movie. I've already argued that no one in the audience seems transfigured by this ending, which Bates has defended to Isobel as being "sentimental in a good way," nor can they know how close they came to being stranded by the film at the wasteland junkyard. More significantly, what this scene has done is transform Isobel from a character in Allen's film into an actress in Bates's film, while it collapses completely any distinction between Bates's life and his movie. In other words, if the scene he is describing to her is the scene they're simultaneously playing, who are they? They're just part of the cinematic machinery that has betrayed Allen's audience into sentimentally embracing a romantic ending which is abruptly revealed to be only a movie approximation of resolution, the recycling of a too-familiar cinematic convention.

The deliberate confusion between reality and film created in this scene is exacerbated by the impossibility—in instrumental terms, at any rate—of the Bates movie ending existing as *Stardust Memories* presents it. By the logic of Allen's film's chronological narrative, the film festival audience is watching a filmed version of a scene which, if it ever happened, could only have taken place on the very afternoon on which they're watching it. (Additionally, since Bates spends much of the festival weekend worrying about his film's ending, how could the festival audience possibly watch a completed version of that ending?) Without a doubt, the thematic issues of *Stardust Memories*—questions concerning the meaning of life, the purposefulness of art, and the possibility of personal redemption—begin to blur as the film/reality confusions proliferate. It's important to note that the scene Bates perceives as the source of his regeneration and his shift toward the existential affirmation he expresses to Isobel on the train—the most intensely emotional scene in *Stardust Memories*—is adulterated by precisely the same ambiguities.

Casting about for moorings amid the psychological conflicts and instabilities which comprise his *Stardust Memories* pilgrimage, Bates experiences a memory. "I guess it was the combination of everything," Bates says in describing his response to the film's title "Stardust" epiphany,"the sound of that music, and the-the breeze and how beautiful Dorrie looked to me. And for one brief moment, everything seemed to come together perfectly, and I-I felt happy, almost indestructible, in a way" (p. 372). There is no more affirmative moment in Allen's films, no more lovingly dramatized cinematic celebration of the randomly experienced moment of beauty which is Allen's most compelling affirmation of life. It is an intensely and, for Allen's films, unprecedentedly lyrical moment in which the screen image of the gorgeous Dorrie is conflated with Louis Armstrong's rendition of "Stardust," the cinematic elision of the Hoagy Carmichael popular standard and human beauty coming as close as Allen's films ever do to evoking what Stanley Elkin termed "the grand actuality of the reconciled," the convergence of inward, imaginative fantasy and external, worldly perfection. However, the authenticity of that moment depends on our disregarding of the fact that the film has already conditioned us to be skeptical of such emotionally and generically overdetermined scenes.

In an earlier scene of *Stardust Memories,* Bates and Dorrie are kissing beneath an umbrella in a rainstorm, the movingly romantic moment gradually revealed to be a movie take, the camera pulling back to expose klieg lights and a rainmaking machine beyond the boundaries of the original frame. It follows that if as viewers of *Stardust Memories* we are drawn into the even more beautifully epiphanic "Stardust" memory which expresses the film's ultimate existential affirmation, then its sudden interruption by the exclamations "Cop-out artist!" "That was *so* beautiful," and "Why do all comedians turn out to be sentimental bores?" from Bates's audience pours the cold water of mediation upon our intense emotional involvement. What we've been so wrapped up in is just another scene in Bates's movie to which numerous contradictory audience responses are possible. Sandy Bates's sentimental affirmation of life is framed and parodied by Woody Allen's deflationary irony; increasingly, we come to recognize that *Stardust Memories* is a film deliberately mined with cinematic booby traps set to snare the generic expectation, the unwary emotional investment. Unquestionably, it's not the sort of film that Pearl, *Interiors'* incarnation of uncritical artistic responses, would enjoy, though her new daughter-in-law-to-be, Joey, would understand it completely: "The writer argued both sides so brilliantly," she says of a play the family is discussing, "you didn't know who was right" (*Interiors,* p. 152).

The self-reflexive ironies produced by the ending of Bates's film are reinforced and amplified by the ending of Allen's. Among those in the festival audience whose responses to Bates's "big, big finish" reflect no awareness of or interest in the issues to which Bates's film is most committed are characters the published screenplay identifies as "Dorrie," "Isobel," and "Daisy," but who seem no longer to be acting completely in character. "Dorrie," like her anorexic character in the film, is preoccupied with her weight, worrying that she looked fat in the movie; "Isobel" is pleased when "Daisy" tells her she looked beautiful on-screen, but she feels her pronunciation of English wasn't good, and both agree that when "he" (an extremely ambiguous pronoun suddenly) played romantic scenes with them, he wiggled his tongue unpleasantly around in their mouths and "never lets you go" (p. 378). For Bates, who recalled (or, more likely, fantasized) a scene earlier in the movie in which Dorrie describes him as "the best kisser" (p. 278), these actresses' collective critique of his smooching would represent a particularly humiliating rebuke; more significantly, it thoroughly deflates the film's "big, big finish" of romantic reconciliation by reducing its metaphoric resonances to matters of Bates's personal osculatory techniques. But then, precisely what the scene throws into question are the identities of "Dorrie" and "Isobel" and "Daisy"—and of course, of "Bates" as well.

Viewers of Allen's film have been encouraged to believe throughout much of the narrative that they understood the difference between Bates's films and his life, the scenes from his "early, funny movies" being clearly bracketed as what they are—brief routines which, except for a self-parodying, exaggerated comedic emphasis, could have appeared in *Everything You Wanted to Know About Sex.*[16] Besides those moments in which romantic embraces with Dorrie are exposed to be scenes from Bates's films, the first all-out assault on the stability of that distinction occurs when the Isobel and Bates reconciliation on the train turns out to be the end of Bates's untitled movie. Unlike Dorrie, whom Bates met while making a movie and who acknowledges that "I guess I'm always acting" (p. 306), Isobel has no apparent connection to filmmaking, and much of her appeal for him—as for the viewer—seems located in her complete uninvolvement with that world of role-playing narcissistic self-awareness and illusions. Accordingly, for Allen's audience, as for Og, Isobel seems "someone you can count on." But then, that his heartening, life-affirming choice of her over the kamikaze Daisy is not, as we briefly thought, the romantic closure of Allen's film but of Bates's, is deeply disorienting; even more so is the appearance of the three female characters at the end of the film presenting themselves no longer as Bates's intimates but as actresses, as professionals no less oblivious to the film's themes and romantically affirmative conclusion than is the rest of the festival audience. Nowhere in Allen's movies is there a more unequivocal dramatization of the utter inability of film (or, as we saw earlier, filmmakers) to raise the audience above their personal agendas and narcissistic preoccupations—of, that is, the impotence and inefficacy of art.[17]

It therefore seems ironic that Allen described the work which makes that point as "the best film I ever did . . . It was the closest I came to achieving what I set out to achieve."[18] That irony is, of course, the source of the effectiveness of *Stardust Memories*. More than any other Allen film, *Stardust Memories* operates on a dynamic of assertion and retraction, affirmation and negation, one perfectly dramatizing Allen's ambivalent attitude toward the art-related themes he habitually addresses. The content of Bates's closing speech to Isobel—"It's not as terrible as I originally thought it was because-because, you know, we like each other, and . . . we have some laughs, and there's a lot of closeness, and the whole thing is a lot easier to take"—reflects a belief in the redemptiveness of human relationships sporadically affirmed in Allen's films. The exposure of this assertion as a scripted scene in a movie reveals it to be not an image of how human beings actually interact in the world but merely as Sandy Bates's hopefully romantic projection of that reality. It reflects his desire of how things should be rather than an image of how they actually are. The intensely emotional "Stardust moment" delivers its affectively compelling conviction that "for one brief moment, everything seemed to come together perfectly, and I-I felt happy, almost indestructible, in a way." Our realization that this too is a created cinematic moment exposes it as well as the product not of unmediated life but of artistically calculated, reconstructed human desire. *Stardust Memories* is less a film affirming life than one dramatizing the human desire artistically to affirm it.

That point is reinforced, in fact, by the lyrics of the song creating the

"Stardust memory" itself. "Sometimes I wonder why I spend the lonely nights dreaming of a song," Louis Armstrong sings, the metonymic substitution of song for lover fitting perfectly in a film in which lovers are repeatedly preempted by others' constructed visions of them. "And I am once again with you. When our love was new, oh babe, it's an inspiration. But that was long ago, now my consolation is in the stardust of a song." "Stardust," the very song which generates the "Stardust memory" itself, expresses the irrecoverability of such moments; even as Bates is experiencing the beauty of "everything seeming to come together perfectly," the content of the song eliciting that feeling in him is asserting the inescapable mutability of such moments. "Though I dream in vain," Armstrong concludes the Hoagy Carmichael lyric, "in my heart it will remain, my stardust melody, the memory of love's refrain."

Following the montage of some of Alvy's and Annie's happy moments together at the end of *Annie Hall*—the montage visualizing "the memory of love's refrain"—Alvy Singer affirms his relationship with Annie ("It was great seeing Annie again, right? I realized what a great person she was and-and how much fun it was just knowing her" [*Annie Hall,* p. 105]) by suggesting that his memories of their love affair are valuable and sustaining. *Stardust Memories* complicates that affirmation of human remembrance by dramatizing how often it constructs, rather than recovers, past events. "Just before I died," Bates explains in introducing his "Stardust memory," "I was on the operating table, and I was searching to-to try to find something to hang on to, you know? . . . 'cause when you're dying, uh, life suddenly does become very authentic. . . . I was searching for something to give my life meaning and-and a memory flashed through my mind" (p. 361). The fact that the "Stardust memory" that follows is a scene from a film suggests the level on which memory, like film, may represent the solution to human dilemmas, or may constitute nothing more than a symptomatic expression of our desperate need to solve them. For Allen, in other words, the desire to find meaning in the world always threatens to compromise the validity of the meaning ultimately found. The experience of beauty achieved may be actual, or it may be only a cinematic construct of an artist seeking to remedy his "Ozymandias Melancholia"; the reconciliation of lovers may be a human potentiality or just a generically defined way to end movies; love may be a human reality, or it may simply be "in the stardust of a song."

Bates's happy ending, then, is too ensnared in film-within-film ambiguities to leave behind it any sense of determinacy or closure, memories and movies dissolving into each other so inextricably that it becomes difficult to decide whether Bates himself hasn't been ironized out of existence by their interweavings. ("Sandy, Sandy," expostulates an eccentric fan at the UFO convention who has intuited the Batesian mental reality he exists in, "you know this is exactly like one of your satires. It's like we're all characters in some film being watched in God's private screening room" [p. 360].) The possibility that Bates has been annulled by the competing unrealities which he is projecting is significant because an element of the affirmation he reaches in his film's closing scene is an affirmation of self—not untypically, one he articulates as if it were Isobel's perception, or—to complicate things further—the perception of "this character who's based on" her in his film. "You're just crazy about me. You just think I'm the most wonderful thing in the world," he tells her, "andand you're in love with me . . . despite the fact that I do a lot of foolish things, cause-cause you realize that-that down deep I'm-I'm . . . not evil or anything, you know? Just sort of floundering around. Just-just ridiculous, maybe. You know, j-just searching, okay?" (p. 376).

This is as close as this protagonist Allen described as "not a saint nor an angel, but a man with real problems" comes to honest self-confrontation, its defense of him as one "searching" providing the best answer the movie gives for his continuing to make films of whose purposefulness he is deeply skeptical and whose positive affect on the audience he seriously doubts. How wonderfully ironic it is, then, that at the very moment in which Bates has reached this highly significant self-affirmation, the viewer is wondering whether the self-affirmer is Bates or a character in Bates's movie or. . . . Nonetheless, whether we give way to the temptation to identify Bates's self-justification here with Woody Allen's own rationale for filmmaking or not, this is Bates's most sympathetic moment in *Stardust Memories,* the one which most forthrightly asks the viewer to reassess him and forgive his various trespasses. That being the case, this moment too must be ironized.

If the perspectival involutions of Bates's self-affirmation weren't enough to nullify its content, its replication of Guido Anselmi's declaration at the end of *8½* may be sufficient to do that as well as to intertextually undermine whatever minimal protagonistic integrity Bates retains. After he has experienced a brief moment of clarity in which "everything is real, everything has meaning," Guido complains, "There—everything is just as it was before, everything is confused again. But this confusion . . . is *me.* It's because I am as I am, and not as I would like to be. I'm not afraid anymore—I'm not afraid of telling the truth, of admitting that I don't know, that I seek and have not yet found. Only this way can I feel alive."[19] Guido's inflection is markedly less stutter-ridden and hesitant than Bates's, his eloquent self-affirmation, delivered through interior monologue and therefore not dependent upon another's response, seeming far more confident. Furthermore, it couldn't typify the two directors more aptly that Fellini's protagonist construes his lack of certainty as a necessary concomitant of being alive, whereas Allen's protagonist identifies his existential confusion with his own ridiculousness. Nonetheless, they have in common their tentative acceptances of themselves as searchers, a similarity which nonetheless seems to push them and their films toward very different conclusions.

Guido moves from his self-affirmation to reconciliation with his wife and a joining of hands with the living and the dead from whom he's felt alienated throughout the film; the circus ring which forms the backdrop of their parade, a progress Guido, the blocked director, directs, seems not to undermine the sincerity of his regeneration, but to confirm it. Sandy Bates's self-affirmation, on the other hand, is revealed to be simply a sentimental ending for a movie, one which moves only a fatuous young actor who badgered Bates earlier and who interprets the film's point as being "how . . . everybody should love each other" among other "serious, heavy things." Once the Stardust Auditorium has cleared, Bates enters alone. He retrieves his sunglasses from a seat, the act suggesting, as Nancy Pogel argues, that he's a member of the audience in a way that Guido never seems to be, but reminding us, too, that it's the studio mavens who wear sunglasses throughout the film so that their eyes can't be seen. He dons the sunglasses, stops to consider the blank screen for a few moments, then exits the building. As the room darkens, the only illumination left is semicircles of lights around the ceiling, the pattern they form strongly reminiscent of the lights outlining the circus ring on which *8½* fades out. As if in imitation of the Jewish comic's strategy of outflanking anti-Semitism by anticipating and surpassing it in his/her routine, Allen incorporates into *Stardust Memories* the criticism that his work is derivative of great European directors, exploiting that objection in order to reinforce his dramatization of how completely human lives are mediated by movies.

In this film of incessantly proliferating ambiguities, a final uncertainty is whether the figure who stares at the screen at the end of *Stardust Memories* is Sandy Bates. If the ending of *Stardust Memories* constitutes a deliberate homage to the Fellini film which consistently blurs the distinction between its director and protagonist, it makes sense that, in the closing scene of Allen's film, Dorrie, Isobel, and Daisy have become indistinguishable from the real-life actresses Charlotte Rampling, Marie Christine-Barrault, and Jessica Harper, and that the absorption of Sandy Bates into his own film's final scene has left only Woody Allen to briefly occupy the Stardust Auditorium in grand isolation.[20] Such a culminating stripping away of levels of illusion is entirely appropriate, since all of the film's themes—the tension between comic and tragic art, the interpenetrability of memory and desire, the capacity of the artifice of film to distort reality, the parallel capacity of erotic fantasy to distort perceptions of others, and so on—have their locus in the same individual, one whose discussion of his unresolved conflict as a filmmaker between "what I really am and what I would like myself to be" actually echoes the realization of a Fellini film protagonist whose redemptive solution to his conflict is to recognize that "I am who I am and not as I would like to be." Whether we perceive the sunglasses retriever as Sandy Bates or Woody Allen, it is nonetheless clear that *Stardust Memories* is Allen's most personal—and, certainly, most complex—

cinematic confrontation with the issues of his relationship to his art, and one whose closing bleak demythologization of the artistic illusion undeniably reflects his inability to resolve the conflicts he's dramatized.[21] Bates—or Allen— is finally unable to affirm the affect of his film on its audience or its effects on him: he could be, in staring up at the screen, posing to himself the same objections and questions the critic raises about the autobiographical film Guido is attempting to create in *8½*: "What a monstrous presumption to believe that others might benefit by the squalid catalogue of your mistakes! And to yourself, what good would it do you to piece together the shreds of your life, the vague memories, the shadows of the ones you didn't know how to love?"

It is the major achievement of Allen's film that the gradually emerging mediations and vertiginously self-consuming ironies of *Stardust Memories* constitute the only artistically legitimate response he could make to such questions.

8

Woody's Mild Jewish Rose

Broadway Danny Rose

Why do all comedians turn out to be sentimental bores?

—Viewer at Sandy Bates Film Festival after watching the "Stardust memory" scene of Bates's movie in *Stardust Memories*

Perhaps "bores" is an inordinately harsh term with which to describe them, but the comedians who gather at the Carnegie Delicatessen in the opening scene of *Broadway Danny Rose* to trade borscht belt jokes, kibitz about the old days on the New York stand-up comedy circuit, and compete with each other to tell "the greatest Danny Rose story" are nothing if not sentimental. The pervasiveness of that sentimentality is but one of the elements which makes *Broadway Danny Rose* seem a cinematic antithesis to the prevailing jadedness of *Manhattan's* ethos, and even more so to the relentless perspectival and affective chill of *Interiors*. Although there's hardly an explicit reference to art—as Eve would define it, at any rate—anywhere in *Broadway Danny Rose*, it's nonetheless a central movie to consider in the context of a discussion of Allen's equivocal stance toward the aesthetic because it dramatizes, albeit in distinctly mediated and elliptical terms, the values Allen counterposes to the life-consecrated-to-art ethic he so conflictedly rejected in *Interiors*. If high culture artistic aspiration aroused in Allen an ambivalence he was incapable of resolving dramatically in *Interiors,* the pop culture world of Jewish American comedy elicits his sympathies so palpably that its depiction moves Allen as close as he ever comes on film to the creation of a consonantly resolved narrative founded upon a remarkably sentimental affirmation of human solidarity and morality.[1] Therefore, *Broadway Danny Rose* is as well-made a film as Allen has produced, in addition to being an object lesson in Allen's conception of the conditions necessary to the creation of artistic closure in film narrative.

The protagonist of the comedians' communally generated "greatest Danny Rose story" represents the contravention of everything the aesthete Eve embodies. The contrasts between Eve and Danny Rose are easy to recognize: she decorates and dresses in tasteful, monochromatically repressed earth tones, whereas his style is '70s polyester, his polka dot shirts competing cheerfully with loud plaid jackets; she is devoted to her personally defined, individualistic conception of beauty, wanting Arthur to see the interior of a church "before it gets cluttered up with people," whereas Danny is entirely other-directed, inquiring of every female he meets, "How old are you, darling?," and offering the world pep talks full of self-help incantations borrowed from wise dead relatives such as "star, smile, strong" and "acceptance, forgiveness, and love." Eve is the "very delicate" Matisse drawing she buys for Arthur at Parke-Barnet, while Danny is completely sold on "Mr. Danny Kaye and Mr. Bob Hope and Mr. Milton Berle"; she finds her only solace in the past, being desperately committed to the restoration of the lost unity of her family, which was her greatest creation and only protection, whereas he embraces a homiletic American belief in progress and the future, insisting that the beauty of show business lies in that "Overnight, you can go from a bum to a hero."[2] Validating Danny's Horatio Algeresque faith in the possibility of self-transformation from "bum to hero" constitutes both the movie's pivotal dramatic project as well as the basis for its central pun.

Perhaps the most significant distinction between the two film protagonists, however, exists in Eve's dedication to an ideal of humanity-ennobling artistic perfection as opposed to Danny's unequivocal commitment to artists over art. It's not merely that the performance specialties of his clients—balloon folding, water glass playing, bird and penguin acts—bear only a parodic relation to what Eve would designate fine arts; beyond that, he seems to have deliberately sought out performers whose physical incapacities *necessarily compromise* their ability to perform their art. Far from achieving anything approaching perfect art, the performances of a number of Danny's clients—his blind xylophonist, one-legged tap dancer and one-armed juggler—must be judged primarily on the basis of their success in overcoming the disability to which their acts unerringly draw attention. Danny is, as Jonathan Baumbach's review of the film described him, "a one-man Salvation Army for crippled performers,"[3] and apparently it is only the utter wretchedness of Barney Dunn's jokes that prevents Danny from representing this genial stuttering ventriloquist. Client or not, Barney (Herb Reynolds) is one of the guests at the patently sacramental Thanksgiving scene which closes the movie, Danny's annual gathering of his showbiz low rollers manifesting not his belief in the magnitude of their talents but his sincere affection for them as people.

Accordingly, in attempting to sell his clients to hotels, rooms, and promoters, Danny invariably invokes their human qualities—the blind xylophone player is "a beautiful man," "a fantastic individual"—rather than the virtues of their acts, Danny's intense involvement in their lives enabling him endlessly to vouch for their characters and plead their causes for them. (The trauma of the death of one of the birds in Herbie Jayson's act, Danny argues with a club manager, justifies his being paid despite his client having been too devastated to perform.) Simlarly, Danny is able to value even those whose lack of talent doesn't even have the excuse of good character to recommend it. The client of Danny's that the comedians' "greatest Danny Rose story" concentrates on is perceived by the rest of the show business community as nothing but trouble: Lou Canova (Nick Apollo Forte) is, in the words of the owner of Weinstein's Majestic Bungalow Colony, "a dumb, fat, temperamental has-been with a drinkin' problem" (p. 154). The unfolding of the plot adds "womanizer" to that catalogue of Lou's character deficits, none of which deters Danny from devoting himself unswervingly to the promotion of the Italian crooner's career, even volunteering to waive his commissions when Lou feels financially pinched. "In business," Danny's father had told him, "friendly but not familiar," but he hasn't been able to follow that advice because, "This is personal management I'm in. You know, it's the key word, it's *personal*" (p. 212). His emphasis on ministering to the personal lives of his clients combined with the limitations of their talents insures that he and they remain on the outer fringes of show business. His marginality is epitomized by the fact that his most successful performers regularly abandon him for more powerful agents, and by the snapshots on his apartment wall of himself with Frank Sinatra and Tony Bennett, of himself with Judy Garland, of himself with Myron Cohen— photographs in which Danny is never quite visible. In this most sentimentally egalitarian of Woody Allen's films, it is anything but a putdown to suggest that Danny and his clients deserve each other.

"You're livin' like a loser," Tina Vitale (Mia Farrow), tells Danny when she first visits his apartment. Tina is the widow of a Mafia hit man whose aspirations to a career in interior decoration have her imagining room decors as tasteful—and as unlike Eve's—as Danny's wardrobe. The two are thrown together on the day of Lou's appearance at the Waldorf, the singer insisting that he can't go on without knowing his lover is in the audience. It's the contrast of his "loser" humanist values—concern for others and "acceptance, forgiveness, and love"—with her hard-bitten "looking out for number one" ethic which provides a central thematic tension for the film. (Whereas the moralism of *Manhattan's* Isaac Davis is self-righteous and self-serving, Danny's is generously permeated by altruistic impulses. Nothing reflects the comedian's subjective needs in recounting his story more clearly than its dramatization of Danny's betrayal by the callous, self-interested, antihumanistic values of show business.) Undergirding the main comic business of *Broadway Danny Rose*— an extended chase scene occupying much of the heart of the film in which Tina and Danny are pursued by Johnny Rispoli's brothers, who are intent upon rubbing out "Danny White Roses" for stealing Tina from Johnny—is a debate between the couple about personal responsibility to others, a debate ultimately resolved by Tina's eventual acknowledgment of the inevitability of guilt to human interaction.

Early in the film when Lou Canova reveals his adulterous relationship with Tina to Danny, Danny points to the sky and warns the singer, "Some day you're gonna have to square yourself with the big guy"; Danny later admits that he doesn't believe in God, but he's "guilty over it." Tina spends the last third of the film attempting to square herself with all that the movie offers her to square herself with—the little guy, Danny. Tina appears uninvited at Danny's annual Thanksgiving bash (he serves his performers frozen turkey TV dinners each year) with his Uncle Sidney's trio of virtues—"acceptance, forgiveness, and love"—on her lips, having in the last weeks undergone an object lesson in the validity of Danny's philosophy of life: "It's important to have some laughs, no question about it, but you got to suffer a little, too. Because otherwise, you miss the whole point of life" (p. 254).

No Woody Allen film ends in a more completely earned or more satisfying sense of closure than *Broadway Danny Rose*. The conciliation scene between Danny and Tina takes place with charmingly corny aptness outside the Carnegie Deli in which the comedians, some years later, would be nostalgically reconstructing the couple's adventure together.[4] In order not to overextend the happy ending, Allen signals only with calculated indirection the inevitable romantic resolution and Danny's post-narrative progress from "a bum to a hero." In the film's final scene, Sandy Baron reveals that the Carnegie Deli has elevated Danny to the status of Broadway luminary through introducing a sandwich intermixing Danny's Jewish and Tina's Italian heritages called the "Danny Rose Special," the offering consisting, Morty Gunty speculates, of cream cheese on bagel with marinara sauce. Whether the sandwich Danny has become is a hero or not is left to the viewer to decide. Significantly, that sandwich is all that remains of Danny Rose in the film's present—he has become inseparable from the story told about him, or, as John Pym suggested, "he has faded into the mythical anecdotes of his peers."[5] It is his withdrawal into the status of the legendary that largely accounts for the film's untypical—for Allen—happy ending, *Broadway Danny Rose* reinforcing the point implicit in *Radio Days* that happy endings are possible only for fictional characters.

Inspired by this heartwarming resolution, jocularity prevails as the closing titles scroll over some good-natured banter between the comics about the length of Baron's Danny Rose story and expressions of surprise at Corbett Monica's uncharacteristically picking up the evening's check. It's clear that the telling of the "greatest Danny Rose story" has accomplished what efficacious myths effect: it has magically altered ordinary human interactions in the Carnegie Deli. Gunty affirms that the comedians will meet again tomorrow for more nostalgia, more talk of the old days, but it's evident that we've heard the story they most needed and wanted to tell. To understand how *Broadway Danny Rose* manages to reach what so few Allen films do—an unambiguously happy ending—it's necessary to recognize how completely the fable's resolution depends on the needs and agendas of its community of tellers. (In re-

sponse to Will Jordan's account of how he came to impersonate James Mason, Howard Storm indirectly calls attention to the mediatory role of the comedians in *Broadway Danny Rose,* asking "But this thing is all in like the mask, right?" [p. 150]. Right.) At the bleakest point in Sandy Baron's narrative (Danny, fired by Lou on the night of his nostalgia act's biggest showbiz success, walks out of Roosevelt Hospital into a rainstorm after visiting Barney Dunn, for whose pulverization by Mafia thugs he's inadvertently responsible), Morty Gunty objects, "I thought this was a funny story. It's terrible!"(p. 291) The story is destined not to end terribly because of the purpose its telling is serving the tellers and the told.

Before they embark upon their communal Danny Rose narrative, the assembled comedians shmooze about the condition of the world of show business as they experience it in the film's present, the early 1980s. It's not good. The old failsafe jokes they've traditionally stolen from each other for their routines aren't working anymore; there are far fewer rooms for comedians to play in the New York metropolitan area, obliging them to travel as far as Baltimore and Washington for jobs and to have much better tires than they previously needed; audiences are neither as reliable or as loyal as they once were. "They never left," Baron recalls mournfully, invoking the old crowds in the old venues devoted solely to comedy, "they never left at all" (p. 149). It is no coincidence that to counter these present miseries and cheer themselves up the story Baron and his fellow comics enthusiastically choose is that of Danny Rose, who—at least in their nostalgic reconstruction of him—is notable primarily for his unstinting and unequivocal loyalty to his acts. "His acts were so devoted," Will Jordan comments, "They loved him . . . I mean, where you gonna find that kind of devotion today?" (p. 154) In his *Commonweal* review, Baumbach characterized *Broadway Danny Rose* as "a comedy about mythmaking,"[6] which I take to mean that what we're watching in the movie is the comedians' construction of the myth which is "the greatest Danny Rose story." So it's quite appropriate that the first flashback scene the comedians evoke of Danny (the first in which Allen appears in the movie) dramatizes his attempt to sell his acts to the booking agent for Weinstein's Majestic Bungalow Colony and includes a discussion of the disloyalty—foreshadowing Lou's defection—of one of Danny's recent acts who had begun to prosper in show business. "They get a little success," Phil the Colony booking agent tells Danny, "and they leave you" (p. 155). Danny, to the contrary, "would work his tail off for his acts . . . if he believed in them," comedian Howard Storm insists. The comics agree that making his clients believe in themselves constituted much of the "star, smile, strong" strategy of "Danny Rose, Personal Management."

"I don't see you folding balloons in joints," Danny insists in a typical client-motivation spiel, "You're gonna fold these balloons in universities and colleges . . . you're gonna make your snail and your elephant at, at, on Broadway," and thus become "one of the great balloon-folding acts of all time" [p. 154]. It's in this goofily sincere belief in other people and his endless encouragement of them that Danny Rose differs most radically from every other Woody Allen protagonist, and if his character is the sentimental idealization of show business of an earlier decade projected by aging, demoralized, and nostalgic comics,[7] he represents Allen's least Woody Allenesque portrayal and Allen's single most accomplished job of comic acting.

Vincent Canby eloquently described *Broadway Danny Rose* as "a love letter not only to American comedy stars and to all those pushy hopefuls who never made it to the top in show business, but also to the kind of comedy that nourished the particular genius of Woody Allen,"[8] his characterization effectively accounting for the unequivocality of the film's address to the viewer's emotions. Gilbert Adair's review of the film summarized the affective quality of Allen's performance equally elegantly: Danny recalls Chaplin's "little man" and, "reincarnated here as Danny Rose, he *is* pathetic, melancholic, droll, poignant, affecting—that whole Thesaurus of sentimental adjectives covered by the outmoded but not quite obsolete critical commonplace 'Chaplinesque.' Danny is a born loser; and the film's premise, one of the most moving it's possible to imagine, is the ultimate triumph of the loser over his fate."[9] All that Adair's eloquent description omits is the fact that it's the Carnegie comedians who are engaging in the communal act of wish-fulfillment which is the story of this loser triumphing over his fate. Lacking the actual Danny himself for reassurance, they are creating their own elaborate narrative version of "star, smile, strong" to buck themselves up as they prepare to schlep themselves to Baltimore and New Jersey to perform their gigs.

For Baron and his fellow comics, Danny is the epitome of a lost world in which performers like themselves—and even those still more inferior and small time—were cared for, valued in a way these comedians' opening exchange proves that they no longer are. (That a couple of the comedians turn out to have attended one of Danny's TV dinner Thanksgiving feasts affirms their largely unacknowledged solidarity with Danny's exotic acts.) Because there *is* no Danny Rose beyond Sandy Baron's narrative, it is impossible to distinguish fact from myth in the film; all we have is the "landlocked Hebrew" of their telling, whose message is "acceptance, forgiveness, and love" and who will arguably become more noble and self-sacrificing with every telling of his story by the comedians who ritualistically gather at the Carnegie Deli to cheer themselves with sentimental constructions of the superiority of yesterday to today. David Denby's objection that "not even Damon Runyon, Broadway fabulist and designer of improbable matches, could have imagined that this girl [Tina] is for that guy [Danny]"[10] assumes that the film's conclusion is dictated by real-world probability; insofar as Danny and Tina are united in the film's close, it's only because the comedians, in their affection for their hero, believe *he deserves her.*[11] For his loyalty to his acts, for his epitomizing humanistic values in an increasingly inhuman industry, the comedians' myth-weaving rewards Danny with Tina. That's the story they tell themselves; that's the story we see. It's not even certain, in fact, that the "Danny Rose Special" *does* marry Jewish and Italian cultures: although Morty Gunty asserts it's "[p]robably a cream cheese on a bagel with marinara sauce" (p. 309), neither he nor the other comedians seems to have the heart to check the Carnegie Deli menu board a few feet away from their table for fear, perhaps, of finding that the honorary sandwich is actually cream cheese and lox on bagel.

Only the narrative intercession of "sentimental bores" like Baron, Gunty, Corbett Monica, Jackie Gayle, Howard Storm, Will Jordan, and (perennial Allen film producer) Jack Rollins,[12] with their communal need to remember a better day in American showbiz and to provide themselves with a Danny Rosean pep talk brightening their future prospects, could transform the workings of Danny's Godless, guilt-laden universe into the encouraging little fable with its lovely, morality-affirming resolution which is *Broadway Danny Rose.* Only their benevolently mediational presence and Allen's obvious affection for them and the world they embody can account for the generation of this most artistically consonant and happiest of Woody Allen endings.

"You're livin' like a loser," we've already heard Tina tell Danny. As we've also noticed, Gilbert Adair took her at her word, describing Allen's protagonist's character as that of "a born loser" whose triumph is that of "a loser over his fate"; Andrew Sarris concurred, designating Danny "a pathetic loser who lives in a rat hole"[13]; Daphne Merkin took a different tack by being offended that the film evoked concern from the audience for Danny rather than "the losers who surround" him,[14] acts whom Joseph Gelmis characterized as Danny's "'family' of show biz losers."[15] Jack Kroll in *Newsweek* was more egalitarian in conferring the status on both agent and clients, seeing Danny as "a loser selling losers,"[16] while David Denby perceived the same redemptive movement in the film Adair did, viewing *Broadway Danny Rose* as "a fable about how losers can become winners." It's interesting that these reviewers—some of whom find Tina an unconvincing character—nonetheless so emphatically endorse her social Darwinist ethic. She knows losers when she sees them, and so do they. Given the near-unanimity of this descriptor's application to Danny and his acts, it's worthwhile to briefly consider the validity of the label "loser" so liberally conferred not only upon characters in *Broadway Danny Rose* but to Allen's "nebbish" protagonists in general. Although somewhat tangential to the issue of Allen's ambivalence toward art, the "loser" tag so uncritically applied to Allen's characters may have done more to blind reviewers and critics to the nuances of Allen's vision than any other misperception.

As early as 1963, William K. Zinsser described the persona projected by Allen's stand-up routine as that of "a born loser . . . who walks onto a stage and immediately makes his presence unfelt"[17]; the first critical book published on Allen's films was titled *Loser Takes All,* and contains the sentence, "Despite all the failures, however, it should not be concluded that Allen's persona is always a loser,"[18] which clearly implies that he usually is one. Maurice Yacowar did point up the paradox of Allen's having ridden himself of the "loser" persona to great personal success, but the glib characterizing of his characters as "losers" continued. Does categorizing Allen's characters as losers help to clarify anything about them or about the films in which they appear? More particularly, is this derogatorily fatalistic judgment consistent with the tone and spirit of *Broadway Danny Rose?*

Perhaps there's some justice in characterizing the one-dimensional hapless bunglers of *Take the Money and Run, Bananas,* and *Sleeper* as unredeemed, unreconstructed losers, though it's difficult not to think that even there the term serves primarily as an excuse for critical—not to mention humanistic—imprecision. But what makes Allan Felix of *Play It Again, Sam* a loser? He's nervous around women, he fails to deliver the appropriate insincerities when the moment and his erotic advantage demands them, and California beauties spurn his attempts to dance with them—he's not, in short, Bogart. What makes *Annie Hall's* Alvy Singer a loser? He's obsessed with death, he's hypochondriac, and hypersensitive, and—like many of us in the audience—his desire to be loved exceeds his loveability. What makes Danny Rose a loser? He's dedicated himself to supporting performing acts because he cares about the performers more than he does about the quality of their performances or about the financial rewards which might accrue from his representing them, and—as his obviously delighted hosting of the Thanksgiving feast dramatizes—he derives obvious pleasure from his relationships with them. (Not coincidentally, he lives in an apartment reflective of his indifference to the money they don't make for him.) That these are comic characters, presented to us partly for laughs, suggests that their sensibilies are extreme, exaggerated for the purpose of humor. To dismiss them as "losers," however, is to ignore the fact that, throughout Jewish American comic literature, the unWASPish "deficiencies" of Jewish protagonists, in addition to being excellent material for jokes, also satirically reflect upon the mainstream culture from which they represent significant deviations. The obsession Nathanael West's Miss Lonelyhearts develops with the sufferings of the letter-writers to his newspaper column pushes well into comic excess, even though the novella never suggests that he isn't responding to a terrible American reality which those around him refuse to acknowledge or which they callously reduce to jokes. Moses Herzog's obsessive letter writing *is* funny, but the sensibility it expresses (one more literary than, but not unlike Holden Caulfield's) also critiques WASP ideals of masculine reticence and expressive self-inhibition. Alexander Portnoy's incessant masturbation makes us laugh while satirizing the Puritan abjuration of the physical promptings of the body he somehow failed to internalize; Bruce Jay Friedman's Stern has so completely introjected American anti-Semitism that his ongoing struggles with it are as hilarious as the cultural bigotry with which he is contending is real.

These "losers" all have in common their recognition of—or perhaps more accurately, their obsession with—human or cultural realities the denial of whose existences is a cultural code to which those around them have conformed. The excess of their overreaction to those realities is both what makes them comic *and* the works' primary documentation of their non-American mainstream humanity. While laughing at the disparity between the conduct of these protagonists and national norms of behavior and belief, we are obliged by Jewish American literature to scrutinize the validity of those values, invited to find them wanting.

In the fictional worlds through which these protagonists move, they may be perceived as losers, but is the reader intended so uncritically to adopt the values of those worlds? After all, isn't it these characters' imperviousness to the values of mainstream American culture which constitutes the very source of their "loserness?" That would seem to place those imposing the term "loser" on them in the anomalous position of defining winning as conformity to, or the achievement of success in, mainstream American culture. Lou Canova is experiencing success in that world by singing "Agita," a song which he (actually Nick Apollo Forte) wrote about indigestion, his exploitation of the 1970s

nostalgia craze allowing him to dump Danny for the more powerful management of Sid Bacharach. Is this the point of the "parable of how losers can
become winners?"[19] Bacharach, whom Tina knows through her murdered
husband, the Mafia hit man, expresses agreement with her ethic of "You see
what you want, go for it," and "Do it to the other guy first, 'cause if you don't
he'll do it to you" (p. 254); if Bacharach represents the film's epitome of winning, Danny Rose and his stable of performers will remain losers. What Tina's
appearance at Danny's apartment at the end of the film affirms with a truly
Chaplinesque sentimentality unprecedented in Allen's work is Danny's Uncle
Sidney's belief in "acceptance, forgiveness, and love," a moral stance which
makes no provision for discriminations between winners and losers. Surely
one of the objectives of art is to demonstrate the bankruptcy of simplistic,
superficial, and essentialistic conceptions of humanity; *Broadway Danny Rose's*
touching demonstration that fellow-feeling and compassion for others *are* rewarded, not in heaven but in front of—or inside—the Carnegie Deli, should
have been sufficient to quash for good the "loser" rhetoric mindlessly applied
to Allen's protagonists.

That so-called "loser" deficiencies may constitute a manifestation of an
inverted form of personal redemption is a major point not only of *Broadway
Danny Rose,* but also of the Allen film that preceded it, *Zelig.* Saul Bellow's
assessment of the Zelig phenomenon in that movie has to be understood as a
view mediated by the fact that a real author is discoursing straight-facedly on
a fictional character, the ironic inversions implicit in the clip dictating that we
should take his mock judgment quite seriously, both as a comment on Leonard
Zelig and—arguably—as a gloss on some of Bellow's own protagonists. "The
thing was paradoxical because what enabled [Zelig] to perform this astound-
ing feat [flying over the Atlantic Ocean upside down] was his ability to transform himself," Bellow explains. In other words, the psychic pathology of
imitating the world around him for which Zelig had to be treated was what
allowed him to emulate Eudora Fletcher's piloting of the plane after she had
passed out and to fly them safely back from Germany. "Therefore, his sickness
was at the root of his salvation," Bellow continues, "and . . . I think it's interesting to view the thing that way, that it, it was his . . . it was his very disorder
that made a hero of him."[20] Just as the "sicknesses" of West's, Bellow's, Roth's,
and Friedman's obsessives are "at the root of their salvation," so it is Danny
Rose's eccentric loyalty to and celebration of show business rejects—the one-
legged tap dancer and one-armed juggler and stammering ventriloquist, all of
whom, just like the rest of us, attempt to make art out of our various impair-
ments—which constitutes the heroism the comedians implicitly reward him
for and culminates in the Broadway apotheosis of his becoming a Carnegie
Deli sandwich. It is his deviation from the inhuman values of American show
business which makes a hero out of Danny Rose.

In the end, the best corrective to the critical tendency to reduce Allen's protagonists to "losers" is to invoke his own use of the term. "Basically," Allen said as early as 1969, discoursing on his favorite topic of human mortality, "everybody is a loser, but it's only now that people are willing to admit it."[21] In making this assertion, Allen was implicitly declaring his solidarity with the Jewish American literary tradition that had for years been using the satirical portraiture of Jewish characters to backhandedly skewer the WASP values which they so hilariously failed to emulate. Their inability to accommodate themselves to those values proves, ironically, that the "disorder" Bellow attributes to Zelig is in the culture rather than in them. More than any other film of Allen's, *Broadway Danny Rose* finds in the admission that "everybody is a loser" not grounds for self-hatred or narcissistic withdrawal but, instead, an affecting rationale for human solidarity.

9

The Fine Art of Living Well
Hannah and Her Sisters

Poor fool, he's dead and he never found the meaning of life.

—A nurse eulogizing the assassinated Sandy Bates in *Stardust Memories*

This dilemma is so repeatedly invoked in Allen's films that it has practically come to seem a familiar Woody one-liner, a predictable component of the repository of jokes we watch his movies to enjoy. It's part whine, part existential interrogation. Mickey Sachs (Allen), the producer of a television show resembling *Saturday Night Live*, rehearses it with his assistant (Julie Kavner) early in *Hannah and Her Sisters:* "Can you understand how meaningless everything is? Everything! I'm talking about . . . our lives, the show . . . the whole world, it's meaningless. . . . I mean, you're gonna die, I'm gonna die, the audience is gonna die, the network's gonna—The Sponsor. Everything."[1] Partly because of Mickey's hilarious search for meaning through his hapless attempts to convert to Catholicism and Hare Krishna, *Hannah and Her Sisters* became an audience favorite, its emergent good spirits leavening the quest for spiritual answers much more affirmatively than in Allen's other seriocomic film of existential inquiry, *Stardust Memories*.

Hannah and Her Sisters is also the film of Allen's about whose ending he has been most forthrightly critical. When asked by Bjorkman whether he perceived the movie as confirming or disputing the Tolstoy quotation—"The only absolute knowledge attainable by man is that life is meaningless"—used in the film as an interchapter title, Allen replied, "It was not a point of departure for *Hannah*, but it was certainly what my story was about, what my thread was about. I think, if I'd had a little more nerve on that film, it would have confirmed it somewhat more. But I copped out a little on that film, backed off a little at the end. . . . I tied it together at the end a little too neatly. I should have been a little less happy at the end than I was."[2] Although *Hannah and Her Sisters* is less concerned with art—except as a negative life dedication—than Allen's other films, its exemplification of artistic resolution as an act of falsification makes it highly relevant to a study of Allen's skepticism toward the promises of artistic rendering. Accordingly, in discussing *Hannah and Her Sisters,* the emphasis of this text continues to be on closure, making Allen's opting for such an uncharacteristically buoyant close for *Hannah* the focal point. The unpersuasiveness of *Hannah's* resolution, it can be argued, reflects Allen's Mickey Sachs-like attempt to convert not to a new religion but to another creed in which he ultimately can't believe: the family.

Given that the dramatic momentum of the film ordains their romantic convergence, it seems fairly obvious that the ending Allen is regretting is not the closing scene's disclosure of the marriage of Mickey (Allen) and Holly (Diane Wiest), but Holly's confession that she is pregnant. A flashback earlier in the movie establishes that during his marriage to Hannah (Mia Farrow), Mickey was medically diagnosed as infertile, his friend Rob (Tony Roberts) providing sperm for the twins Hannah produces. Since the artificial insemination has no further dramatic repercussions and Mickey and Hannah's divorce has resulted in no conflict over Mickey's right to see his sons, it seems clear that the only necessity for the infertility subplot is to prepare for the reversal generated by Holly's concluding disclosure.

The circumstantial improbability of her revelation (Holly is joining Mickey at Hannah's annual Thanksgiving celebration, which makes it seem highly unlikely she could have seen a doctor earlier in the day to receive the news) is reinforced by what seem like signals of the misgivings Allen had about ending his film so happily.[3] For one thing, the entire closing scene is shot in a mirror, the fact that it is Mickey's and Holly's reflections we're watching calling into question the reality of the moment.[4] Further, Mickey refers explicitly to the story quality of the scene he and she are living out: "It'd make a great story, I think . . . a guy marries one sister . . . doesn't work out . . . many years later . . . he winds up . . . married to the other sister" (p. 180). His gloss seems to reflect Allen's self-conscious awareness of how close his narrative's ending has come to imitating sentimental art rather than life. These evidences of something bordering on authorial bad faith raise an important question about the film, which audiences and a number of critics alike have judged to be Allen's best: why impose the improbable pregnancy on an ending that, because Mickey and Holly (like Lee and her new husband) have recently married, already contains numerous reasons for "thanksgiving," already constitutes a gratifyingly comedic resolution? Perhaps the only convincing answer to this question is that Holly's pregnancy constitutes the sole solution Allen could imagine for Mickey's existential anxieties, the child she will bear him implicitly providing a remedy to his fear that mortality wipes him out entirely, rendering his life meaningless and leaving nothing of him behind to be remembered. Having in earlier films repudiated art as a source of symbolic immortality, in other words, Allen is seeking in the conclusion of *Hannah and Her Sisters* to determine whether paternity—the family way—works any better than artistic creation does as an antidote to personal extinction.

If we accept this interpretation of the ending of *Hannah and Her Sisters,* we do so in the knowledge that nowhere else in Allen's work is there any suggestion that children represent a form of immortality their parents can produce. The narrator of Gabe's novel in *Husbands and Wives* characterizes procreation as "a nitwit strategy," a judgment apparently borne out by the fact that children are generally seen and not heard throughout Allen's films.

Hannah's brood at her Thanksgiving dinner, for instance, are segregated off at their own table, barely perceivable at the margin of the screen, the half dozen or so of them never once interrupting the ritualistic gestures and genteel conversation being conducted at the adults' table. Although there are brief dramatizations of warm relationships between Isaac Davis and his son in *Manhattan,* and between Larry Weinrib and his adopted son in *Mighty Aphrodite,* these sons are included primarily to heighten dramatic tensions (Isaac's apprehensions about his boy's being raised by lesbian partners) or to facilitate plot development (Larry's search for and relationship with Max's biological mother). The son Larry and Carol have produced in *Manhattan Murder Mystery* has for character the fact that his parents annually take him to '21' for his birthday, and the primary purpose Joe and Steffi's daughter, DJ, serves in *Everyone Says I Love You* is to orchestrate Joe's erotic liaison with Von. Harry Block's real affection for his son, Hilly, is clearly subordinated to Harry's other preoccupations: his adoration of Fay and his writer's block. None of the characters Allen portrays before or after Mickey Sachs—whose narrative's positing of paternity as the solution to his existential questions, in fact, is never dramatized in *Hannah,* it being left to the audience to make the inference—remotely perceives progeny as an answer to questions about the meaning of human life.[5]

Judged on the basis of his entire film output, Allen is no more likely to conclude a film addressing existential issues with the dramatization of his protagonist's achieving symbolic immortality through the generation of offspring than he is to resolve one through the protagonist's successful creation of a work of art. Overall, Allen's films endorse the attitude Mia Farrow cites him as maintaining throughout her memoir, *What Falls Away:* "I have zero interest in kids," he told her early in their relationship, and when they were about to adopt their first child together, he explained, "Look, I don't care about the baby. What I care about is my work."[6] During the public airing of their disintegration as a couple, Allen told *Time Magazine,* "The last thing I was interested in was the whole parcel of Mia's children. . . . I spent absolutely zero time with any of them."[7] "It's no accomplishment to have or raise kids," he insisted earlier, "Any fool can do it."[8]

Such disavowals of interest in family notwithstanding, Allen does conclude *Alice* with the title protagonist repudiating both her marriage and her writing ambitions in favor of dedicating herself to motherhood; the closing image of Alice pushing two of her children on swings clearly evokes a character whose liberation from upper East Side wealth and her marriage to a compulsive adulterer is utterly redemptive. The title character of *Alice* replicates and celebrates Mia Farrow's intense commitment to her children, a dedication which Allen and others often publicly commended. "Mia has a talent for mothering the way some people have a green thumb for gardening or an ear for music or a talent for medicine," Allen told *People Magazine* in 1992, and Rose Styron, the godmother of one of Farrow's adopted children, Soon-Yi, suggested that "I've never known anyone who cared so selflessly about children, and who put so much of herself into them. . . . They always came first."[9]

Accordingly, Farrow's *What Falls Away* proliferates with expressions of her belief in the sacredness of the family, one of which includes her explanation to her mother of how she came to adopt and bring into her family children designated "difficult to place."

> When my mother asked why, I told her that I learned from Moses, firsthand, that meeting special needs is a special privilege, which brings a parent special rewards. It seemed that on the deepest level the other children understood this. Matthew, at seventeen and Yale-bound, had written in his college application essay, "Only now do I fully understand that my mother's way of making life meaningful was to give a home to orphaned children. As a result she has saved four lives and enriched her own. If I can do as much, my life will be a success."[10]

When Allen concurred in Farrow's desire to adopt another child in the mid-1980s, Farrow hoped that Dylan Farrow would be the one to "open [Allen's] heart" to children and family. In recalling this desire in *What Falls Away,* she articulates clearly both her conception of family and her understanding of Allen's opposition to it:

> I still hoped that he would love this child, that she would be the one to open his heart, and that through her he would learn to love without suspicion; that through her, he would see that a person other than himself, with needs and interests distinct from his, can exist not as a threat, but as one worthy of respect and love. And in discovering this, he would surely acknowledge all my children, he would see who they are as human souls, and in knowing them, how could he not love them? And then he would know all they mean to me, and finally he would understand who I am; and knowing my heart, he would feel safe, and love me back with certainty. In loving this child, he would place her needs before his own—he would begin to hope on her behalf, and in doing that he would have access to a purer, deeper connection to life; and we would all be there together, a family. That is what I hoped.[11]

The upshot of Farrow's hopes fueled the tabloid press for months during 1992–1993; six years earlier, *Hannah and Her Sisters,* with Farrow's children Daisy Previn and Moses Farrow portraying Hannah's children, constituted Allen's first attempt to evaluate artistically Farrow's familial ethic. The film's contrived ending communicates Allen's insuperable doubts about the validity of the *Hannah* affirmation and unambiguously expresses his inability to endorse the family. Following the Soon-Yi revelations, Mia and Moses Farrow would agree on the motivation for "the atrocity . . . committed against our family" by Allen. "[H]e had an unfathomable and uncontrollable need to destroy everything positive in his life, so he tried to destroy our family."[12] Farrow summarized her son's interpretation, which echoes her own explanation of Allen's disruption of a lovely family Christmas moment: "Everything was too nice, too beautiful. He just had to ruin it."[13] *Hannah* is Allen's exquisitely framed cinematic vehicle for expressing the familial ambivalence both Farrows would subsequently ascribe to him; *Husbands and Wives* would be Allen's unsparing repudiation of the familial values equivocally treated in *Hannah.*

It's possible to attribute *Hannah*'s inordinately happy ending to external causes: Allen's contentment with his stable relationship of seven years with Farrow,[14] and the good feelings arising from working with a first rate cast. The structural dynamic spanning three Thanksgiving celebrations (a holiday similarly sacramental in *Broadway Danny Rose,* though one commemorated by characters markedly less culturally privileged) to which his screenplay committed him may have also been a factor. More compelling, in critical terms, is to see the pregnancy ending as a resolution dictated by one of the two plot strains of *Hannah and Her Sisters,* the conclusion reflecting a perception of reality largely alien to Allen's characteristic vision. To illuminate that bifurcated structure of *Hannah and Her Sisters,* it's useful to begin by accounting for the fact that this film presents a more positive depiction of the relationship between art and its audience than does any of the other films previously discussed in this text.

There are two worlds dramatized in *Hannah and Her Sisters,* and art is largely contained within the domain in which Hannah is the central figure and symbol. Her husband, Elliot (Michael Caine), and sister, Lee (Barbara Hershey), both recognize Bach's "Concerto for Harpsichord in F Minor" and experience pleasure in listening to it; both have read Richard Yates's *The Easter Parade* and talk briefly with each other about the novel's effect upon them, and they share a passion for the poetry of e.e. cummings, which Elliot employs in seducing Lee. Hannah and her mother, Norma, have portrayed Ibsen's Nora in *A Doll's House* on the New York stage, and Hannah will soon play Desdemona in *Othello,* her highly successful acting career presented as the apparent source of the comfort in which she and her family live. Norma and

her husband, Evan, entertain guests at parties with nostalgic vocal/piano du-
ets of standards by composers such as Cole Porter, Richard Rodgers, and Lorenz
Hart; Holly briefly dates David, an architect who enjoys showing her his favorite New York buildings and has a private box at the Metropolitan Opera.
Hannah, her family, and those with whom they associate are what Allen described to Bjorkman as "people who are sensitive and cultivated," those for
whom art represents "entertainment on a very, very high level." (Their degree
of sensitivity and cultivation, the film clearly implies, is a function of their
very comfortable material circumstances.[15]) For them, art is pleasurable largely
because they assign it to an appropriate place in their lives: none of them
expects a Bach concerto or Puccini's *Manon Lescant* to "save" them, and David's
enthusiasm for his aesthetic occupation is clearly a product of his understanding that architecture is art in which people live and work.

The characters from Allen's earlier films that Hannah's extended circle
most obviously resemble are the highly cultured members of Eve's family in
Interiors. An important difference, however, is that in *Hannah* there is no
matriarch exaggerating art's significance to human beings or grotesquely seeking to make people's lives imitate some ideal aesthetic stasis. The one professional artist in Hannah's immediate family—Hannah herself—balances her
acting career with raising a large family, unlike *Interiors*' Renata, whose art
seems an excuse for ignoring familial obligations.[16]

The character in *Hannah* who *does* make an island of art and who
solipsistically refuses to countenance others' perceptions of it is quickly and
even a little heartlessly dispatched. Lee tells her lover, Frederick, whom she
had once wanted to teach her "everything about poetry, about music," that it's
asking too much for her to act as his only connection to the world. She consequently moves from the dismal Soho warehouse studio he inhabits to the
bright Upper East Side apartment of her parents. Significantly, the audience
of the predominantly upbeat *Hannah* is allowed only briefly to witness the
suffering his self-imposed artist's isolation has brought upon Frederick, as compared to *Interiors*' extended dramatization of the emotional wages of Eve's life-
denying aestheticism.[17]

In her desperate search for a viable career for herself, Holly misconstrues
the proper balance between art and life that her sister seems to embody and
thus offends Hannah by creating a script extravagantly predatory upon real
life—Hannah's married life in particular—and inadequately informed by creative imagination. However, since reading her second script to him becomes
the catalyst through which the romance between Holly and Mickey develops,
her literary trespasses seem to be pardoned through her announcement that
she will soon present Mickey with life rather than what she'd previously offered him—an exceedingly poor dramatic imitation of it.[18] Art, in Hannah's
world, is a complement to life rather than a substitute for it, and if the charac-

ters within her circle come off better than they should because of the film's willingness to gloss over flaws and frictions that other Allen films would routinely explore, their attitude toward art goes so completely unquestioned as to seem indistinguishable from Allen's own.

The other world of the film is one in which art isn't much of an issue because anxieties about the meaning of life and the omnipresence of death render metaphoric projections of existence pointless. As well, the sublimatory capacities underlying the civilized aestheticism of Hannah's crowd prove to be beyond the character whose wont it is to scream at his empty apartment, "I have a tumor in my head the size of a basketball!" This world is, of course, the highly familiar world of Woody Allen films, the realm inhabited by Mickey Sachs. Introduced by one of the chapter headings as "The hypochondriac" (and thus, by implication, as someone excessively and deludedly focused on himself and his imagined pathologies), Mickey is to Hannah's family what Pearl is to Eve's: a counterpoint to their formality, the antithesis of their reticence about emotional realities and of their habitual projection of a social surface of extroverted reasonableness. Admittedly, the Pearl/Mickey parallel is somewhat diluted by the fact that Pearl is a complete outsider entering a family, one much more negatively dramatized than Hannah's, while Mickey, Hannah's former husband, has already been a member of the positively framed family he's marrying into, suggesting that the assimilatory gap is necessarily smaller. Nonetheless, the contrast in styles of emotional self-presentation (and thus of scenic energy) between Hannah's family and Mickey is maintained from the beginning to the end of the film by its structural alternation between the narrative of her emotion-repressing circle and that of Mickey's emotionally demonstrative medical/spiritual crisis.[19] It's as if the two human options Isaac Davis posits for a short story he considers writing in *Manhattan* had been divided into two narrative realms: the Hannah circle "constantly creating these real, uh, unnecessary neurotic problems for themselves 'cause it keeps them from dealing with the more uh, unsolvable, terrifying problems about uh, the universe" (*Manhattan*, p. 267)—the very problems Mickey is confronting in facing his mortality. Whether Mickey should abandon his obsession with those "unsolvable, terrifying problems" and join the human family symbolized by Hannah's Thanksgivings represents the central thematic tension of *Hannah and Her Sisters*.

In *Hannah and Her Sisters* Allen was continuing the argument he conducted with himself over the value of family-as-stability in the Isobel/Dorrie antinomy of *Stardust Memories,* one which comes to a remarkably similar conclusion to that which its predecessor film, *The Purple Rose of Cairo,* reached about movies-as-something-to-live-for. That *Hannah* was produced in the midst of the era in which Hollywood had been producing a series of family values movies (*Ordinary People, Fatal Attraction*) probably influenced Allen in making *Hannah* far less than did his immediate personal circumstances. Having been involved with Mia Farrow and her family for five years when he began writing the screenplay, and having, by her account, been consistently reluctant to connect emotionally with her brood of children, Allen was ready to undertake a fictionalized cinematic inventory of the life he had chosen, a commitment already qualified somewhat by the fact that he and Farrow continued to maintain separate apartments. The generally positive feelings of this period of Allen's life are palpably evoked in the film's narrative coherence, in the striking clarity and stability of Carlo Di Palma's cinematography, and in the overall momentum of the movie away from dissonance and contentiousness toward comedic resolution. It's not only Allen's skepticism about the film's upbeat ending which contests *Hannah and Her Sisters'* positive trajectory, however; Allen's doubts about the family as an ultimate source of human meaning are also hinted at in the film through autobiographically laden plotting and casting choices.

The most obvious art/life convergence in *Hannah,* one noticed by the film's reviewers, is Mia Farrow's complex relationship with her less professionally successful sisters. Beyond that, for the role of Hannah's husband, Elliot (who is unfaithful to Hannah with her sister), Allen and his longtime casting director, Juliet Taylor, cast Michael Caine, the actor who had introduced Allen and Farrow to each other in Elaine's in 1979. The discrepancy between Hannah's marital state and the Farrow/Allen real-life relationship seems difficult to over-look, especially for the actress playing Hannah. In addition, during the shooting of *Midsummer Night's Sex Comedy,* Farrow was concerned that Allen was interested in her sister, Steffi, who was working on the set as Farrow's stand-in: "What I shared with nobody," she acknowledged in *What Falls Away,* "was my fear that *Hannah and Her Sisters* had openly and clearly spelled out his feelings for my sister."[20] During the shooting of *Radio Days* in 1987, Farrow's son, Fletcher, who was playing one of Little Joe's friends, told his mother that Allen seemed attracted to an actress in the cast; Farrow had noticed the flirtatiousness between Allen and Dianne Wiest, the only actress appearing on both films, on the *Hannah* set.[21] In a movie that seems so sentimentally to affirm the stabilizing influence of family, *Hannah* is significantly permeated with extratextual reverberations of faithlessness and disloyalty, cryptic reminders directed perhaps at Mia Farrow of the tenuousness of their union. Allen's script not only dramatizes a dedicated family man suddenly and inexplicably betraying his wife by precipitating an affair with her sister; the film also brings Mickey and Holly together in a marital union which could scarcely have gratified Farrow. We'll return to the Hannah/Mia Farrow connection later in this chapter; for the moment, it's sufficient to have demonstrated the existence of countercurrents underlying the film which complicate the ostensible affirmation of family in *Hannah and Her Sisters.*

The first chapter of *Hannah and Her Sisters*—which Allen has designated one of his two "novels-on-film"[22]—bears the title "God, she's beautiful . . . ," and establishes Elliot's infatuation with his wife's sister while introducing the various members of Hannah's family attending the first of the three Thanksgiving celebrations that provide the film's temporal structure.[23] The scene's pacing is relaxed; the movements of the hale, attractive holiday guests through the sumptuous surroundings of Hannah's apartment emanate a measured leisureliness dictated by the social occasion they're attending and a serenity reflecting self-contentment founded upon their assumption of their fully deserved cultural and financial elevation. The scene gives the impression that they *belong* in such privileged circumstances among such preterit company—equanimity swarms at Hannah's Thanksgiving.

The scene culminates in the group's sitting down to dinner at a long, perfectly appointed table "overflowing with food, floral decorations, and candles" (p. 20) upon which everything seems to glow. The extreme formality of the setting is complemented by the highly ceremonial toast offered by Hannah's father, Evan (Lloyd Nolan), proclaiming Hannah's private and public triumphs—as cook of this feast and as tragic heroine in *A Doll's House.* Hannah's response is an equally ritualistic, similarly balanced affirmation of the fulfillments of public and private realms, a sincere acknowledgment that the gem of an Ibsen play which had lured her away from home was insufficient to prevent love for her family from returning her happily to it; her mini-oration wins warm applause from the assembled company, and these reassuring words constitute the grace note on which the scene closes—the only grace their communally enjoyed meal requires. There is no more deliberately poised, composed, or posed moment in Allen's films, nor any scene which attempts as unapologetically as this one does to visualize the possibility of human beings living well—and beautifully—in communion with each other.[24] "This beautiful Thanksgiving dinner," her father aptly summarizes the scene, "was prepared by Hannah."

The film's rhythm alters abruptly with the shift into "The hypochondriac" chapter, the opening of which presents Mickey moving frenetically through the halls of an office building, besieged from all sides by people cutting between him and Di Palma's camera and by problems proliferating in the television show he produces, which is about to go on the air.[25] The delicacy and utter self-containment with which Elliot's voice-over confesses his errant passion for Lee and his commitment to its concealment is nowhere evident in the television studio scene, in which nothing is under control, everything is out in the open (including one performer's having swallowed "a drugstore of Quaaludes"), and the chaos of it all prompts Mickey to confess "my ulcer is killing me" and to complain, "Christ, this show is ruining my health" (pp. 32–33).

The Hall and Singer family polarities of the *Annie Hall* Easter scene are refrained in greater detail in *Hannah* through the juxtaposition of Hannah's and Mickey's realms. Whereas physical robustness is the norm in Hannah's circle, vigorous healthfulness allowing its members to concentrate on melodically soundtracked pursuits of the heart and ego, Mickey's loss of hearing in one ear condemns him to a series of grimly silent diagnostic examinations conducted by unsympathetic medical technicians utilizing otherworldly technology. In Hannah's world, the self's dilemma consists in finding another self to gratify its longings and to confirm the ego's perception of itself as desirable and valuable. In Mickey's narrative, the potential of a brain tumor isolates the self completely, reducing Mickey to a condition of incessant, self-conscious anxiety over the threat of its imminent extinction. The fact that diagnosis reveals no tumor restores Mickey to the human condition as it has been configured by numerous Jewish American novelists: as a state in which the human being is left with (as Moses Herzog puts it) his "bone-breaking burden of selfhood," with his "poor, squawking, niggardly individuality" as his only defense against the world and mortality.[26]

To characterize the prevailing values of the opening scene of *Hannah* as WASP and the temper of Mickey's introduction as inflected toward the culturally "Jewish" is to run the twin risks of cultural essentialism and interpretive reductiveness. The fact that Mickey spends much of the film comically attempting to convert from his family's Jewish faith(because he "got off to a bad foot with my own thing") to Catholicism and Hare Krishna makes a reading of the film as cultural/religious allegory particularly tempting.[27] Such a reading does, for instance, account for the presence of the brief scene introducing Mickey's parents as he tries to explain to them why he's shopping around for an alternative God, the loud, comically grating, and fractious debate among the three characters and Mickey's father's gruffly unpaternal dismissal of his son's mortality anxieties ("Who thinks about such nonsense? Now I'm alive. When I'm dead I'll be dead" [p. 132]) representing the antithesis of Hannah's solicitous, soft-spoken, and utterly nurturing mode of parenting.

The film doesn't present either of its contradictory worlds as one-dimensional cultural caricatures as *Annie Hall* tended to do: Mickey is not merely a self-fixated *schlemiel,* and Hannah's family is not simply the incarnation of WASP self-restraint, emotional tact, and decorum. Mickey's fears for his health seem, at least temporarily, to have a basis in medical fact rather than simply representing hypochondriac neurosis and excessive self-awareness; his quest for meaning ("I gotta have something to believe in, otherwise life is just meaningless" [p. 129]) is presented as no less sincere and urgent than its prospective grails are absurd. The alcoholism of Hannah's mother, Norma (Maureen O'Sullivan), is dramatized in an ugly confrontation between her and Evan, which Hannah must be summoned to mediate. Her parents' obvious favoring of their most gifted daughter has plainly had devastating effects on the lives of Lee and Holly, who have unsuccessfully sought to deal with their feelings of rejection through substance addiction (Holly with drugs, Lee with alcohol) and by seeking out substitute fathers in professors (Lee) or contesting Hannah's "chosen-ness" by attempting desperately to prove her worth in an artistic career of her own (Holly). The two worlds of *Hannah and Her Sisters* are presented with some nuance, then, but it's difficult at first glance not to see the clean, well-lighted Thanksgiving ceremony at Hannah's apartment as a highly attractive event to which Mickey would have good reason to enjoy returning and which, given where the film ends, might even be argued to emerge as inseparable from the grail itself.[28]

In *Stardust Memories,* Sandy Bates's best argument for himself is that he's "not evil or anything, you know? Just sort of floundering around. Just-just . . . ridiculous, maybe. You know . . . searching, okay?" (p. 376); by the time Allen made *Hannah and Her Sisters,* he clearly wanted his protagonist to find as well as seek. Mickey's epiphany while watching the Marx Brothers' *Duck Soup* that there's value in being "part of the experience" of living represents, as numerous critics have noticed, a seminal moment in the evolution of Allen's perception of his comic art. It dramatizes as well the existential affirmation that restores Mickey to involvement in life and thus allows for the romance with Holly which follows and the pregnancy announcement in which their marriage (and the film) culminates. Just as the happy ending of *Broadway Danny Rose* required the creative imaginings of "sentimental comedians" in order to evolve, *Hannah's* buoyant close is similarly dependent upon the *deus ex machina* of Holly's pregnancy as well as the glossing over of numerous dramatic tensions implicit in the narrative which Allen's films would normally investigate and exploit. Perhaps all comedy becomes comedy precisely by skirting potential conflicts that threaten otherwise to erupt into drama, even into tragedy; Chekhov's plays seem particularly devoted to the creation of scenes teetering on this generic brink. Nonetheless, the final Thanksgiving celebration closing *Hannah and Her Sisters* seems overendowed with potential sources of conflict that are introduced but never addressed, their consequences never fully mined, even ignored.

The reconciliation of Elliot and Hannah stands on the extremely tenuous ground of her ignorance of his year-long affair with her sister, a disparity in knowledge which must, at the very least, adversely affect the two sisters' relationship with each other as well.[29] Both of the marriages which this third Thanksgiving's guest list ratify promise to founder on the same problem that doomed Lee's previous relationship (her need to take as lovers substitute father figures, the latest a Columbia professor) and haunted Holly's relationships with men: their parents' refusal to acknowledge them, a new cycle of which will be initiated at this closing celebration by Norma's preprandial toast announcing Hannah's role in *Othello*. The primary source of tension in Norma and Evan's marriage—her drinking—resurfaces at the final Thanksgiving as well, Norma holding a glass of booze from the bottle sitting on the piano as Evan performs "Isn't It Romantic?" (It is, so long as you ignore the underlying strains existing in the scene.) Somewhat like Lear's ceremonial division of his kingdom, or the shimmering wedding of Ben's daughter in *Crimes and Misdemeanors* at which conspirator-in-murder Judah is a venerated and celebrated guest, the beautiful ceremony which opens *Hannah and Her Sisters,* we realize after watching two more of them, creates order at the expense of veracity, artificially mutes too many human realities at play in the room, represents a too great willingness to disregard problems in the name of projecting an illusory decorum. The holiday good cheer which seems to resonate in the film's ending carries with it opposing undercurrents of falsity and doubt; Hannah, the founder of the feast as well as the putative object of its celebration, occupies the center of the conflicting messages of *Hannah and Her Sisters.*

Allen has been remarkably forthright in acknowledging that for both himself and Farrow, Hannah remained something of an enigma. "We couldn't find a clear handle on [her character]," he told Bjorkman. "I could never decide whether Hannah was good or bad. It was very hard for me to know whether Hannah was a good sister or a bad sister."[30] Given that Hannah is all but universally praised by the characters in the film for all of her other characteristics—generosity, sensitivity, maternal instincts, competence, homemaking skills, acting ability, and personal independence—the trait in contention is clearly the one articulated by Elliot: "It's hard to be around someone who gives so much and-and needs so little in return."

"But look—I have enormous needs," Hannah responds.

"Well, I can't see them, and neither can Lee or Holly" (p. 157).

Hannah's emotional self-containment is the quality which troubles her husband and apparently creates ambivalence as well in the screenwriter who, working with the inspiration of her model, Mia Farrow, imagined Hannah into being.[31] Whereas the more numerous voice-over passages allotted to Lee and Holly reflect their thoughts about themselves and their own circumstances, Hannah's single soliloquy is devoted to a meditation upon her parents' marriage, one that provides insight into a source of her own maternal dedication—Norma and Evan having been more interested in show business than in child-raising—but which offers no illumination of the "enormous needs" to which she lays claim. The loss of Elliot's affections leaves her on the second—and most tension-ridden—of the three Thanksgivings, confessing to him, "It's so pitch black tonight. I feel lost" (p. 158).

Given that Lee had broken off the affair with him earlier in the evening, Elliot is liberated from his conflict between his erotic attachment to both sisters, allowing him to comfort and sincerely rededicate himself to Hannah. But the question that she asked him earlier continues to reverberate despite their reconciliation: "Do you, do you find me too . . . too giving? Too-too-too competent? Too-too, I don't know, disgustingly perfect or something?" (p. 155). Interestingly, this is precisely the question some viewers have posed about her and, by extension, about the film that bears her name so centrally; it's certainly the question that Allen is raising about it in expressing doubt about the effectiveness of the film's ending. Another way to pose this question would be to ask whether Hannah's projection of cultural serenity and orderliness is more significant than Mickey's emanations of incessant, nearly masochistic self-questioning, of philosophical irresolution and uncertainty. Arguably, the text answers one way, the subtext another.

The ambiguity Allen admitted to in his feelings about Hannah's character seems to be dramatized in the fact that both Mickey and Elliot (albeit only briefly) have fled from her, while her sisters betray her, respectively, in her husband's arms and through an unflattering portrait of her in a play. It is, arguably, Hannah's professional success, completely unimpeachable virtuousness and patient modesty which make her difficult for her lovers and sisters to contend with. In reconciling with her, Elliot says "I don't deserve you," and it appears that this conviction had played a precipitating role in his irrational pursuit of Lee, whose history of alcoholism and negligible worldly accomplishments make her a far less intimidating and much needier romantic partner than Hannah, celebrated star of Broadway stage and family hearth. However, it may be less her personal qualities to which they are so violently responding than to her not completely intentional epitomization of family—of human communality predicated upon home sharing. Given that she provides a home for her unenumerated natural and adopted children, Hannah is the magnet around which all the film's issues of family congregate, Allen's attitude toward the family consistently getting expressed through the characters' relationships with and responses to her.

That Allen is articulating his own ambivalence toward family through his conflicted depiction of Hannah is the point being argued here, one made more uncomfortable by the fact that Hannah and Mia Farrow, in whose Manhattan apartment much of the movie was shot, often seem so inextricably linked to each other in the film. Maureen O'Sullivan, Farrow's mother in both life and the film, accused Allen of the sort of excessively imitative art of which Holly's two scripts are undeniably guilty, characterizing her daughter's role of Hannah as "a complete exposure of herself. She wasn't being anything—she was being Mia."[32] Hannah is, of course, a fictional character, one who merely resembles, without replicating, an actual person. Nonetheless, it is difficult not to see significant convergences between Hannah's characteristic docility and Farrow's tendency to depict herself as acted upon more than acting throughout her memoir.[33] Underlying both character's and author's passivity lies a penchant, no doubt justified, to consistently depict herself simultaneously as self-sacrificing mother and as victim-of-others. In her memoir, Farrow commented, "It was my mother's stunned, chill reaction to the script [of *Hannah*] that enabled me to see how [Allen] had taken many of the personal circumstances and themes of our lives, and, it seemed, had distorted them into cartoonish characterizations. . . . He had taken the ordinary stuff of our lives and lifted it into art. We were honored and outraged."[34] In obvious and less-than-obvious ways, *Hannah and Her Sisters* seems to confirm Farrow's comment to Kristi Groteke: "I look at them [the films she made with Allen] and see my life on display for everyone to watch."[35] It is Allen's ambivalent attitude toward the life that Hannah/Farrow embodies which gets acted out in *Hannah and Her Sisters*.

Unlike the sudden and, in Hannah's eyes at any rate, unambiguous resolution of her spiritual/marital crisis, the dramatization of Mickey's dark night of the soul involves thoughts of suicide ("I just felt that in a Godless universe, I didn't want to go on living" [p. 169]), and a comical attempt at self-destruction, his psychic struggle culminating in a hard-won affirmation of the surfaces of life as "a slim reed to hang your whole life on, but that's the best we have."[37] (The emotional urgency of Mickey's search contrasts as well with the dispassionate precision with which Elliot earlier articulates his conflict between Hannah and Lee, his mode of expression alone continuing to affirm the assumption of cultural elevation embodied by Hannah's Thanksgiving:

"For all my education, accomplishments, and so-called wisdom . . . I can't fathom my own heart" [p. 144].) As he watches the Marx Brothers' film, Mickey manages to affirm his life on remarkably similar grounds to those on which Elliot indicted his own: "I'm thinking to myself, geez, I should stop ruining my life . . . searching for answers I'm never gonna get, and just enjoy it while it lasts. And . . . then, I started to sit back, and I actually began enjoying myself" (p. 172). Nothing follows in the film to undermine or ironize this judgment, and it is with good reason that many critics tend to quote from this passage as if it were a sort of consummate Woody Allen creed. In fact, it is most certainly this affirmation of life (or, more exactly, of the Marx Brothers' Jewish American comedic burlesque of it[38]) which subsequently culminates in Mickey's interest in Holly, the union rendering possible both his readmission to Hannah's family and the potential solution of his existential anxieties through fatherhood. Because of his existential baptism in *Duck Soup,* Mickey is back for another Thanksgiving dinner at Hannah's. He's going be a dad, and apparently all is right with the world: "The large family and the plentiful food" Douglas Brode contends, "suggest Mickey's (and Woody's) understanding of the need to rejoin the human community."[39]

But for all the engaging holiday felicity of this ending, there are suggestions in the unacknowledged tensions permeating the scene that for Mickey to rejoin Hannah's family exacts an extraordinarily high price, since it implies repudiating the self-as-searcher, the identity which many of Allen's protagonists assert. The cost of the effort to "enjoy [life] while it lasts" may necessitate his embracing of her family ethic's reluctance to ask discomfiting questions—to believe as Hannah does that people should conceal their true feelings because others "don't want to be bothered" with them. (Significantly, all that Mickey and his assistant, Gail—also Jewish—are depicted discussing are Mickey's deeply felt personal dilemmas and conflicts, the humor of their dialogue predicated upon the classic Jewish American comic formula: talk about what the Goys *never* talk about, and you've got funny.)

The affirmation of family in *Hannah and Her Sisters* seems inextricably burdened with the values of this specific family, one with whom Allen has, at best, ambivalent sympathies. It almost seems as if Hannah's family's characteristic tactfulness and discretion have their equivalent in the plot's reluctance to seriously engage some of the issues it has raised: even Di Palma's justly praised rotating camera scene of emotional confrontation among the three sisters over lunch fails to bring into the open the primary tension underlying it: Lee's continuing affair with Elliot.[40] In a decade when Hollywood was regularly turning out films—*On Golden Pond, The Hotel New Hampshire*—celebrating the family as a repository of human cohesiveness and order, *Hannah* is Allen's sincere attempt to create a more substantial vision of that affirmation, his attempt to convince the viewer—and even more so, himself—of its validity.

Holly's disclosure of her pregnancy, then, represents the leap of faith Allen undertook—and would later regret undertaking—in order to register his endorsement of the family-as-repository-of-meaning. As if in retraction of the affirmative construction of family he'd attempted to create in *Hannah and Her Sisters,* three years later in *Crimes and Misdemeanors,* Allen proceeded to make a film in which a man complicit in a murder is released from the terrible guilt he experiences over the deed by the warmth, regard, and love of his family. In *Hannah,* Allen managed to push this affirmation as far as marrying Mickey to Holly and allowing himself the *deus ex machina* of her pregnancy revelation. However, it seems crucial to recognize that the film stops short of visualizing Mickey seated at Hannah's groaning board of holiday feast, festivity, and unconfronted tensions—that it refused to portray him grinning happily as Norma, blissfully oblivious to the effect it must have on her daughter/ Mickey's wife, Holly, toasts Hannah's latest theatrical triumph to the enthusiastic approbation of all in attendance. Consequently, the two worlds of *Hannah and Her Sisters* almost, but don't quite, converge in the final Thanksgiving scene. Allen obviously understood that dramatizing Mickey's participation in this annual ceremony would create an image as incredible as that of Mickey mounting a crucifix on his apartment wall or dancing at airports in the garb of Hare Krishna. Even in a film as lushly affirmative in tone and surface as *Hannah and Her Sisters,* there are still some conversions the viewer, like Woody Allen, would simply never accept.

10

If You Want a Hollywood Ending

Crimes and Misdemeanors

Comedy is hostility. . . . What is it the comedian says when his jokes are going well? I murdered that audience. I killed 'em . . . They screamed . . . I broke 'em up.

—Daisy's boyfriend, Jack, talking to Sandy Bates in *Stardust Memories*

If it's difficult to identify the Woody Allen film ending that least approximates the morally consonant, emotionally gratifying closure of *Broadway Danny Rose,* it's not because there's a shortage of candidates. *Manhattan* and *Stardust Memories* close on resonantly discordant notes of irresolution and human isolation, diminished chords. The most optimistic sentiment offered at the end of the unremittingly dour *September* is "Time will pass and you'll forget this summer," Allen's second chamber film proving incapable of conceiving a more fortuitous conclusion to human affairs than forgetting them. The Great Irmstedt's affirmation closing *Shadows and Fog* that people need illusions "like they need the air" invokes more compellingly the brutality of reality than the virtues of compensatory illusions, while Gabe's question to the documentary interviewer at the end of *Husbands and Wives*—"Is it over?"—epitomizes the mood of enervated defeatism pervading that film, one widely interpreted as mirroring the anguish and turmoil of Allen's personal life in 1993.

Allen's oeuvre contains numerous candidates for antithesis to *Broadway Danny Rose*'s consonant close, then, but because it's so much about endings, *Crimes and Misdemeanors* wins the anti-closure competition. If the mediating presence of the sentimental Carnegie Deli comedians imposes on *Broadway Danny Rose* a resolution conciliating human desire with morality, the complete absence of any such moral touchstones in the universe of *Crimes and Misdemeanors* renders that film's ending the most striking contrast to the resolution of the Danny Rose cinematic fable. Because of its philosophical ambitiousness and its self-conscious investigation of the relationship between questions of morality and the generically determined resolutions of literary plots,[1] *Crimes and Misdemeanors* is a crucial work to the understanding of Allen's conception of the value of art to life, a film which offers his most pessimistic judgment on the relevance of cinematic/literary constructs to the lives that people actually live.

To begin at the end of this film so preoccupied with endings: Judah Rosenthal (Martin Landau) and Clifford Stern (Allen) share a piano stool in a corridor outside the hall in which a reception is being held to celebrate the marriage of the daughter of Judah's opthamological patient, Ben (Sam Waterston), a rabbi. Cliff is depressed by the revelation he's suffered this evening that Halley Reed (Mia Farrow), a PBS producer he's fallen in love with as his own marriage has been unraveling, is engaged to Lester (Alan Alda), his soon-to-be ex-brother-in-law and a slick, highly successful television personality for whom Cliff has nothing but contempt. Lubricated with alcohol, Cliff sourly contemplates the injustice of a universe in which, as he facetiously explains to his young niece earlier in the film, "great depth and smoldering sensuality don't always win," the resolutions of the 1940s Hollywood movies they've been watching together to the contrary. The outrage of injustice to Cliff's ego in which the film concludes plays "misdemeanor" to Judah's "crime."[2]

Judah has conspired with his brother, Jack (Jerry Orbach), to have his mistress, Dolores Paley (Anjelica Huston), murdered when she threatens to expose both their affair and the financial improprieties involved in his fund raising efforts for the building of an opthamology wing at his hospital, the completion of which has resulted in his being celebrated as a hero. Aware that Cliff makes films, Judah, his tongue similarly loosened by champagne, takes his cue from Cliff's ironic comment that he's "plotting the perfect murder"—that of Lester—to offer him a "murder story with a very strange twist." Believing that he's being told a fictional narrative, Cliff responds to Judah's story as an inducement to philosophical speculation, one—for him—distinctly colored by the bitterness of his unjust rejection by Halley. For the audience of *Crimes and Misdemeanors,* Judah's narrative provides the postscript to his story, describing the culmination of his weeks of suffering guilt over the deed he'd precipitated. The man responsible for the murder "isn't punished—he prospers," Judah tells Cliff. "His life is completely back to normal, back to his protected world of wealth and privilege. . . . Oh, maybe once in a while he has a bad moment, but it passes. In time, it all fades."

Responding directly through his trampled ego, Cliff replies with a phrase nearly identical to the one he'd used when Halley revealed that she was marrying Lester: "His worst beliefs are realized." There is no principle of justice functioning in the universe, he takes to be the point of Judah's plot's "strange twist": foul murder doesn't out, killers prosper, and Halley dump serious documentary filmmakers for vacuous sitcom moguls. It's dramatically inevitable that Cliff and Judah meet for the first time in the film's final scene, since both have been debating the issue of universal justice with themselves and others throughout *Crimes and Misdemeanors.* Cliff's entree to the issue is Professor Louis Levy (Martin Bergmann), a philosopher whose entire family was wiped out in World War II and about whose life and work Cliff is producing a documentary.[3] Levy's existentialist philosophy emphasizes the coldness of the universe, its utter obliviousness to human happiness, and the necessity of human beings to project value into its moral vacancy, a central value being love. "It is only we with our capacity to love that give meaning to the indifferent universe," Levy argues. "We define ourselves by the choices we have made—we are in fact the sum total of our choices." Levy's heartening message is abruptly nullified for Cliff by the philosopher's suicide, an act of violent self-contradiction that simultaneously divests Cliff of a documentary subject and an intellectual/spiritual mentor. Levy's fiercely ineloquent suicide note—"I've gone out the window"[4]—obsesses Cliff, its revelation of the ultimate unintelligibility and inarticulability of Levy's final, self-defining choice negating for him all projections of human meaning.

Inhabiting the void left by this advocate of moral responsibility in the universe, Cliff experiences a final repudiation of Levy's affirmation of love when Halley, informing him of her engagement at Ben's daughter's wedding, says that the love letters Cliff sent to her in London were beautiful; it's just that he sent them to "the wrong person." That "resilient little muscle"—the heart—which facilitates the happy ending of *Hannah and Her Sisters* by allowing Mickey Sachs to love Holly as he had once loved her sister, Hannah, is presented in *Crimes and Misdemeanors* as subject to woeful misperception and poor object choice. Both Cliff and Judah choose women the love of whom culminates not in "the giving of meaning in an indifferent universe" but in additional suffering: Halley is seduced by Lester's wealth and success into believing she loves him,[5] while Dolores has made a far more calamitous romantic commitment. The outcome of Cliff's sister's desperate quest for love may represent the film's most decisive comment on Levy's celebration of human love: the man she meets through newspaper personal ads ties her up and defecates on her.

Judah, too, is haunted by ethical advocacy, his internal voices of conscience closely identifying themselves with the Jewish faith, which—ironically, given his name—has largely ceased to have meaning for him. The memory of the words of his father, Sol (David S. Howard), "the eyes of God are on us always," has stayed with Judah despite his lapsed religious beliefs. In a modal inversion of the comic *Annie Hall* scenes in which Alvy and Annie visit Alvy's childhood, Judah appears at one of his family's seders, witnessing a debate over the ultimate wages of complicity in murder between his father, who contends that even if the perpetrator isn't caught, his evil deed will "blossom in a foul manner," and Sol's sister, May (Anna Berger), who concludes—prophetically, in terms of the film's ending—"And I say if he can do it, and get away with it, and chooses not to be bothered by the ethics, he's home free."

Judah's other interlocutor/advocate of the existence of universal justice is his patient, Ben, in whom he confides his affair with Dolores, and who encourages him to confess the transgression to his wife and ask her forgiveness. "You see [the world] as hard and empty of values and pitiless," Ben tells Judah, "and I couldn't go on living if I didn't feel with all my heart a moral structure with real forgiveness, and some kind of higher power, otherwise there's no basis to know how to live. And I know you well enough to know that there's a spark of that notion in you, too." That the proponent of the most eloquent religious sentiment expressed in Allen's films loses his eyesight is an irony to which many reviewers of the movie strenuously objected, and it's probably fair to say that Allen's penchant for allegorizing his characters was overindulged in the creation of Ben, the film's elaborate vision motif getting overextended in his affliction.[6] And yet, the closing scene's juxtaposition of the sightless Ben, dancing with his just-married daughter, complemented by a Louis Levy voice-over commentary effectively links the two as spokesmen for philosophical positions contrary to the ethical reality dramatized by the film.

Judah's explanation to Cliff of how "the man's" spiritual ordeal following the murder resolved itself is practically no explanation at all. Describing the terrible period of self-incrimination he underwent, the dramatization of which takes up much of the last quarter of the film, Judah, echoing Ben, tells Cliff that

> sparks of his religious background which he's rejected are suddenly stirred up. He hears his father's voice. He imagines that God is watching his every move. He's plagued by deep-rooted guilt. . . . Suddenly, it's not an empty universe at all but a just and moral one, and he's violated it. Now he's panic-stricken, on the verge of a mental collapse, an inch away from confessing the whole thing to the police. Then, one morning, he wakes up, and the sun is shining, and his family is around him, and mysteriously, the crisis is lifted. He takes his family on a vacation to Europe and he finds as the months pass that he isn't punished. In fact, he prospers.

"Now," Judah concludes, this time echoing his Aunt May, "he's scot-free. His life is completely back to normal, back to his protected world of wealth and privilege."

Whereas Judah is emphasizing what is, for him, the positive aspect—the crisis's "mysterious lifting"—of his story, Cliff's "his worst beliefs are realized" response to it focuses upon the universe implied by the narrative, which is, in Ben's terms, "harsh and empty of values and pitiless." Annoyed by Cliff's misreading of his story, Judah asks him with derisive incredulity, "What do you expect him to do—turn himself in?" This is exactly what the filmmaker in Cliff would prefer: unsatisfied with Judah's story's conclusion's moral indeterminacy and ellipticality, Cliff suggests that the "absence of God" dramatized in the narrative "creates tragedy. If [the murderer] turns himself in, the story assumes tragic proportions." Good Louis Levian that he is, Cliff wants for the moral void where God's judgment once existed to be filled by the perpetrator's own ethical decision, humanity taking upon itself the task of imbuing the universe with its own self-projected moral imperatives even at the terrible personal cost of self-condemnation. Judah's response to Cliff's proposed revision of his plot is unhesitating and completely unequivocal, and represents a major aesthetic/ethical declaration in Allen's films: "But that's fiction, that's movies . . . I mean . . . I mean, you see too many movies. I'm talking about reality. If you want a happy ending, you should see a Hollywood movie."

At first glance, Judah's conflation of "a story [which] assumes tragic proportions" with "the happy endings of Hollywood movies" seems contradictory. So complete is his repudiation of teleology, however, that any ending manifesting moral purpose is for Judah equally fraudulent. The point Judah makes about the disparity between the moral shapes that literary/cinematic genres impose upon narratives and the shapelessness of lived human experience is one that *Crimes and Misdemeanors* not only refuses to contest, but one which it deliberately reinforces by generating its own Hollywood ending in order to demonstrate the falsification produced by that mode of artistic resolution of human experience.

Throughout *Crimes and Misdemeanors,* the audience is made aware of ironic convergences between the plot of the film they're viewing and scenes from Hollywood movies the characters watch. In the first of these juxtapositions, Judah's efforts to persuade Dolores to release him from their affair cuts suddenly to a scene Cliff and Jenny are watching at the Bleeker Street Cinema from Hitchcock's *Mr. and Mrs. Smith,* in which Carole Lombard complains that Robert Montgomery wants to "throw me aside like a squeezed lemon." Judah and Jack's conversation initially broaching the idea of killing Dolores elicits a scene from *This Gun for Hire* in which a woman's murder is being plotted; "All I do is dream of you the whole night through" are the lyrics of a *Singin' in the Rain* song Cliff and Halley listen to which echo his earlier description of his feelings for her; Judah's secretary's announcement shortly after Dolores's death that a detective has made an appointment to speak with him seems to generate Betty Hutton's energetically loopy performance of "Murder He Says!" from *Happy Go Lucky.* In the final instance, Cliff responds to Halley's informing him that she's going to London for four months by complaining, "I feel like I've been handed a prison sentence," his language abruptly triggering a scene from *The Last Gangster* in which Edward G. Robinson sweats out his term laboring in the Alcatraz laundry. The passage of time, which the movie visualizes through the words "MONTHS" chasing each other across the screen, converges with the passing of the four months of Halley's absence, so that once the clip ends, she has returned from England and the date of Ben's

daughter's wedding has arrived. The absolute synchronicity of Hollywood movie reality and Allen's characters' reality dramatized by these artistic interspersions is comically effective, representing the most consistently humorous element of the film, and might be said to reflect nothing beyond that were it not for Judah's concluding insistence upon the complete irreconcilability of the endings of Hollywood movies and real life which constitutes the penultimate extended speech in *Crimes and Misdemeanors.*

The final speech of the film is reserved for Louis Levy, whose philosophical musings initially provide a voice-over background to the deeply moving image of the sightless Ben dancing with his daughter. Then Allen resorts to the traditional Hollywood ploy of a retrospective silent montage of scenes from the film, a device which, in movies such as *Butch Cassidy and the Sundance Kid* and *Thelma and Louise,* tends to raise the emotional ante of the ending by evoking earlier moments of the film, often of carefree joy, now past and irrecoverable. Allen's closing montage diverges from the Hollywood convention (and from his own use of the device in *Annie Hall*) by reprising scenes of more equivocal import: Levy's voice-over continues as we shift from the wedding to Dolores and Judah arguing in her apartment, Cliff kissing Halley, Judah learning from Jack that the murder of Dolores has been completed, and so on.[7] Allen is not interested in using the montage fraudulently to milk the audience's emotions by creating nostalgia for scenes past; instead, he presents the highly conventionalized ending to mock its own pretensions to resolution and determinacy, the silently reprised images on the screen often contending with the existentialistically optimistic conclusions of Levy's philosophizing which are their aural backdrop. The cinematic layering of Levy's words, the film's reprised images, and the playing of the mordant "I'll Be Seeing You" on the soundtrack of *Crimes and Misdemeanors* create Allen's most densely textured and thematically complex film conclusion, one which deliberately contests its own pretensions to resolution.

Admittedly, there are moments in the montage in which Levy's voice-over and the on-screen images converge and reinforce each other: his assertion, "It is only our capacity to love that gives meaning to an indifferent universe," accompanies a brightly lit, immaculately composed shot of Ben's daughter and her fiancé at the ceremony approaching the rabbi who is about to marry them. More typically, however, Levy's message and the content of the dialogueless scenes being contrasted with it create disjunctions invoking the film's unresolved conflicts. His argument that "we define ourselves by the choices we have made. We are in fact the sum total of our choices" overlays Judah's receiving the phone call from Jack telling him the murder has been committed. "It's over and done with—no problems—so you can forget about it," Jack is telling Judah in the wordless scene reprised in the montage, "It's like the whole thing never existed. So, go on back to your life and put it behind you." For Jack, and subsequently Judah, we are the sum total of the choices we are able to forget making. Judah's account to Cliff of the aftermath of the murder suggests that it's Jack's gangland realism rather than Levy's moralistic existentialism which prevails in *Crimes and Misdemeanors*.

Levy proceeds to argue, "Events unfold so unpredictably" [image of Jack and Judah first broaching idea of murdering Dolores], "so unfairly" [Sol at seder listens to his sister challenging his spiritual beliefs by insisting that "might makes right"], "human happiness does not seem to have been included in the design of creation," the final clause contrasted with the image of Dolores walking home to her apartment, carrying a wine bottle in a bag. The bottle traces the shot to the scene in which she leaves a liquor store and walks home, unaware that she's being followed to her apartment by the hit man Jack has hired. Dolores's "human happiness" is clearly not an issue if she's about to be murdered, so Levy is evidently right about this, but beyond that, the interplay of voice-over and images calls attention to the fact that Levy's abstract conceptualizing of the human condition practically omits the role or significance of human agency in the fates of people. Individuals' fates may be beyond their control, in other words, but occasionally others—Judah and Jack—can become the self-appointed instruments of fatality. Jack's brutal pragmatism, articulated in the scene where he initially advocates to Judah the solution which is Dolores's murder, again enacts its practical superiority to the existentialist rationalism of Levy: "That's what I'm saying, Judah—if the woman won't listen to reason, you move on to the next step" of eliminating her.

Levy's closing paragraph, with its evocation of the small satisfactions that keep human beings choosing life over death, accounts for whatever good feelings the film's conclusion affords its audience, though a consideration of the content of the images accompanying his words again complicates his message's reassurances. Cliff is walking with Jenny in the city streets, affectionately placing his arm around his niece's shoulders as Levy affirms that "most human beings seem to have the ability to keep trying and even to find joy" [return to image of Ben dancing with his daughter at the wedding], "from simple things like their family, their work, and from the hope that future generations might understand more." The silent image of Cliff and Jenny walking together appears more positive when their conversation about Cliff's unrequited love for Halley is muted, and Cliff's loving gesture is his response to the girl's naive and ultimately wrongheaded assertion that Lester "is no competition to you" for Halley's love. Levy is correct that people draw sustenance from family, but in *Crimes and Misdemeanors* it is "waking to find his family around him" that allowed Judah to overcome guilt and subsequently to celebrate his recovery by taking them off to Europe, following Jack's counsel by "putting it [the murder] all behind him." Again seeming to affirm family in this late-1980s era of family values movies, Judah tells Miriam in his final line in the film, "We're going to make a wedding like this for Sharon," the immediate cut to Ben dancing with his daughter summarizing a central injustice dramatized by *Crimes and Misdemeanors*. Ben, the good man stricken with blindness, celebrates his daughter's marriage, while Judah, complicit in murder but restored nonetheless "to his protected life of wealth and privilege" within a family completely deceived about his character, will soon replicate this occasion of familial happiness and conciliation. There are surely no sentimental stand-up mythmakers mediating in *Crimes and Misdemeanors* to ensure that the righteous prosper while the wicked are punished.

If "family" as a value to live for is presented equivocally in *Crimes and Misdemeanors,* "work" is depicted as equally corrupted. Cliff is out of a job, Lester having fired him from his directorship of PBS's "Creative Mind" Lester biography. Here and everywhere else throughout the film, the world of work is dominated by Lester's values. Cliff's serious film projects on subjects such as leukemia, toxic waste, and starving children earn him only an honorable mention at a documentary film festival in Cincinnati, while Lester is pulling in cash and Emmys for making sitcoms whose political conscience is epitomized by one about a sexy bimbo ACLU lawyer whose husband writes for rightwing magazines, the couple's divergent politics allowing the show, as Lester has it, "to get into issues." While offering Cliff the job of directing his biography, Lester has a brainstorm for a new show inspired by their conversation, the show reflecting the humanistically inverted values which prevail in the world of work in *Crimes and Misdemeanors*: "A poor loser agrees to do the story of a great man's life," Lester tells his dictaphone, "and in the process learns deep values."

As for Levy's concluding "hope that future generations will understand more," the philosopher's own myopias, combined with the film's consistent dramatization of the complete domination of action over reflection, materialism over idealism, cast doubt upon even so hedged a prospect. Halley's final judgment on Levy's suicide constitutes what might be construed as Allen's ultimate conclusion on the human attempt to subject world to idea, to mind: "No matter how elaborate a philosophical system you work out, it's gotta be incomplete." Much the same thing might be said for Allen's view of the "elaborate philosophical system" which is the conventional ending of the Hollywood movie.

The concluding montage of *Crimes and Misdemeanors* utterly fails to enact the neat emotional resolution that such endings traditionally generate, largely because the articulation of values superimposed upon it is constantly contradicted by the content of the images that voice-over projects. What the comedians of the Carnegie Deli manage to do through their sentimental reconstruction of past events in *Broadway Danny Rose*, creating a story with an ending consonant and heartwarmingly resolved, Levy's philosophical musings fail to accomplish in *Crimes and Misdemeanors,* because the later film focuses so consistently upon the great disparity between human projections of universal values and reality as the film has defined it. "I mean, you see too many movies. I'm talking about reality," Judah dismisses Cliff's advocacy of tragic closure, "If you want a happy ending, you should see a Hollywood movie."[8] It's difficult not to see Judah's contemptuous dismissal of happy endings as Allen's way of rebuking himself for seeking in Hollywood movies—e.g., the *Duck Soup* scene in *Hannah and Her Sisters*—resolutions life itself doesn't offer.

Cliff's faith in aesthetic and ethical resolution is chastened as well by Lester in response to his sister's scathing denunciation of Cliff's documentaries with their aspirations to "change the world." Articulating a network television version of Jack's brutal pragmatism, Lester argues, "He's got to grow up, this is the real world, this is the big time; they don't pay off on high aspirations—you got to *deliver.*" *Crimes and Misdemeanors* begins at a major public function celebrating Judah's generosity and professional accomplishments and closes with a massive public wedding ceremony generously financed by Lester, a ceremony which Judah will soon recreate for his own daughter. The film's two unambiguously prevailing figures embody a wealth, successfulness, and savage realism as radically at odds with Levy's optimistic existentialism—or Cliff's ineffectual moralism—as the song superimposed upon Ben's concluding dance with his daughter is with Ben's personal circumstances—"I'll Be Seeing You." At the risk of partaking in the film's proclivity for overplaying visual motifs, I'd suggest that through its dramatically effective interplay of movie reality and actuality, *Crimes and Misdemeanors* is Allen's darkest—and most compellingly dark—film.

Crimes and Misdemeanors, obviously, is a serious film—so much so, in fact, that the foregoing discussion of the movie threatens to sound as if the movie were scripted by Dostoevsky rather than Woody Allen. It seems undeniable that in this movie, more than in any of his others, Allen allowed himself to directly articulate the philosophical questions that arise elsewhere in his work in more fragmentary, tentative, or self-parodic terms. However, the film did not draw the virulently negative critical attacks which Allen's chamber films—*Interiors, September,* and *Another Woman*—tended to attract. The film's reviewers didn't consistently agree on the effectiveness of the film's dramatization of its moral issues, but practically none of them invoked the arguments raised against the earlier serious films: that the filmmaker was out of his depth or was creating an artwork that he is temperamentally ill-suited to achieving. If *Crimes and Misdemeanors* is Allen's most effective serious film, as most reviewers suggested,[9] its success is the product of its individual synthesis of gravity and Woody Allen comedy, the movie demonstrating—as do *Stardust Memories, Broadway Danny Rose, The Purple Rose of Cairo, Hannah and Her Sisters, Bullets Over Broadway,* and *Deconstructing Harry*—that Allen is always at his best when his films are epiphanizing the very profound psychological tension in him between humor and solemnity. It's worth briefly considering how *Crimes and Misdemeanors* manages to absorb its Woody Allen comedic features into the remarkably uncomedic business of a murder without consequences for the murderer. What emerges from such scrutiny is a film that, in both content and form, displays little respect for the power of humor to accomplish anything worthwhile in the world.

The mixed-genre trick is accomplished largely through the structure of the script, which dictates that the central characters of the film's two plot lines—Judah and Cliff—never meet until the final ten minutes of the film, the separation tending to compartmentalize the film's two dominant moods. The Judah plot plays itself out largely without humor, its mood undergirded by classical music on the soundtrack. Judah's anxiety about his mistress, Dolores, is established even before he delivers the speech that represents his professional apotheosis as doctor-as-Jewish-cultural-hero. The viewer has only the briefest opportunity to perceive him as the moral exemplar that he is presented as being to the audience at the opening testimonial dinner in his honor before his guilt-ridden erotic double-dealing is revealed. Martin Landau's performance emphasizes both the basic dignity and decency of Judah as well as the want of spiritual values, which makes him vulnerable to the temptation of easy self-indulgence with which Dolores confronts him. Dolores's emotional desperation and possessiveness, portrayed with such frighteningly escalating neediness by Anjelica Huston, constitute the only inducement that could compel Judah toward considering even the most extreme measures to preserve his reputation. For all the guilt Judah expresses after Jack's hit man has completed the killing, his cold-blooded visit to Dolores's apartment to clear away signs of their relationship before her body is discovered epitomizes the egotism and heartlessness which will subsequently allow him to live with the murder "as if it never happened." The closing scene's dramatization of precisely how (in his Aunt May's phrase) "home free" Judah is comprises the most chilling moment Allen has filmed.[10]

Crimes and Misdemeanors would very likely have been a schizophrenic film had its subplot involved a humorous, likable protagonist (Mickey Sachs, for instance) whose narrative represented comic relief from the progressively dark trajectory of Judah's story. The Clifford subplot isn't that, and although it is less heavy than the Judah plot, what it primarily demonstrates is the capacity Allen had developed to dramatically manipulate his persona away from comedy toward an unprecedented depth of characterization. Cliff's narrative, backed by the familiar Dixieland jazz and pop standards of other Allen soundtracks, is where the script's few jokes are found and where conflicts have more modest and purely personal consequences. The mutual contempt and antipathy Cliff and Lester feel for each other is a primary source of the film's consistently sardonic humor, their competition for Halley constituting a comic parallel to Judah's grim quest to restore himself to home and reputation, the outcome of their contest proving equally unjust and as inevitable as Dolores's fate. (A characteristic joke of Crimes and Misdemeanors is Cliff's self-deprecatory one-liner about his love letter to Halley having been plagiarized from James Joyce, which explains all of its references to Dublin. If the joke elicits laughter, it's laughter born of bitter disappointment and the acknowledgment of romantic unfairness. It's one of many such ironies in the film that the fatuous Lester is right in claiming "comedy is tragedy plus time," the movie's chosen form of humor corroborating the idea that only once the pain stops can we laugh.) One of the film's most striking achievements is that the Cliff subplot seems less like comic relief than like a minimalist version of Judah's, the documentary filmmaker's parallel egotism and want of spiritual faith culminating not in tragic conflict but in ignominious personal defeats. They are comic not so much because they're funny than because they're less than fatal.

Although he resembles earlier Allen protagonists in a number of ways, Cliff seems an attenuated, more ineffectual version of them, their virtues becoming deficiencies in his embrace. He is the only Allen protagonist whose attraction to old movies appears to embody the characterization of movie theaters as "temples for cowards" which Allen offered in an interview, Cliff's description of seeing movies in the afternoon with his niece as "playing hooky" substantially juvenilizing him. The gift of a book of pictures of old New York he gives to her similarly seems to express a futile nostalgia for a lost world which he's attempting to inculcate in Jenny,[11] a failed filmmaker's substitute version of Allen's *Manhattan*. When he's not playing hooky with her, the documentaries he produces about acid rain and leukemia reflect good, liberal, humanitarian values, but their limited distribution and tiny audiences seem to corroborate the highly unsympathetic judgment of his wife, Wendy (Joanna Gleason), that Cliff has "these fantasies about changing the world, he's a man who thinks he can change the world. He makes these films, and in the end they come to nothing."[12] (*Crimes and Misdemeanors* potently dramatizes Yeats's "The Second Coming" plaint that "The best lack all conviction while the worst are full of passionate intensity."[13]) As Richard A. Blake argued, Cliff's involvement with the Lester biography epitomizes the deeply conflicted nature of his moralistic impulses, his merciless satire of Lester ultimately exposing the bad faith of his undertaking the project in the first place.[14] Cliff's fecklessness generally feeds narcissistically on itself, his Judah-like want of personal spiritual moorings leaving him nothing to affirm except himself and his erotic needs; he is *Manhattan*'s Isaac Davis with less energy and talent, more bitterness, and a heightened capacity for self-pity. As Sam B. Girgus suggested, Cliff loses his love to a moral inferior as does Isaac,[15] their failures in love dramatically rebuking their shared penchant for a self-righteousness that serves to conceal their resentment of others' success.[16]

Cliff manages to locate an external object for his resentments in the media success of his brother-in-law, Lester, who provides him with the means of gaining revenge. By offering Cliff the job of directing a PBS biographical film on himself, Lester implicitly becomes the target of the subplot's comically constructed murder correlative, Cliff's film doing everything he can to annihilate Lester's reputation by visualizing him in compromisingly predatory sexual circumstances, by likening him to Mussolini, and by having his ersatz show business wisdom spouted by Francis the Talking Mule. Lester is to Cliff as Dolores is to Judah: a dalliance in something beneath him, his agreement to direct the documentary constituting an act which adulterates his better self and which he must ultimately repudiate by transforming his adversary into an ass.

It is plain to see that humor doesn't count for much in *Crimes and Misdemeanors:* so ineffectual is Cliff's version of homicide-by-satire that its would-be victim can simply annul the attempt by firing him from the project, leaving the director with nothing to do but haplessly voice the complaint with which Dolores repeatedly rebukes Judah: "But you *promised!*" That Cliff is absolutely right in his assessment of Lester's egotism, the shallowness of his values, and perhaps even about the tendency his sitcoms have to "deaden the sensibilities of a great democracy" doesn't count for anything in the movie, either;

they're just more evidence in a film full of proofs of the lack of causal connection between human virtue and cultural success, between the embrace of positive, life-affirming values and the capacity to act effectually in the world.[17]

That Halley chooses Lester over Cliff is, in Cliff's eyes, the culminating
manifestation of universal injustice, the clinching evidence that success matters more than elevated moral vision and humanistic concern. Compared to
Judah's getting away with murder, it's a trivial instance of the want of an ethi-
cally centered universe, and only a disaffected but still hopeful romantic—
which is what Allen's protagonists generally are—could attempt to transform
that grim truth into the grounds of tragedy. Here too, Cliff sucks it up: his
attempt to affirm the imposition of human meaning upon a Godless universe
is derisively bounced back at him (by a conspirer in murder, no less) as being
equivalent to the happy ending of a Hollywood movie. That Miriam Rosenthal
(Claire Bloom) arrives to gather up Judah and return him to "his protected
world of wealth and privilege" in Connecticut is the only kindness Allen's
script's conclusion extends to Cliff's battered idealism.

Consequently, Cliff is left on the piano bench to contemplate the sour,
central joke of the film: that his belief in a scheme of universal order is just a
symptom of his having spent too many afternoons playing hooky at the Bleeker
Street Cinema. Similarly galling is the fact that Cliff's humanistic desire that
Judah's narrative be elevated to "tragic proportions" through the introduction
of human responsibility has been mocked by Lester's reading of *Oedipus Rex,*
which finds in Oedipus's discovery that he is himself the murderer he has
sought to expose "the structure of funny." *Crimes and Misdemeanors* dramatizes more effectively and unequivocally than any other film Allen's fear that
his favorite autobiographical protagonists' penchant toward philosophizing is
pointless, that meditating on the human condition produces nothing more
substantial than Hollywood happy ending illusions—or generates instead the
despair Cliff experiences which no Hollywood montage could ever transform
into felicitous resolution. That both Judah and Cliff undergo parallel educa-
tions in the absence of what Ben terms "a moral structure with real forgiveness" in the universe is what unifies the two plots of *Crimes and Misdemeanors*
into an engrossing and coherent film narrative, and if Cliff's education seems
surprisingly short on laughs for a Woody Allen part, it's probably because
Woody Allen doesn't find Cliff's lesson very funny, either.

11

Everyone Loves Her/His Illusions
The Purple Rose of Cairo and *Shadows and Fog*

> I want what happened in the movie last week to happen this week . . .
> otherwise what's life about anyway?
>
> —Woman in audience of *The Purple Rose of Cairo*

Stardust Memories dramatizes the contradictory agendas of artistic purposes from the maker's perspective; *The Purple Rose of Cairo* delineates them from the vantage point of the viewer. As one of the most infatuated of the millions upon whom screen illusions are intended to work their magic, Cecilia is confronted in *Purple Rose* with many of the same conflicts between reality and illusion which besiege Sandy Bates—the issue of movies as a desperate evasion of an insupportable actuality in particular. The Allen protagonist even better suited than Bates to playing counterpart to the self-effacing, illusion-pursuing Cecilia, however, is Kleinman, the clerkish, nebbishlike central character of *Shadows and Fog*. So alike are the beginnings and thematic resolutions of *The Purple Rose of Cairo* and *Shadows and Fog*, in fact, that it is useful to discuss the two films together in order to point out the similarity of the conclusions they reach in their emphatically hedged affirmations of art as consolation, of art as refuge.

At the beginning of both movies, the character played by Mia Farrow (Cecilia/Irmy) discovers that her husband/lover has been unfaithful to her—Monk (Danny Aiello) with a friend's sister, Paul (John Malkovich) with Marie (Madonna), a trapeze artist in the circus in which he and Irmy are performers. Cecilia packs a bag and leaves Monk, immediately encountering a prostitute (Dianne Wiest) plying her wares in the New Jersey streets. Terrified that this is the inevitable fate of a woman on her own, Cecilia seeks refuge in the Jewel Theater, where *The Purple Rose of Cairo,* a romantic movie she's seen numerous times, is playing. She watches it again, the champagne comedy facilitating her repression of the dismal awareness that once the last show has ended, she'll be fulfilling Monk's prediction: "Go on, go on . . . You see how it is in the real world . . . You'll be back!" Irmy's first encounter after she's fled Paul and the circus in *Shadows and Fog* is, likewise, with a prostitute (Lily Tomlin), but instead of fleeing her, Irmy is taken by the woman to Felice's, the brothel where she is the madam, for shelter for the night. She's fed by Felice's goodhearted whores, and the wine she drinks loosens her inhibitions enough that she beds down with a college student for the $700 he has won this night from gambling. In *The Purple Rose of Cairo*, Tom Baxter (Jeff Daniels), silver screen exile, plays the naïf who blunders into the brothel and receives a similarly sympathetic welcome from the lively prostitutes; otherwise, the parallel plot trajectories of the two films diverge after Irmy's brothel experience, though both movies remain thematically devoted to exploring the relationship of life to art—in *Purple Rose*, the art of Hollywood movies, in *Shadows*, the allegorized arts of the circus performers. In both films, too, the nature of that relationship is profoundly influenced by the existence of a cultural extremity so menacing it renders the ministrations of the arts more than normally emotionally needful: the Depression in *Purple Rose*, a crazed murderer in *Shadows*. It is against the backgrounds of these manifestations of human subjection that *Purple Rose*, in mimetic terms, and *Shadows*, in allegorical ones, work out their shared vision of the markedly dubious necessity of art to the lives of men and women. These two films constitute the quintessential cinematic dramatizations of Allen's favorite thematic conflict between "the seductiveness of fantasy and the cruelty of reality."[1]

Tom Baxter's departure from the screen, and thus from the plot of *The Purple Rose of Cairo*, to court Cecilia, Hollywood filmdom's dizzily ardent fan, gives Allen the opportunity to examine dramatically what Hollywood movies have meant to their audiences. The fact that Tom walks off the screen into Depression America not only creates comic contrasts between his jet set socialite assumptions about the world and the slough of economically dictated demoralization he's entered, but given the heightened dependency of viewers upon Hollywood's medium of distraction and reassurance during the era, it also focuses and intensifies Allen's film's investigation of the inherent human need for the consolations of escapist art. Tom is, however, only half of the story: Gil Shepherd (Daniels), the actor who plays Tom, is lured from Hollywood to the New Jersey town in which Tom fled the screen in order to attempt to compel his errant character back into the plot of *Purple Rose*, and basically replicates Tom's courtship of Cecilia.[2] In choosing between them at the end of Allen's film, Cecilia is only apparently choosing between silver screen images and real life; in fact, Tom and Gil confront her with a choice not between fantasy and actuality but between two different modes of illusion.

One of Tom's primary virtues is that he is completely consistent because consistency is—as he habitually describes the structure of his personality—"written into my character." His kisses are exactly what Cecilia dreamed kisses should be, but he's confused by the fact that they don't culminate in fade-outs. He's always up for adventure, but he doesn't comprehend that in New Jersey you need keys to start the cars required to make daring escapes. The stares his great white hunter's garb and pith helmet attract from urban New Jerseyans

are lost on him, the discrepancy between his pride in being "Tom Baxter, of the Chicago Baxters," and the Depression America into which he's escaped never seeming to register completely, either. He claims to be courageous, and he is: he battles Monk, a much larger and more brutal man, over Cecilia and is defeated only because Monk fells him with sucker punches the deceitfulness of which Tom can't anticipate because mistrust is not "written into my character." He suffers no wounds from Monk's pounding, because Hollywood heroes routinely emerge from fisticuffs unmarked, and he's baffled when his movie currency won't pay their check in a New Jersey restaurant. ("We'll live on love," he assures her once his pennilessness in this world has registered, but even Cecilia knows "That's movie talk" [p. 387].) The familiarly Hollywood montage world of *The Purple Rose of Cairo* into which he takes Cecilia— "Trust me," he says, urging her to follow him onto the screen (p. 442)—is as beautiful and romantic as she expected, the only problem being, as she remarks, the champagne is really ginger ale and he can use his bogus currency as legal tender to pay for it. Finally, it's his infatuation with Cecilia that initially inspires Tom to liberate himself from the scripted inexorability of his marriage to Kitty, the nightclub singer, in the narrative of *The Purple Rose of Cairo,* the pursuit of Cecilia representing the primary expression of his newfound freedom. (To Cecilia, the plottedness of *Purple Rose* dictates that, for its characters, "things have a way of working out right"; to Tom, the script subjects him deterministically.) Tom's commitment to Cecilia is sincere and unwavering, giving him the distinction of being perhaps the only major Woody Allen character incapable of committing adultery. As he tells the prostitutes who, charmed by his weird innocence, have offered to service him communally without charge, "Oh, I couldn't do that. . . . I'm hopelessly head over heels in love with Cecilia. She is all I want. My devotion is to her, my loyalties. . . . Every breath she takes makes my heart dance" (p. 429). Prostitute Emma is deeply impressed by his recitation, assumedly recognizing pure "movie talk" when she hears it. "Where I come from," Tom tells Cecilia immediately upon spiriting her out of the movie theater following his escape from the screen, "people, they don't disappoint. They're consistent. They're always reliable."

"Y-y-you don't find that kind in real life" (p. 379) is Cecilia's response. The film's sudden cut to Gil Shepherd, whose initial appearance in the film seems sparked by Cecilia's scene-closing line, represents Allen's most compelling embodiment of her assertion. Gil has none of Tom's pride in family, having changed his name from Herman Bardebedian to a more WASPish *nom de film*. Rather than continually talking about Cecilia and his devotion to her, Gil obsesses about himself and his movie career, shamelessly feeding off Cecilia's adoration of him and the comic movies he's made. It's because Tom's defection from *The Purple Rose of Cairo* threatens to undermine that career and to interfere with Gil's ability to land the plum "serious" role of Charles Lindbergh in an upcoming biographical movie that Gil has traveled to New Jersey, and once he's convinced Cecilia to "trust me . . . *please*" (p. 400), she takes him to Tom.

Gil, immediately violating his pledge to Cecilia, tries to talk Tom out of his conviction that his freedom from the screen is precious and to compel him back into the movie. Gil courts Cecilia with his real-world charm and Hollywood-trained abilities, impressing her with the musical comedy duet they perform in a music store. The songs they play together invoke the change of fortune ("I know that soon . . . we're going to cover ground. And then I'll holler . . . 'Cause the world will know, Here I go, I'm Alabammy bound" [p. 431]), youthful felicity ("She's only twenty, And I'm twenty-one. We never worry, we're just havin' fun") and happy resolutions ("Sometimes we quarrel . . . and maybe we fight . . . But then we make up/the following night" [p. 432]) which Hollywood movies routinely promised their audiences as being just around the corner. (Cecilia's association of happy endings with ultimate meanings is compressed in her attempt to describe God to Tom: He's "a reason for everything . . . otherwise, i-i-it-it'd be like a movie with no point and no happy ending" [p. 408].) Gil's clothes contribute equally to his appeal, the nattily coordinated pastel ensemble he sports contrasting no less radically with the bark-drab garb of Depression America than Tom's safari getup, but bearing the cachet of wealth and glamour—"You've got a magical glow," Cecilia tells him—rather than the ethos of adventure yarn weirdness. Cecilia never comments on the potency of his kisses, but by the time Gil kisses her, he's already reduced the act to pure technique: "It's a movie kiss," he explains when she asks about kissing fellow star Ina Beasley on-screen, "You know, we professionals, we can put that, that stuff on just like that" (p. 434). In arguing his suit for her against Tom, Gil, feigning embarrassment at speaking with such sincerity, tells Cecilia that he knows it "only happens in movies" but "I love you" (p. 458). The paradox here—the scripted character has the freedom to love genuinely, the real actor loving through mimicking movie plots—is clear to and dramatically effective for the viewer; what Cecilia overlooks is the extent to which Gil is reenacting one of his movies throughout his relationship with her.

Tom leads her through their Hollywood montage "night on the town" on the other side of the screen of the Jewel Theater, Cecilia's response to it— "My heart's beating so fast!"—echoing the song lyric, "Heaven, I'm in heaven, And my heart beats so that I can hardly speak," which provides the soundtrack frame of Allen's film. At the end of this wonderful night, Cecilia finds herself on the borderline of the two realms, obliged to choose between her suitors and the worlds they represent: the beautiful black-and-white unreality of *The Purple Rose of Cairo* or the actual Hollywood to which Gil promises to take her. "Your dreams are my dreams," Tom contends, just evading articulating the truth that he *is* Hollywood's approximation of the dreams in Cecilia's head. "I love you," Tom continues his plaint, "I'm honest, dependable, courageous, romantic, and a great kisser."

"And I'm real!" is Gil's rebuttal (p. 456).

"You know, you know you said I had a magical glow?" Gil's seductive case for himself begins. "But that . . . it's you, you're the one that has one." Gil's argument that the "magical glow" exists not in the images on the silver screen or in those "stars" who embody that glow in movies but in its downtrodden and economically beleaguered audience reaffirms the impetus which initially drew Tom out of the screen, confirming the Hollywood press agent's contention that "The real ones want their lives fiction, and the fictional ones want their lives real" (p. 395). The tug-of-war evoked here between the claims of an artistically contrived reality as against those of actuality becomes a central theme of *Bullets Over Broadway*, Cheech's brutal street knowledge injecting a saving vitality and realism into David Shayne's formalistically overdetermined play. In *The Purple Rose of Cairo*, Gil's location of the source of magic in the real world is merely rhetoric aimed at achieving his primary goal: getting Tom back into the film, thus eliminating the obstacle he poses to Gil's career's ascendancy.

"And even though we've just met," Gil concludes his suit, "I know this is the real thing." What finally wins Cecilia over is his stronger alliance with reality: "You'll be fine," she tells Tom in rejecting him. "In your world, things have a way of working out right." (She's unaware that the producers are considering the idea that, once Tom has returned to the screen, they'll "turn off the projector and . . . burn all the prints" [p. 439] of *The Purple Rose of Cairo* so Tom's flight to freedom can't be repeated.[3]) "See, I'm a real person," she continues, disregarding all the evidence with which she's been confronted that Tom's "movie talk" devotion is—ironically—more real than Gil's glib charm and tutored courting: "No matter how . . . how tempted I am, I have to choose the real world" (p. 459). In Allen's films, of course, acts of integrity and self-renunciatory pragmatism like Cecilia's choice are abruptly rewarded by manifestations of the ugliness of the reality she has opted for. Consequently, Tom disconsolately returns to his scripted role in *The Purple Rose of Cairo* as Cecilia hurries home to pack for her trip to Hollywood. In an exact inversion of the *Stardust Memories* scene in which Sandy Bates stares up bleakly from the auditorium at the screen on which his cinematic fate has just played itself out so felicitously, Tom Baxter stares mournfully out from the screen into the empty movie theater which once harbored the happy ending so tempting he'd fled the screen in pursuit of it before returning to the plot of *The Purple Rose of Cairo* and his arranged marriage to Kitty, the nightclub singer, or to an incendiary fate far bleaker still.

"Go, see what it is out there," Monk upbraids Cecilia as she packs her bag at their apartment for her Hollywood trip, "It ain't the movies! It's real life! It's real life and you'll be back!" Cecilia slams out of their apartment on her way to the Jewel Theater to meet Gil, and once again the prophecy that she'll be returning to her abusive, unfaithful husband lumbers toward fulfillment. (Her repetition of the same interaction with Monk at the beginning and end of Allen's film suggests that her life contains no more freedom of choice than does Tom Baxter's.) That Gil won't be waiting at the Jewel Theater when Cecilia arrives to run off with him is written not in her stars but in the script he's been acting out with her.

In their second meeting, Gil and Cecilia recall one of the movies—*Dancing Doughboys*—in which he appeared, Cecilia joyfully reciting lines from it to him in testimony to her fan's devotion. "I won't be going South with you this winter," she recalls him telling his leading lady, and Gil completes the rest of his line: "We have a little—uh—score to settle on the other side of the Atlantic."

"'Does this mean I won't be seeing you ever again?'" she recites; "'Well, 'ever' is a long time,'" is his line. "'When you leave, don't look back,'" she recites, concluding the *Dancing Doughboys* highly melodramatic scene (p. 433).

Gil plainly had a little score to settle with his *Purple Rose* portrayal on this side of the Atlantic, and having settled it, he's gone. He's "not heading South with you this winter"—he isn't "Alabammy Bound"—or heading with Cecilia in any other direction; that was just a song he sang with her, the kind of sentimental ditty Hollywood producers inject into their movies to make the audience forget they're irremediably married to Monk and the grinding, unending Depression of which he seems simultaneously symptom, victim, and scourge.[4] Gil never gets to deliver his "ever is a long time" line because the next we see of him, he's on a plane en route from New Jersey back to Hollywood, appearing a little melancholy but never looking out the window, never once looking back.

And so Allen's *The Purple Rose of Cairo* ends on what is possibly his most emotionally compelling and completely earned pessimistic cinematic closure. (When advised by an Orion Films executive that the change to a happy ending would make millions of dollars difference in the box office receipts of *The Purple Rose of Cairo,* Allen responded, "The ending was why I made the film."[5]) Cecilia, sunk in abandonment and disappointment, yet reluctant to return home to once again fulfill Monk's prediction, wanders numbly into the Jewel Theater, where a new attraction, *Top Hat,* is playing. Tearfully, she begins watching Ginger Rogers dancing with Fred Astaire as he sings "Cheek to Cheek," another Depression-era song evocative of fortuitous resolutions, happy endings. Given that the song provided the soundtrack beneath the opening credits as well, "Cheek to Cheek" here seems testimony less to ripening conditions than to the lack of change which has transpired in Cecilia's life over the course of the film, an idea ironically pointed to through the line, "And the cares that hung around me through the week/Seem to vanish like a gambler's lucky streak/ When we're out together dancing cheek to cheek." Cecilia's "lucky streak" ("Last week I was unloved . . . Now . . . two people love me . . . and i-it's-it's the same two people" [p. 455]) has clearly vanished as well. In the course of *The Purple Rose of Cairo,* Cecilia has seen the Hollywood illusion from both inside the screen and from outside it: she now understands the overplotted, falsely reassuring, pretty unreality which the screen projects, and she's known firsthand as well the hypocrisy which is the product of the star-making machinery, having personally experienced Gil's Hollywood egotism, complete untrustworthiness, and real indifference to the audience of which she is part. "After such knowledge, what forgiveness?" T.S. Eliot asks in "Gerontion," but as Cecilia watches the gorgeously romantic choreography of Fred and Ginger on the screen, knowledge gradually gives way to forgiveness, her tears drying, her eyes widening with fascination and adulation as she reenters her familiar infatuation with the images on the silver screen.[6] All traces of troubling thoughts—of her rejection of Tom and betrayal by Gil, of her imminent return to Monk, of the continuing Depression in the world outside, or of her unemployed status—have disappeared, leaving her staring up at the flickering shadows on the Jewel Theater screen with a fully rekindled, completely ecstatic joy as Allen's film comes to a close.

The final lines of dialogue of *Shadows and Fog* could provide an appropriate—though thoroughly unnecessary—gloss for the point *The Purple Rose of Cairo* makes about Depression America's dependency upon Hollywood films, or, more broadly, about human beings' addiction to fantasy. A circus roustabout hails the magic tricks of the Great Irmstedt (Kenneth Mars), "It's true—everyone loves his illusions," his celebration eliciting a haughty revision from the magician himself: "*Loves* them! They *need* them . . . like they need the air." Breathlessly, Cecilia watches Fred and Ginger performing a romantic *pas de deux* her life will never know, Monk, the Depression, and everything she's learned about corruption on both sides of the silver screen all suspended in the epiphany which their dance and the lyrics Astaire sings conjures up:

Heaven, I'm in heaven,
And my heart beats so that I can hardly speak,
And I seem to find the happiness I seek,
When we're out together dancing cheek to cheek.

For Cecilia, "choosing the real world" culminates in rededication to saving illusions of romantic harmony, to a belief in "dancing cheek to cheek"; for Allen, as for his protagonist, affirming faith in the artifice of cinematic resolution is similarly inevitable, since a world "with no point and no happy ending" is a world without meaning. Cecilia's reversion to embracing the erotic union epiphanized by the choreography and lyrics of "Cheek to Cheek" is pure psychic necessity, because only these images of glamour, grace, and erotic concord can reconcile her to returning to her life with Monk and his irrationally affectionate and abusive behavior, his impotence before the ravages of the Depression, and his crap games exemplary of an ironically misplaced faith in chance. These images are the only happiness she knows how to seek; she needs them "like she needs the air" because without them, she would suffocate.

It is a testament to the film's clarity of dramatic purpose that the ending of *The Purple Rose of Cairo* has inspired so little disagreement among Allen's critics: the significance of Cecilia's gradual, ultimately ecstatic reabsorption into a "heaven" whose utter fraudulence it has been her dismal necessity to confront throughout the film is a stunningly ambiguous effect lost on few who have written about the movie. For Christopher Ames, *Purple Rose* shows that "turning to movies for the satisfaction of desire poses the danger of increasing one's alienation from the circumstances in which one lives," while also demonstrating that "the escape offered by movies is magical, wonderful, and deserving of celebration. . . . Cecilia finds in film images that console and enrich her in a world that is fundamentally cruel and unfair."[7] "Essentially," Arnold Preussner agreed, "the silver screen environment contains no lasting value for its audience beyond that of temporary escape. Absorbed in great quantity, its effects may actually prove harmful. Remarkably, Allen manages to

convey the radical shallowness of escapist comedy while simultaneously preserving audience identification with Cecilia, the ultimate fan of such comedy."[8]

If *Purple Rose* is Allen's most compelling cinematic expression of his ambivalent feelings about the human dependency upon escapist illusions,[9] it is—as Preussner implies—in large part a product of Mia Farrow's portrayal of the awestruck embracer of illusions. It is Farrow's great achievement to make believable a character who seems to carry the Depression's awesome weight in the drab wool coat and bonnet she wears but whose face is nonetheless capable of sudden ecstatic illumination when confronted with a movie character or Hollywood star; in Farrow's bridging of Cecilia's polar selves lies the success of *Purple Rose*'s dramatization of its central thematic antinomy. If Allen's incapacity to elevate Mariel Hemingway's beauty to Gershwinian magnificence in *Manhattan* limited that movie's development of its structural contrast between idealistic projections of New York and human venality of its inhabitants, the central tension of *Purple Rose* is completely achieved through

Farrow's nuanced and completely persuasive portrayal of a hell-dweller's desperate need to believe in heaven.

The remarkably lucid realism of *The Purple Rose of Cairo* with its alternation between Cecilia's Depression reality and the black-and-white champagne comedy world of Hollywood's *Purple Rose* is truly Allen's cinematic medium—his most characteristic films represent a convergence of the traditions of American theatrical naturalism and classic Hollywood film style. But Allen's fondness for O'Neill, Tennessee Williams, and other naturalist dramatists and Hollywood realist filmmakers contends with his admiration for what he describes as the "poetic" cinema of Ingmar Bergman. "On the screen, one does poetry or one does prose," Allen told Stig Bjorkman. John Huston's films are "prose of a wonderful kind . . . But Bergman works with poetry." In *The Seventh Seal,* Allen believes, Bergman created "the definitive dramatic metaphor" for death, and in his own efforts at creating poetic films, "I've never come up with a metaphor as good as his. I don't think you can. . . . The closest I've come so far is *Shadows and Fog,* but it's not as good a metaphor as his. Bergman's is right on the nose. It's great."[10] Although Allen's appropriation of German Expressionist film style filtered through *film noir* techniques for the purpose of making a Bergmanian "poetic" film was not well-received critically, the movie's symbolic landscape and allegorical characters produce an intriguing modal reconceptualizing of the escapist fantasy/real life conflict underlying *The Purple Rose of Cairo.*

Shortly before his climactic assertion equating illusions with air in *Shadows and Fog,* Irmstedt offers Max Kleinman, Allen's character, a job in the circus as the magician's assistant. Kleinman's initial response maps the allegorical geography of *Shadows and Fog:* "I'm gonna join the circus? That's crazy!" he objects. "I have to go back to town and, you know, join real life." However, "real life," as it is acted out in the unnamed European town created by Santo Loquasto's atmospheric Kaufman Astoria Studio set for *Shadows and Fog,* is best described by a *Rolling Stone* reporter's characterization in *Annie Hall* of sex with Alvy Singer: it's "a Kafkaesque experience." The failure of the local police to capture the murderer terrorizing the town leads citizens to form vigilante groups, each of which has its own strategy for dealing with him.

At the beginning of the film, Kleinman is awakened in the middle of the night by one such group and coerced into joining their plan, though he is never told what the plan is or what role he's supposed to play in it. As a result, he spends the entire night wandering around the fog-enshrouded town in search of instructions, failing utterly to understand why a "socially undesirable" Jewish couple has been arrested in connection with murders obviously committed by a single man, why his name appears on a list being compiled by the local priest and a police captain, or why citizens are being murdered by members of factions favoring different solutions to the bane of the homicidal maniac.[11] When Cecilia is obliged to choose between Tom and Gil, one of the screen-bound actors of *The Purple Rose of Cairo* comments that "The most human of all attributes is your ability to choose" (p. 456); "Are you with us or against us?" the leader of one faction threateningly interrogates Kleinman, who, once again invoking Kafka's Joseph K, responds, "How can I choose? I don't know enough to know what faction I'm in."[12]

Unimpressed by ignorance as an explanation, the faction leader berates him again, "Lives are at stake; you *have to make a choice!*"

The existential necessity to choose among unintelligible, indistinguishable options is the Kafkaesque fate of Kleinman, a self-identified "ink-stained wretch" who "doesn't know enough to be incompetent"; it's his insistence upon adhering to the ideal of human rationality which prevents him from falling in step with his rabid fellow citizens. "Everybody has a plan," he tells Irmy, "I'm the only one who doesn't know what he's doing." (Kleinman's fellow townsman's scheme—"Let's kill [Kleinman] before he gives us all away"—reflects how perilous not knowing what he's doing can be in this world of plans which replicate the scourge they seek to eliminate.) Unwilling to embrace some fragmentary truth as totalizing explanation—and thus refusing, in the terms of Sherwood Anderson's *Winesburg, Ohio,* to become the "grotesque" that each of his fellow citizens has transformed himself into—Kleinman champions reason: when a mob accuses him of the murders, he responds, "This is a joke. Listen, we're all reasonable, reasonable, you know, rational people." The film's immediate commentary on Kleinman's assertion is to cut to Spiro (Charles Cragin), a psychic who sniffs out crime and criminals telepathically and has employed his faculty to smell an incriminating glass in Kleinman's pocket: "Once again I thank the Lord," Spiro prays, "for the special gift He has seen fit to bestow upon me." Rationality doesn't count for anything in this world under the imminent threat of death; none of the numerous questions of human ultimacy raised during this night—including the interrogation of the Doctor (Donald Pleasence) regarding the nature of human evil as it is manifested in the murderer—elicit even remotely adequate answers. (The characters' attempts to solve ontological mysteries in *Shadows and Fog*—"So many questions!" the killer harrumphs dismissively before strangling the Doctor with piano wire—are no more effective than Tom Baxter's efforts at philosophical reflection in *The Purple Rose of Cairo,* speculations confounded by his inability to understand that Irving Sachs and R.H. Levine, *The Purple Rose of Cairo*'s screenwriters, aren't God.) Kleinman is the only citizen courageous enough to admit that he's incapable of choosing because "I've been wandering around in the fog"—the fog which is the film's externalization of the limit imposed upon human understanding by the presence of death, its benighting effects exacerbated by plans devised by humanity in futile efforts to clarify and illuminate their desperate existential circumstance. The alternative, then, is shadows.

If the town of *Shadows and Fog* is a projection of reality filtered through *The Trial* and parables of the lonely Kafka sojourner whose experience consists largely in being disabused of his conviction that the institutions of the world are rational and just, the circus as an allegorical embodiment of the realm of fantasy and art is an even more Kafka-influenced reality. "When I see him out there in his makeup," Irmy tells the prostitutes who befriend her of her lover, Paul, a clown in the circus, "just getting knocked around and falling in a big tub of water with all the people laughing, I can only think, 'he must have suffered so to act like that.'" Painters, poets, novelists, and musicians are understood to create their art through the aesthetic transfiguration of their personal suffering, but a circus clown? Paul the clown, Irmy the sword swallower, and Irmstedt the magician are artists in the same sense that Kafka's hunger artist is an artist, their "arts," like his fasting, providing a model of how art works, helping to clarify what function it serves for those dependent upon its performance. "We're not like other people," Paul tells Irmy early in the film, "we're artists. With great talent comes responsibility. . . . I have a rare opportunity now. To make people laugh. To make them forget their sad lives." This is the affective justification of art Allen offers in *The Purple Rose of Cairo*, but whereas Hollywood's glowing images in that film have the potency to win back Cecilia's devotion despite all she's learned of the duplicity and fraudulence existing on both sides of the screen, Paul's art, for all his self-congratulation, isn't working: "I'm an artist. Every town I've played in, I get huge laughs, and here, nothing. I mean, no one comes, and the few that do sit there stone-faced. Believe me, nothing is more terrifying than trying to make people laugh and failing." Paul's art (like Irmy's and, subsequently, Irmstedt's) is failing at the circus for the same reason that Kleinman's appeals to rationality are persuading none of the vicious factioneers in the town: the presence of the murderer.[13]

Allen initially sketched out the Kleinman plot of *Shadows and Fog* in "Death (A Play)," the one-act's one-liner gravitational pull and its want of the film's controlling metaphors of fog and shadows making it a substantially less resonant work, but one whose greater spareness frames its allegorical intent more distinctly. Stabbed fatally by the maniac in the play, Kleinman is asked by John, who finds him bleeding to death, for a description of the murderer. Kleinman's response is that the murderer looks like himself. Once Kleinman has died, John proclaims, "Sooner or later he'll get all of us."[14] Death, incarnated by the killer whose various names—maniac, strangler, beast, evil one, murderer—suggest a spectrum of mortality and its causes, is the ultimate power in both "Death (A Play)" and *Shadows and Fog*: it dictates most of the characters' actions in both play and film, inspiring fear, despair, philosophical speculation, and even Paul's determination to abandon his circus art in favor of beginning a family. Ultimately, "Death (A Play)" has little original to say about death: it's omnipotent and personalized, each person confronting her/himself in facing it. *Shadows and Fog* concentrates, instead, on human responses to the inevitability of death, expanding the civic confusion and brutality ("Soon we're going to do his killing for him," the *Shadows and Fog* Kleinman accurately predicts) that results from competing strategies for dealing with the murderer's presence in town and the presence of the reality of death. "Nobody's sure of anything! Nobody knows anything!" Kleinman summarizes the theme in the play, "This is some plan! We're dropping like flies!" (p. 75). The film adds to the play's allegorizing of death the competing circus allegory with its emblematization of art as temporary antidote to, then compensation for, human mortality.[15]

Whereas the townspeople's rival plans are either impotent before the threat the killer poses or contributory to it, Irmstedt is able to use his magician's illusions to capture the killer (Michael Kirby) temporarily when he appears on the circus grounds. (Irmstedt's name and accent identify him with another Swedish magician, one less equivocal than Allen about the limits of artistic creation. Ingmar Bergman described his own craft in these terms: "I am either an impostor or when the audience is willing to be taken in, a conjuror. I perform conjuring tricks with apparatus so expensive and so wonderful that any entertainer in history would have given anything to have it."[16]) Irmstedt and Kleinman first hide in a trick mirror, transforming themselves into images unaffected by the killer's subsequent destruction of the prop; then Irmstedt entraps the killer in a circular cage before making him disappear and rematerialize ("He was here—and now he's there!"), chained hand and foot to a stool. "We have captured the beast!" Irmstedt exults, but by the time the other circus personnel arrive to witness his triumph, the killer has slipped his bonds and fled. "No man could have escaped," Irmstedt complains, confirming that it wasn't a man he'd shackled, "Those were the real locks. Even *I* could not have escaped." Taking up this cue, the roustabout replies, "Looks like he's a greater magician than you"—perhaps invoking Death's ability to make people disappear for good.

"Meanwhile," the roustabout later goads Irmstedt, "your tricks didn't stop the killer." "No," the magician admits, "but we checked his reigns for a moment. Perhaps we even frightened him." In other words, art's illusions can distract us briefly from the inevitability of death, making us believe that through the imposition of artistic permanence upon materiality, we have immobilized the passage of time, defeating mortality. But Irmstedt's magic, by his own admission, allows him only to escape from trick locks, not from the real ones, which can't contain death. ("[A]ll those silly magic tricks" *still* can't help Nat Bernstein when it's his time to die.) As for Irmstedt's bravura claim of having frightened the killer with what the magician derisively calls his "paraphernalia," it's only necessary to recall Irmy's initial description of him after Kleinman has told her what a great artist he believes Irmstedt is: "He's a great artist when he's sober." Irmstedt is a drunk, Paul—the champion of the responsibility which comes with great talent—is a womanizing philanderer,[17] and the circus incarnating the saving power of human fantasy is, in Paul's estimation, "a completely mismanaged stupid traveling show." Art, Allen's films consistently insist, is no more pure or perfect than the artist who creates it; therefore, art is utterly incapable of achieving the triumph with which Modernist aesthetics often credited it: the transformation of temporal progression into humanly intelligible meaning. The typical attitude of Allen's films toward the artistic process, instrumentally considered, is perhaps best summarized by the character of Rain, Gabe Roth's writing student in *Husbands and Wives,* who disparages the mimetic achievement he finds in her stories: "It's just a trick, you know," she replies. "When I was ten I wrote this whole story on Paris. It's just a trick—you don't have to know [Paris in order for the trick to work]."[18]

Having heard everyone else's theory about the killer and how to capture him, Kleinman offers his own—and his creator's—summary at the end of the movie: "My theory is that nothing good is going to happen until we catch him."[19] However, the fact that Irmstedt's magic/art can't "catch" the murderer/Death does not, in Kleinman's—or in Allen's—view, render it useless. Admittedly, Irmy and Paul have chosen to leave the circus to raise a family, their decision constituting the extinction of their artist-selves since, as Paul earlier argued, "a family—that's death to the artist." But the conclusion of *Shadows and Fog* also contains a compensatory countermovement dramatizing with great effectiveness Allen's real ambivalence toward the necessity of illusions—of art—to human happiness.[20]

As Irmy and Kleinman say good-bye to each other at the end of the "strange night" dramatized in the movie during which Irmy feels "like my whole life has changed," she asks what will become of him, and he responds with a summary of his circumstances, one more desperate but otherwise similar to Cecilia's at the end of *The Purple Rose of Cairo:* "I should be all right—apart from the fact that I'm wanted by a lynch mob, and the police are after me, and there's a homicidal maniac loose, and I'm unemployed. You know, everything else is fine." (Kleinman neglects to mention that in distracting the murderer from making Irmy his next victim, the "ink-stained wretch" has demonstrated courage which redeems the cringing cowardice and passivity that have characterized him throughout the film, and which reached their culmination in his impotency with one of Felice's prostitutes.) After considering what the "real world" of the town holds in store for him, Kleinman—like Cecilia sitting in the Jewel Theater, shifting mentally from her confrontation with actuality's unremitting ugliness back into the fantasy of "Heaven, I'm in heaven" as it is danced by Astaire and Rogers—reverses his decision declining

Irmstedt's job offer. In a world whose dominant characteristics are inscrutabil-ity, unintelligibility, the impossibility of making distinctions, and violent hu-man contentions resulting from that incapacity—in a world, that is, in which you can know nothing but that "the killer lurks in the fog," Kleinman's life-transforming choice is obvious. "What better way to spend the rest of my life," he asks Irmstedt rhetorically, his eyes as wide as Cecilia's as Hollywood's most glamorous couple swirls across the screen before her, "than to help you with those wonderful illusions of yours?"

Poetic License, Bullshit

Bullets Over Broadway

This is a work of art. The ropes come off, and I tie sash weights to her ankles with soft catgut. She disappears two weeks, maybe three. Then up she pops, none of this stuff on her anymore, no marks—a suicide. Isn't that beautiful?

—Scene from *This Gun for Hire,* watched by Halley and Cliff
in *Crimes and Misdemeanors*

One of the limitations of the allegorical mode of *Shadows and Fog* is that the necessarily abstract assertion the film makes about the human dependency upon art allows it to provide only a minimum of insight into the nature of the magic illusions on which its conclusion turns. (The German Expressionist films—primarily *Nosferatu* and *The Cabinet of Dr. Caligari*—whose influence pervades *Shadows and Fog* are similarly blunt instruments, works as dedicated as Allen's to atmospherically externalizing a condition of soul and as little concerned with the detailed exposition of complex ideas.[1]) Because of its more realistic aesthetic, *The Purple Rose of Cairo* is able to give the viewer a fairly comprehensive sense of the components of the cinematic illusion, including some unromantic behind-the-scenes realities that Cecilia never sees: the egotism of the characters in the film who, divested of their narrative by Tom's defection, acrimoniously dispute each others' claims to being the central character of the movie's plot, and the bottom line cynicism of the producer and studio heads, whose contempt for the movie audience is exceeded only by their indifference to everything but box office receipts.

In contrast, Irmstedt, the magician—and thus the central artist—of *Shadows and Fog,* whose illusions people need "like they need the air" and who carries much of the conclusion's thematic burden, appears only in the final ten minutes of the film, his assertion about illusions giving the viewer little insight into how his illusive art of diversion/consolation works. He affirms that people not only love but also need his illusions, a contention the film's viewers have been conditioned to accept largely through their introduction to the alternative "real-life" realm of inscrutable purposes, bureaucratic terrorism, and senseless murder that is the town—a realm from which any sane person would willingly flee. Allen is content, then, to dramatize a single

Irmstedt trick—the one that fails to stop the killer/Death in his tracks—because that failure so effectively epitomizes Allen's ambivalent conception of art's value to humanity: we need its illusions in order to live, but we're only deluding ourselves if we believe they can redeem us from death. (To reformulate the final line of *Annie Hall* and title of Diane Jacobs' critical study, we need the eggs despite the fact that they won't alleviate our hunger.)

Partly because of its more realistic aesthetic, *Bullets Over Broadway* not only makes an assertion about art, but through its dramatization of the gradual evolution of a work of literary drama, it illuminates in detail both the operation of an individual creative mind and the interventions of corrupt reality which comprise—and compromise—the final product, which is David Shayne's play. Although a more cheerful film than *Deconstructing Harry, Bullets Over Broadway* enacts the same anatomization of the tawdry mongrel of appropriated life and self-serving fantasy that is the work of art, while simultaneously depicting artists as men and women vulnerable to particularly virulent forms of corruption. Released right in the middle of the decade, *Bullets Over Broadway* provides the best explanation for the propensity of Allen's 1990s movies to affirm life over art.

"I'm an artist," David Shayne (John Cusack) asserts in the opening line of *Bullets Over Broadway,* and, having reached this point in Allen's cinematic oeuvre, we should be prepared to regard with some skepticism the artist's self-congratulatory declaration of his personal integrity: "I will not change one word of my play to pander to a commercial Broadway audience." The artists in Allen's films who make such extreme claims are either utter recluses (Eve, of *Interiors,* for whom art creates a life-denying, actuality-displacing perfectionism, or Frederick, of *Hannah and Her Sisters,* who "can't stand to be with people" other than his lover, Lee), or hypocrites like Paul, in *Shadows and Fog,* whose avowals of artistic integrity are belied by his habitual sexual betrayals of Irmy. It is to Shayne's credit that he—unlike his friend, Sheldon Flender (Rob Reiner), whose proof that he is a true genius consists in that none of the twenty plays he's written has ever been produced—is willing to subject his work to the external testing of production and the vicissitudes of the Broadway marketplace. But if there's anything *Bullets Over Broadway* doesn't dramatize, it's a playwright impervious to commercial and other pressures, an artist constitutionally incapable of altering his play for personal or professional gain. In a movie that Allen characterized as "a comedy with a serious point to it, a philosophical point,"[2] the "serious point" at its core dramatizes the moral hypocrisy underlying artistic ambitions.

The central motivating joke of *Bullets Over Broadway* is that the uncompromisingly idealistic artist who believes that "it's the theater's duty not just to entertain but to transform men's souls" consents to sell his own soul by agreeing to have the production of his play financed by a murderous Mafia boss

(Joe Vitirelli) whose nonnegotiable stipulation is that his talentless chorus-line-reject girlfriend, Olive Neal (Jennifer Tilly), be given a role. When Shayne initially balks at the terms of the deal, his agent, Julian Marx (Jack Warden), gives him a lecture on the relationship between art and reality—a lecture that Allen could have written for delivery to a number of elitist aesthetes in his films: "Let me level with you, Mr. Artist. This is a dog-eat-dog world, not an ideal world. Now if you want to get your play on, you're going to have to make a few concessions. Life is not perfect—plus, it is short. And if you can't figure that out, you might as well pack up right now and go back to Pittsburgh." The "few concessions" to reality Shayne has to make in order to see his play staged, the nature and magnitude of which ultimately do send him packing for Pittsburgh and the adoption of a middle-class life as unlike his Bohemian Greenwich Village playwright's existence as he can make it, begin with Olive, whose single theatrical credit prior to Shayne's play consists in a Wichita musical review titled *Leave a Specimen*. (To his credit, Shayne wakes in the middle of the night following his acquiescence to Valenti's terms screaming, "I'm a whore! I'm a prostitute!") Exacerbating Olive's complete theatrical incompetence is the fact that the only role in Shayne's play small enough to hide her in is that of a psychiatrist whose professional assumptions are as incomprehensible to Olive as her diction is foreign. (When a line of hers referring to a masochistic patient is explained to Olive, she declares the patient "retarded.") Olive's complete unsuitability to this tragic drama and Mafioso Nick Valenti's improbable casting of himself in the role of theatrical angel combine to create one of the most inspired satiric premises that Allen, working with co-writer Douglas McGrath, has ever fabricated. The recurring class confrontations throughout the film between elitist Broadway cultural pretension and streetwise untutored gangland brutishness generate a succession of extraordinary comic scenes. However, as in his other most substantial comedies—*Broadway Danny Rose, Hannah and Her Sisters,* and *Mighty Aphrodite*—the jokes in *Bullets Over Broadway* support and reinforce the film's organizing theme: the impartibility of destruction and creation, the interdependence of art and life, which Flender affirms in claiming that the work of art "is not an inanimate object. It's art. Art is life—it lives."[3]

Given the Freudian assumptions of Allen's perception of things, it's no surprise that the secondary temptation Shayne experiences to the compromising of his artistic integrity is sexual. Helen Sinclair (Dianne Wiest), a celebrated Broadway actress who hasn't had a stage hit for a while, condescends to take on the lead female role of Sylvia Posten in Shayne's play despite finding the character colorless, sexually unalluring, and lacking in passion. Helen establishes clearly at the first day's rehearsal that her status as theatrical veteran and stage star resolves the issue of whether she or the first-time director/ playwright wields the greater power in dictating the evolution of this production.

To bolster her command over the play, she proceeds to seduce Shayne by flattering his position relative to hers ("My God—who am I? Some vain Broadway legend? You're a budding Chekhov!") in an ill-concealed attempt to coerce him into rewriting her character as someone she believes more closely resembles the stage persona she has developed. "Audiences have come to empathize with me in a very personal way," she tells Shayne the first time they have drinks together, his tacit acquiescence to her demand that her star quality dictate the production representing the first in a series of many compromises of his dramatic vision to her star's egotistical self-projection. That night he tells Ellen (Marie-Louise Parker), the woman with whom he lives, of his newly arisen doubts about Sylvia's character; Ellen responds that Sylvia is the best female character he's ever created. His mind throbbing with Helen's disingenuously manipulative question, "You see through me, don't you?" and her seductive assurance that he has "such insight into women," Shayne decides that Ellen is insufficiently intellectual to appreciate the problem and sets about rewriting Sylvia's character, giving dramatic form to the concession he made to Helen as they separated that afternoon: "I don't see why she has to be frigid."

As their professional relationship warms into an affair, Helen increases her lobbying for further changes in her role, suggesting at one point that if Sylvia "succeeds in seducing the lieutenant rather than being rejected a second time, it might add some variation to the character." Moreover, she makes Shayne promise that after this play is produced, he'll write another: "a vehicle for Helen Sinclair. But it must have size—an important woman—Curie—Borgia—you name it." (Midway through the film they seem to have settled on a drama about the Virgin Mary.) Shayne's deepening infatuation with Helen blinds him to her resistance to his protestations of love, her explanation of this response reflecting her actual attitude toward the craft so crucial to his sense of himself: "Everything meaningful is in some unexplainable form," she tells him, "it's more primordial than mere language." Thereafter, she responds, "Don't speak, don't speak," whenever he tries to express his feelings for her. (Insofar as she loves him at all, she loves—in the terms of a running debate Shayne has with his Village friends—"the artist, not the man," since it's the artist who can further her career and merely the man who is regaling her with declarations of affection couched in "mere language.") "To your play," Helen toasts him as they drink together at her penthouse, "To an ideal world with no compromise." Given her skepticism about language's ability to communicate human ultimacy and her insistence upon shaping her roles to conform to her fraudulent temptress stage persona, Helen Sinclair is the film's comic incarnation of the artistic compromise she pretends to abhor.

Shayne's play is called *God of Our Fathers*, the Biblical pretension of the title invoking the thematic gravity of second-rate naturalistic American drama of the 1920s and '30s, plays whose earnestness of tragic purpose exceeded that of their models—O'Neill, Odets, Maxwell Anderson—and consequently resulted in works of nearly oppressive solemnity.[4] In his attempt to create a tragedy, Shayne has obviously pushed past solemnity into pomposity, encumbering his actors with lines like "What endeavors you to concoct a theory so tenuous?" and "The heart is labyrinthine, a maze beset with brutal pitfalls and mean obstacles." Shayne's defense of the play's elevated language is that it represents "a stylish way of expressing a particular idea," but the character who initially emerges as his antagonist, only to later become his collaborator, reads it differently: "You don't write the way people talk," Cheech (Chazz Palminteri) tells him.[5] Compelled to sit through every rehearsal because Valenti wants his hit man to keep an eye on Olive, Cheech becomes a progressively vocal critic of Shayne's play, and when he recommends a plot revision during rehearsal, Shayne is outraged by the actors' unanimous support for the suggestion from "this strong-arm man with an IQ of minus fifty." Secretly impressed by the suggestion, Shayne allows Helen to persuade him to incorporate the change (which, because it amplifies Sylvia's character's sensuality, she favors). It follows that Shayne comes increasingly to rely on Cheech's script doctoring to improve his play by injecting into it what Shayne's literary affectations and his overwrought obeisance to his theater models have drained from it: real life.

In order to establish the connection immediately, the initial scene in which Cheech appears depicts him enacting his hit man's profession by executing Valenti's enemies. That scene is framed, tellingly, by a lecture Shayne's agent gives him: "Let me tell you something, kid. That's a real world out there, and it's a lot rougher than you think." Cheech is the film's chief incarnation of that "rougher-than-you-think real world." Although his Mafia connections introduce an anomalous element into his character, Cheech otherwise embodies what Lionel Trilling construed historian V.L. Parrington as representing to American literary history: opposition to the "genteel and academic" aspect of literature, an alliance with "the vigorous and actual." Parrington, Trilling argued, had "what we like to think of as the saving salt of the American mind, the lively sense of the practical, workaday world, of the welter of ordinary, undistinguished things and people, of the tangible, quirky, unrefined elements of life. He knew what so many literary historians do not know, that emotions and ideas are the sparks that fly when the mind meets difficulties."[6] In Trilling's view, the prejudice in favor of "reality" which led Parrington to champion Theodore Dreiser as a major American writer despite the infelicities and awkwardness of his prose style is the same prejudice which prompts the actors of God of Our Fathers to extol in the coarsest terms they can manage the script revisions they're unaware are Cheech's, each of them attempting to emulate his crude genius by generating appropriately earthy compliments. "In the American metaphysic," Trilling continued, "reality is always material reality, hard, resistant, unformed, impenetrable, and unpleasant. And that mind is alone felt to be trustworthy which most nearly resembles that reality by most nearly reproducing the sensations it affords."[7] Shayne also embraces this mythology, praising how "naturally" writing seems to come to Cheech: "You have a huge gift," he tells the hit man,"It's uncanny—your instincts—it's really—enviable." Allen's commentary on the American prejudice toward associating reality with naturalness and instinct is to have the natural, instinctive artist turn homicidal in defense of his work.

Once Cheech has begun actively collaborating on *God of Our Fathers,* he confronts Shayne again on the issue of stilted dialogue, rejecting Shayne's rationale for it as "taking poetic license": "Poetic license, bullshit. People believe what they see when the actors sound real." Cheech's single aesthetic concept is distilled in this sentence, one which aligns him with the naturalist movement in American theater of the early 20th century and with Gil Shepherd of *The Purple Rose of Cairo,* whose identification with reality ("And I'm real," he tells Cecilia in response to movie character Tom Baxter's case for himself) is inseparable from his basic human inconsistency and untrustworthiness. Rather than remaining the proletarian artist who is able to value art in proportion to its worth ("It's a play anyhow," is his level-headed justification for an early revision: "It don't have to be real, but it'll be stronger"), Cheech eventually surpasses and exceeds Shayne as the ultimate aesthete non-compromiser, finally resorting to gangland solutions when the integrity of his theatrical work is irredeemably undermined by Olive's incompetence. In a dual character reversal typical of Allen's plots,[8] Cheech and Shayne basically exchange places, the mob hit man transforming himself into the temperamental artist, the committed playwright arguing for the superiority of life to art and ultimately repudiating the theater altogether. Although Allen didn't emulate his protagonist in disavowing his art, the movies that follow *Bullets* approximate dramatically Shayne's resolution by consistently endorsing life over its artistic representation.

The actors' reaction to the revisions they are unaware are Cheech's is unanimous and metaphorically consistent: Eden Brent (Tracey Ullman) tells Shayne, "Congratulations—it finally has balls." "I would give my body freely to the man who wrote those words," Helen effuses. She later assures Shayne that the version of his play she gave to George S. Kaufman to read "was the rewrite—not the eunuch version," and declares in their final scene together that, as a result of his recent maturation as a playwright, "the world will open to you like a giant oyster—no, like a magnificent vagina." That the creation of effective art is so repeatedly likened to sexual potency simultaneously reflects the characters' gut-level conviction that reality is inseparable from genitality and anticipates an idea introduced late in the film in the dialogue between Shayne and Ellen when he informs her of his affair with Helen Sinclair, and she in turn informs him of hers with his best friend, Flender.

ELLEN: You know [Flender's] theory that art is relational, that it's something that requires two people, the artist and the audience? Well, he feels that way about sex, too.

DAVID: Sex?

ELLEN: That between the two right people, it becomes an art form.

DAVID: You and Flender have raised intercourse to an art?

ELLEN: Not just intercourse. Foreplay too.

The artist whose greatest pride lies in the unproducibility of his plays has rendered sex and art indistinguishable through an act of will which many artists in the film seem to believe is the utterly appropriate privilege of the creative mind: "An artist," Flender grandly announces to Shayne when the *God of Our Fathers* playwright confesses to him his affair with Helen, "creates his own moral universe." It's only later in the film Shayne discovers that the freedom with which Flender privileges himself as "creator of his own moral universe" includes a sanction to have an affair with Shayne's lover.

Throughout the film, Shayne is bookended by two views of art and the artist which are similar in the extremity of their claims for art's ascendancy and inviolability, dissimilar in the work they do and don't engender, and similar again in their indifference to the moral consequences of artistic creation. Flender's file-cabineted theatrical creations give him the liberty to declare himself beyond morality and to define art as anything that suits his libidinal purposes at the moment, lovemaking *and* foreplay included. When asked by Shayne what to do about loving both Ellen and Helen at the same time, Flender's thoroughly relativistic solution is "What you gotta do, you gotta do"—which doesn't, in Flender's immediate circumstance, include telling Shayne he's cuckolding him. Cheech at least is willing to question the morality of the situation he's about to resolve immorally: "You think it's right," he asks Shayne, "some Tootsie walks in and messes up a beautiful thing like [the play]?" Shayne's insistence that the audience doesn't really notice Olive's incompetence and that compromise is necessary in the real world only enrages Cheech further, eliciting the response, "Listen to me. Nobody is going to ruin my work— nobody." At which point, it's—to cite the title of the Al Jolson song opening the film—"Toot, Toot, Tootsie, goodbye."

"Olive, I think you should know this," Cheech says before blasting her off his favorite execution pier, "You're a horrible actress." *Bullets Over Broadway*, then, contains two embodiments of uncompromising artistic integrity: a self-styled genius and conscientious objector from play production for whom an artistic vocation is merely an excuse for sexual libertinism, and an actual proletarian genius whose barbarous upbringing has provided him with no ethic to oppose the idea that execution is an acceptable means by which a dramatist can improve the performance of his play. In *Bullets Over Broadway*, the art of theater progressively comes to seem not a means of transcending life but a capitulation to life's most lascivious and aggressive impulses.

Shayne expresses justifiable outrage at Cheech's hit man's mode of production enhancement, and when Cheech asks him "Who says?" you don't murder to ensure your play's greatness, Shayne responds, "I'm an artist, too—not a great artist like you, but first I'm a human being, a decent, moral . . . "

"You are?" Cheech answers, "So what are you doing with Helen Sinclair?"

In an early draft of *Bullets Over Broadway*, Allen included an extensive final meeting between Helen and Shayne, which in addition to establishing that Helen is no longer interested in Shayne because he's been revealed to be so much less the playwright than Cheech, allowed the two characters to talk through (or more accurately, talk away) some of the film's central themes. "When confronted with a truly creative individual in any field, many people have trouble distinguishing the man from the artist," Helen, too neatly echoing the Bohemian artists' debate, explains to Shayne. "You did with Cheech—but I've always fallen in love with the artist—that's why so many love affairs have been with shitheels—you get what I'm saying?"[9] That Helen's speech reduces themes to "saying" is precisely its problem, and few viewers would lament Allen's decision to delete it or the undramatically discursive scene in which it appears. The speech's obvious intention to temper the film's consistently satiric characterization of Helen is nonetheless interesting, and even more so is its unequivocal identification of artists as "shitheels." Although generally speaking, *Bullets Over Broadway* is a brightly lit, highly colorful and cheerful comedy populated by comedic type characters (an actress who speaks baby talk to her Chihuahua, an actor whose stage fright provokes eating binges, prompting him to steal the Chihuahua's doggie treats) reminiscent of those in Allen's "early, funny movies," its depiction of artists and the artistic vocation is remarkably and unrelentingly negative, there existing not a single creative person in the film who doesn't seem worthy of Helen's designation of "shitheel."

In the same early draft of the script, Shayne, on the verge of abandoning playwriting and fleeing to Pittsburgh with Ellen, admits to Helen that, "My work was weak and tentative—I was lucky to find a writer who made me look like a hero."[10] In this lighthearted comedy with a bleak soul, Shayne's depressingly egotistical construal of *God of Our Fathers* is probably the most complimentary thing that's said about artists and the artistic vocation. If the point of creating art isn't that it increases the artist's capacity to rationalize endlessly promiscuous sexual activity or affords an ethic through which s/he can justify trampling on other people, then it's valuable because—assuming the creator finds a great ghostwriter whose work he can claim as his own—it may make him "look like a hero."[11] The film leaves little doubt as to how deceptive that perception would be, or how far it is from Shayne's apparently ideal formulation from the opening of the play: "The theater's duty is not just to entertain but to transform men's souls."[12] On the evidence of *Bullets Over Broadway,* involvement in the theater *does* transform men's souls—for the worst.

Of course, it is impossible to account in any certain terms for the heightened negativism toward art dramatized by *Bullets Over Broadway.* Shayne's repudiation of his vocation in the film's final lines ("I'm not an artist. There, I've said it and I feel free. I'm not an artist") represents Allen's films' most unequivocally condemnatory concluding judgment on art and artists before *Deconstructing Harry's* denouement surpassed it. Imputing the cynicism reflected in the film to Allen's notorious troubles in the early '90s is risky, especially since *Husbands and Wives* is generally recognized as the more obvious cinematic expression of Allen's publicly aired private life nightmare. Cheech's final revision, however, invites comparisons between his absolutist aesthetic credo and that of the filmmaker who created him.[13] Unconvinced by Cheech's explanations of what he was doing the night Olive was murdered, Valenti sends his goons after him, gunning him down in the Belasco Theater during the final act of *God of Our Fathers'* opening night. (Even in death Cheech contributes revisions to the play, the gunshots ending his life construed by a reviewer as the lieutenant's experience of a combat flashback and thus becoming a sound effect in subsequent performances.) As Shayne cradles the dying Cheech in his arms, the gangster offers one final rewrite before expiring: "The last line in the play . . . tell Sylvia Posten to say she's pregnant. It'll be a great finish."

Allen didn't think that having Holly tell Mickey Sachs that she is pregnant with their child made a "great finish" for *Hannah and Her Sisters,* acknowledging to Eric Lax that the result of that choice was to make *Hannah* "a movie that ended like almost every movie, with happy endings all around." Having Mickey's sterility suddenly resolved by Holly's concluding announcement "was too neat and tidy an ending," Allen explained: "Life is more ambiguous and unpleasant than that."[14] Allen's comic indictment of the Mafia hit man so monomaniacally committed to his art as to be indifferent to the moral consequences of his acts may well have contained an element of oblique self-incrimination.

"That's so great—" is Shayne's response to Cheech's final revision of *God of Our Fathers,* but Cheech cuts him off: "No, don't speak, don't speak," he says with his last breath. Cheech's dying admonition echoes Helen Sinclair's incessant exhortations to Shayne to leave their passion unspoken, the two champions of art-at-any-cost being identified at the end of the film as sharing a desire not to foster sincere emotion but to silence it. An egotistical Broadway legend for whom art is nothing more than a medium for self-dramatization and self-glorification; a proletarian dramatist whose professional executionary tactics seem an acceptable means of protecting his play against inaesthetic corruption; an unpublished and unproduced playwright whose status as an artist is nothing more than a pretense rationalizing his "creating his own moral universe"—these are the exemplars of the aesthetic in *Bullets Over Broadway*. Only a triumvirate of characters possessed of artistically inspired rapaciousness of this magnitude could prompt Woody Allen to allow his protagonist to embrace enthusiastically an art-repudiating self-exile to Pittsburgh.

If the artists populating *Bullets Over Broadway* are a sorry census of the superiority of aesthetic sensibility, the work of art whose evolution the film delineates is analogously dubious. The reviewers of the opening night performance of *God of Our Fathers* summon up their favorite expressions of Modernist artistic transcendence in lauding the play as "a masterpiece," "a theatrical stunner," and "a work of art of the highest quality." However, Allen's film prompts his audience to see Shayne's play in distinctly less elevated terms. The *God of Our Fathers* whose evolution we've watched is a pretentious pastiche of Maxwell Anderson and Eugene O'Neill riddled with artistic compromises: its financial backing is supplied by a brutal mobster in exchange for his incompetent moll getting a role in the play, and the tragic plot is endlessly manipulated to stroke the vanity of an egomaniacal Broadway diva with whom the playwright/director is erotically involved. Cheech's script doctoring, initially implemented to eliminate the drama's pomposities, becomes grounds for his gangland elimination of Olive: because "she's killing my words," Cheech feels justified in killing her. In the end, *God of Our Fathers* is implicated in two deaths (Olive and Cheech) while engendering three adulterous relationships (Shayne and Sinclair, Olive and Warner Purcell, Ellen and Flender); if Flender is right in asserting that that an artwork "is not an inanimate object" but "art is life, it lives," the life lived by *God of Our Fathers* is thoroughly corrupt.

While Sinclair and Marx at a post-theater party are reading in the play's notices that dramatist/director Shayne "is the find of the decade," he has fled the Great White Way he's conquered for the Village in hopes of reconciling with Ellen, asking her to marry him and carrying her off to Pennsylvania. "I'm not an artist," Shayne exults to Ellen in the movie's final lines, "There, I've said it and I feel free. I'm not an artist." It is characteristic of Allen's attitude in the mid-1990s that the exquisitely lit, elaborately staged, and beautifully photographed *Bullets Over Broadway* so emphatically and unequivocally condemns the art of which it is so generously possessed.

13

Let's Just Live It

Woody Allen in the 1990s

HARRY: I'm no good at life.
RICHARD: But you write well.
HARRY: I write well, but that's a different story because I can manipulate
the characters.
RICHARD: You create your own universe, which is much nicer than
the one we have, I think.

—Harry Block and Richard in *Deconstructing Harry*

Let *Bullets Over Broadway* exemplify the ambivalence of Woody Allen's attitude toward art in the 1990s. The movie enacts David Shayne's realization
that his only hope of redemption from the corruptions to which artistic ambition is heir necessitates renouncing the theater and fleeing with Ellen to Pittsburgh to become a family man. However, the cinematic vehicle of that dramatic
message embodies a contrary judgment. The contradiction is implicit in Julian
Fox's fine description of the cinematic art of *Bullets Over Broadway:* "The film
is a visual feast, from its Times Square opening—actually a black-and-white
cut from the period which was digitally colorized to match—to the art deco
apartments and hallways, the artily-lit street scenes, speakeasies and news-
stands, vivid backstage milieu and darkly comic waterfront shoot-outs. It is a
highly romanticized recreation of a vanished age, bathed in a deep red, sepia
and yellow glow by cameraman Carlo Di Palma, designed and costumed to
the nines, the soundtrack awash with the kind of insouciant golden standards
which nostalgia buffs adore."[1]

As Fox's generously detailed summary attests, *Bullets Over Broadway* gives
no impression of being a film made by a filmmaker bearing a grudge against
his medium; it was Allen's most expensive production to date, as lushly exact-
ing in its evocation of 1920s Manhattan as *Radio Days*—Allen's previous period piece bank breaker—was of New York in the middle 1940s.[2] *Bullets Over
Broadway* epitomizes Allen's cinematic craft in its stability of framing, in the
linear nature of its narrative and in its devotion to precise realistic depiction;
the film's formal symmetries and clarity of focus consistently contrast with the
moral myopia of the characters' beatification of art and glorifications of themselves as artists. The distinctive formal coherence of Allen's work provides its

own testimony in favor of artistic craftsmanship as part of the dialectic of those movies, then, even as the content of the film becomes increasingly skeptical about the promises and premises of an artistic vocation. Before proceeding to consider the two films—*Husbands and Wives* and *Manhattan Murder Mystery*—which deliberately violate Allen's characteristic cinematic formal coherence (and which, consequently, were typically interpreted as reflecting the emotional turmoil of the Allen/Farrow dissolution), we will look at something of a synopsis of the complex issue of Allen's ambivalent position toward artists and his own cinematic art going into the production of the watershed movie, *Husbands and Wives*.

Allen's misgivings about art (and about similarly abstract or metaphoric conceptualizations of human experience) are expressed in his films not only through the unfolding of plots, but also through the presence of a number of characters whose primary trait is unrelenting skepticism and whose dramatic role it is to goad the movies' more visionary protagonists—usually, but not exclusively played by Allen—into questioning the grounds of whatever idealism they possess. The rationalist philosopher, Leopold, of *A Midsummer Night's Sex Comedy;* streetsmart Tina Vitale of *Broadway Danny Rose;* Cecilia's brutal husband, Monk, in *The Purple Rose of Cairo;* Mickey Sachs's father in *Hannah and Her Sisters;* Diane's physicist husband, Lloyd, in *September;* Judah Rosenthal's outlaw brother, Jack, and his Aunt May in *Crimes and Misdemeanors;* Felice, the brothel madam of *Shadows and Fog;* David Shayne's bottom-line heeding agent, Julian Marx, and Cheech in *Bullets Over Broadway* are just some of the varyingly sympathetic characters who preach the doctrine of hard-boiled practicality and realism in Allen's films. Each character in his or her own way suggests what Judah's brother Jack repeatedly refers to as the "real world" as the standard according to which everything in life must be judged.[3] That Allen is attracted to such tough-minded pragmatism is reflected in the regularity with which it gets voiced in his movies and interviews, and also in the tendency of Allen's protagonists to occasionally articulate analogous sentiments.

While walking through the town together in *Shadows and Fog*, Kleinman and Irmy pause to look at the night sky through a brief opening in the fog, and when Irmy tells him that the star they're seeing may have ceased to exist a million years ago, Kleinman finds the thought deeply disquieting. "When I see something with my own eyes, I like to know that it's really there, because otherwise a person could sit down in a chair and break his neck."[4] The problem with art, many of the skeptics in Allen's films would argue, is that it's not "really there" in this sense: it lies, it projects stars where they no longer are or where they may never have been, creating "Stardust memories" out of airy nothingness. It's this pragmatic impulse, of course, which prompts Kleinman initially to decline joining the circus as Irmstedt's assistant because "I have to go back to town and, you know, join real life."

In Allen's cinematic universe, the human choice nearly always consists between embracing illusion or—as the pragmatists in his films recommend—living with the bleakest truths of this dark period of human history. Allen sought to articulate those truths as he perceived them in an essay published in *Tikkun: A Bimonthly Jewish Critique of Politics, Culture and Society* in 1992, his essay imaging up a world approaching Jack Rosenthal's in its bleakness. Composed during the year he was writing and filming *Shadows and Fog,* "Random Reflections of a Second Rate Mind" is Allen's only prose reaction to the Holocaust, his response—as Mashey Bernstein has pointed out[5]—echoing the position of Frederick in *Hannah and Her Sisters* that the only serious question raised by "the systematic murder of millions" is "why doesn't it happen more often?" (*Hannah,* p. 101). "The mystery that had confounded my relatives since World War II was not such a puzzle," Allen wrote, "if I understood that inside every heart lived the worm of self-preservation, of fear, greed, and an animal will to power. And the way I saw it, it was nondiscriminating. It abided in gentile or Jew, black, white, Arab, European, or American. It was part of who we all were, and that the Holocaust could occur was not all so strange. History had been filled with unending examples of equal bestiality, differing only cosmetically."[6]

So bleak is the anatomy of the human heart in Allen's essay, in fact, as to summon up the judgment of Judy in *Husbands and Wives* in response to a pessimistic assertion of her husband, Gabe: "You really trust no one. No wonder people accuse you of cynicism." *Shadows and Fog* dramatizes this atomistic stance through Kleinman's inability to determine who is in what faction, the only certainty he reaches being that everyone in town is equally out for himself and equally murderous—equally willing to emulate the killer who is their quarry and putative enemy. Kleinman, understandably seeking refuge from the social Darwinist actuality Allen's essay invokes, abandons the town of "real-world" pragmatism and brutal political machinations to enlist in the circus of Irmstedt's illusions, resolving, in the formulation of *Shadows and Fog*'s philosophical student, to "tell jokes" rather than "facing death." (Felice, the brothel madam of *Shadows and Fog*, counters the student's brief for contemplativeness by insisting that "The trick is to have as much wine, as many men, as many laughs as you can before they carry you out in a pine box.") Although the field in which Woody Allen makes his choices is significantly more complicated than Kleinman's, it's nonetheless clear that his post-*Husbands and Wives* films, with the exception of the art-negating *Bullets Over Broadway*, have largely mirrored the decision of that "ink-stained wretch" to identify himself with "wonderful illusions." The crucial point to acknowledge here is that Allen's decision to align himself with the big top of artistic performance and the illusory comforts of generically defined contrivance is a self-conscious artistic decision. Rather than invoking the ability of imaginative artifice to conquer the bleak reality of death, his resolution affirms the inherent human necessity to distract the self from grim actualities with saving illusions. The visualization of Cecilia at the end of *The Purple Rose of Cairo* being gradually reabsorbed into the romantic *pas de deux* of *Top Hat* is Allen's most compelling emblem of the human need to recover sanity through engagement with cultural fantasy. In *Manhattan Murder Mystery*, *Mighty Aphrodite*, and *Everyone Says I Love You*, Allen filmically adopts the illusion-affirming perspective of Cecilia/Kleinman, conjuring up movies that deliberately seek to deflect the audience's attention from their personal spectres of the omnipresence of Monk, the Depression, the killer.

Allen's determination to accentuate the comical and minimize tragic potentials in these movies is not without additional repercussions and conflicts. An antinomy he is as likely to discuss in interviews as that between illusion and reality is the distinction between entertainment and serious art, and his devotion to creating the latter. In the late 1980s, Allen told Eric Lax, "I'm going to try before my life is over to rise to the occasion and make one or two [films] that would be considered great by any standard. . . . Maybe now that I've moved into my fifties and I am more confident, I can come up with a couple that are true literature."[7] In 1996, Allen reiterated this idea, telling John Lahr, "The only thing standing between me and greatness is me. . . . I would love to do a great film. I don't feel I've ever done a great film."

Citing *Citizen Kane*, *Rashomon*, *The Bicycle Thief*, and *Grand Illusion* as his benchmarks of great films, Allen continued, "I'm still in pursuit, and the pursuit keeps me going. If it happens, it'll happen by accident, because you can't pursue it head on."[8] However, this objective is complicated by Allen's conviction that "the only thing standing between me and greatness is me." Allen's comic self-deprecation here focuses the conflict at the heart of his film-making and his perception of art: "My conflict is between what I really am and what I really would like myself to be. I'm forever struggling to deepen myself and take a more profound path, but what comes easiest to me is light entertainment. I'm more comfortable with the shallower stuff. . . . I'm basically a shallow person."[9] His films aren't better, he repeatedly contends, because of his inability to be "good enough, or not deep enough on subjects."[10] One way to describe Allen is as a Modernist by doctrine and a postmodernist by inclination and practice. He is a filmmaker whose aesthetics are permeated by Modernist notions of depth and the aspiration toward a "transcendence of phenomenal experience,"[11] but whose impulses constantly drive him toward the production of movies he considers "shallow" because they are predominantly comic rather than serious—because their primary objective is to entertain rather than to inspire and enlighten.

The films Allen has produced since the early 1980s constitute a debate he has been conducting with himself over his desire to make movies such as *September, Another Woman,* and *Crimes and Misdemeanors,* which "take a more profound path," and the contrasting impulse, reflective of his unregenerate "shallowness," to provide his audience with vehicles in which to lose themselves—magic lantern entertainments like *A Midsummer Night's Sex Comedy, Manhattan Murder Mystery, Mighty Aphrodite,* and *Everyone Says I Love You*—the predominating tendencies of which are to charmingly distract viewers from life's dark enigmas rather than to seriously confront them.

The Modernist Allen wants to make serious films which attempt to answer significant human questions; the Postmodernist Allen doubts the utility of posing the questions. "Sometimes I've had the thought that to try to make films that say something, I'm not doing my fellow man a service," he told Anthony DeCurtis in a 1993 interview. "I would be better off abandoning asking the audience to try to come to grips with certain issues because those issues finally always lead you to a dead end. They're *never* going to be understandable, they're *never* going to be solvable. We all have a terrible, fierce burden to carry, and the person who really does something nice is the guy who writes a pretty song or plays a pretty piece of music or makes a film that diverts."[12]

Perhaps in tribute to his professional beginnings, Allen's cinematic tales, as we've seen, tend to celebrate popular culture much more frequently than serious art. Og's advice to Sandy Bates in *Stardust Memories*—"You want to do mankind a real service? Tell funnier jokes"—represents both a central thematic argument of that movie and a summary of the direction in which Allen's films in the 1990s have gravitated. Consequently, the boundaries of the corner into which Allen has painted himself are, at least in part, demarcated by a tension between Og's admonition and Allen's highly traditional, hierarchical perception of artistic achievement, that canon-revering stance obliging him to minimize his own accomplishments in film for the purpose of exalting the work of his cinematic inspirators.[13] Without worrying about the irresolvable issue of whether Allen has created any film remotely comparable to the best of Welles, Bergman, Godard, Kurosawa, or Truffault, it seems clear that his insistence that he hasn't done so partakes of the attitude expressed in the Groucho Marx joke Allen borrowed to open his first "significant" film, *Annie Hall,* a one-liner which sometimes does seem a key to his career: "I wouldn't wanna be a member of a club which would have me for a member." In other words, if he made a film worthy of Welles et al, it would minimize their achievements rather than elevating his.

There is more to this conflict between "what I really am and what I would really like myself to be" than professional self-effacement, however. It's difficult not to believe that, for Allen, making a great movie would necessitate resolving the dilemma that *Hannah and Her Sisters* "copped out on" through the convenient miracle of the restoration of Mickey's potency manifested through Holly's pregnancy, a dramatic closure he perceived in retrospect as influenced by the "American films" he'd grown up with, which try "to find a satisfying resolution. It may not be happy, but it's satisfying in some way. But as I've gone on, I've started to resolve the films less."[14] In the view of its director/screenwriter, what invalidates that movie is that *Hannah* is ultimately a symptom of the human desire to transcend the problem of mortality rather than the solution itself; finally, *Hannah* is one more narrative with a contrived ending which, rather than resolving the existential bind, reinforces and confirms the irresolvability of that condition.

In the aggregate, Allen's films seem to dramatize an irreducible choice to which every artist is limited: s/he can either create artworks imitating the formlessness of human experience, thus affirming the omnipotence and inescapability of suffering and death, or s/he can assume the irrelevance of any artistic artifice to the essential human condition and continue to create what Sandy Bates terms "my stupid movies" because people need the resulting diversions—the consolations of aesthetic design—"like they need the air."[15] To create the first kind of artwork, in Allen's experience, has been to ensure himself a minuscule audience because, as Bates's producer, Walsh, puts it in *Stardust Memories,* "Too much reality is not what the people want" (p. 335). On the other hand, to produce artworks which basically sketch fetching designs on the void is to capitulate to the human desire for illusion, falsification, and bogus reassurance; and although Allen's films clearly establish that there *are* distinguishable degrees of illusion-mongering (a generic romantic kiss film ending being relatively less mendacious than the wasteland's inhabitants getting transported to a preposterous "jazz heaven"), in the end, an artwork lies, which doesn't—as *Stardust Memories* does—close on an image of human solitude and circumscription. To adopt Allen's favorite metaphor for artworks, if the magic trick works, it's a trick and therefore invalid as a suspension of the physical laws that oppress us; if the film reassures or consoles us about the human condition, it's done so by falsifying it.

Each of Allen's films delineates a slightly different configuration of the issue of art's capacity for celebrating human existence and falsifying it, but both inside of these movies (in the dramatization of the illusions underlying *The Purple Rose of Cairo* as well as in Alvy Singer's and Sandy Bates's imposition of unmotivated, unrealistically romantic resolutions on their artworks) and outside of them (in the "too neat and tidy finish" Allen accused himself of imposing upon *Hannah and Her Sisters*), Allen's cinematic art seems preoccupied with the possibility—or perhaps inevitability—that art lies.

As we've seen, that lie, in the dialectic Allen's films create, is not without its virtues. As Friedrich Nietzsche argued in an idiom different from Allen's but from a stance that the filmmaker would readily endorse, "From the beginning we have contrived to retain our ignorance in order to enjoy an almost inconceivable freedom, lack of scruple and caution, heartiness and gaiety of life—in order to enjoy life! And only on this solid, granite foundation of ignorance could knowledge rise so far—the will to knowledge on the foundation of a far more powerful will: the will to ignorance, to the uncertain, to the untrue!"[16] Even when we recognize the falsity of these artistic constructions—once we fully understand how tendentiously constructed they are, how much they are themselves products of the human desire we in the audience seek to gratify by entering the movie palace in the first place—we look outside the theater of illusions, see Monk and the Depression, or the Killer, or the un-air-conditioned, cacophonously clamorous streets of Brooklyn's Coney Island Avenue waiting. Like Cecilia, we snuggle back comfortably into the ersatz glamour of *Top Hat*, desperately embracing it even though we know that the set on which Fred and Ginger dance *is* a movie set, that the champagne they'll drink to slake their thirst is ginger ale, and that the "Heaven" their graceful choreography of male/female union projects so perfectly is only a word in a pop song lyric.

Like Kleinman in *Shadows and Fog,* Allen's most predominant 1990s response to this artistic conflict has been to say, "What better way to spend the rest of my life than to help with all those wonderful illusions of [Irmstedt's]?" because in committing himself to this enterprise he'll be "doing something I really love." But Kleinman/Allen suffers under no delusion that the illusions he/Irmstedt creates have any real power over the prevailing force at work in the world: the killer/Death. Consequently, the impotence of his art sometimes—as Bates's projected analyst suggests about his patient's art—makes him feel guilty, its contrivances and misrepresentations of actuality appearing to him as manifestations of some shallowness in himself, of some long-standing, deeply suspect need to make people laugh. At other times, however, the aspirations toward the magical which his films embody seem to Allen as their raison d'être: "I always loved magic as a boy, and I feel that the only way out of things is magic," he told Anthony DeCurtis. "Everything is so glum, so really depressing, that the only hope you have is . . . it would require magic, you know. There's no way, short of a magical solution. All the rational solutions, you know, are degrees of workable but not thrilling."[17]

If there is greatness in Allen's art comparable to that of the filmmakers he venerates, it may reside in the one place he'd be least liable to see it: in his films' continual debate between the human need to seriously confront the conditions of existence and the conflicting desire to wrest pleasure from the brief span of existence human beings have—"the ancient legitimate cure for mortality's anxieties," as Cynthia Ozick has described this remedy: "Seize the day."[18] Each film of Allen's since *Annie Hall* defines a slightly revised stance vis-à-vis Tom Baxter's appeal to Cecilia in *The Purple Rose of Cairo:* "I don't want to talk any more about what's real and what's illusion. Life's too short to spend time thinking about life. Let's just live it" (p. 440). The fact that Allen is dependent upon the highly technological process of film production to express this ideal of unreflectiveness represents what may be the central paradox of his art and life.

In sum, one of the things which makes Allen's cinematic oeuvre interesting to consider even when individual films seem less than completely successful is the debate he's conducting with himself from movie to movie over the value of art to lives—that is, the necessity of illusions to human psychic equilibrium—and the film-by-film reconceptualizing of his attitude toward art as the redemption of life and art as a deliberate distortion and falsification of life. The resolution of *Bullets Over Broadway* (1994) represents, as we've seen, Allen's most unambiguously negative appraisal of the artistic enterprise following *Interiors* and preceding *Deconstructing Harry* (1997). Contesting that verdict are four of his 1990s films—*Shadows and Fog* (1992), *Manhattan Murder Mystery* (1993), *Mighty Aphrodite* (1995), and *Everyone Says I Love You* (1996)— which embody markedly more positive attitudes toward the tissue of narrative artifice that is cinematic creation, these movies implicitly affirming and celebrating the consoling artifices of art. But then, *Celebrity* (1998) and *Sweet and Lowdown* (1999) depict the devotion to art as, respectively, inextricable from the corruptions of American tabloid culture and as a narcissistic evasion of life, as justification for circumventing the human relatedness which is at the center of the aesthetic exchange. Characteristically, Allen closed out the century offering cinematic cautions about the art whose indispensability to humanity he had begun its final decade by affirming.

In terms of Woody Allen's 1990s cinematic output, this overview omits only the film to which we turn next: *Husbands and Wives* (1992), Allen's most controversial and perhaps most distinctive movie with its raw, painful, and—for Allen—unprecedentedly personal projection of the vexed relationship between art and life.

14

Because It's Real Difficult in Life
Husbands and Wives

Oh, yeah. All right, well . . . well, go, go! See if I care. Go, see what it is
out there. . . . It ain't the movies! It's real life! It's real life, and you'll be
back! You mark my words! You'll be back!

—Monk warning Cecilia what awaits her out in the world
as she leaves him in *The Purple Rose of Cairo*

Now that the protracted media paroxysm with which *Husbands and Wives* was
so inextricably linked has receded into whatever part of the national memory
it is in which we store yesterday's scandals, it's more difficult to perceive the
movie as the source of extreme discomfort that so many of its reviewers described it as being. David Denby's reaction to the film typifies the frustrations
of reviewers attempting to respond critically to a work of art the tabloids had
already designated a cinematic *roman à clef.* Allen's characteristic disavowal of
autobiography in his films—"Movies are fiction," he told *Time,* "The plots of
my movies don't have any relationship to my life"[1]—convinced no one. "When
I saw *Husbands and Wives,*" Denby wrote in *Newsweek,* "the audience, caught
between loyalty and distaste, was clearly uncomfortable. So was I. Parts of the
movie are excruciating—the scenes between Woody Allen and Mia Farrow,
for instance, lack the minimal degree of illusion necessary to fiction. . . . I felt
like I was snooping."[2]

The twelve-year relationship between Allen and Mia Farrow was by all
accounts in a stage of terminal disintegration as the movie was being shot, and
surely that reality inflects the film's aura of marital discord and collapse. If
there is any justification for the insatiable curiosity the media and public dis-
played regarding the Farrow/Allen split, it lies in the fact that the thirteen
films they made together between 1981 and 1992 blurred the distinction
between the couple's private and public lives. In fact, four of those films look
like either celebrations of Farrow's private life virtues and/or metacommentaries
on the health of her private relationship with Allen. Dr. Eudora Fletcher's
loving solicitousness to Leonard Zelig's extraordinary psychic needs is clearly
what allows him to survive the media frenzy to which he's subjected, *Zelig*—
the couple's second film together—seeming to evoke Allen's sincere affection
for and gratitude to the partner whose relationship with him was practically as

public as is Fletcher's and Zelig's.[3] *Hannah and Her Sisters* offered a much less oblique and markedly more equivocal portrait of the relationship, the film never managing completely to reconcile the self-containment, WASP decorousness, and familial devotion of Hannah with the existential anxieties of Mickey Sachs except through the *deus ex machina* resolution of Mickey's miraculously restored fertility. *Alice* seems a sincere attempt on Allen's part to create a type character—the wealthy Manhattan mom with too much money, too many servants, and too little to do—whose dramatic evolution consists in her gradual acquisition of Farrow's maternal virtues and social conscience (though his original ending of having her travel to India to work with Mother Teresa among the poor seems to transform her from one type of character to another). In ways allegorical or literal, depending on the viewer's reading of the film, *Husbands and Wives* marks the emotionally antagonistic end of their relationship. If viewers share the illusion of possessing special insight into the evolution of the Farrow/Allen relationship—from the private/public amicability of *Zelig* to the rancorous abrogations of *Husbands and Wives*—their illusion is one which Allen's movies have clearly contributed to fostering.

Even if viewers don't share Denby's sense of intruding on private grief in watching the Farrow/Allan scenes of *Husbands and Wives,* few would deny that the raw edges of the breakup's contentiousness are manifested in the remarkably unAllenesque raggedness of Carlo Di Palma's cinematography, as well as in the plot's relentless dramatization of the narcissism which inspires the characters to perceive others purely as means to their own self-gratifications. Admittedly, the film's technique was an innovation for Allen, one seemingly intended to undermine the uniform, visually centered, and stable framing of the Hollywood style characteristic of Allen's own previous work. Less unprecedented was the film's exploration of the narcissism of erotic attraction, Allen and Farrow having delved into this psychological theme in *September* and *Another Woman,* neither film proving any more successful than is *Husbands and Wives* in presenting a solution to the *Civilization and Its Discontents* conflict between the need for the formation of stable families built on trust and the incessant demands of the libido. Perhaps it's because *Husbands and Wives* is one of only three films—the others being *Zelig* and *Broadway Danny Rose*—in which Allen's protagonist and Farrow's character comprise a couple that reviewers like Denby found the arguments between Gabe and Judy Roth so painful to witness. Nonetheless, there was very substantial and very public evidence that Allen and Farrow split over quite different issues than the ones that divide Judy and Gabe.

Although Gabe's attraction to a much younger woman prompted many reviewers to draw parallels with Allen's relationship with Farrow's adopted daughter, Soon-Yi, little else in the film's plot (which concerns several forming and dispersing couples, not just one) seems directly to mirror the far more lurid Farrow/Allen breakup. In fact, Elliot's infidelity with Hannah's sister in *Hannah and Her Sisters* could be said to more closely resemble the circumstances chronicled so sensationally by tabloids in 1992–1993 than anything in *Husbands and Wives,* both subversions of familial trust and solidarity involving adultery with a family member.

It's always misguided to impute one-to-one correspondences between Allen's life and his screenplays, and reading *Husbands and Wives* as pure autobiography is certainly to misinterpret and distort the film. It would be even more seriously unreasonable to believe that *Husbands and Wives* offers details of Allen's private life as if it were a cinematic version of the tell-all book Isaac Davis's ex-wife publishes about their marriage in *Manhattan* or the memoir that book now seems to have prefigured, Mia Farrow's memoir, *What Falls Away.* At the same time, responsible criticism of Allen's work must also recognize how insistently a few of his films—*Stardust Memories, Hannah and Her Sisters, Radio Days,* and *Deconstructing Harry* are the other most obvious examples—intrude the issues of autobiography into their narratives as inescapable components of the films' constructions. In essence, none can be adequately interpreted without critical attention being paid to the ambiguous role that Allen's self-extrapolation of a protagonist in the movies plays in relation to him.

As we've seen, it's not entirely clear whether Sandy Bates or Woody Allen is exiting the Stardust Auditorium at the end of *Stardust Memories,* the film having irremediably conflated them, while to turn *Radio Days* from a series of nostalgic/comic vignettes into a consonant, artistically coherent film, it's necessary to recognize filmmaker Allen's mediating presence—his deliberately celebratory cinematic visualizing of what Little Joe and his family could only imagine when they heard it described on the radio. The very intentional failure of *Husbands and Wives* to reach any form of closure or resolution is a consequence of the film's formal dislocations having their correlative in the narrative's irresolvably ambiguous relation to the real-life experiences of its actors. That the film lacks, in Denby's characterization, "the minimal degree of illusion necessary to fiction" reflects its rejection of the blandishments of artistic distance, its calculated refusal to function according to the aesthetic defense Alvy Singer offers for his first play in *Annie Hall:* "You know how you're always trying to get things to work out in art because it's real difficult in life." In *Husbands and Wives,* the impossibility of "getting things to work out in life" is translated into a cinematic indictment of the very art which seeks to order and render humanly coherent that impossibility. *Husbands and Wives* comes as close as an Allen film ever does to fulfilling the conditions evoked by Cecilia of *The Purple Rose Of Cairo* in her effort to describe a universe without God to Tom Baxter: "It'd be like a movie with no point and no happy ending" (p. 408).

Husbands and Wives is distinctive among Allen's films for the extent to which its cinematography and scene construction reproduce the raw emotionality of the film's plot and the bitter disjunctions which are its subject matter. As was suggested in the discussion of *Bullets Over Broadway,* Allen's films are generally characterizable as "well-made" movies: their narrative devices (the use of voice-overs in *Annie Hall, Broadway Danny* Rose, and *Hannah and Her Sisters,* for example) tend to be transparent, undistracting (because their relationship to the plot is clearly specified), and purposeful, and however heated the emotional interiors of his movies, the presentation of scenes tends toward orderliness and coherence. Allen's dependence upon master shots as opposed to editing reinforces his films' aura of continuity, of cohesive seamlessness. (Given the general absence of visual innovation in his movies and his self-acknowledged debt to American playwrights, it seems not completely inappropriate to describe Allen as a naturalistic dramatist working in the medium of film.) The fact that Allen has used basically the same style of opening and closing titles since *Sleeper* epitomizes the overall consistency of his annual cinematic productions, the often bewildering narrative shifts of *Stardust Memories* representing the exception that proves the rule of his characteristic formal methodicalness and uniformity of scene sequencing and composition.[4] Their humor is undoubtedly the primary reason Allen's films draw the audience they do, one fairly sizable in proportion to their production budgets; the clarity of dramatic presentation, visual precision, straightforward realism, and overall accessibility of his movies are other, not inconsiderable sources of their attractiveness.[5]

With its neat chapter-by-chapter construction, punctilious interweaving of narratives and symmetry-favoring scene construction unusually brightly lit by Carlo Di Palma, *Hannah and Her Sisters* is, arguably, the quintessence of the Woody Allen well-made film. Consequently, *Hannah* is Allen's oeuvre's most extreme stylistic antithesis to *Husbands and Wives.*[6] In discussing *Husbands and Wives,* contrasts between these two films can be repeatedly invoked for two reasons: because *Husbands and Wives* so emphatically recants the commitments tentatively dramatized in *Hannah,* and because it is the stylistic virtues of *Hannah,* with their implied identification of artistic decorum with familial affirmation, that Allen sought to repudiate and subvert in making *Husbands and Wives.*

Allen explained to Stig Bjorkman the motivation underlying the deliberately uncentered cinematography of *Husbands and Wives*: "I've always been thinking that so much time is wasted and so much devoted to the prettiness of films and the delicacy and the precision. Pick up the camera, forget about the dolly, just hand-hold the thing and get what you can. And then, don't worry about colour correcting it, don't worry about mixing it so much, don't worry about all the precision stuff and see what happens. When you feel like cutting, just cut. Don't worry about that it's going to jump or anything. Just do what you want, forget about anything but the content of the film. And that's what I did."[7]

The opening titles of *Husbands and Wives*, scrolling over a remarkably lugubrious version of "What is This Thing Called Love?,"[8] reflect Allen's trademark mode of introducing his films, but the scene which follows little resembles what we expect from a Woody Allen movie. Whereas camera movement in his films is normally stable, unintrusive, and "natural," Carlo Di Palma's camera in the opening scene seems to be attempting to reproduce Judy's emotional response to the announcement by their closest friends, Sally (Judy Davis) and Jack (Sydney Pollack), of their separation: "I just feel shattered—I *do*." Described by Allen as "fighting for its life to keep the characters in frame,"[9] the camera caroms uncertainly from one character to another as they bat the sad news back and forth among themselves, its framing eye seldom arriving on time to visualize the person speaking before it has to swivel off wildly in the direction of the next speaker. Often, the best it can do is to approximate the position of the speaker it strives to locate, the ill-composed images of the speaking characters, positioning them to the left or right of center of the frame, reflecting the fact that the scene—like many in the movie and practically all in life—had never been blocked.[10] In *Manhattan, Crimes and Misdemeanors*, and other films, Allen occasionally allows characters to walk out of scenes, the camera focusing on the background they've left as their dialogue continues. In the beginning of *Husbands and Wives*, the camera seems utterly helpless to keep up with the characters' movements, at one point losing Judy (Farrow) completely as she flees angrily for her bedroom, focusing pointlessly on a fireplace she's passed before zooming clumsily in futile pursuit of her down the hallway she's already vacated. (Gabe will have parallel difficulties staying with Judy toward the end of the film, ultimately losing her as completely as the camera does.) Compared to the more characteristic scene composition and camera movement of Allen's productions, the opening scene *of Husbands and Wives* seems to have contracted delirium tremens, Di Palma's handheld camera enacting its experience of free-floating anxiety and terminal loss of moorings as the characters vent to each other about their analogously dislocated psychic conditions.

The opening scene cuts to a medium close-up of Judy being asked a question by a male voice off-camera (Jeffrey Kurland, Allen's longtime costume designer). She candidly answers his intimate question concerning the night of Jack and Sally's revelation and waits unperturbed for his next inquiry. His cross-examinations continue with other characters sporadically throughout the film, and he becomes the narrator of significant passages of it as well. Since no attempt is made to establish whether this voice is a therapist, a sociologist, a documentary filmmaker, or what, the movie's refusal to integrate this *cinema verité* presence into the plot leaves that significant narrative dimension of the film gapingly open and ambiguous. Like the God whom Gabe, in the movie's first line of dialogue, characterizes as not playing dice with the universe but who instead "just plays hide and seek" with it, this narrator/interlocutor is everywhere and nowhere in the film, human testimony to the triumph of the therapeutic, which *Husbands and Wives* continually dramatizes and tacitly laments.

As the movie continues, it gradually settles into a somewhat more conventional cinematographic mode, only in moments of emotional extremity reverting to the eccentric, anxiously decentered cinematic style in which it began. Nonetheless, it's clear that in *Husbands and Wives,* Allen is deliberately jettisoning many of the techniques of narrative coherence and manifestations of "well-madeness" which he relies upon to focus and stabilize his other films.[11] The raggedness of *Husbands and Wives'* pseudodocumentary *cinema verité* style effectively replicates the raggedness of the characters' deeply ravaged interior lives while implicitly repudiating the actuality-distorting blandishments of dramatic construction which rounded off the rough edges of films like *Hannah.* Di Palma's handheld camera's conjuring of instability in the world of *Husbands and Wives* is the film's most apparent technical decentering ploy, but the plot is equally permeated with misdirections and equivocations evocative of a humanly atomized reality.

One such plot element is introduced by Gabe's comment to Judy after they've learned of the Sally and Jack separation: "You think you're so friendly with people and so close, and then it turns out you have no idea what they're thinking." In confirmation of this comment, Allen's script has Gabe tell Judy (and thus the viewer) what he knows about Jack's extramarital meanderings preceding the separation. Acting on Jack's confession that his marriage isn't sexually fulfilling, a business associate of Jack's (Bruce Jay Friedman) gave him the name of an expensive call girl, Gabe explains; resisting the temptation with difficulty, Gabe adds, Jack tore up her phone number. The film cuts from Gabe's assertion of his friend's incorruptibility to a young woman being interviewed by the film's narrator/interrogator: she is the call girl to whom Jack actually made numerous visits, her revelations including the fact that she set Jack up with another call girl with whom he also had repeated assignations. The moral issues raised by the prostitute's revelations are significant, especially in terms of their reflection on the likelihood of Sally and Jack's film-closing reconciliation surviving their unresolved sexual problems and Jack's philandering proclivities, but perhaps more important to the movie's central themes is their exposure of Jack's duplicity in his dealings with both Sally and Gabe.

"Do you ever hide things from me?" Judy asks Gabe after he tells her his version of Jack's resistance of temptation, "—feelings, you know, longings, complaints?" Gabe responds in the negative, but in doing so he's hiding things from her: as the documentarian's interrogations of individual characters and the narrative's dramatic scenes jointly confirm, *all* the characters in this movie conceal things from the others, clandestinely pursuing emotional and erotic agendas in violation of their moral and legal contracts. If *Husbands and Wives* validates any single assertion made during the Allen/Farrow contention, it's Allen's much-quoted self-justification, "The heart wants what it wants. There's no logic to those things. You meet someone and you fall in love and that's that."[12]

At the end of *Hannah and Her Sisters,* the human heart is affirmatively dramatized as a "resilient little muscle," one capable of withstanding rejection and rising from it to sing the celebratory Cole Porter song that Holly and Mickey watch Bobby Short perform—"I'm in Love Again." In *Husbands and Wives,* the heart is the repository of emotional and sexual inconstancy and concealment, its theme song the dourly interrogatory Cole Porter composition, "What is This Thing Called Love?"[13] Of Allen's films, only *September* presents the human heart as being more disastrously subject to misguided romantic object choices and misplaced, self-destructive affections than does *Husbands and Wives.* Jack regularly visits prostitutes while secretly buying lingerie for someone other than Sally; despite (or because of) his knowledge of her "kamikaze woman" proclivities, Gabe is strongly attracted to Rain (Juliette Lewis), a student in his Columbia University fiction writing class; Judy "has feelings for" Michael (Liam Neeson), a co-worker to whom she has introduced Sally; Sally alone plays by the rules of monogamous fidelity, a circumstance attributable, it seems, to her sexual dysfunctionality. The more striking exception to the rule of human erotic inconstancy in *Husbands and Wives* is

Rain's parents, whose twenty-five years of marriage have resulted, apparently, in stability and happiness. Their example, however, hasn't proved transferable to the next generation, the "kamikaze woman" of a daughter they've raised having, at the age of twenty-one, already experienced numerous fractious love affairs with men over fifty.[14] At the end of the film, Gabe and Judy are divorced, she having married Michael; Jack and Sally have successfully reconciled; and Gabe's reward for terminating his embryonic affair with Rain is his relegation to solitude.[15] Like Nick Carraway, who concludes *The Great Gatsby* forswearing the "privileged glimpses into the human heart" which constitute his story, Gabe, having grown weary both of his erotic pursuits and of turning them into patently autobiographical fictional narratives, has abandoned his confessional novel in favor of a "more political" work of fiction—one assumedly less preoccupied with the human capacity to love.

"Maybe the poets are right," Mickey Sachs muses in *Hannah and Her Sisters,* "maybe love is the only answer" (p. 109). The generically determined comedic/romantic ending of *Hannah* seems to confirm this judgment, since the film's five major characters are all visually dramatized in attitudes of love achieved, revived, or recaptured in the movie's radiant closing Thanksgiving scene. Members of the two couples reformed and dissolved in the course of *Husbands and Wives* are interviewed at the end of the film, their *cinema verité* discourses upon love and marriage engendering more doubts about the solidity of erotic relationships than they resolve. Jack attributes his reunion with Sally—despite an unresolved sexual incompatibility—to the idea that "you can't just wipe out years of closeness"; in their final dialogue together in the film, Gabe accordingly recalls for Judy two of their warmest moments of closeness: their decision to skip a Columbia faculty party and walk through a snowbound Central Park, and the night they watched *Wild Strawberries* together until dawn.[16] Judy's response not only constitutes her refusal to be drawn into a nostalgia-inspired reconciliation with Gabe, but it also represents something approaching a recantation of the affirmation which proves provisionally redemptive in other Allen films. "All that stuff," she objects, "those memories, they're just memories, they're just moments from years gone by. They're isolated moments—they don't tell the whole story."

The "whole story" of Sandy Bates's relationship with Dorrie, Judy's objection would suggest, can't be epitomized by the "Stardust memory" of a lovely Sunday morning idyll any more than the aesthetic joy engendered by *Wild Strawberries*—or by *Duck Soup*—is anything other than a passing emotional experience; consequently, it is nothing upon which to predicate the continuation of a marriage—or of an existence.[17] Gabe's attempt to reduce a complex past to representative "isolated moments" partakes of precisely the same emotional need for the memorial restructuring of experience which makes films seem a distortion to Allen: the metonymic attempt to make "the world stand still here," to reduce its complexly on-rushing fluxion to humanly grati-fying shapes and stories, necessarily falsifies actuality. (The larger cultural pro-jection of this impulse is equally fraudulent, according to Harry Block in *Deconstructing Harry:* "Tradition," he explains, "is the illusion of perma-nence."[18]) In *Husbands and Wives*, nothing—Di Palma's camera in particu-lar—stands still, and rather than affirming his now-terminated relationship with Judy by recalling fond moments, as Alvy does in the denouement of *Annie Hall* and Sandy Bates does through his "Stardust memory," in the film's final line, Gabe instead invokes the omnipotence of temporality, the utter human subjectedness to time: "Can I go? Is this over?"

Many in the audience at the time of the film's release would need a copy of the day's *New York Post* in order to confidently answer that question, so ensnared in the popular mind had the production of *Husbands and Wives* become with the disintegration of the Allen/Farrow relationship. Although Allen routinely insisted that Gabe and Judy are fictional characters, Farrow's reading of the film disagreed. In *The New York Times*, Maureen Dowd quoted Farrow as "expressing dismay that Mr. Allen had made her play out a fictional version of the triangle with her adopted daughter, Soon-Yi, before she learned of the affair."[19] One needn't accept Farrow's interpretation, however, to find in *Husbands and Wives* substantial evidence testifying to the impartibility of art and life. Gabe's novel (which often serves as the film's equivalent in the plot, both—in Rain's characterization—presenting "all this suffering and making it so funny"[20]) includes a barely fictionalized version of his and Judy's meeting in the Hamptons, which the viewer sees in flashback, Judy explicitly objecting to her husband's self-serving appropriation of this scene from their marriage for artistic purposes. Gabe's attempt to placate Judy by praising the character modeled on her—"She's the best woman in the book; that's why he married her"—only evinces his inability to separate art and life. Gabe Roth's heedless aesthetic imperialism links him to Holly in *Hannah and Her Sisters* and to Harry Block of *Deconstructing Harry*, but his surname clearly identifies him with another artist who has made a career of scandalously transforming his personal experience into art—Philip Roth.[21]

Rain's critique of Gabe's manuscript is a sophisticated reading of the text as a reflection of the character and values of its author, her indictment inevita-bly widening outward to include the author's author in its condemnation. "Isn't it beneath you as a mature thinker," Rain asks Gabe, "to allow your lead character to waste so much of his emotional energy obsessing over this psy-chotic relationship with a woman that you fantasize as powerfully sexual and inspired when in fact she was pitifully sick?" The appearance of Gabe's "kami-kaze woman"—a woman whose erotic attractiveness is inseparable from her mental instability—is what Rain is disparaging in his novel, it having not occurred to her that, were she to have a role in his life, that would be it. Her critique reinforces the film's ongoing demonstration that Gabe's existential fixations and erotic conflicts are the stuff of his fiction, while extending beyond him to remind the viewer how regularly "kamikaze women" like Mary Wilke in *Manhattan* and Dorrie and Daisy of *Stardust Memories* appear in Allen's films. (Jack, in turn, completes the circle by ascribing Gabe's erotic vulnerability to "kamikaze women" to popular media: "Like all of us," he explains, Gabe "grew up with movies and novels in which doomed love was romantic.") It's also difficult to ignore how similar the section of his novel visualized in the film recalls Allen's episodically structured *Everything You Wanted to Know About Sex* and anticipates the dramatization of scenes from Harry Block's fiction in *Deconstructing Harry*. If there is anything *Husbands and Wives* is *not* about, clearly, it is absolute demarcations between art and life. Allen's awareness of the artistic potential for exploiting his and others' personal grief for the purposes of making a film is even more self-consciously revisited in *Deconstructing Harry*, which, as Allen threatened to do a year before its release, goes "right into the teeth" of the public's view of him by having him portray a "nasty, shallow, superficial, sexually obsessed guy. I'm sure everybody will think—I know this going in—they'll think it's me."[22] They're wrong, of course; but Allen has contrived in making that film—as he had in creating *Stardust Memories, Radio Days, Hannah and Her Sisters,* and *Husbands and Wives*—to make it impossible for the viewer to confidently distinguish fact from fiction, autobiography from story.

A sex-obsessed guy named Harry Block isn't Woody Allen, any more than a red-haired kid named Joe or a demoralized filmmaker named Sandy is, and the popular media's inability—or refusal—to distinguish between an estranged couple in a movie and a real-life couple whose separation hadn't occurred when the film was being scripted is surely irresponsible, if not comical. At the same time, for Allen to pretend that a film which insists (as many of his screenplays do) on the autobiographical basis of art should be read completely in isolation from the real-world circumstances that clearly inspired its mood and certainly influence its plot reflects an equally oversimplified understanding of the complex transactions between art and life which are his films and which so often comprise the subject of his movies. What makes absolutely no sense, of course, is for the viewer to believe that what happens on the screen bears a one-to-one relationship to Woody Allen's life, to believe that s/he knows anything true about Allen or his relationships from watching his movies. Far more reasonable and justifiable is Denby's reaction, which affirms the discomfort arising from viewers' inability to separate their knowledge about the director and female lead from their emotional responses to the film. Because of its subject matter, *Husbands and Wives* seems to deliberately exploit that conflict in the audience, making watching the film feel like an invasion of real people's privacy—"I felt like I was snooping," as Denby complained. Creating those feelings of discomfort in Denby and other viewers is Allen's chief rhetorical strategy in *Husbands and Wives,* the deliberate blurring of fact and fiction in the movie giving the audience an emotional experience equivalent to the characters' feelings of betrayal, demoralization, and disorientation. Many of the same reviewers who found the movie's aura of autobiographical self-disclosure painful to witness also expressed incomprehension about the identity of the film's narrator/interrogator and the relevance of Carlo Di Palma's lurching handheld cinematography. (Jokes in reviews about Dramamine being sold at concession stands in theaters showing the movie were very popular.) These devices, along with its fiction/autobiography conflations, make *Husbands and Wives* Allen's least artistically consonant film, which is to say the one least possessed of the aesthetic contrivances and artifices that shape and lend coherence to works of art. In Denby's formulation, the film lacks "the minimal degree of illusion necessary to fiction" because it deliberately complicates the issue of what "degree of illusion" is necessary to effective fictional rendering, pushing the envelope of anti-aesthetic form as far as Allen is likely to push it. In a film whose central question is "Do you ever hide things from me?" *Husbands and Wives* reduces both characters and cinematic techniques to a level of nakedness unprecedented in Allen's work, the characteristic civility of his films giving way to profanity (Sally's explosion, "Fucking Don Juans—they should have cut his fucking dick off," for instance), violence (Jack's ugly attempts to force Sam [Lysette Anthony], with whom he's been living, into his car as they leave a party at which they've quarreled), and camera movements and scene compositions evocative of such emotional eruptions. Nor, as in most Allen films, do viewers have the luxury of reassuring themselves that what is on the screen is only fictional fabrication—because they have no way of knowing which scenes derive from actual events and which don't—or that the consolations of aesthetic form will kick in to generate a meaningful artistic resolution. "I'm exaggerating for comic purposes," is Gabe's defense of his novel to Rain, "I'm deliberately distorting it in order to show how hard it is to be married." What the viewer of this most peevish of Allen's cinematic inbreeding of fact and fiction never knows is what is distorted life and what isn't. Let the movie's characterization of Judy serve to exemplify *Husbands and Wives'* discomfort-inducing conflation of art and life.

Husbands and Wives revisits a central tension of *Hannah and Her Sisters,* this time generating a less gratifying resolution of it. In *Hannah,* the issue of the title character's aura of independence and self-containment, which is dramatized simultaneously as one of her virtues and as a source of her loved ones' resentment, is dissolved by the termination of Elliot's affair with Lee and his reconciliation with Hannah. "I don't deserve you" is Elliot's summation upon their rapprochement, he having apparently forgotten that this conviction about his wife's superiority had contributed to his attraction to the significantly less-

194 THE RELUCTANT FILM ART OF WOODY ALLEN

accomplished Lee in the first place. In *Husbands and Wives,* Hannah's self-suffi-
ciency and relentless decency reemerges more emphatically in Judy as passive-
aggressive behavior; both of her first two husbands in the film comment on
her tendency to get what she wants from men by assuring them, "No, no, I'll
be okay, don't help me." Like Hannah, Judy is quick to offer help to others,
but her personal agenda in doing so is more transparent. Her ostensible penchant for other-directedness elicits an explosion from Michael when she assures him that she is "not pushing" him to spend a Sunday with her while he
attempts to get over the loss of Sally. "Yes, you are," he angrily responds, "in
that quiet, steady way of yours. You're always there for me. Supportive is your
word—understanding. God—stop being so damned understanding!" When
she runs from the room in tears, Michael follows her out into the rain, embracing her and swearing, "I don't deserve you—I'm sorry." Once they have married, the interrogator/narrator asks Judy and Michael how things are. Judy admits
great satisfaction with her third marriage but expresses concern with how it
came about. "I hope I didn't push," she says, "I wanted it to work, it's true."

"I told you," is her first ex-husband's summary: "she gets what she wants."

John Baxter describes Hannah as "so generous, understanding and vir-
tuous [that] she's almost insupportable," Allen's fourth biographer suggesting
that she and Marion Post, the protagonist of *Another Woman,* "hint at a subtext
of resentment felt by Allen towards the woman with whom he was, however
tentatively, sharing his life."[23] The characterization of Judy in *Husbands and
Wives* extends that critique by emphasizing the disparity between Judy's self-
effacing exterior and the effectuality with which she carries out her private
agendas. *What Falls Away,* with its consistent depiction of Farrow as a passive
recipient of fortune and the world's ills, reinforces Baxter's identification. The
affectively New Age memoir never reveals a trace of the young actress who
once affirmed, "I want a big career, a big man, and a big life. You have to think
big. That's the only way to get it."[24] Similarly, the memoir's sincere celebration
of Farrow's family often lapses into sanctimoniousness and melodramatic prose
posturings which belie the very real achievement her assemblage and sustenance of that family is. The viewer never hears any of the poetry Judy shows
Michael in *Husbands and Wives,* but it's not surprising that the woman on
whom she's modeled is capable of the poetic flights of *What Falls Away,* a
number of which could have benefitted from the editorial critique of someone like Gabe, whom Judy considers "too critical" and "not supportive enough"
to show her poems to.[25]

It's easy to attribute the pervasive negativism evoked by the formal
frazzledness of *Husbands and Wives* to the tabloid battles being fought out
while it was in production, and to settle for the interpretation that it is simply
a film in which art is mirroring life in a particularly pessimistic and unsettling
way. ("Life doesn't imitate art," a line in one of Rain's stories contends, "it

imitates bad television.") Although real-world bad feeling surely inflects the mood of the movie, it's not really necessary to go outside the film to account for its consistently anti-aesthetic impulses. As is usually the case in Allen's films, anti-aesthetic attitudes in *Husbands and Wives* are traceable to art's being indivisible from the human.

Both Gabe and Judy offer their literary efforts—his novel, her poems—to Rain and Michael, characters to whom they are physically attracted, thereby exploiting their work as seduction tools, the sharing of their writing signaling openness to greater intimacy far more than any desire for serious textual criticism. In one of his exchanges with the interviewer, Gabe expands upon his own confusion between the aesthetic and erotic. He intimately confesses his attraction to "kamikaze women—women who crash their plane—they're self-destructive—but they crash it into you . . . If there are hurdles or obstacles" to the relationship's developing, Gabe explains, they represent increased erotic inducements to pursuing it: "Maybe because I'm a writer . . . some dramatic or aesthetic component becomes right, and I go after that person. It's almost as if there's a certain . . . some dramatic ambiance . . . it's almost as if I fall in love with the person and in love with the situation in some way, and it hasn't worked out well for me at all."[26]

As Julian Fox noticed, Gabe's "attraction to the free-spirited Rain" dramatizes the same art/life confusion, since her allure "is as much due to her literary promise as her precocious sexuality."[27] For Gabe—as for *Bullets Over Broadway*'s Sheldon Flender—eroticism and aesthetics have become inseparable and indistinguishable, both having their genesis in the ego. It's only appropriate, then, that this movie in which Gabe appears embodies an attitude toward the formal qualities of filmic rendering as jaded as the one it enacts toward the possibilities of meaningful romance. Allen's assurances to the press about the fictionality of *Husbands and Wives* were completely justified by the media's deliberate oversimplification of the relationship between art and life in their reactions to the film, but Allen's screenplay nonetheless provides significant evidence that literary plots and sexual attraction—art and life—have the same source, and that the contrivances of artistic representation are indistinguishable from the erotic treachery the movie so relentlessly exposes.

Consequently, *Husbands and Wives* is the Woody Allen film in which art and life most closely—and most dishearteningly—converge with each other, the dynamic of narrative getting sourly configured as sexual desire's correlative and mirror.[28] And, once again, *Hannah and Her Sisters* provides the most dramatic antithesis: the concluding Hannah/Elliot reunion and Holly/Mickey union affirm the divisibility of art and life, dramatizing the superiority of unmediated heart over the calculations of art. Subsequent Allen films will relegate art and life to disparate realms, largely by projecting good-feeling narratives hell-bent on generating upbeat resolutions: the most effective of these films, *Bullets Over Broadway,* resuscitates the art/life antinomy only to clearly dramatize the repudiation of art in favor of life. As for his education in the erotics of art and the art of erotics, Gabe has resolved to move on from his confessional novel to one "more political," but for him, as for his creator, the perception of human nature articulated by the leader of the chorus in *Mighty Aphrodite* explains why any such project is highly unlikely to work for either of them: "Curiosity—that's what kills us. Not muggers or that bullshit about the ozone layer. It's our hearts and minds."[29] The hearts and minds of the characters in *Manhattan Murder Mystery, Mighty Aphrodite,* and *Everyone Says I Love You* are substantially less egocentrically disloyal than those in *Husbands and Wives,* and even that latter film ends on the slightly leavening note of Gabe's decision not to indulge his curiosity about Rain's erotic attractions, resolving to let this "kamikaze woman" crash her plane into someone else. In any event, *Husbands and Wives* is the film which comes closest to repudiating the affirmations—the resiliency of the heart, the redemptiveness of memory, the reassuring, existence-structuring, meaning-imbuing capacities of art—on which earlier Allen movies close. "Maybe in the end," Gabe ends one of his stories, "the idea was not to expect too much out of life"—or out of the art which is its distorting mirror and product, either.

15

Rear Condo

Manhattan Murder Mystery

But that's fiction, that's movies . . . I mean . . . I mean, you see too many movies. I'm talking about reality. If you want a happy ending, you should see a Hollywood movie.

—Judah critiquing Cliff's interpretation of Judah's perfect murder plot in *Crimes and Misdemeanors*

The projection of human need upon reality's ceaseless flux and the subsequent, inevitable disillusionment of that effort often dramatized by Allen's films is most eloquently described by a physicist, Lloyd (Jack Warden), in *September*. Asked what he sees when he looks out into the universe, Lloyd replies, "I think it's as beautiful as you do. And vaguely evocative of some deep truth that always just keeps slipping away. But then my professional perspective overcomes me. A less wishful, more penetrating view of it. And I understand it for what it truly is: haphazard, morally neutral, and unimaginably violent."[1] Kleinman's characterization of reality after the fog has once again obscured the stars agrees with Lloyd's account and with Gabe's emotional experience in *Husbands and Wives*, while adding a note on personal consequences of this perception: "Everything's always moving all the time . . . No wonder I'm nauseous."

In their omnibus interview, Allen suggested to Stig Bjorkman that he might return to the "get what you can and move on" cinematography of *Husbands and Wives* in subsequent films because "it's inexpensive and it gets the job done"[2]; however, Gabe's closing line—"Is it over now? Can I go?"—seems to summarize his feelings about having been subjected to the decentered, "moving all the time" cinematography of the film, and perhaps Allen's as well. The calculated raggedness of that technique, one reminiscent of John Cassavetes' idiosyncratic style of shooting scenes, perfectly suits material evocative of erotic duplicity and the isolating dynamics of human desire; it's poorly suited, however, to the projection of the more upbeat tonality which is ultimately Allen's cinematic touchstone and trademark. "In the end, we are earthbound," Allen told John Lahr in 1996, invoking the emotional tenor of *Husbands and Wives* before shifting to a discussion of the antithetical (and, if successful, antidotal) mode which would predominate in his following four films: comedy. It is comedy's capacity, he explained, to "defy all that pulls you down, that eventually pulls you all the way down. The comedian is always involved in that attempt somehow, through some artifice or trick, to get you airborne. Being able to suggest that something magical is possible, that something other than what you see with your eyes and your senses is possible, opens up a crack in the negative."[3]

This affirmative stance belies a desperation which Allen expresses later in Lahr's essay/interview, echoing the speech he had written for *September's* physicist: "The only hope any of us have is magic. . . . If there turns out to be no magic—and this is simply it, it's simply physics—it's very sad."[4] The literalness with which three of Allen's films—A *Midsummer Night's Sex Comedy, Alice,* and "Oedipus Wrecks"—attempt cinematically to incarnate this assertion indicates that the desire to generate movie magic doesn't inevitably produce movie magic: the "spirit box" Andrew has invented, Dr. Yang and his herbs, and the magic which installs Sheldon Mills's mother in the skies over Manhattan all fall somewhere between transparent plot devices and jokes the film is playing on its characters. To an extent, of course, Allen's comedy is always tottering on the brink of self-parody, and "Oedipus Wrecks" gladly tumbles over the edge in order to comically hyperbolize Mills's obsession with his mother. *Sex Comedy* and *Alice,* on the other hand, seem uncertain how seriously to take their magical realist elements, the former suggesting that sexuality, not the spirit world, is the motivating force behind human behavior, the latter using Dr. Yang's sorcery to precipitate a transparently generic dramatic character reversal.[5]

Conveying the reality of magic has proven particularly difficult for Allen largely because of his own skepticism about its existence, the awareness he dramatized in *The Purple Rose of Cairo* and *Radio Days* of how thoroughly the human desire that magic be real can seem its own confirmation despite overwhelming evidence to the contrary. Consequently, Allen's attempts to evoke magical moments often leave the impression conveyed by the scene from *Alice* in which Alice (Mia Farrow) and Eddie (Alec Baldwin) fly over Manhattan: this isn't magic but movie magic, special effects rather than spells.[6] With the exception of *Bullets Over Broadway* (which construes magic's stand-in, art, as egocentricity pretentiously commodified), Allen's 1993–1996 films were dedicated in varying degrees to affirming that "the only hope we have is magic," even if the forms that magic takes are the merely everyday sorceries: movie murder mystery plotting and detection (*Manhattan Murder Mystery*), of the transformative powers of Eros (*Mighty Aphrodite*); and the ubiquity of the human dependency upon romance (*Everyone Says I Love You*). It is not Kleinman's idea that "When I see something with my own eyes, I like to know that it's really there" which pervades these films, but instead it is Allen's more hopeful construal of art as a medium manifesting that "something other than what you see with your eyes and your senses is possible." These movies embody the lesson learned by Mickey Sachs in *Hannah and Her Sisters,* Allen predicating his mid-'90s filmmaking career, as Sachs does his life, on the "slim reed" of "maybe": "And I'm thinking to myself, geez, I should stop ruining my life . . . searching for answers I'm never gonna get, and just enjoy it while it lasts. And, you know, after all, who knows? I mean, you know, maybe there is something. I know, I know 'maybe' is a very slim reed to hang your life on, but that's the best we have. And . . . then I started to sit back, and I actually began to enjoy myself" (*Hannah,* p. 172).

Cynics would charge that these films are far more about Woody Allen enjoying himself than they are about projecting some philosophically portentous "maybe" on which lives might be predicated; because he's generally honest about what he perceives as his greatest temptations in filmmaking, the best of these movies include amidst their celebrations of existence dramatic countercurrents of skepticism about their own impulses toward affirmation. In their cinematic projection of the debate Allen is conducting with himself over the human need to believe in the magical and that need's distortion of the very thing whose existence we seek to confirm, Allen's 1993–1996 films constitute both effective comedies and honest attempts on Allen's part to create what he isn't sure exists anywhere but on movie screens.

As if in reaction against the disquietingly unmoored cinematic technique of *Husbands and Wives,* Allen's next film, *Manhattan Murder Mystery,* begins with a distinct return to his more visually stable and precisely calculated cinematic style.[7] Its steady, even pan across the New York skyline from the air culminates in a perfectly framed image of Madison Square Garden as Bobby Short plays Cole Porter's "I Happen to Like New York" on the soundtrack, the sequence recalling, as Philip Kemp noticed, the "Rhapsody in Blue" beginning of *Manhattan.*[8] Reinforcing the sense that the world filtered through Woody Allen's glasses has been restored to normalcy is the fact that the camera, completely ignoring the Rangers game being played on the ice and the rest of the Garden crowd, cuts immediately to and focuses steadily upon two spectators: Allen and Diane Keaton. (As the tabloids breathlessly informed their readers, Keaton had taken on the role of Carol Lipton when the estrangement between Allen and Farrow necessitated recasting the part he had written for her.[9]) The state of the marriage of Larry (Allen) and Carol (Keaton) Lipton is epitomized by the bargain of cultural sublimation they've struck with each other: she'll sit through a Rangers game if he watches an entire Wagner opera with her. (She keeps her part of the agreement; he walks out of the opera because "I can't listen to that much Wagner. I start getting the urge to conquer Poland.") Although Carol has many of the diffident character traits of Allen's female protagonists (she wants to do significant work in the world but isn't sure what kind, this confusion feeding her want of self-confidence), she is the one who recognizes the stale peace which their marriage has become, worrying that they're becoming "just another dull, aging couple" seeking titillation from hockey games and fascist opera—"a pair of comfortable old shoes."

The suspicious death of neighbor Lillian House (Lynn Cohen) gives Carol's unengaged attention something on which to focus, and she begins to believe that Lillian's husband has killed her. Carol is joined in this intrigue not by Larry (who initially construes her obsession with the neighbor's death as an overreaction to watching *Double Indemnity*) but by Ted (Alan Alda), a recently divorced family friend who sees this private investigation as an opportunity to spend time alone with her. "Maybe we're just two people with hyperactive imaginations whose lives need a shot of adrenaline or something," Carol tells Ted as they stake out a hotel, unaware that Larry is simultaneously having a distinctly flirtatious meeting with Marcia Fox (Angelica Huston), an author whose books he edits. Recognizing how much ground he's losing to the togetherness fostered by Carol and Ted's sleuthing ("If you're gonna have an affair with the guy," Larry scolds her, "you don't need a murder to do it"), he reluctantly joins her on stakeouts. Just as she'd explained *Last Year at Marienbad* when they first met, Carol explains to him why this murder plot is so important to them: "It's like this tantalizing plum that's been dropped in our laps. Life is such a dull routine, and here we are, right . . . we're on the threshold of a genuine mystery."

The mystery that screenwriters Allen and Marshall Brickman contrived for the film fulfills the genre's demands: it is conventionally intricate, acceptably imaginative, passably involving, and is also somewhat beside the point. Characteristically, Allen is more interested in imitating previous movie versions of his plot than the plot itself. Consequently, Allen and Brickman's script's debt to murder mysteries such as *Double Indemnity* and *The Lady from Shanghai* is acknowledged by the fact that those two films are being screened in the theater that is conveniently owned by the murder plotter, Paul House (Jerry Adler). Orson Welles' film also feeds suitably melodramatic lines to House's murderer, Mrs. Dalton (Marge Redmond), as she dispatches him. The mystery, as David Ansen argued, "is just Allen's fanciful pretext for making another movie about relationships."[10] The "plum" is obviously less significant than the portion of the anatomy into which Carol describes it dropping, the film repeatedly insisting—as Larry does—on the pursuit of the murder plot as a sublimated form of erotic adventure. Carol finally loses interest in the whodunit less because Marcia, a fan of murder mysteries, surpasses her ability to enter the mind of a murderer and outflank it than because Marcia has captured Ted's attention, rendering the pursuit completely unerotic for Carol and thus completely uncaptivating. In other words, Carol is finally no more interested in a murder plot for its own sake than is Woody Allen, seeing it, as he does, as nothing more than a self-consciously embraced antidote to the "dull routine" of life, as a pretext for the playing out of other agendas. "I wanted to use the murder," Allen told Anthony DeCurtis, "strictly as a vehicle to give the audience pleasure rather than make any kind of philosophical point with it."[11] For Allen, as for Carol, the mystery in *Manhattan Murder Mystery* transparently represents the desire to affirm the concept that "something other than what you see with your eyes and your senses is possible" rather than that idea's dramatic confirmation.

Inspired by a novel she's read called *Murder in Manhattan,* Marcia precipitates the finale by devising a scheme to trap House in which Larry, Carol, and Ted join. That plot involves putting House's young mistress through a bogus play audition, for which Larry is obliged to "write lines that don't mean anything." Once the trap has been sprung, Larry's temerity in confronting House after he has kidnapped Carol causes her to see her husband with new eyes ("Larry, you were surprisingly brave," she gushes), his transformation from condo complaisance neatly resolving the tensions in their marriage. The film ends with the happily reunited couple disappearing together into the glass-enclosed entrance of their Upper East Side condominium building as the doorman securely closes the perfectly polished doors behind them.

It's probably easy to be too influenced by Allen's misgivings about making this film, by his assertion years before he began drafting it that "I could be very funny in a comedy mystery and it would be enormously entertaining in a totally escapist way for an audience." Making such a film, he continued, would be to indulge his propensity toward producing "light entertainment," catering to his greater comfort in working with "the shallower stuff." At the time of that interview Allen added, "But I can't bring myself to do that."[12] By 1993, in the midst of his public flagellation, he could.

Given his personal excruciations and dislocations of 1992–1993 so jarringly evoked in *Daily News* headlines and in the decentered cinematic style of *Husbands and Wives,* it's not surprising that Allen's next film would resort to an antithetical cinematic mode, to the stability of an idea he'd lived with for a long time—a murder plot having been part of the original script he and Brickman wrote for *Annie Hall* [13]—and to the familiar presence of the actress who had collaborated so substantially with him in the "light entertainment" films responsible for his early success.[14] Since Allen never intended *Manhattan Murder Mystery* to be anything other than "a trivial picture," "a little thing done for fun. Like a little dessert or something,"[15] it's not so much the film's "light entertainment" quality as its utter dependency upon generic determinants which compromises *Manhattan Murder Mystery*'s comedic attempt to "get you airborne." Given that all of the films Allen has produced since *Husbands and Wives*—*Manhattan Murder Mystery, Bullets Over Broadway, Mighty Aphrodite, Everyone Says I Love You, Deconstructing Harry, Celebrity,* and *Sweet and Lowdown*—seek similarly to create comedy through the mixing of movie and literary genres, it's worth considering some of the pitfalls Allen can en-counter when he resolves to make films reflecting taking pleasure in life rather than interrogating it for signs of ultimate meaning. In other words, having written so many passages of resonant dramatic dialogue over the years, Allen found the task of "writing lines that don't mean anything" effectively distract-ing from the Mia media miasma but ultimately unfulfilling.

Allen has never made any concerted attempt to explain what for him constitutes "light entertainment," though his description of the New Orleans jazz he plays with his band ("There's nothing between you and the pure play-ing—there's no cerebral element at all"[16]) approaches definition. His apparent assumption that its qualities are self-evident allows him to categorically dis-tinguish *Manhattan Murder Mystery* from the other films he made during that period on the ground that "it wasn't ambitious enough for me."[17] However, in dialogue with Bjorkman, Allen did characterize the sources of pleasure he finds in filmmaking, his description evoking the production not of his serious movies like *Crimes and Misdemeanors* or *Husbands and Wives* but of "light entertainment" films such as *Manhattan Murder Mystery, Mighty Aphrodite,* and *Everyone Says I Love You.* Recalling his childhood awareness of the dispar-ity between the life he lived in Brooklyn and that of the characters in the films he went to see, Allen admitted that he had never overcome his amazement that "there are people whose lives are different and happy like in the movies." It follows that filmmaking for Allen has always been inseparable from "the sense of wanting to control reality,

> to be able to write a scenario for reality and make things come out the way you want it. Because what the writer does—the filmmaker or the writer—you create a world that you would like to live in. You like the people you create. You like what they wear, where they live, how they talk, and it gives you a chance for some months to live in that world. And those people move to beautiful music, and you're in that world. So in my films I just feel there's always a pervasive feeling of the greatness of idealized life or fantasy versus the unpleasantness of reality.[18]

The "greatness of idealized life or fantasy" is a perfect description of the tex-tures of three of Allen's 1993–1996 films and one which effectively demar-cates the risks these movies run. In their zeal to project affirmative, self-consciously idealized or "movieized" visions of actuality, Allen's films face two hazards: trivializing the conflicts they dramatize in the name of comedy or generic resolution,[19] and forgetting that that their renderings of the world *are* idealizations. Arguably the least effective of these comedies, *Manhattan Murder Mystery,* proved least able to evade these two hazards.

Sam B. Girgus's fine study of Allen's work, *The Films of Woody Allen,* traces, among other things, the progressive development of women protagonists in Allen's films, arguing that in *Hannah and Her Sisters* Allen "finally completed his *Manhattan* project of making a great movie about women. *Hannah and Her Sisters* is their movie in a way that *Manhattan* never quite becomes the possession of the women in it."[20] In these terms, *Manhattan Murder Mystery* seems something of a regression to the early Allen comedies in which male domination—the unequivocal centrality of the Allen protagonist—was a critically unexamined given, the female lead's character and the plot being largely determined by her desirability and availability to him. Carol's ambition to open a Manhattan restaurant surfaces occasionally in *Murder Mystery,* but the movie's genre-dictated conclusion leaves the element of Carol's desire to find fulfilling work for herself unresolved, with her ambition silently subsumed into the ending's felicitous renewal of her marriage to Larry. Larry's rescue of Carol in House's theater may similarly reflect how reverently this film is adhering to conventions of the genre to which Allen—the screenwriter/director of such sympathetic and substantial portraits of women as *Interiors, Another Woman,* and *Alice*—committed himself in taking on this project.[21] It's nonetheless discomfiting to watch Carol, whose insistence that reality *can* imitate murder mysteries initially animates the film's plot, become marginalized in the final third of the movie. The reduction of her role to that of female-who-needs-to-be-rescued pays excessive obeisance to the Nick and Nora Charles model of gender relations, which previous Allen films have dramatically contested. The ending, in fact, implies that, as in *The Thin Man,* it is the male protagonist's passivity, languor, and dependency upon the comforts of his opulent existence which need redeeming through a confrontation with extremity, the conclusion subordinating Carol's search for rejuvenation to Larry's need to reaffirm himself through an act of Hollywoodesque heroism. Adam Gopnik characterized this element of Larry effectively: "Now, when [Allen] seems to want to return, Zelig-like, to his former likeableness, as he does in *Manhattan Murder Mystery,* he no longer seems quite himself. He appears sexless and deracinated—a nervous man in his fifties, isolated in his apartment.[22]

As for the issue of idealization, no one ever suggested that Woody Allen's movies offer an objective representation of New York City. *Manhattan* can be interpreted as dramatically exploiting the tension between surface and substance—between Isaac Davis's idealized projections of New York and the adulterate hearts of its inhabitants; Gershwin's melodies underlying the gorgeous Gordon Willis cinematographic images of the city embody a "grand actuality of the reconciled" which the residents' lives and souls never remotely approach. Arguably, it's when Allen uncritically indulges his Isaac-like propensity to romanticize the city that his films begin misfiring. *Manhattan Murder Mystery* conveys little awareness of the consistently blandished representation of setting which characterizes it, and the fact that there's less going on in this film than in most of Allen's other movies makes the viewer more than usually conscious of the process of idealization to which New York has been cinematically subjected. From Bobby Short's opening titles performance of "I Happen to Like New York" on the soundtrack, the city's virtues are either assumed or are visually exaggerated. Except for the scene in the Waldron Hotel with its blue powder along the hallway baseboards and English as a second language front desk employees, *Manhattan Murder Mystery,* in emulation of 1930s-1940s Hollywood murder/comedies, restricts itself to opulent New York neighborhoods, restaurants (Elaine's, '21'), and residences.[23] Of course, Allen's New York is *always* markedly less-populated than the real-life city of twelve million inhabitants: when, for instance, Mickey Sachs in *Hannah and Her Sisters* dances joyfully down Fifth Avenue in broad daylight after having been given a clean bill of health at the Guggenheim Pavilion of Mount Sinai Hospital, he has the entire block completely to himself. But, even granting Allen's habitual Manhattan-enhancing proclivities, having Carol stand in the middle of an uptown street for nearly a minute describing a clue to Ted and getting honked out of the way of vehicular traffic by only a single car exceeds all credibility. Even by Allen's highly subjective criteria, the Manhattan of *Manhattan Murder Mystery* is too much an artistically overdetermined Bobby Short valentine to the city, too much a place constructed out of images of New York borrowed from sophisticated 1940s Hollywood comedies.[24] Pauline Kael's captious comment on *Hannah and Her Sisters* seems still more applicable to *Manhattan Murder Mystery:* Allen "uses style to blot out the rest of New York City."[25]

Despite its emulation of *The Thin Man* series and brief homages to *Double Indemnity* and *The Lady from Shanghai,* the film which *Manhattan Murder Mystery* most closely resembles is Hitchcock's *Rear Window.*[26] That Allen could model his "trivial picture" on Hitchcock's constitutes no contradiction for Allen, who argued that "I think Hitchcock himself never intended anything significant, and indeed his movies are not significant. They are delightful, but completely insignificant."[27] In both movies a couple characterized as being too complacently secure is drawn into the death of a neighbor which one member of the couple insists is a murder, the female character placing herself in jeopardy by repeatedly entering the murderer's apartment in search of evidence. In Allen's film, as we've seen, the characters' involvement in the plot is a sublimated version of sexual adventuring. This point is reinforced by Marcia's asking Ted, after he's revealed to her that he slept with House's mistress, Helen Moss, that afternoon as part of their scheme to keep Moss unavailable to House while the trap is being sprung on him, "You'll do anything to catch a murderer, won't you?" In Hitchcock's film, the gradual absorption of Jeff Jeffries (James Stewart) in the activities of Lars Thorwald (Raymond Burr) is the consequence of the photographer's being laid up with a broken leg, thus reducing his involvement in life to that of a voyeur vicariously participating in the experiences of others by watching them through his rear window. Allen's dismissal of the existence of "anything significant" in Hitchcock's films notwithstanding, lines like those of Stella (Thelma Ritter)—"We've become a race of peeping Toms. People ought to get outside and look at themselves"— and the comment of Lisa Carol Fremont (Grace Kelly) to Jeffries, "I'm not much on rear window ethics, but we're two of the most frightening ghouls I have ever known,"[28] have given two generations of film critics substantial textual inducement to read *Rear Window* as one of Hitchcock's oblique cinematic commentaries on photography—and, by extension, film—as a voyeuristic medium. Whereas Hitchcock's film thoroughly succeeds in using the conventional thriller format to conceal a sophisticated argument about film without puncturing the movie's pretense of popular entertainment transparency, *Manhattan Murder Mystery* insists, in a way that Allen's other films don't, on the absolute difference between significant and popular art. The movie locates itself so intently in the latter realm that even the recurrent theme of life imitating art gets reduced to a one-liner at the close, the inclusion of film clips from *Double Indemnity* and *The Lady from Shanghai* apparently carrying no reverberations or thematic ramifications beyond dramatizing how dwarfed Allen's characters are by Wilder's and Welles's on the movie screen. If *Manhattan Murder Mystery* is among the least resonant of Allen's films, it's at least partly because of his dubious assumption that the genre he was working in can't be anything else.

The limitation of *Manhattan Murder Mystery*, finally, is that its affectionately nostalgic appropriation of the generic moves of earlier mystery and murder/comedy films gave Allen permission to pose none of the questions his most interesting films always leave in play—the relationship between genders, between serious and popular art, between literary and film genres, and the issue of the desire for meaning running afoul of the human capacity to embrace illusion.

There is, however, still another Hollywood icon influencing the course of *Murder Mystery*. Returning to their condominium building after the opening Rangers' game scene, Larry tells Carol about a Bob Hope movie on television he's looking forward to watching. The line reinforces Larry's characterization as someone—like Jeff Jeffries—dependent upon spectating for excitement, while introducing the Hollywood figure who seems to encapsulate for Allen a side of his personality as surely as Ingmar Bergman incarnates for him philosophical gravity and intense spiritual introspectiveness. Having been asked by the American Film Institute to assemble a tribute to Hope, Allen told Frank Rich that he "had more pleasure watching Hope's films than making any film I've ever made. I think he's just a great, huge talent. Part of what I like about him is that flippant, Californian, obsessed-with-golf striding through life. His not caring about the serious side at all."[29]

When Carol tries to tell Larry about developments in her sleuthing, he responds "I don't want to know—leave me alone," and a particularly intense dose of what Carol has discovered provokes from him the comment, "It's the eye of the beholder. We have to get you to the doctor to get happy glasses." In *Mighty Aphrodite*, Allen offers a more deliberate repudiation of pessimistic perceptions of existence in the Greek chorus's donning of "happy glasses"; in *Murder Mystery*, Larry Lipton's trial-of-bravery has resuscitated him sufficiently that he whom Carol believes "used to be a fun guy" can now joke merrily with her about Ted as they disappear into their condo building. The mugging face he makes toward the audience when Carol zings him in the last line is Allen's way of signaling what the entire movie has dramatized: the idea that the world of *Manhattan Murder Mystery* is a self-consciously Bob Hope reality, one in which even the presence of murder can't alter its "not caring about the serious side at all."

A testament to Allen's uncharacteristic insistence on the absolute discontinuity between popular and high art, *Manhattan Murder Mystery* suffers from its insistent joviality and from the unreflective, unrelenting reverence it displays toward the conventions of the urbane New York whodunit. The film's closing good-naturedness rings slightly hollow because what Carol describes as "the most exciting adventure I've ever been on" has never seemed more than a Yuppie couple's brief hiatus from their wealth's insularity, an artificially induced holiday from late-middle age anomie. It is perhaps the greatest risk to Allen's filmmaking career that his movies can become no more than this: diverting, generically imitative adventure mechanisms ultimately intended to restore their characters—and, thus, their audiences—to a sense of their own comfort and equanimity. Rather than effectively replicating the silly cheerfulness of the resolutions of 1940s Nick and Nora Charles movies, the Liptons' 1993 retreat into their apartment building in the closing image of *Manhattan Murder Mystery* seems smug.

The couple appears to gather the security of their glass fortress around themselves much as Allen in the film has wrapped himself snugly in the conventions of the sophisticated comedic whodunit genre he's resurrecting. In a game of mirrors reflecting mirror images as disorienting as the scene in which Mrs. Dalton enacts her revenge on House, Allen has made in *Manhattan Murder Mystery* a movie about "people who are different and happy like in the movies." *Everyone Says I Love You* would prove more successful in transforming this cinematic Chinese box into charmingly compelling yet highly self-conscious film narrative. What the pursuit of the mystery is for Carol is too much what the film is for Allen: a contrived antidote for an oppressive reality, distraction impersonating remedy. The movie's numerous allusions to previous detective films leave little doubt as to the validity of Larry's admission that "I'll never say that life doesn't imitate art again"[30]; the major limitation of

Manhattan Murder Mystery may be, in fact, that its images of life are finally too imitative of art, too dictated by the style and genre of an earlier era's films to have much contemporary vitality of their own. But the comment Larry makes which even more effectively summarizes *Manhattan Murder Mystery* (and Allen's ambivalent attitude toward making it), comes earlier in the film: "You're making a murder," he admonishes Carol as her fixation upon the mystery deepens, "where nothing exists."

16

That Voodoo That You Do So Well

Mighty Aphrodite

Think of Oedipus. Oedipus is the structure of funny. Who did this terrible thing to our city? Oh my God—it was me! That's funny.

—Lester discoursing on comedy in *Crimes and Misdemeanors*

The mystery underlying *Mighty Aphrodite* is not, as it is in *Manhattan Murder Mystery*, generically but genetically coded. Allen was inspired to write the film's screenplay by thinking about the legally indeterminable heredity of Mia Farrow's adopted daughter, Dylan, and the fact that the child would never know what her inheritances actually are.[1] The way in which those meditations also inspired the introduction of the Greek chorus into the film isn't difficult to imagine, the enigmas of parenthood precipitating questions about origins appropriate to these on-stage projections of the audiences of Greek tragedy. And so the movie opens with the chorus bemoaning the lives of men and women, cataloguing those heroes—Achilles, Menelaus, Antigone, Medea—fated by the inexplicable wills of the gods to misery and suffering. "For to understand the ways of the heart," the chorus leader (F. Murray Abraham) intones, "is to grasp clearly the malice or ineptitude of the gods who, in their vain and clumsy labors to create a flawless surrogate, have left mankind dazed and incomplete."

"Take, for instance," the chorus, suddenly sounding very un-Greek choral, responds, "the case of Lenny Weinrib, a tale as Greek as fate itself."[2]

The case of Lenny Weinrib (Allen) involves his attempt to alter the future of Linda Ash (Mira Sorvino) so that when his adopted son, Max (Jimmy McQuaid), goes searching for his mother later in life, he won't be confronted by a prostitute appearing in porno films under the *nom de cinema* Judy Cum. Whether Lenny's efforts seriously constitute "a tale as Greek as fate itself" is, of course, dubious. In fact, some of the film's reviewers perceived the chorus's presence in *Mighty Aphrodite* as an arbitrary means of producing a few easy laughs, as "a device pushed well beyond its comic limit."[3] It's likely that the good trick of having the chorus from behind their masks of tragedy express themselves in the whiny inflections of a Woody Allen protagonist—"Oh, cursed fate! Some thoughts are better left unthunk!"; "And why a child now, out of left field?"—does become subject to the law of diminishing returns. And yet, the implicit identification of the chorus with Allen's screen persona suggests that there is a more substantial justification for their presence than the anachronism-inspired laughs they provoke. Like the extraterrestrial Og in *Stardust Memories* who, employing an intonation similar to theirs, advises Sandy Bates to make funnier movies, they represent the antagonist in the dramatic dialogue Allen is having with himself over making light comic movies like *Mighty Aphrodite*. (It may be because *Manhattan Murder Mystery* has so completely resolved this conflict that it seems such a less interesting film.) If the chorus is right that fate betrays the greatest among us, and if their leader is right—and Allen's expressed perceptions of the world on film or outside of it have never suggested that either of them *isn't* right—that circumstances of existing in the universe leave mankind "but dazed and incomplete," there seems little cause for optimism about human life and still less occasion for the making of celebratory movies. Nonetheless, *Mighty Aphrodite* moves toward a remarkably cheerful resolution, one that culminates in the conversion of the chorus leader (who proves, admittedly, not inordinately resistant to transformation) from his diagnosis of humanity's "dazed and incomplete" condition to his closing affirmation of human life as being "unbelievable, miraculous, sad, wonderful." The chorus leader's change of heart, in fact, distills the overall trajectory of the film: the human capacity for change provides the primary source of energy dictating the comedic resolution of *Mighty Aphrodite*. Its pervasive breezily comic tone notwithstanding, *Mighty Aphrodite* dramatically opposes Allen's pessimistic perception of human life with his desire to make movies that provide the condemned with consolatory laughter, and if the outcome of the film's extratextual *agon* seems inevitable, that's just a testament to the mightiness of the power which transforms the chorus from disputants of grim universal mysteries to celebrants of—in the words of the Cole Porter classic they end up performing—"that voodoo that you do so well."

Mighty Aphrodite's Greek chorus appears to be on loan from a performance of *Oedipus the King* taking place in an amphitheater in Greece. (Actually, the Greek Theater in Taormina, Sicily.) Accordingly, they seem to follow the Sophoclean concept of the chorus's role, commenting on and influencing the action of Allen's plot without ever directly entering it. In describing the role of the chorus in Greek tragedy, Bernhard Zimmerman argues that it "leaves the narrow circle of the action to meditate on past and future, on distant times and people, indeed on humanity itself, in order that it may derive great truths from human experience and pronounce the lessons of wisdom."[4] The closest Allen's chorus comes to pronouncing on "great truths of human experience" is their lamentation about children "growing up and moving out, to ridiculous places like Cincinnati or Boise, Idaho. Then you never see them again." As Bernard Knox demonstrated in *Oedipus at Thebes,* the chorus of Sophocles' tragedy rejects all attempts by Jocasta and Oedipus to deny the truth of prophecy, viewing the oracles of the gods as absolute and humanly incontrovertible.[5] Conversely, the chorus of *Mighty Aphrodite* is far more relativistic in its judgments, answering the question, "Is there a growing void in the Weinribs' marriage?" which has led them so suddenly to adopt a child, "We didn't say there was. We're all just speculating on possible motives."

Reviewers of *Mighty Aphrodite* tended to perceive the presence of the chorus in the film as an arbitrarily imposed frame for the narrative, which produced a few jokes of the deflation-of-high-culture-icons characteristic of Allen's comedy from his stand-up days, literary allusions and philosophical schemes alike getting reduced to their most common and trivial consequences. ("Rosencrantz and Guildenstern are dead," the court fool announces in *Everything You Wanted to Know About Sex*, "their tailor shop is closed"; Mickey Sachs decides in *Hannah and Her Sisters* that he can't embrace Nietzsche's notion of the Eternal Return because it would mean that he has to sit through the Ice Capades again.) Certainly, the disparity between the dignity of the Sophoclean chorus's somber dithyrambs and the Oprahesque kibitzing of Allen's chorus is much of the fun of *Mighty Aphrodite*. However, there is an element of Sophocles' play that his and Allen's choruses have in common. Confronted with the possibility that they inhabit a universe in which oracles are substanceless and the prospering of evil only proves the nonexistence of the gods, Sophocles' chorus angrily threatens to repudiate their choral role: "If irreverent action is to be respected and profitable, why should I dance?"[6] As if confirming that we inhabit a just universe, one well worth celebrating, Allen's tragic chorus not only dances; while dancing, they also sing "You Do Something to Me" and "When You're Smiling." The Dick Hyman Orchestra and Chorus's ebullient renditions of these songs and Graciela Daniele's exquisite choreography of the chorus's not completely un-Greek song and dance combine to create what may be Allen's single most infectious and compelling emblem of existential affirmation. Its effectiveness is firmly founded in the fact that, despite their thoroughly unexpected flair for musical comedy, the chorus with their masks and bleakly flowing robes never completely sheds their associations with unsmiling speculations and dark necessities.

The god whose existence is implicitly affirmed by the chorus's dazzlingly affecting performance of "When You're Smiling" at the end of the film is the Mighty Aphrodite of the title, a deity who never literally appears in the movie but whose influence generates its buoyant resolution. Lenny's wife, Amanda (Helena Bonham Carter), has realized she loves him, not her seductive art gallery colleague, while Lenny's night of lovemaking with Linda Ash rejuvenates his commitment to his marriage. For her part, Linda loses the onion farmer with whom Lenny has fixed her up when Kevin (Michael Rapaport) happens upon a video in which she appears in her Judy Cum incarnation, but driving back from an unsuccessful attempt to win Kevin back in upstate New

York, Linda picks up a grounded helicopter pilot whom she ultimately marries instead. ("Talk about a *deus ex machina!*" the chorus leader, briefly becoming the film's narrator, responds to the helicopter's fortuitous descent as Linda drives by.) There are other things humans can't know about their circumstances, the film suggests: Linda doesn't know Lenny's adopted son, Max, is her child, while Lenny doesn't know that the daughter he meets Linda with in FAO Schwartz years later is the child they parented during their night together. ("Yes, yes—isn't life ironic?" is the chorus's perky gloss on the meeting of unwitting parents and children at the toy store.) Aphrodite is indeed mighty, her interventions in the lives of men and women regularly determining the plot resolutions of Allen's happiest films.

And yet, much of what happens in *Mighty Aphrodite* seems the result of human agency rather than divine intervention. Lenny defends the unscrupulous tactics he uses to learn the name of his adopted son's birth mother by dismissing the warnings of the chorus leader who has dropped in while Lenny illicitly searches the files of the adoption agency: "That's why you'll always be a chorus leader. I act. I take action, I make things happen." As much as this might seem the kind of self-congratulatory line a Woody Allen protagonist could be expected to spend the rest of his film disproving by acting out through progressively comical scenes his passivity and want of control over anything, in *Mighty Aphrodite,* Lenny is absolutely right. By obtaining courtside New York Knicks' tickets for her pimp, Lenny frees Linda from subjection to him, and Lenny coaxes her in the direction of hairdressing, which will become her post-hooking career.[7] As Mary P. Nichols demonstrates, Lenny's matchmaking efforts on Linda's behalf fail because of the outrageous lies he tells her and Kevin about each other in order to pique their romantic interests, the film thus suggesting the limits of human beings to intervene effectually in the fates of others.[8] Nonetheless, it's driving back from visiting Kevin in Wampsville, New York, in Lenny's car that Linda experiences the *deus ex machina* of the descent of helicopter pilot Don from the sky. That Lenny unknowingly leaves Linda pregnant with the daughter who constitutes unintended compensation for the son he's gained from her provides more evidence that Lenny—even more than her helicopter pilot—has been the answer to her dreams. On their first date, she and Kevin exchange descriptions of their dreams, Linda confiding that "My dream is that someone would come along and think I was special. That, you know, they'd want to come and change my life for me."

Immediately after Linda has been rejected by Kevin and Lenny has learned that Amanda plans to leave him, he tells Linda, echoing an argument we encountered in *Broadway Danny Rose,* "Remember you once said we were a couple of losers? Well, I think that's definitely true." Allen thinks that's definitely untrue, the lovemaking that immediately follows Lenny's declaration putting both characters on the road to forming or reforming the happy families of three Linda and Lenny are enjoying when they meet in FAO Schwartz two years later. *Mighty Aphrodite* is not a film in which such fatalistic formulations as "we are a couple of losers" are ever validated, Lenny's commitment to action and the consequent altering of circumstance often being carried out in defiance of such deterministic conceptions.

One central set of mechanistic assertions that are repudiated through Lenny's quest in the film are those relating to heredity. In the opening scene of the movie, Lenny's friend, Bud (Steven Rendazzo), counsels him and Amanda against adoption because they might get what he refers to as "a bad seed." He later implants the notion of seeking out Max's birth mother in Lenny's mind when he suggests that "It's like raising thoroughbreds—this kid must come from good stock. He's good- looking, he's got a high IQ, he's got a great personality, and he's amusing. . . . A good father and a dynamite mother produces a kid like Max." Lenny's tireless interrogation of Linda's genetic inheritance provides nothing but contrary evidence to Bud's genetic thesis. She doesn't know who Max's father was ("It could have been one of a hundred guys" she acknowledges), but her father was a drug pusher, pickpocket, car thief, and epileptic who was finally jailed for mail fraud. The only exceptional person in his family was a brother who was supposed to be a genius but whose chances to excel in math were nullified when he became a serial rapist; the rest of her family, in Linda's words, "is all slugs and lowlifes." The film misses no opportunity to establish that Max's mental gifts don't come from his mother, either, Linda constantly comically misconstruing what others say. (When she asks Lenny if he works out; he responds, "Not religiously"; she replies that she's not religious either, though her parents were Episcopalians.) Linda lays claim to and proves to have a good sense of humor, and perhaps the "amusing" quality Bud attributes to Max is hereditarily coded; otherwise, the film seems to consistently insist that there's no necessary connection between gene pools and character or innate ability, the affirmation of randomness implicit in that judgment—given that it projects no obstacles to Linda's happiness despite her "slugs and lowlifes" heredity—being depicted in *Mighty Aphrodite* as a cause for celebration. The irrelevance-of-heredity theme culminates in the final scene in Lenny's response to the daughter Linda shows him whom he doesn't know he fathered: "You've got to have a very handsome husband," he tells Linda, "she's got a great face."[9]

The film's other, more obvious repository of deterministic ideas are the Greek tragedy figures who ultimately provide—ironically—the movie's comic frame. A messenger (Dan Mullane) invokes the entire lexicon of Greek tragedic dire consequence in describing Lenny's obsession with learning more about his son's mother: "I come from the midtown area, where Lenny Weinrib, tortured by passions too overwhelming to regulate, did indeed call this little hustler on the phone in earnest attempt to see her again. At first, he wrestled with his drives, trying to master a curiosity not slaked by this initial meeting, but only whetted by it. His thirst to know this woman more did inexorably provoke him to call her." The messenger's rhetoric of impending disaster to the contrary, Lenny's passionate curiosity, instead of precipitating his self-destruction, has thoroughly benign effects on both himself and its object.

Similarly, the chorus and its prophetic sidekicks, Cassandra (Danielle Ferland) and Tieresias (Jack Warden), are constantly and futilely warning Lenny against the future ramifications of both his search for Max's mother and of seeking to meddle in her fate once he's found her. "You never should have looked for her," Cassandra admonishes Lenny, "Now I see *big trouble.*" But there is no big trouble, even Linda's bondage to her procurer proving surprisingly easy to annul with choice NBA seats, the film charmingly and rather uncontestedly cruising toward its happy ending.

The chorus leader's insistence that "Of all human weaknesses, obsession is the most dangerous" isn't borne out by the plot, either: Lenny's obsession with gaining absolute knowledge of his son's mother proves highly productive and beneficial to both her and to his own marriage. (Even the chorus has a response for their leader's dark declaration: "And the silliest!" is their mincing reply.) As David Denby noticed, Lenny never listens to the "choral laments and injunctions," and "the movie shows he's right to ignore them. None of the chorus's most dire predictions come true, and the movie slips into a pleasant fable. Life is not riddled with catastrophes. Life is a comedy."[10]

Denby's argument that the film affirms comedy over the ominous injunctions of the chorus with its lamentations—"Woe unto man!"—and its invocations of tragic heroes whose lives illustrate the bleak fates humanity is heir to is surely the most convincing justification for their presence in the film that criticism has thus far provided. However, two other explanations present themselves, the latter more demonstrable than the former.

Appearing on *Sixty Minutes* during his public battle with Mia Farrow, Allen recalled for Steve Croft a threat he claimed that Farrow had made against him, one which sounds weirdly like a tragedian's reconfiguring of the plot of *Mighty Aphrodite*: "You took my daughter, and I'm going to take yours." (Linda doesn't know that Lenny "took" her son through adoption; Lenny doesn't know that Linda "took" the daughter with whom he impregnated her by never informing him of her existence.) Allen continued, "[Farrow] threatened to have me killed and kill me. And then to stick my eyes out, to blind me. Because she became obsessed with Greek tragedy and felt like that would be a fitting, you know, vengeance." Farrow denied ever having made the threat, but she acknowledged having compared herself to Hecuba in *The Trojan Women*—actually, in Euripides' *Hecuba*—who avenges herself on Polymestor's murder of her son, Polydorous, by blinding him.[11] It seems not inconceivable that Allen used the writing of *Mighty Aphrodite* partly as a means of deflecting

Farrow's threat by transforming the child stealing/murder into comedy. Through introducing the chorus into the film, he ridicules both their constant invocation of fatalistic imperatives such as vengeance and tragic flaws and their reading of "the ways of the heart" as manifestations not of human desire but of "malice or ineptitude of the gods."[12] In other words, Farrow's threat is empty because the spokesmen (in Allen's incarnation of them, spokespersons) of Greek necessity are just fashionably draped guys and gals who want most to sing Tin Pan Alley favorites and dance a bit. Whether the presence of the chorus in the film actually constitutes Allen's parodic rejoinder to Farrow's breakup-inspired "obsession with Greek tragedy" is admittedly less clear than that it is so repeatedly aligned with human psychology as to seem the projection of the only character in the film who ever becomes conscious of its existence—Lenny.

After Laius (David Ogden Stiers) and Jocasta (Olympia Dukakis) recount their family history of parricide and incest, and the blind Oedipus (Jeffrey Kurland) wanders around helplessly, blundering into people and things, a member of the chorus abruptly asserts the link between Laius' family heritage and depth psychology: "And a whole profession was born, charging sometimes as much as $200 an hour, and a fifty minute hour at that." (Allen's additional jibe at that profession is contained in his script's establishing that Linda too charges $200 a session.) The emergence of psychoanalysis out of this family history suggests that the myth of Laius, Jocasta, and Oedipus isn't about people acting in compunction to divine but psychic necessity. This point is reinforced by the chorus leader's quintessentially Allenesque repudiation of political explanations for human behavior: "Curiosity, that's what kills us, not muggers or all that bullshit about the ozone layer. It's our own hearts and minds." He's wrong that curiosity kills anyone in *Mighty Aphrodite*, but in terms of the universe of Woody Allen films, he's locating the source of pain and conflict in exactly the right places.

The choral leader is, of course, himself an expression of Lenny's "heart and mind," ceasing gradually to oppose Lenny's quest for knowledge by counseling that he meet Linda for the first time not at the Plaza but "somewhere out of the way" like her apartment, and subsequently deciding that "it would be nice if [Lenny] could bring off" getting Linda together with Kevin, his stance contesting the chorus's firmly maintained conviction that the matchmaking effort constitutes "hubris." When he begins asking Lenny, following his lovemaking with Linda, "Was she great? Was she great in bed? You can tell me. I mean, a woman with all that experience!" it's clear enough where the chorus leader's spiritual priorities have migrated to. Accordingly, the chorus leader's closing affirmation of life as "unbelievable, miraculous, sad, wonderful" seems an articulation of the look on Lenny's face after seeing Linda at FAO Schwartz beneath the toy emporium's trademark clock face. This timepiece evokes playtime rather than humankind's inescapable destiny, and provides an appropriate symbol of the happy culminations of both Linda's and Lenny's narratives, their mutually benign fates filling Lenny with the same sense of wonderment the choral leader expresses. By the end of the movie, this source of dark admonitions has metamorphosed into a traditional voice-over film narrator passing on the good tidings of Lenny's happy ending, the chorus leader getting all but absorbed into the person whose fatalistic side he represented.

The film offers still more evidence that Lenny's Greek interlocutors are projections of his own incipient fatalism. When Lenny first encounters Cassandra, her warning that if he perseveres in his quest, "You'll be sorry— I'm telling you, quit now!" prompts him to say "You're such a Cassandra"; she responds that she isn't "such a Cassandra" but *is* Cassandra, then admonishes him against buying a Hamptons property that Amanda wants because the prophetess foresees beach erosion and a heavy mortgage. Phobic about sand ticks and aware of Hamptons resident Jerry Bender's designs on Amanda, Lenny has no desire to buy a house there, his opposition getting voiced in Cassandra's prophecy. When Lenny offers her these explanations for not purchasing the property, Amanda's response is "You're such a Cassandra!" Lenny's next line, were it not truncated by the cutting away to the next scene, might be that he is not "such a Cassandra," but *is* Cassandra. Tieresias's disclosures are similarly limited to Lenny's most immediate psychic concerns, the seer's graphic description of Amanda kissing her would-be seducer, Jerry Bender (Peter Weller), representing, in Tieresias's words, "something you don't want to know, but you'd have to be blind not to see it." In this highly Freudian reading of the workings of Greek drama, the chorus and its Attic cohorts are neither divine oracles nor embodiments of tragic fatality, but are the voices of Lenny's psyche, delivering admonitions ("Please, Lenny—don't be a schmuck!") in the only language he understands—his own. Denby's argument seems indisputable: in *Mighty Aphrodite,* tragedy's vision of humanity as unconsciously fulfilling an unintelligible destiny dictated by the gods gives way to the comic vision of the case of Lenny Weinrib, whose only fate is to fulfill his desires.

So upbeat is *Mighty Aphrodite's* delineation of human possibility, in fact, that it dramatically reverses a recurrent Allen attitude. Early in the film, Amanda attributes to Lenny a characteristic we've noticed in a number of Allen's protagonists: he's "opposed to change in any form." Lenny is obviously discomfited by the growth in Amanda which culminates in her independently gaining the funding to open her own art gallery in Soho, chastening her for the fact that "you've changed" and hinting darkly that "things have really changed between us." But as the movie proceeds, Lenny comes increasingly to ignore the chorus's injunctions to "Turn back, don't meddle any further!" Refusing to "[a]ccept the truth" of who Linda is as they demand, Lenny indulges not only the curiosity they condemn but also the impulse they denounce even more energetically: his quest "to change her life." And so Lenny gradually evolves into the agent Linda is unconsciously invoking in describing her dream of "someone who could come along . . . and want to change my life for me."[13] When Kevin rejects Linda because of her X-rated career, Lenny tells him, "People change—you're going to hold her past against her?" In Lenny's view—a view the film endorses—her past is no more finally determinant of who she is than her son's heredity has dictated the "terrific kid" he's become. (Analogously, it's chance—not fate—which directs helicopter Don to descend into Linda's life, their meeting facilitated less by the intercession of Zeus than by the loan of Lenny's car.[14]) That Linda ends up married with a child and Lenny experiences a rebirth of his marriage to Amanda are testaments to the ability of human beings to change, a capacity the film symbolizes most charmingly in the chorus's metamorphosis from purveyors of tragic knowledge into a jaunty song and dance team.

The somewhat mixed reviews of *Mighty Aphrodite* suggest, however, that not all viewers perceived the film's closing familial union and reunion as being as charming as was apparently intended.[15] If the movie is not completely successful in its projection of a traditional romantic comedy resolution with good feelings all around, a few of the film's materials may be responsible. Amanda is certainly the least sympathetic wife of an Allen protagonist since Wendy (Joanna Gleason) in *Crimes and Misdemeanors,* her negatively portrayed qualities rendering ambivalent the viewer's feelings about both her characterization and Lenny's reunion with her. She's often shot with her hair obscuring her face, the visualization seeming to reinforce her secretiveness, her concealment from Lenny of the rapid progress she's making toward opening an art gallery in Soho obliging her mother (Claire Bloom) to reveal to him her success in obtaining funding for the project. (Significantly, though, Lenny is no less clandestine in his pursuit of Max's mother.) Although the viewer is given only cursory glimpses of the Manhattan art world with which Amanda is so tirelessly involved, it seems to have at its heart not aesthetic commitment or the communication of depthless human truths but the making of connections and raising of money, its central embodiment being the incessantly predatory, professionally and erotically on-the-make Jerry Bender. (Lenny's sports writing profession, on the other hand, is depicted as fulfilling, unpretentious, and fun, its portrayal reflecting Allen's much-chronicled affection for sports.[16]) Surprisingly, Allen also burdens Amanda with *the* quintessential wifely defect of Hollywood films: Max asks Lenny who is the boss between him and Mommy; Lenny replies, "I'm the boss. Mommy says what we do, and I have control of the channel changer." The film's plot corroborates this assessment, Lenny's concealment of his Linda Ash redemption project from Amanda seeming like the revenge of the powerless against the powerful. Add to these unlikable qualities the fact that Amanda is saddled with a habit which Allen's films

consistently convey as an unattractive manifestation of insecurity and anxiety—smoking—and it's difficult to understand why Lenny wants her back.[17]

Reviewers of the film caviled less with Amanda's character than they did with the film's treatment of Linda and Kevin. Much of the film's humor, Nick James contended, "is at the expense of their ignorance. We are invited to mock and chide their limited aspirations as they make slow progress towards some kind of Upper East Side vision of whatever it is nice, uncultured, ordinary folks do."[18] Condemning every comic film which satirizes its characters' want of intelligence would, of course, leave us with precious few comedies, and it is arguable that the Times Square restaurant scene in which Linda and Kevin speak intimately with each other commingles palpable sympathy for them with the laughs it elicits at the expense of their cultural unawareness. Nonetheless, the categorical nature of Allen's reported single instruction to Sorvino about her role—"I don't want a glimmer of intelligence to show through [in Linda's character] because not only is she dumb but she's stupid"[19]—seems to support James's contention that Linda Ash was conceived in remarkably, and perhaps excessively, one-dimensional terms.

To raise such an objection, however, is to read *Mighty Aphrodite* purely as a realistic or representational film, a critical strategy which nearly always misperceives Allen's movies. *Mighty Aphrodite* moves a little slowly for the first half hour, the adoption plot, Amanda's overbearing nature, and the odd choral interruptions seeming pleasant enough, but unmemorable. The movie gathers a completely different level of energy when Lenny arrives at Linda's apartment for the first time, the scene which follows being classable with the finest and funniest Allen has ever shot. In at least fifteen of his previous twenty-four films, we've watched Allen's protagonists define themselves largely through their desperate erotic pursuits of one female or another; what Lenny is encountering in Linda Ash is the aggregate of all that sexuality distilled into a single "ur-woman," an "Amazonian bimbo"[20] whose power is as overwhelming as it is mindless. Lenny pursued Linda in hopes of finding in her virtues confirmation of his perception of his son as an exemplar of human intelligence; she is instead the embodiment—if not the living parody—of human sexuality, a cheerful, obscenity-spouting porno queen whose comedic character and symbolic presence seem summarized by the titles of her adult movies: *Snatch Happy* and *The Enchanted Pussy*. (She is a personification of the humongous breast of the *Everything You Wanted to Know About Sex* monster movie spoof, the overmatched Allen protagonist's role in both films being to domesticate this omnipotent force.) Allen has repeatedly enacted his protagonist's imperilment in all sorts of situations, but he has never seemed so utterly and completely engulfed as he does by Sorvino's Linda/Judy Cum, her assisting him in undoing the strings of her sweater reducing him to a twittering idiot, her tongue in his ear transforming him into a tiny old man whose spastically kneading hands seem to be simultaneously expressing pleasure and signaling for help.[21] Sorvino's Linda *is* Mighty Aphrodite, the cipher and summation of the sexuality that has energized practically all of Allen's films, and Lenny's initial confrontation with her hilariously demonstrates how thoroughly powerless his civilized inhibitions are against her resolutely anti-intellectual, unapologetically vulgar, relentlessly physical presence.

Given that the might of Aphrodite prevails in the film, it's appropriate that one of the images in the closing montage is of Lenny and Amanda (whose lovemaking earlier on fails because he "couldn't find it") passionately making love. More disquieting, but equally appropriate, is the fact that as Cassandra, Tieresias, and others back in the Greek Theater watch the chorus performing "When You're Smiling," Oedipus is putting the heavy make on Jocasta. It's not his tragic fate he's acting out, and it's certainly not comedy—it's just sex, and *Mighty Aphrodite* with its vibrantly hyperbolic personification of that force is Allen's refreshingly raunchy tribute to it. In other words, *Mighty Aphrodite* offers as benignly comedic a cinematic validation as Allen could manage to create of his much-quoted self-justification during the tabloid wars, "the heart wants what it wants." Perhaps more than any other Allen film, *Mighty Aphrodite* is simultaneously an affirmation of the comedic vision of things, a celebration of existence, and a dramatic delineation of the erotic grounds for that celebration.

17

And What a Perfect Plot

Everyone Says I Love You and *Zelig*

Look, I-I love you. I know that o-only happens in movies, but . . . I do.

—Gil to Cecilia in *The Purple Rose of Cairo*

Allen's implicit self-appointment as a devotee of the goddess of love in *Mighty Aphrodite*—his declaration representing more of a reenlistment than a new commitment—involves him in a contradiction which the films he has yet to make will find extremely difficult to resolve. Acknowledging the differences between Linda's physical ripeness and his own small stature and advanced years, Lenny jokes that "At my age, if I made love to you, they'd have to put me on a respirator." In fact, he seems to survive their amorous night together nicely, leaving her with a daughter as if in reciprocation for the son he has from her, and the subsequent visualization of his rambunctious lovemaking with Amanda once they've reunited reinforces the idea that there's enough life left in the old boy that he's recovered his ability to "find it" again.

Throughout Allen's work, film-resolving affirmation has nearly always necessitated the erotic convergence between the protagonist and her/his love interest. The ending of Sandy Bates's movie in *Stardust Memories* makes the link between existence-affirmation and romantic resolution most explicit: he's still on the train whose destination remains a mystery to him with the Hogarthian grotesques for fellow passengers—the basic condition of his life hasn't changed. What *has* changed is that he's with Isobel. "But it's not as terrible as I originally thought it was," he tells her, "because-because, you know, we like each other, and-and . . . uh, you know, we have some laughs, and there's a lot of closeness, and the whole thing is a lot easier to take" (p. 376). That this affirmation is only the ending of a movie-within-a-movie doesn't completely ironize its point, which other Allen films dramatize even less equivocally. "[T]hat's pretty much how I feel about relationships," Alvy Singer explains, "you know, they're totally irrational and crazy and absurd and . . . but, uh, I guess we keep goin' through it because, uh, most of us need the eggs" (*Annie Hall*, p. 105). The dilemma repeatedly evoked in his recent films takes the form of an as-yet-unanswered question: what is there to affirm once aging has rendered us less capable or less eligible egg-gatherers than we once were? Allen's idea that Eros is the only magic is emblematized best by Andrew's spirit box in *Midsummer Night's Sex Comedy*, which "penetrates the unseen world." What the spirit box ultimately projects are images of lovers, of sexual trysts in the woods, each of the characters perceiving the box's projections as dramatizing her/his own sexual fantasies or possibilities. Only the hyper-rationalist Leopold sees no shadow of himself and his desire for Dulcy, until the ending engineers his conversion into a "glowing presence on summer nights," a spirit evocative of the undying power of sexuality. *Sex Comedy* affirms the idea articulated by Frid in Bergman's *Smiles of the Summer Night:* "There are only a few young lovers on this earth. . . . Love has smitten them both as a gift and as a punishment." The summer night smiles for all, Frid continues—"for the clowns, the fools, the unredeemable . . . who invoke love, call out for it, beg for it, cry for it, try to imitate it, think they have it, lie about it."[1]

For a filmmaker whose primary if not only source of affirmation has been the "very, very resilient little organ"—the human heart—and the redemptively distracting webs of romantic involvement and entanglement it projects into the world, the prospect of aging provides a particularly daunting challenge. (Shadowing that issue further are the strikingly un-*Hannah*esque implications of Allen's most-quoted rationale during the public imbroglio with Mia Farrow, "the heart wants what it wants.") For a while now, reviewers have been none too diplomatically wondering whether Allen isn't getting a little old to be playing romantic leads, and for all the anatomical/spiritual congruences of its "what are your charms for . . . what are my arms for?" sentimentality, *Everyone Says I Love You* contains an obvious undercurrent of this very real artistic conflict. That subtext plays itself out in *Everyone* not only through the film's necessity to generate romantic closure, but also in its recurrently conjured anxiety that to be without "the eggs" is to have no identity, no self at all.

On its very lovely surface, however, *Everyone* represents Allen's attempt to make a movie that is light, engaging, and enchanting without being trivial or transparent. From its lushly visualized opening scene in which Holden (Edward Norton) and Skylar (Drew Barrymore) winsomely but untunefully sing "Just You, Just Me," the film immediately announces its strategy: it's a musical in which people who aren't singers regularly burst—or, in Allen's case, shrug—into song.[2] David Denby, a reviewer generally willing to attempt to understand Allen's purposes in a film before lambasting it, noted the singers' vocal incapacities and took them for an exercise in egalitarianism: everyone loves, he argued, so everyone sings. Locating the ancestors of this film in Hollywood musical comedies, Denby explains what it means when Astaire dances: he's in love, he's gotta dance. The only way to visualize the exultant feelings Astaire's character is experiencing is for him to dance and sing them; the only way to manifest the togetherness forged by his and Ginger's love for each other is for them to kick up their heels. "Everything builds up to those num-

bers," Denby contends, "and the greatest of them, exploding on the screen, made us happy in ways that perhaps nothing else in movies can equal."[3]

Allen, who closed *The Purple Rose of Cairo* with one of the most beloved of such scenes—the Astaire/Rogers "Cheek to Cheek" duet from *Top Hat*—would very probably agree, though his framing of their dance redefined its significance considerably. What Denby underestimates in comparing such classic song and dance numbers to those in *Everyone* is that even when Allen celebrates these grand movie moments in his films, their framing conveys an implicit skepticism about them. The image of romantic consummation embedded in the Astaire/Rogers choreography clearly does nothing to alter the circumstances waiting outside the Jewel Theater for Cecilia—except, perhaps, to reinforce the illusion that there is something for her in the world other than Monk and the Depression, thus incapacitating her to deal effectively with those inescapable realities. The consolations of even Hollywood's most radiant scenes are suspect in Allen's skeptical aesthetic because they are necessarily fabrications, artifices whose capacity to reassure exists in inverse proportion to their relationship to truth. However much his own films are the product of his having grown up with the beautiful illusions of what he calls "champagne comedies"—the shimmering Radio City Music Hall scene in *Radio Days* best epiphanizing this connection—Allen nonetheless exhibits a consistent mistrust of his own tropism toward the celebration of such moments on-screen. The skeptical side of Allen's attitude toward such romantic epiphanies, the religious language excepted, closely parallels Cynthia Ozick's description of the anti-artifice tendencies of her short story, "Usurpation." "It is against magic and mystification, against sham and 'miracle,'" Ozick suggested, "and, going deeper into the dark, against idolatry. It is an invention directed against inventing, the point being that the story-making faculty itself can be a corridor to the corruptions and abominations of idol-worship, or the adoration of magical event."[4]

The Purple Rose of Cairo is, along with *Stardust Memories*, Allen's most fiercely ambivalent depiction of film's capacity to incite "the adoration of magical event." Although *Everyone Says I Love You* is a substantially lighter film than either, its musical comedy impulses, like its construction of late middle age romantic impulses, are nonetheless more equivocal than its relentlessly cheerful narrative implies. Both of these equivocations culminate dramatically in the poignant *pas de deux* on the Seine, which is simultaneously Allen's lovingly parodic homage to Hollywood romantic dance numbers and the film's emotional climax. Until then, the cares predominantly evoked by the film are limited to those Holden exuberantly croaks about: "My baby just cares for me."

Djuna (Natasha Lyonne)—the DJ of the narrative—explains at the film's end that when she decided her family's story should be a movie, her half-sister, Skylar, suggested that she should "make it a musical or no one will believe it."[5] (That American college-age young women in 1996 would want to make such a film seems unlikely; that the music they'd choose for their musical would be Broadway show tunes forty years old is an anomaly the film never seems to find anomalous. It's one of a number of unscrutinized felicities which allow *Everyone* to cleave to its ebullient course.) And so the film begins with DJ introducing her family by affirming, "We're not the typical family you find in a musical—for one thing, we've got dough." (Perhaps the only musicals she's seen are *West Side Story* and *A Chorus Line*.) The inherited wealth of her mother, Steffi (Goldie Hawn), and the lucrative law practice of her stepfather (Alan Alda) enable the family to live in a plush Manhattan penthouse and to travel to Paris for Christmas to celebrate the holidays in a suite at the Ritz. When DJ's father's summer month with his daughter rolls around, he whisks her off to Venice; consequently, the film, exquisitely photographed by Carlo Di Palma, visualizes not only the beauty of Manhattan in summer, fall, and winter, but it also captures the loveliness of Paris and Venice, the departures from Allen's undeviating New York settings constituting one of the movie's many manifestations of expansiveness and surprise.

Once the narrative begins to unfold, it becomes clear that *Everyone* is a much lighter addressing of the "resilient little muscle" of the heart theme which underlies *Hannah and Her Sisters*. Nearly everyone in the movie (other than Grandpa, who dies) is falling into or out of love, a number of different characters—Allen's Joe Berlin included—getting to try their voices on melancholy versions of "I'm Thru with Love." (Even DJ's fourteen-year-old half-sister, Lane, when dumped by a crush in favor of her sister, Laura, tearfully warbles a chorus of the renunciatory tune.) One of the film's running jokes is DJ's endlessly mutating infatuations (a Venice gondolier, an American college student, a rap singer who hilariously translates "I'm Thru with Love" into his own idiom, a celebrant at the closing Paris Cinemateque ball) and the self-serving rationales she uses to justify her breezy rotations from one flame to the next. For adults in the film, of course, love isn't such a comically self-perpetuating matter: Joe has had little luck in his search for a replacement for Steffi, his former wife, his pursuits having coupled him with a nymphomaniac and a drug addict. DJ's junior procuress campaign to supply her father with romance constitutes much of the film's minimal plot.

In *Another Woman*, Marion Post's accidental overhearing of a patient's psychoanalytical sessions with her therapist in an adjoining apartment begins the protagonist on the progress dictated by the final line of her favorite Rilke poem: "For here there is no place that does not see you: you must change your life." The analysand, Hope (Mia Farrow), is a young woman who, Marion learns when they become acquainted, fears becoming the passionless, cerebral woman Marion is. Therefore, Hope represents a sort of self-projection who precipitates the necessary change in Marion which is the film's psychic/dramatic dynamic.[6] *Everyone Says I Love You* reprises the same situation of psychiatric eavesdropping, treating it comically.

Lane and Laura have a friend whose mother is a psychiatrist; they listen to her talking with patients through a hole in the wall, and DJ joins them. Her eavesdropping allows her to tell her father all of the most intimate fantasies of one of the clients, Von (Julia Roberts), whom they encounter in Venice. Consequently, Joe is able to invoke Von's private imagery as his own perceptions and thereby convince her that he is, as she puts it, her "true soulmate." Their magical encounter—"This could be me talking," Von responds to one of Joe's supposedly self-revelatory monologues—is purely the product of DJ's girlishly antic intervention and results in amusing moments in which Joe, to Von's utter astonishment, parrots her most secret desires and fantasies back to her.[7] The joke goes sour for Joe only when Von decides that, having met the man of her dreams in Joe—"It's not that he's tall or handsome," she tells her analyst, "but he's magic"—she can now comfortably return to her husband, no longer tortured by her fantasy of the perfect man and perfect romance existing undiscovered for her out in the world.[8] "But that's so neurotic," is Joe's response when she reveals she's leaving him, an accusation Von will turn back against him in this film in which, as in *Annie Hall,* the romantic and neurotic are seldom perceived as being separable from each other.

And so romantically deflated Joe and Steffi attend a masked ball together (her husband having conveniently fallen into a Paris fountain and caught cold) at which all of the guests come disguised as Groucho Marx. (In *Hannah*

and Her Sisters, a Marx Brothers movie becomes Mickey Sachs's *raison d'être;* so giddily affirmative is the surface of *Everyone Says I Love You* that in the end of it everyone actually *becomes* Groucho Marx.) After exchanging some diverting Groucho impressions at the ball, Steffi and Joe head off for a nostalgic visit to an old wooing site of theirs on the Seine. The riverside *pas de deux* which follows, facilitated by the use of a blue screen and invisible guy wires to make Goldie Hawn seem to fly her way through the dance, is one of Allen's great set pieces, but for Denby it's here that democracy-in-action once again mars the film. Whereas Hawn, in his view, dances creditably, Allen only "alludes to a man dancing, the way we all do in the living room, clowning for the children." (As if "clowning for the children" in viewers weren't what Astaire's dances were always about.) Denby seems to assume that Allen's attempt is to replace Astaire rather than, as seems more likely, mediating him.

In *Play It Again, Sam,* Bogart watches Allan Felix renounce his love for Linda, and then comments, "If I did that, there wouldn't be a dry eye in the house." The disparity between Bogart and Felix is the source of much of the humor in Allen's script, the unapologetically moralistic conclusion of which is Felix's realization that "The secret's not being you . . . it's being me. I'm short and ugly enough to make it on my own."[9] The gap created in the film by the discrepancy between an idealized screen Bogart and an all-too-human Allan Felix comments satirically on both Felix, who can't measure up to Bogart's standards, and the Bogart image he tries to replicate, which is nothing more than a cultural fiction. "I-I-I just met a wonderful new man," is how Cecilia, making the same point, describes her similarly screen-spawned beau, Tom Baxter. "He's fictional, but you can't have everything." Choosing, as Cecilia ultimately does, the "real world" over Hollywood fictions is the inevitable decision of Allen's protagonists, even if, as Cecilia does, they inevitably return to the source of the rejected option to warm themselves in its glow.

The audience of *Everyone Says I Love You* is sufficiently conditioned by movie musicals to expect dance numbers to culminate in that glow, to have the same expectations of a romantic dance duet that Denby articulates. The female in such scenes is supposed to be supple, floating, airily feminine; Hawn largely fulfills her role, save for a moment when she seems to be getting propelled down the river perched on the side of a runaway safe, though even her performance totters on the brink of self-parody. The male is supposed to be effortlessly graceful, passionately engaged yet coolly urbane as he whirls, twirls, and dances his love. Joe makes an effort, but he's too depressed at being "Thru with Love" to pull this off; he rises to the occasion only enough to give his despondency a touch of poignancy and to keep Steffi from sprawling on the quay. That Joe Berlin is not Fred Astaire, rather than being the flaw of the scene, is its point: *nobody* in Allen's movies is Fred Astaire, and the implication is always there in his films that Fred Astaire wasn't Fred Astaire, either. (In his era, reviewers often wondered whether Astaire wasn't a little old to be playing romantic leads, too.)

Richard Schickel's review of the film eloquently described its ambivalence toward its cinematic sources: all of the characters in *Everyone* want their lives "to be set to a score by Kern or Gershwin; they all want to believe that there is an authentic possibility of romance when they visit Paris or Venice; they all hope for the kind of transformative musical epiphanies that would suddenly be vouchsafed Kelly or Astaire as they soft-shoed through their happier—or anyway more stylized—realities."[10] When they seek to sing out their desires, Schickel noted, they sound no better than most members of the audience would; when they try to dance their emotions, the effect is more evocative of Yeats's "rag and bone shop of the heart" than of Astaire's dancing cheek to cheek. Next to the Joe/Steffi number, Edward Norton's winningly enthusiastic yet calculatedly clumsy soft-shoe performance of "My Baby Just Cares for Me" on the sales floor of Harry Winston Jewelers is probably the film's classic dramatization of the difference between Hollywood musical epiphany and blundersome actuality; its visual poignancy is reinforced by the fact that we immediately learn that his baby, rather than caring just for him, is, like Cecilia, "a dreamer" fantasizing about a man who is "ideal, but then he isn't real, and I'm a fool—but aren't we all?" The film's not completely celebratory answer to that question is *yes,* Skylar choosing an ex-convict her limousine liberal mother has been championing as the fully inappropriate object of her fantasy affections.

Von never quite figures out that her dream man, Joe, isn't real, either—that he's merely a cunningly prepped repository of her psychic life fraudulently regurgitated back to her, his "magic" quality projecting a thoroughly explicable illusion. Thus, if the film's audience expects Joe to get transformed into some version of *their* dream man, they haven't been paying attention to the movie's demonstration of the falsity of dream man construction. (*Everyone Says I Love You* validates more precisely than any other Allen film Pauline Kael's judgment that "Woody Allen's parodies and fantasies are inseparable; their unstable union is his comic subject."[11])

The climactic dance scene never quite tips over into self-parody but (like the chorus's closing dance in *Mighty Aphrodite,* also choreographed with mode-blurring equivocality by Graciela Daniele) remains delicately poised upon the point in our psychic geography at which our all-too-willing suspension of disbelief in the musical comedy felicities of Fred and Ginger confronts our knowledge of the world. The very real, fully-earned poignancy of the dance contends with its aura of being too much a reconstructed romantic movie scene, too much—and yet, given the dancers' limitations, too little— of what our romance- conditioned hearts long to see.[12] What we are watching, after all, is not a romantically choreographed consummation of human love but a dance embodying human disconnection and disjunction, post-divorce's poignant terpsichore. In their dance's final movement, Joe prepares to pluck the flying Steffi from the air, but she soars over his arms and daintily touches down five yards beyond him, the moment symbolizing even better than the awkward dialogue between them which follows it the separation which Joe is no longer sure he ever wanted and which Steffi doesn't completely regret. They agree that they've been better friends than they were husband and wife, a conclusion belied by their kiss, which obviously rejuvenates a more-than-friendly passion. Even Fred and Ginger would have had difficulty dancing the ambivalent emotions Steffi and Joe are feeling in this scene.

The nocturnal scene on the Seine cuts back to the brightly lit Groucho Marx ball, where, appropriately, the orchestra is playing "Everyone Says I Love You" from *Horse Feathers* and DJ has found someone new to say it to—the only person who came to the party dressed as Harpo. If Allen's film seems inordinately bemused by the limitless capacity of youth to discover new crushes and recommence love relations, that's just musical comedy compensation for all the minor key notes in the late-middle-agers' narrative which suggest that, for them, time for new chance romance is running out—that it's later than they think and that they have good reason to sing "I'm Thru with Love." "Goodbye to spring, and all it's meant to me," the song's lyrics, evoking the insuperable problem of time's irreversibility, lament, "it can never bring the things that used to be."

Joe's daughter acts as if her father were incapable of attracting a woman unless he can reflect her most intensely private fantasies back to her, and when Joe tries to impress Von by emulating her jogging, he suffers an apparently unfeigned stress attack which suggests that his jokes about being old and out of shape aren't just jokes. The only explanation for Steffi's singing "I'm Thru with Love" at the end of the film is that the notion of love her kindly, devoted husband (Alan Alda) expressed in lines from Cole Porter's "Looking at You" ("Looking at you, while troubles are fleeing and the sweet honey dew of well-being settles upon me") is so familial, insular, and cozy as to practically eviscerate the word as the source of mystery and magic it's often construed as being in Allen's films. Grandpa's senile belief that he can leave a message for his wife, dead twenty years, seems a commentary upon love's capacity for delusion; his conviction that he's going to a doubleheader at the Polo Grounds between the Cardinals and New York Giants (who departed the Bronx for San Francisco in 1957) seems to glance satirically at the kind of nostalgic reconstruction of the past so necessary to the good feelings of Allen's movie. Similarly, Allen's filmic idealizations of New York seem to be alluded to in a policeman's explanation of where he'd encountered Grandpa: "We found him at Grand Central Station. He thought he was at the Botanical Gardens." Grandpa's rising from his casket at a funeral home to join his fellow dead in singing and dancing a rousing version of "Enjoy Yourself (It's Later Than You Think)" is both delightfully funny and as frightening to contemplate as Allen claims it was for him when he first registered the song's meaning as a child.[13] DJ's equivocations regarding which of the seasons in New York is her favorite allows Di Palma wonderful opportunities to visualize the seasons as they pass, the film's movement from spring through winter tacitly confirming the admonition of "Enjoy Yourself": "The years go by, as quickly as a wink." It's a testament to the film's spritely Tin Pan Alley soundtrack, its sumptuous photography, and DJ's girlishly cheerful narrative which closes the film that *Everyone,* its significantly darker crosslights notwithstanding, could be read by one reviewer as "emotionally and artistically all but weightless, as ephemeral as a ditty dashed off on a bar napkin."[14]

No doubt many comedies, like happiness itself, can be expected to turn somber when scrutinized too closely. It's clear from Allen's few comments on the film that he was seeking to make "a very light picture—as they say, very broad."[15] "I thought, I want to enjoy myself," he told John Lahr. "I want to hear those songs from over the decades that I loved so much. I want to see those people on Fifth Avenue and Park Avenue. It comes from what I wish the world were really like."[16] Those upbeat intentions are clearly borne out in the film's numerous comic scenes: in the repetition of Skylar's swallowing the engagement ring Holden gives to her; in an entire hospital floor's patients' and medical personnel's song and dance rendition of "Makin' Whoopee"; in Skylar's ill-considered and ill-fated affair with ex-prisoner Charles Ferry (Tim

Roth); in the trick-or-treaters of DJ's family's building performing musical comedy standards for their candy; in the diagnosis of arterial blockage as the explanation for Scott (Lucas Haas) being a political conservative rather than a liberal Democrat like the rest of his family; and of course, in the funny, lovely songs which permeate the film.

"The songs, sweetly romantic chestnuts," Janet Maslin argued, "are mostly a way to evoke the madcap impossible world that Mr. Allen means to conjure. It's a world both of serene privilege and surreal possibility, and it offers a delightful and witty compendium of the filmmaker's favorite things."[17] Maslin's characterization of the film perfectly catches both the mood of enchantment *Everyone Says I Love You* seeks to project while acknowledging simultaneously the expressionistic excesses which make it all difficult to believe despite the fact that—as Skylar recommended—the film *is* a musical. It's when the film's "world of serene privilege and surreal possibility" seems most unbelievable that we begin to notice that *Everyone Says I Love You* perpetuates a significant tendency in Allen's recent films, one manifested in the perplexities of their male protagonists.

In *Manhattan Murder Mystery,* Larry tells Carol, "I don't need a murder to enliven my life at all," and thus largely absents himself from the detection plot until the end of the film. Of the protagonists Allen has played, Larry seems unquestionably the least individually characterized (he dislikes stamp collections; he likes Father's Day and Bob Hope movies) and the most per-functorily derivative of previous Allen portrayals. In *Bullets Over Broadway,* David Shayne loses confidence in his own dramatic writing and becomes in-creasingly dependent upon Cheech to rewrite whole sections of his play for him, pretending the revisions are his own. In *Mighty Aphrodite*, Lenny, the most effectual of the four protagonists, tells the chorus leader that "I take action, I act," and although he bears out this claim through his intervention with Linda Ash, at home there seems to be no alteration of the familial power structure he delineates for Max: "I'm the boss. Mommy says what we do, and I have control of the channel changer." A certain withdrawal, or self-efface-ment, is what the three protagonists seem to share in common, one epito-mized by Linda's insight about Lenny: "You only talk about me—you never talk about yourself."

The same basic passivity is noticeable in Joe Berlin. When he and DJ arrive in Venice, she worries that "he just seemed to hang around the hotel," and she is relieved when Von's appearance inspires the scheme to shake him from his doldrums. Joe prepares for his pursuit of Von by steeping himself in her fantasy life via DJ and by pretending a knowledge of Tintoretto which he doesn't possess. When Von explains why she is leaving him, he tries to disown his ideal man pose by asking her what she'd say if he admitted that his "magi-cal" quality was only a "facade," that he'd merely had special "access to your

deepest feelings and thoughts" and had been "playing this character just to win you over and make you like me, to make you happy?"

"I'd say you were crazy," is her response.

If that is crazy, it's a form of crazy Allen anatomized in detail in one of his most memorable protagonists.

In her attempt to begin treating Leonard Zelig's neurotic imitation of other human beings' physical and mental traits, Eudora Fletcher (Mia Farrow) is confronted first with his identification of himself with her as a doctor. Telling him he's not a doctor fails to have any effect, so she hits upon the clever plan of using the psychic material she'd gathered from interviews while he was under hypnosis to reverse the identification dynamic at work between them. She asks for his help as a doctor, confessing that she lied to others about having read *Moby-Dick,* hoping those who had read the novel would like her because she had read it as well. Zelig, noticeably discomfited by his unconscious mind's recognition that its contents are being mirrored back as another's experience, suggests that, as a doctor, she can handle her problem. Eudora pursues her strategy by explaining to him that she isn't actually a doctor—that she only pretends to be a doctor because she wants to fit in with her friends, who are doctors. Since Zelig's greatest fear is that, beyond his imitations of others, "I'm nobody—I'm nothing,"[18] Eudora is confronting him with the terrible anxiety of surrendering the parameters of the self he has appropriated by disavowing them herself. The cognitive dissonance created in him by her counter-chameleon plan is hilarious to watch; it also represents the first step en route to his recovery and to their romance.

In order to effect a cure for Zelig and to generate a romance for herself, she has to do for him precisely what Joe does in courting Von: she transforms herself into the contents of his psyche.[19] The difference, of course, is that in Zelig's case, the strategy results in a cure and a marriage. (Among other things, *Zelig's* comic resolution commemorated the recent romantic union of Allen and Farrow, a relationship that would see them make thirteen films together.) Unlike the resuscitated and happily coupled Zelig, Joe is abandoned in Paris, inhabiting an apartment he moved into because it represented Von's dream of an artist's garret, her final words to him as she departed echoing in the place: "I'd say you were crazy."

Arguably, even when Allen tries to make a light confection of a film, full of reassurance and bright Broadway show tunes, the old anxieties and questions inevitably resurface. The similarity between Fletcher's initiatory Zelig therapy and the mechanics of DJ's matchmaking scheme is striking; even more so is how closely Joe's courtship of Von replicates Zelig's trademark interpersonal dynamic: mirror the other back to herself to earn her approval and affection. Given the centrality of the psychological issues dramatized so effectively in *Zelig* both in terms of contemporary humanity's anxieties and in Allen's career as well, it's probably not surprising that Zeligian characteristics begin reemerging in his films at the point that they do. Before returning to those more recent movies, it's worth briefly considering how the themes so powerfully addressed in *Zelig* illuminate the choices and challenges of Allen's post-*Husbands and Wives* career.

For Allen, a filmmaker whose participation in the Freudian revolution of the twentieth century has meant modeling his work on that of artists such as Eugene O'Neill and Ingmar Bergman in focusing on the interior landscapes of human beings as the primary subjects of his films, Leonard Zelig represents both the ultimate joke and the quintessential threat. In artistic terms, the question Zelig allowed Allen to pose to himself was this: how to make films about the self if the self is only a reflection of other selves, if the self has come to be understood as nothing more than a mirror of its surroundings?[20] In more personal, psychological terms, the question becomes whether the narcissism so widely interpreted as the ascendent psychological symptom of the age isn't an elaborate compensation for anxiety about the self's integrity, if not about its very existence. In Zelig's various self-metamorphoses into a Greek, an Indian, an African-American, a fat man, and a Nazi, the viewer perhaps recognizes his/her own experiences of adaptive coloration, of assuming the attitudes, ideas, or styles of others in order to flatter them or to impress some other audience. And—if s/he is honest about it—the viewer acknowledges as well the sobering moment of doubt as to whether there is an integral self behind the imitations at all. That Allen's film hilariously mined a source of real cultural anxiety of the early 1980s seems undeniable; whether *Zelig* replicates a significant characteristic of Allen's own filmmaking career is necessarily more conjectural.

Were Zelig a filmmaker, the form that his neurosis might be expected to take would be the creation of movies which closely resemble other filmmakers' movies: he might make a period comedy, for instance, about three couples cavorting in the green world of the countryside which would recall Bergman's *Smiles of a Summer Night;* a grim family drama set at the seashore might remind some viewers of Bergman's *Persona;* the narrative of a demoralized filmmaker attending a film retrospective in his honor might evoke Fellini's *8½;* the process of self-confrontation experienced by the title character of *Alice* would conjure up *Juliet of the Spirits,* and so on. At least two of Allen's movies—*Interiors* and *Stardust Memories*—can be fruitfully discussed with only minimal reference to the films which influenced their creation; however, there is no getting around the fact that Allen is a filmmaker whose films incessantly and unapologetically invoke other films.

The setting of the emotional climaxes of three of his finest films—*Stardust Memories, Purple Rose of Cairo,* and *Hannah and Her Sisters*—in movie theaters reflects Allen's profoundly postmodern assumption of how completely our lives are mediated by cinematic narrative, how significant a role films play in our construction of selves. (Had Allen wanted to insist on this point, he might have had Zelig begin imitating the characteristics of the Leonard Zelig in the Hollywood biopic produced on Zelig's life, thus reinforcing the film's argument that the self is partially a construct derived from images of self projected on the silver screen.) Whether Allen's films' evocation of the emotional colorations of earlier movies represents effective cinematic homage or the Zeligian imitation of moods in the absence of tonalities of Allen's own is a question which *Everyone Says I Love You* does not alone raise. But to dismiss his movies on the ground that they're derivative or imitative of classic European or Hollywood films is to ignore how deliberately his work addresses and complicates precisely these questions of artistic derivation and imitation and also investigates their relationship to the artist's mental stability. That a culturally ascribed deficiency may be a virtue is the point of many of Allen's fables as well as the self-defined object lesson of Leonard Zelig's story: "It shows," Zelig explains at the end of the documentary creating him, "exactly what you can do if you're a total psychotic." For Joe Berlin, of course, the chameleon strategy culminates—far less happily—in the same characterization: Von's response, "I'd say you were crazy."

Given the movie preoccupation of Allen's movies, it seems appropriate that the resuscitation of Leonard Zelig from non-being ("Devoid of personality, his human qualities long since lost in the shuffle of life, he sits alone, quietly staring into space, a cipher, a non-person, a performing freak") to the hero for whom a New York ticker tape parade is held is so much a process of filmmaking. When Eudora Fletcher's assistant asks her why she can't simply take notes on Zelig's responses once his therapy has been initiated, she explains that she must have his progress on film because "when a man changes his physical appearance, you want to see it." That progress gets recorded not only on her assistant's film but by the newsreel cameras which, in the process of filming his receiving the key to Manhattan and cavorting at the Hearst mansion with Tom Mix, golfer Bobby Jones, and others, authenticate his evolution from "non-person," "cipher" and "performing freak without a life of his own" to American celebrity. "Ultimately," Daniel Green argued, "Zelig the 'human chameleon' is a unique creation of film, a character whose 'life' is completely dependent upon its manifestation in filmed images. We never actually experience Zelig's transformations; rather, we laugh at them as *fait accompli* which have been caught by a camera. In a very real sense, we accept Leonard Zelig as an authentic subject for a documentary because of our willingness to accept the authenticity of the cinematic image itself."[21]

The adherence of *Zelig* to the structure of documentary is probably the only reason the film isn't routinely considered among Allen's best—ironically, this movie constructed out of documentary footage depicting what Bruno Bettleheim characterizes as "the ultimate conformist" often seems like Allen's most original and intensely creative work. That Zelig is so completely the creature of film clips significantly limits his compellingness as a dramatic character, his two disappearances from the movie (during which he insinuates himself into the Pope's inner circle in Rome and into the Nazi high command) comprising what the film has for plot development. However, anyone watching the film recently will be surprised to find that the formulaic character of Zelig's progress has become weirdly inflected by extratextual coincidence: the scandal resulting from the exposure of Zelig's many marriages and other indiscretions while acting out his numerous personalities seems depressingly familiar, the screenplay suddenly proliferating with newspaper quotations which now seem cruelly like art/life *double entendres*: "ZELIG'S PAST CATCHES UP," "CLAIMS AGAINST ZELIG MULTIPLY," "Zelig says that he will fight it in court, but public opinion begins to shift subtly against him." Apparently one of Allen's less autobiographical characters, Zelig anticipated Allen's own immersion in violent cultural controversy. Zelig redeems himself in the public's perception by reverting to his neurotic condition and flying himself and Eudora back to the United States by imitating her abilities as a pilot. As Saul Bellow interprets Zelig's reclamation in the film, "His sickness was at the root of his salvation, and . . . I think it's interesting to view the thing that way, that it, it was his . . . it was his very disorder that made a hero of him."[22] Who would better understand this idea than a comedian-turned-filmmaker whose fame continues to be predicated upon his calculated deviance from mainstream ideals of human behavior and self-image?

That Allen is unlikely to set a world record by flying upside down over the Atlantic Ocean probably eliminates any possibility of his becoming a hero with the American public; of course, it isn't even clear that the largely upbeat movies he produced between *Husbands and Wives* and *Deconstructing Harry* represent what numerous reviewers have seen in them: attempts on his part to restore himself to the moviegoing audience's good graces. (If this was Allen's objective, *Deconstructing Harry* and *Celebrity* constituted the introduction of a concerted counterstrategy.) And yet, as we've seen, there was an aura about *Manhattan Murder Mystery* that seemed to emphasize both the felicitous restoration of the Allen/Keaton team and their return to security once they'd outlasted the murder plot, their retreat behind the glass doors of their apartment building all but bearing a subtitle epitomizing the entire film's mood: "We're all right." The ending of *Bullets Over Broadway* includes what can be read as Allen's guilty identification of himself with Cheech, the film's ultimate proponent of the "artist creates his own moral universe" ethic, while *Mighty Aphrodite* seems to repudiate the tragic imperatives of vengeance and retribution invoked by Mia Farrow's preoccupation with *The Trojan Women* in favor of the more comedic inevitabilities of love and romance. Can such elements of Allen's films be read completely in isolation from Allen's very public private experience? Only at the cost of ignoring the considerable evidence pervading his movies that art derives in subtle and not so subtle ways from artists' lives.

Joe Berlin's Zelig-like effort to spark a little love and romance in the heart of Von runs afoul of its own self-subsuming falsity in a movie which otherwise celebrates Eros as the only thing in the world (besides wealth) worth celebrating. "There are only eight little letters in the phrase, you'll find," as the Burt Kalmar/Harry Ruby song, "Everyone Says I Love You," expresses it beneath the film's closing scene, "but they mean a lot more than all the other words combined." It is Allen's very real anxiety that the ability of that phrase to imbue the world with the only magic in which he's ever completely believed is faltering, the impulse to love or be loved becoming as remote as the origins of the songs which are his films' non-visual means of asserting the impulse's validity. This worry manifests itself in his films through the increasing passivity, self-effacement, and confusion of the protagonists of *Manhattan Murder Mystery, Bullets Over Broadway, Mighty Aphrodite,* and *Everyone Says I Love You.* Harry Block of *Deconstructing Harry* might be said to represent a calculated counteraction to the passive tendencies of Larry and David Shayne and Lenny and Joe, Allen having described the film a year before its release as being "about a nasty, shallow, superficial, sexually obsessed guy. I'm sure that everybody will think—I know this going in—that it's me."[23] His eponymous symptom—writing block—unites him with them, however. As we'll see in the next chapter, it's left to Harry to fashion a life without love predicated on the one other form of magic in which Allen has intermittently sought to believe—art.

Allen's work, consequently, promises to continue to do what Diane Jacobs suggested it was doing as early as *Annie Hall:* inviting while refusing to confirm analogies between himself and his protagonists.[24] Therefore, his films will continue to confront his personal anxieties in a way which seems simultaneously to accuse him and the viewer of contemporary psychological deviances in a way unlikely to make either completely comfortable. (Compare the inducement Zelig's sister uses to attract crowds to view the spectacle that is her brother: "SEE ZELIG TURN INTO YOU.") "His story," Irving Howe comments about Zelig, "reflected the nature of our civilization, the character of our times . . . yet it was also one man's story." Saul Bellow adds, "He was of course fairly amusing, but at the same time touched a nerve in people. . . . Perhaps in a way that they would prefer not to be touched" (p. 5). Of all the contradictory and often self-canceling interpretations of Zelig, however, the one most unambiguously confirmed by the film narrative is F. Scott Fitzgerald's closing impression. Zelig and Eudora are pictured in a home movie framed by the porch of a house on the day of their wedding, the couple finally disappearing arm-in-arm around the corner of the building. The narrator, in voiceover, delivers Fitzgerald's judgment: "In the end, it was, after all, not the approbation of many but the love of one woman that changed his life."

"Just he, just she," Holden croons to Skylar at the beginning of Allen's 1996 movie musical, "And what a perfect plot, just say you love me." That "perfect plot" played itself out nicely in the close of Sandy Bates's movie in *Stardust Memories,* in *Midsummer Night's Sex Comedy, Zelig, Hannah and Her Sisters,* "Oedipus Wrecks," *Mighty Aphrodite,* and in the prevailing spirit of *Everyone Says I Love You.* The predominantly upbeat ending of that film is engendered by the story's reversion to DJ's girlishly ebullient narrative, its energy having been juiced up by her encounter with her latest inamorata— "Talk about sexy!" Harpo. Joe and Steffi can't appear in this closing emblem of youthful romantic union and sexual felicity, largely because the conclusion of their dialogue on the Seine has identified them as being beyond all that, their agreement that it's time to head home because "it's late" sparking in the viewer's ear the admonitory lyric, "it's later than you think." In retrospect, their postdance conversation seems to have had the effect of redefining for each of them the meaning of "Just You, Just Me."

For Woody Allen, then, it sometimes seems true that everyone says "I love you," and that subjective impression can feel like "the sweet honey dew of well-being" settling upon him. But he also knows that sometimes *she* stops saying "I love you," and that sometimes *he* says it in order to have something to say so as not to fall silent; other times he's saying it because others have said it in the medium of film, and when they did, it sometimes made him and everyone else feel better. So they "invoke love, call out for it, beg for it, cry for it, try to imitate it, think they have it, lie about it." Allen's films—these two in particular—agree in spirit with the explanation John Updike once offered for the preoccupation with eroticism in Western society: "Might it not simply be that sex has become involved in the Promethean protest forced upon Man by his paradoxical position in the Universe as a self-conscious animal? Our fundamental anxiety is that we do not exist—or will cease to exist. Only in being loved do we find external corroboration of the supremely high valuation each ego secretly assigns itself. This exalted arena, then, is above all others the one where men and women insist on their freedom to choose—to choose the other being in whose existence their own existence is confirmed and amplified."[25] *Zelig* and *Everyone Says I Love You* use very different means to make the same dramatic point that pervades Allen's films: the idea that everyone says "I love you" out of the fear that not to love or be loved is to be no one at all.

18

How We Choose to Distort It

Deconstructing Harry

I didn't want this guy to be necessarily likable. I wanted him to be surly and upset: not a saint or an angel, but a man with real problems who finds that art doesn't save you.

—Allen describing Sandy Bates of *Stardust Memories*

It's one of the oddities of Allen's film oeuvre that his primary objection to the perception of art in Western culture is so seldom directly articulated in his movies. Renata, the poet of *Interiors,* offers its most explicit summation in asking her analyst, "I mean, just what am I striving to create, anyway? I mean, to what end? For what purpose? What goal? . . . I mean, do I really care if a handful of my poems are read after I'm gone forever? Is that supposed to be some sort of compensation? Uh, I used to think it was, but now for some reason, I-I can't." (p. 124). The same idea is presented with allegorical indirection in Irmstadt's invocation of the human dependency on illusions in the closing line of *Shadows and Fog,* and few arguments surface so regularly in Allen's interviews, but the exchange between Vivian and Sandy Bates in *Stardust Memories* briefly following the nurse's eulogy—"Poor fool, he's dead. And he never found the meaning of life"—is, before *Deconstructing Harry,* its only other explicit articulation in his films.

Vivian, the director of the weekend Film Festival, delivers her funereal judgment upon him, telling the audience, "Sandy Bates's work will live on after him." In attendance at what has become his memorial service, Bates objects, "Yeah, but what good is it if I can't pinch women or hear any music?" Intent upon validating her thesis of art's redemptive efficacy, Vivian ignores his objection, proceeding to introduce one of the film clips which to her mind will constitute Bates's immortality: "And now, in this classic scene from his Academy Award-winning motion picture—" "I would trade that Oscar," Bates impatiently interrupts, "for one more second of life" (p. 371). Bates's casually defined yet utterly unwavering existentialism—a philosophical stance shared by most of Allen's protagonists—admits of no substitute for being: as the ghost of one of Harry's friends assures him in *Deconstructing Harry,* "To be alive is to be happy—take it from me." Like his creator, Bates would much prefer to live on not in the minds of men but in his apartment.[1]

"I sometimes feel that art is the intellectual's religion," Allen told Stig Bjorkman in 1994, a point dramatized in *Interiors* by Eve's experience of a crisis of faith when the aesthetic contemplation of a Romanesque church she invited her estranged husband to share with her suffers an abrupt deflation through his actuality-intruding request that they finalize their divorce. Allen might have been characterizing Eve's desperate, futile faith in the aesthetic as he continued:

> Some artists think that they will be saved by their art, that they will be immortalized through their art, that they will live on through their art. But the truth of the matter is, art doesn't save you. Art for me has always been entertainment for intellectuals. Mozart, Shakespeare or Rembrandt are entertainers on a very, very high level. It's a level that brings a great sense of excitement, stimulation and fulfillment to people who are sensitive and cultivated. But it doesn't save the artist. I mean, it doesn't profit Shakespeare one iota that his plays have lived on after him. He would have been better off if he were alive and the plays were forgotten.[2]

Given these sentiments, it's not surprising that the search for meaning so pervasive in Allen's films—"Yeah, but I've gotta find meaning," Sandy Bates objects when the extraterrestrial Og urges him to make funnier movies— never culminates in the affirmation of art-as-preservation, art-as-bulwark against time's incessant passage, art as—in T.S. Eliot's formulation—"fragments shored against my ruins." The closest an Allen film comes to concluding on a celebration of aesthetic preservation is the ending of *Radio Days*, in which the narrator's implicit declaration of his film's memorializing of the radio voices of his youth is equivocated by his admission that even for him, the memorializer, those voices have grown dimmer as each year has elapsed since he last heard them. As we saw through *Stardust Memories*, for Allen the fallibility of human memory necessarily adulterates the Grecian urn perfection that art is supposed to be able to achieve; it is one of his central and most consistently dramatized aesthetic axioms that the creations of imperfect beings must necessarily be correspondingly imperfect.

There is no contradiction, then, in the fact that a vicious mob hit man can be also—in the estimation of David Shayne of *Bullets Over Broadway* and the actors in *God of Our Fathers*, at any rate—"a great artist," since Allen's scripts deny any necessary causal relation between personal morality and artistic capacity. In fact, Cheech, that great proponent of art's responsibility to reflect "how people really talk," seems to live on in the increased sexual explicitness of *Mighty Aphrodite* and in the heightened profanity and carnality of both *Deconstructing Harry* and *Celebrity*. As if in reaction against the artistic compromises and filmic civility of the *Hannah* era, Allen's post-Farrow films have sought deliberately to reflect the deepening vulgarity of the world he depicts, Allen opting for the opposite choice from the one he attributes to David Shayne by opening his art to cultural crudity. Shayne's ringing declaration toward the end of *Bullets* that "I'm an artist—but first I'm a human being" says as much about that film's depiction of the vulnerability of art to human corruption as it does about his personally held moral commitments. Accordingly, Shayne saves himself by fleeing the artistic vocation that had been the principal source of meaning in his life. Like Harry Block, Allen's alternative course has been to make cultural corruption the subject of his art, leaving it to Harry—of his artist/protagonists, arguably the most imperfect and surely the least deserving of salvation—to be saved by art.

Harry (Allen) and Lucy (Judy Davis) are on the roof of his apartment building in the continuation of the scene addressed in the introduction to this study, she having raised the ante of her attack on his novel exploiting their now-terminated affair by pulling a gun on him. In an attempt to calm her, Harry recounts the plot of one of his stories, which is then dramatized cinematically: the protagonist, Harvey Stern (Tobey Maguire), assumes the identity of a hospitalized friend whose bachelor digs he's using for a tryst with a prostitute. "Donning the other man's silk robe," Harry's narrator explains, "Harvey became the swinger Mandel Birnbaum." The impersonation backfires when Death arrives, mistaking Harvey for the apartment's inhabitant and bearing him off instead of the hospitalized Birnbaum.[3] Harry recalls for his psychiatrist that the story made Lucy laugh, deflecting her anger. The analyst replies, "So writing saved your life."

Deconstructing Harry is very much about ways in which writing saves Harry Block's life, but the movie constitutes no reversal of Allen's consistently articulated position on the meaninglessness of literary reputation, on the fraudulence of the Modernist credo that art confers upon the artist the only form of immortality available to humanity. Harry's narration of his "Death Knocks" story earns him not literary immortality but a very tangible prolongation of his mortality—Lucy desists from shooting him; nowhere else in *Deconstructing Harry* is art depicted as having anything more than purely material effects upon artist or audience.

A gaggle of adoring Adair University academics gathered to give Harry an honorary degree burble pompously about the cultural contributions of their former student and present honoree, but no one else in the film—Harry included—has anything remotely positive to say about his art. We have already considered Lucy's excoriation of Harry's novel on the ground that it callously exploits and exposes his friends and lovers, its author, in her words, having "not even cared enough to disguise anything" of the actual events he fictionalized. In general, the excerpts from Harry's fiction dramatized throughout the film are marked by a cynical belittling of their characters: Harvey Stern is a married sexual-obsessive who imagines copulating with all women except his wife; Helen Epstein (Demi Moore) is a psychiatrist so titillated by the fantasies her patients divulge in therapy that she terminates their treatment in order to initiate erotic relations with them; Max Pincus (Hy Anzell) is a bourgeois Jewish family man who has concealed from his wife of thirty years that he murdered his initial family and devoured their corpses. Harry's characters are, in short, cartoonish incarnations of the Freudian notion which pervades Allen's films: that whatever their aspirations toward idealism, integrity, or decency, human beings are finally no better than their basest impulses. Harry has turned this concept into a personal and artistic *raison d'être*.

As his third wife, Joan (Kirstie Alley) characterizes him, Harry is their son Hilly's "alcoholic, pill-popping, beaver-banging excuse for a father." Harry has, as he acknowledges, "squandered everything I had on shrinks and lawyers and whores"; consequently, he confesses, exceeding the demoralized conditions of Larry and Lenny and Joe Berlin, "I'm spiritually bankrupt—I'm empty . . . I got no soul." His sister, Doris (Caroline Aaron), agrees: Harry has "no spiritual center" and is "betting everything on physics and pussy." As if in confirmation of Doris's characterization of him, Harry numbers among his achievements his affair with Lucy, the sister of his second wife, Jane (Amy Irving), and his affair with the patient of psychiatrist Joan—wife number three—which prompted her to initiate divorce proceedings. Harry's literary output—which represents anything but "entertainment on a very, very high level"—is little more than a fictionalized catalogue of his own enormities and the dramatization of the deficiencies of and resentments he holds against those with whom he is intimate. Harry's life and art are summarized most succinctly by Doris's later assessment of her brother: "You have no values. Your whole life is nihilism—it's cynicism, it's sarcasm and orgasm."

Elliott Gould's unavailability to play Harry and Allen's decision to take the role himself increased the likelihood, as he put it, that "everybody will think—I know this going in—that [Harry]'s me." Reviewers of the film had difficulty accepting Allen's portrayal of the self-proclaimed "worst person in the world," Harry's profanity-spouting and incessant drinking consistently conflicting with Allen's familiarly genial gestures and inflections in such a way as to render the characterization unconvincing. In other words, Harry is to Allen what Harry's fictional characters are to their models—caricatures exaggerating their originals' most antisocial and self-serving tendencies.[4] As Allen's hyperbolized projection of the "bad Woody" of the Mia Farrow crisis, Harry is a sexual transgressor of familial boundaries, a "self-hating Jew" whose putatively anti-Semitic art is accused of compounding the sufferings of Jews[5]; he is a man so depraved that he can contest with the Devil over who has committed the foulest and most unforgivable acts, Harry at the time clearly having never quite comprehended that he'd done anything wrong. There are at least three possible explanations for the fact that Harry Block can't remain in the unregenerate condition the film ascribes to him: because underlying *Deconstructing Harry* is another film in which an unsympathetic character achieves self-knowledge and thus a modicum of redemption; because Allen is a sufficiently traditional screenwriter that his plots gravitate toward character reversal[6]; and, because of Allen's ambivalent attitude toward art-as-redemption-of-life, Harry's concluding reversal and recognition are a thoroughly ambiguous event.

Isak Borg, the protagonist of Bergman's *Wild Strawberries*, undergoes a similar one-day voyage of self-discovery in traveling to the University of Lund to be honored on the occasion of the fiftieth anniversary of his graduation from the institution.[7] En route to the ceremony, Borg tells his daughter-in-law, Marianne, "I have no respect for mental suffering, so don't come lamenting to me." A man whose life has been completely dedicated to his work, Borg has cultivated an experimentalist's objectivity, his "love of science" severely delimiting his human sympathies. "Your judgments are very categorical," Marianne responds to his dismissal of "mental suffering," "I'd hate to have to depend on you." No one can depend on Harry Block, either, and for somewhat parallel reasons. As his sister suggests, something like half of Harry's belief system is comprised by physics, the other half by a similarly physical reality. Harry assures a friend that, "between the Pope and air-conditioning, I'll take air-conditioning," and insists subsequently that "I'm all quarks and particles and black holes—all that other stuff is junk to me."[8]

Borg spends much of his day experiencing memories of his past and dreams which confront him inescapably with the suffering, loneliness, and heartache his unfeeling, passionless life have brought on others and himself.[9] Harry spends his day reliving the deeds that have resulted in his current demoralized and solitary condition, many of them being configured as scenes from his fiction which gradually mutate into the experiences of Harry's life that they literarily reconstruct and consistently misrepresent.[10]

In a dream that Borg suffers toward the close of his journey, he is judged incompetent as a doctor because he can't see beyond the image of his own eye in a microscope and mistakes for a corpse a fully alive woman; he is also found guilty of the similarly narcissistic minor offenses of "callousness, selfishness, and ruthlessness." Harry indicts himself with these vices and more, repeatedly judging himself "a failure at life" and "a shit" OD'ing on himself.

At the end of *Wild Strawberries,* Borg prepares for bed following the ceremony and is serenaded by three young people who have been his traveling companions, the girl among them—who bears the name of a fiancée who once rejected him—telling him that, of the three men who have shared her life today, "I love you most of all." Intuiting that this Sara has redeemed the original Sara's desertion of him, Borg determines to write down his impressions from the day because "they seemed to be a jumble in which I could discern an extraordinary logic." That logic's ultimate reward consists in his dreaming that the Sara of his young manhood has led him to a childhood fishing spot where his parents await him. Just as the imagining of the stories he never wrote provides Ernest Hemingway's Harry with a redemptive fantasy death in "The Snows of Kilimanjaro," Borg's reluctant but genuine gestures toward others in *Wild Strawberries* have earned him regeneration—not of his life, but through his dreams.

Allen's Harry's parallel redemption occurs, similarly, through the intercession of a dream, Allen's script diverging from Bergman's in having Harry's dream precipitate rather than follow the "writing down of impressions." Before explicating Harry's dream-induced redemption, however, we need to consider the significance of the fact that Harry's honorary ceremony—unlike Borg's—never occurs, as well as his sardonic observation upon arriving at Adair University: "I can't believe it—my old school wants to honor me, and I show up with a hooker and a dead body."

Threading through *Deconstructing Harry's* oscillation between the dramatization of Harry's trespasses against others and scenes from his stories and novels is a plot: Harry meets a fan of his work in an elevator, telling her, "If this were one of my stories, the elevator would get stuck between floors, we'd start a major affair and then fall in love." As if it *were* one of his stories, he and Fay Sexton (Elisabeth Shue) do have an affair, Harry constantly warning her against falling in love with him because he's like the boy in one of his stories who is incapable of love. Fay had already fallen for his work, she explains—"I love your imagination"—and, reprising a debate from *Bullets Over Broadway*, she mistakes this infatuation for love of him. Harry introduces her to his friend and alter ego, Larry (Billy Crystal), and the Amazon explorer and "fun guy" soon steals her heart. Depicting Larry as a demonic anti-Harry allows Allen the fun of projecting cinematically the Hell over which this Devil rules, with Harry acting out the part of Goldberg, the protagonist of a story he's writing who seeks to recover his wife after the Devil has dragged her off to Hell.

Deconstructing Harry (again like *Wild Strawberries*) takes place over forty-eight hours, spanning the day on which Fay tells Harry that tomorrow she will marry Larry and the day on which both the marriage and the honorary ceremony are scheduled to occur. Harry spends these two days desperately seeking to persuade Fay to marry him rather than Larry, and his grudging acceptance of their marriage is one of the climactic steps in his psychic catharsis and revival.

Harry is so generously provided with character deficiencies that it's difficult to decide which is most deserving of redemption, but the primary symptom of his current malaise is an appropriately named condition—writer's block. "For the first time in my life," he complains, employing a sexual pun we

noticed in the film's opening scene, "I can't seem to write—it's not coming."
One of the characters from his latest novel offers his gloss on his creator's
psychic/artistic dilemma, his judgment getting validated by the plot's unfolding. "You picked [Jane] so [the marriage] wouldn't work," Ken (Richard Benjamin) explains to Harry, "—so you wouldn't have to give up sport fucking
and chronic dissatisfaction and grow up."[11]

The central defect of Harry's work, clearly, is the cardinal defect of his
life: narcissism. Because it is so busy indicting others for what Harry believes
they have done to him, his work never moves beyond the closed circle of
egotism to register the reality or complexity of other lives. Therefore, his characters are caricatures expressing Harry's resentment at their models' refusals to
fulfill his desires. To "grow up," accordingly, would be to acknowledge in
fiction and in life the subjectivity of others and to be able to love them as he
loves himself. By falling in love with Fay, Harry takes his first halting move
away from narcissism, though he remains as bewildered by her refusal to re-
ciprocate his ardor as a child at denials of affection by its mother.[12]

Accompanying Harry on the voyage of self-discovery which is his journey to Adair University are his son, Hilly (Eric Lloyd); Cookie Williams (Hazelie
Goodman), a prostitute Harry has befriended; and Richard (Bob Balaban), a
crony of Harry's who fears his heart is giving out on him and in fact dies just
as they arrive at the campus. Acting as a spiritual guide from beyond the
grave, Richard articulates the form that Harry's self-transfiguration must take:
"Make peace with your demons," Richard's specter admonishes Harry, "and

your block will pass." In order to comply with Richard's instruction, Harry must go to Hell.[13]

One obstacle impeding Harry's attainment of maturity is his unresolved resentment against his father, who held against Harry the fact that his mother died giving birth to him.[14] In Harry's eyes, his father's hostility rendered him "a terrible parent," and, as Doris recognizes, Harry's fictional depiction of the cannibalistic murderer Max Pincus represents the son's attempt to avenge himself on his dead father. In order to progress beyond this psychic block, Harry has to reconcile himself with his father's memory; thus, his descent into Hell begins with a confrontation with his father. He has been cast into eternal damnation because, as his infernal jailer explains, "he behaved unconscionably toward his son, accused the boy of a capital crime just by being born." "Look," Harry responds, "I forgive him. What's over is over. It's finished. Let him go to Heaven, please." Harry's father reminds him that Jews don't believe in Heaven, and they settle for sending him to a Chinese restaurant instead. "Take him to Joy Luck," Harry instructs his father's warder, "I love him in spite of everything."

This prototypical Allen one-liner, yoking the eternal with the finite in comic juxtaposition, exhausts Allen's interest in the Oedipal tensions underlying Harry's block; nonetheless, the scene reflects how deliberately Allen's script is preparing for Harry's redemption. The more significant step in his progress toward restored creative fluency involves his other major confrontation in Hell with Larry, the ruler of the underworld. Enacting the self-invented part of Goldberg, Harry confronts Larry (resentment against whom for stealing Fay inspired the original narrative), the two contesting each other for the title of the universe's most unregenerate creature. Larry concludes that Harry will never try to kidnap Fay back from him because "it's not your style. You're not a fun guy, too serious—Fay knew that. Too angry at life." Harry objects, "I got a lot to be angry at," but Larry has a ready response: "Who doesn't? Sooner or later, Harry, you got to back off. It's like Vegas. You're up, you're down, but in the end, the house always wins."

In the subsequent scene, Fay and Larry bail Harry out of jail—Joan has had him arrested for kidnapping his son so that Hilly could attend the Adair ceremony—prompting Harry to do the mature thing: he backs off, "making peace with his demons." Initially balking at the realization that Fay and Larry have gotten married earlier in the afternoon, Harry suffers Fay's explanation that she loves him but is in love with Larry. She asks for Harry's blessing on their union, and Harry, draping his arms around the couple, finally groans, "I give up, I give up." What he is giving up is the belief that his desires dictate events in actuality, the conviction that his love for Fay will automatically provoke reciprocal love from her as it might have in one of his stories; what he's giving up, in other words, is the assumption that reality can be manipulated as his fiction is, the belief that he can ever beat the house odds against personal happiness.

Right before Fay and Larry bail him out, Harry has his conversation with Richard's ghost, their dialogue preparing him to make his saving gesture of renunciation and resignation. "I'm no good at life," Harry confesses:

RICHARD: "No—but you write well."
HARRY: "I write well, but that's a different story, because I can manipulate the characters."
RICHARD: "You create your own universe, but that's much nicer than the world we have, I think."
HARRY: "But I can't function in the world we have—I'm a failure at life."
RICHARD: "Oh, I don't know. I think you bring pleasure to a lot of people. That's good."

The debate between Harry and Richard's spirit reprises issues—the artist's creation of her/his own universe, the justification of art as valuable insofar as it "tells funnier jokes"—Allen's films repeatedly confront, but Harry's emphasis is somewhat different: he portrays the artist as someone who can't function in life and who uses his art as compensation for that fact. Seeking to win his blessing on their marriage, Larry tells Harry, "I will never be the writer that you are. I know that. You put your art in your work. I put it into my life. I can make [Fay] happier."

Fay beams her agreement, and Allen's movie similarly affirms this judgment: with his "chronic dissatisfaction," Harry is, as Larry earlier insisted, "not a fun guy. Too serious." He would never cruise the Amazon, never take his bride to Santa Fe for a honeymoon as Larry has promised to do.[15] Larry embodies an affirmation of the idea that emerges regularly in Allen's later films: his suspicion that the unexamined life *is* worth living; he incarnates the antimeditative side of Woody Allen earlier incarnated by the series of characters played by Tony Roberts, whose basic position is best articulated by Tom Baxter in *Purple Rose of Cairo:* "I don't want to talk any more about what's real and what's illusion. Life's too short to spend time thinking about life. Let's just live it."[16]

Harry's bitter acknowledgment that life won't submit to his imagination in the way that it does in his fiction constitutes significant growth, and his progress in embracing this truth is registered by the fact that Harry decreasingly translates his experience into fictional comic narratives as the movie proceeds. His reward for resigning himself to the differences between fact and fiction is not long in coming, but, given his investment in his imagination, the reward is a thoroughly equivocal one: it consists in a restoration of the condition Harry worked so hard to escape. That is the concluding irony of *Deconstructing Harry.*

Harry's incarceration for kidnapping Hilly has caused the cancellation of the honorary ceremony at Adair, but adulterous Ken and Leslie and Helen Epstein the libidinous psychiatrist and Harvey Stern the would-be-swinger and Max Pincus the murderer/cannibalist and all the other characters from Harry's fiction join to stage an alternative observance. Harry asks if he can bring Hilly, prompting one of the academics ushering him to this substitute ceremony to reply, "It's your dream." Like Bergman's Isak Borg, Harry is on the verge of experiencing a dream redemption: reality having failed to carry through on its pledge to honor him, Harry compensates by dreaming his own self-celebration. Another of the welcoming party admonishes him that "Everyone is waiting to honor you—after all, you created them." Greeted by the warmly enthusiastic applause of his fictional projections, Harry responds, "I love all of you—you've given me the happiest moments of my life, and you've even saved my life at times." Without a doubt, this ceremony is one of those times.

Harry is referring not only to his "Death Knocks" story having literally rescued him from Lucy's murder threat, but to the way in which his art—as in the substitute honoring ceremony—has occasionally offered a sort of compensation for the reversals of his real life. Spurned by Fay, who ultimately proved herself to be an independent, real-world free agent rather than a projection of his literary imagination, Harry seeks refuge in the world of fiction he's always preferred because it's given him "the happiest moments of my life"; accordingly, its inhabitants salute his preference by celebrating him. Harry's dream of an honoring ceremony, of course, turns into one of those life-saving compensations he invokes in attending it: his expression of gratitude to his characters for honoring him inspires in him the concept for a new novel, about "a guy who can't function well in life, but can only function in art."[17] Mulling over this idea back at his apartment once the ceremony has spun its regenerative magic, Harry has clearly emerged from his writer's block: "Rifkin had a fragmented existence," Harry's "notes for a novel" voice-over in the film's closing lines records: "He had long ago come to this conclusion: all people know the same truth—our life consists of how we choose to distort it. Only his writing was calm—his writing, which had more than once saved his life."

In his twenty-seventh film, Allen finally dramatized the Modernist affirmation of art as an antidote to life's confusions, as the redemption of existence, as compensation for the pain of living.[18] Harry's deliverance from writer's block, then, provides *Deconstructing Harry* with a saving catharsis, but what Harry's characters have actually redeemed him from is his life—they've restored him to the fun-bereft, insularly narcissistic world of his artistic fantasizing, to his barren, antisocial, and loveless "world of fiction." They have helped him rededicate himself to an existence fixated upon "how we choose to distort [life]." Like the fate of Ambrose in John Barth's short story, "Lost In the Funhouse," it is Harry's destiny to "construct funhouses for others and be their secret operator—though he would rather be among the lovers for whom funhouses are designed."[19] It's evident that, for Allen, "creating funhouses for lovers" is the best a self-confessed "failure at life" can expect, just as the best celebration of himself that Harry—and by implication, Allen—will ever experience is one hosted by creatures of his own imagination.

The thoroughly straightforward and remarkably peevish message of *Deconstructing Harry* is that radiant Elisabeth Shue—Fay—is not whom you end up with if you're an aging workaholic artist. She may love his work, but in the end she loves more the younger demon who is out in the world living life instead of being cooped up in his "sewer of an apartment" fictionalizing his experience and attempting to avenge the slights of his existence on paper. At the end of his comparison of life to Las Vegas, Larry adds that the fact that "the house" always wins "doesn't mean you didn't have fun." Because he's "too serious"—too preoccupied with the unfairness of "the house" inevitably winning—Harry's "not a fun guy." Larry's right: he "can make [Fay] happier," and it's not merely Fay's beauty which makes Larry's reward seem so incontestably superior to Harry's. In the conclusion of *Deconstructing Harry,* Larry is sentenced to life; Harry is sentenced to art. The climax of the film very effectively brings together the pervasive anxiety of *Everyone Says I Love You*—that aging excludes the would-be Aphrodite worshipper from reality's romantic sweepstakes—with a devastating critique of the only compensation Woody Allen can possibly imagine for that expulsion: the creation of art.

In the end, it's Allen's view that the artist—like all human beings—brings to a celebration of his cultural achievements only two things: "a hooker and a dead body"—he brings, that is, sexual desire contained in a living receptacle destined to die.[20] The artist's work constitutes no transcendence of the physical—he's accompanied to the ceremony by projections of the inescapability of the corporeal, which is really all Harry's fiction was ever about. The characters an artist creates may, by providing distraction from this existential truth, briefly offer deliverance from the despair it occasions: as Allen told John Lahr, his continual filmmaking "keeps [him] from the fear here and now."[21] But once the latest narcissistically indulgent production has been completed, the artist—recall the image of Sandy Bates at the end of the screening of his film—is returned to the awareness of human physical vulnerability and isolation. Any other outcome, Allen insists, is as substantial as the honorary degree Harry's characters never give him.

In describing the self-referential ploys of Vladimir Nabokov's *Ada,* John Updike suggested that in the novel's conclusion, as in *Invitation to a Behead-*

ing and *Bend Sinister,* "the cardboard flats and gauze trappings collapse, and the author/hero, heavy with death, lumbers toward the lip of the stage."[22] It's not only Allen's prediction"they'll think [Harry's] me" which confers some of the quality Updike invokes upon *Deconstructing Harry,* nor the fact that many of Harry's most negative characteristics—narcissism, nihilism, self-hating anti-Semitism—are precisely those which unsympathetic reviewers have ascribed to Allen's films over the years. Allen's script invites the comparison by consistently dramatizing how thoroughly Harry's fiction derives from his life experiences, a fact which Harry acknowledges in admitting to the Adair faculty that Goldberg, his protagonist pursuing his wife to Hell, is "me thinly disguised. I don't think I should disguise it any more. It's—you know—me."

In the sense that a fictional character's actions can neither predict nor replicate an author's, Goldberg isn't Harry any more than Harry is Woody. In *Wild Man Blues,* a documentary of Allen touring Europe with his New Orleans Jazz Band produced shortly after *Deconstructing Harry* was completed, Allen's mother offered a balanced characterization of her son's relationship to his films: "He adds or subtracts from his life. He doesn't want to make a movie of his life."[23] And yet, Ingmar Bergman was surprised to realize that he had given his *Wild Strawberries* protagonist his own initials, and although Allen has burdened Harry with a plethora of vices he apparently doesn't possess, one nonetheless recognizes in Helen Epstein's analysis of her husband's short stories exaggerated characteristics which both Harry and the screenwriter/director who created him seem to some degree to share: "What one comes away with is your total isolation, your fear of people, your panic over closeness." *Wild Man Blues* dramatizes a semblance of Helen's characterization, presenting its subject as withdrawn and taciturn offstage, the documentary with noticeable resentment eliding Allen's films and New Orleans jazz as art forms more appreciated abroad than they are in their homeland. Allen's 1991 essay, "Random Reflections of a Second-Rate Mind," *Deconstructing Harry,* and *Wild Man Blues* combine to delineate a more autobiographically forthright and candidly pessimistic Woody Allen than the scriptwriter of *Manhattan Murder Mystery, Bullets Over Broadway, Mighty Aphrodite,* and *Everyone Says I Love You;* the disjunction is most apparent in the contrasting enactments/perceptions of art found in these works.

"And that's why," Helen Epstein continues in diagnosing her husband's fiction, "your real life is so chaotic and your writing is so much more controlled and stable." Allen's four 1990s comedies are characterized largely by a "controlled and stable" filmic style which symmetrically frames the movies' prevailing affirmations of human love; *Deconstructing Harry* reverts to the frazzled cinematography of *Husbands and Wives,* self-consciously awkward jump cuts replacing the earlier film's use of an untethered steadicam in order to stylistically evoke the emotional fissures and modal discontinuities of its plot.

Helen's characterization invokes once again the formulation which, Modernists asserted, privileges art above life, but Allen's film finds little justification for celebration in Harry's restoration of literary powers, the film's last images picturing him alone at his typewriter, beginning his new novel, while the slightly derisive "Dream a Little Dream of Me" which glossed his imaginary honorary degree ceremony continues to play on the soundtrack. The best that can be said of Harry's redemption is that it's the only form in which redemption could exist for him—through art. In order to save himself, he has reverted to his late-adolescent attitude of "not caring about the real world" and caring "only about the world of fiction," enacting this reversion by projecting a new novel blurring distinctions between his art and his life. Unblocked, Harry Block begins to craft a narrative delineating "a character too neurotic to function in life, but [who] can only function in art," his novel very likely resembling the film narrative whose ending we have just watched. The ambivalence of Harry's salvation-through-art is nicely summarized in Cecilia's *Purple Rose of Cairo* description of her similarly redemptive affair with a fugitive from a Hollywood movie: "I just met the most wonderful new man. He's fictional, but you can't have everything" (p. 434).

In an important sense, the sour cinematic parable of *Deconstructing Harry* is a thoroughly distorted yet completely revealing self-portrait of Woody Allen. In its testily jump-cutting dramatization of the conflict between life and art, *Deconstructing Harry* effectively epitomizes the filmmaker's irresolvably ambivalent sense of the insufficiency of salvation-through-art—and of the artist's inescapable necessity for affirming that possibility in the absence of any other alternative.

19

From the Neck Up

Another Woman and *Celebrity*

The real ones want their lives fiction and the fictional ones want their lives real.

—Press agent in *The Purple Rose of Cairo*

As Woody Allen prepared to enter the twenty-first century, he was not a sanguine spectator of the realm of cell phones, facial makeovers, and celebrity worship he believed New York City had become. Whereas in *Manhattan* he had dramatically juxtaposed breathtaking vistas of the city and the soaring melodies of George Gershwin with the shallow narcissism of the city's inhabitants, in *Celebrity* Manhattan seems to have dwindled to the size of its characters' sensibilities, New York merely providing an urban backdrop for their self-promoting and self-serving erotic pursuits. Like Isaac Davis in *Manhattan*, *Celebrity*'s protagonist, Lee Simon, is writing a book "about the values of a society gone astray"; even more transparently than Isaac, Lee is as much a symptom of those strayed values as their critic. Isaac accuses Yale, his friend and doppelganger, of mercurial, contradictory attitudes—wanting to complete his book on O'Neill's plays, wanting a Porsche—which closely parallel Lee's conflicts: he longs to write a substantial novel satirizing the media-poisoned world he inhabits, but he is clearly more enthusiastic about cutting a figure in that world as he drives through it in his 1967 Aston Martin. Similarly, Lee wholeheartedly endorses the complaint of spoiled Hollywood star Brendan Darrow (Leonardo DiCaprio) that the scripts he receives lack integrity, but Lee then meekly acquiesces to every change in his own script—about "an armored car robbery with a very strong personal crisis"— which might pique Brendan's interest in the property. *Manhattan*, Allen told Frank Rich, deals with trying "to live a decent life amidst all the junk of contemporary culture—the temptations, the seductions. So how do you keep from selling out?"[1] Lee Simon doesn't. Allen's mood as he produced this sour satire is best summarized by the fact that "amidst all the junk of contemporary culture," art in *Celebrity* doesn't stand a chance.

Through the cognitive dissonances between art and life that Lee experiences throughout *Celebrity*, Allen is making an argument with which we are familiar: art is too much the product of corrupt human beings to be anything other than corrupt. What appears to be new in *Celebrity* is the dramatization of the ways in which life and art are imbricated in each other. In fact, Allen established the terms of their interpenetrability in *Husbands and Wives*. Gabe Roth's explanation to his interlocutor/analyst of the relationship between his art and erotic pursuits provides a key to one of Lee's central confusions throughout *Celebrity*. "Maybe because I'm a writer. . . . some dramatic or aesthetic component becomes right, and I go after that person." Gabe continues, "It's almost as if there's a certain . . . some dramatic ambiance . . . it's almost as if I fall in love with the person and in love with the situation in some way, and it hasn't worked out well for me at all."[2]

As we've seen, Gabe's largely unconscious laminating of life and art "hasn't worked out well for [him] at all" because it demands that his life replicate the dynamics of dramatic narrative. Gabe "grew up on movies and novels in which doomed love was romantic," Judy Roth explains in characterizing her ex-husband to the film's narrator/interlocutor; consequently, Gabe is attracted to the "kamikaze woman," Rain, *because* she's trouble, because, as he acknowledges, her siren's song ringing in his ears is the sound of his "$50,000 of psychotherapy dialing 911." In a moment of rationality, Gabe resists indulging himself in the romantic potentialities of the candlelit, lightning-illuminated occasion of Rain's birthday, withstanding the desire to play out a "scene which cried out desperately to be played." As if to protect himself against further temptations to confuse his art and life, Gabe at the end of *Husbands and Wives* is working on a "less confessional, more political novel," one, presumably, whose more inclusive perspective on human interaction will provide less inducement to make his life mirror its contours. Numerous reviewers construed the ending of *Husbands and Wives* as dramatizing the obverse of Allen's real-life choice, more than one of them upbraiding him for hypocrisy in having his protagonist assume the moral high ground on the issue of May-December relationships in a way that Allen did not. Such moralistic confoundings of art and life were probably the inevitable harvest of a film career so devoted to dramatizing life/art convergences, but it's not as if Allen's films don't provide significant admonitions against similar conflations of the artistic and existential. In movies neatly spaced five years on either side of *Husbands and Wives*, Allen depicts protagonists whose midlife crises prompt them to surrender to the very confusion Gabe evades. *Another Woman* and *Celebrity* create characters whose lives are blighted by their incapacity to keep art and life separate. The very real ambivalence of Allen's feelings toward the human capacity to confuse art and life is epitomized by the fact that in *Another Woman* he portrays Marion Post's blurring of the two with a psychological depth that provokes sympathy for her in the viewer, while dramatizing Lee Simon's parallel failure in such one-dimensional terms as to make him seem an unlikable projection of the hollow, media-crazed world he inhabits and abhors. Between the densely philosophic naturalism of *Another Woman* and the tabloidal shallowness of *Celebrity*, Allen delineates a vision of contemporary life spanning auteurial sympathy and nearly fathomless cynicism.

Marion's opening voice-over narration immediately establishes that she (her interior life, really) is the central focus of *Another Woman*'s narrative. It is clear from the beginning that her opening attitude (she's not afraid of uncovering "some dark side of her character," but if something—her life—seems to be working, she prefers to leave it alone) is going to get rebuked in the film, obliging her to confront "some dark side of her character." That hers won't be a fruitless journey into the dark is signaled repeatedly by the spiritual helpers who emerge to assist Marion along the path toward self-confrontation.

Marion (Gena Rowlands) is a professor who rents a one-room flat in which to write her book on German philosophy, rationalizing the rental's necessity on the grounds that when she begins such a project she must cut herself off from everything but the work. On her first morning of academic seclusion, however, her work is interrupted when she hears emanating from a wall vent a psychoanalytic session in progress in which a client is acknowledging 'some dark side of his character' by admitting to entertaining sexual fantasies of males while masturbating.[3] Because homosexual temptation is not her conflict, Marion manages to silence these unsettling self-exposures very simply by propping sofa cushions against the vent. The self-revelations of a female patient in a session later that afternoon prove impossible for her to block out, however, because they impinge so closely on Marion's repressed condition. This character, played by Mia Farrow, is never actually named in the film, but the closing credits designate her Hope, identifying her with a Gustav Klimt painting she and Marion discuss in an antique store depicting a young woman who appears to be as pregnant and despairing as Marion's companion. "It was as if a curtain had parted," Hope tells her analyst, both anticipating and precipitating Marion's self-confrontation, "and I could see myself clearly, and I was afraid of what I saw and what I had to look forward to." Hope's candid confessions of despair and self-doubt challenge Marion's affirmations of equanimity, prodding her on toward the acknowledgment that her marriage is a union of mutually lonely partners and to the realization that what she has construed in her own behavior as rationality is an emotional frigidity. "She's led this cold, cerebral life," Marion overhears Hope describing her in a later psychoanalytic session, after the two women have met and talked, "and has alienated everyone around her . . . I guess you can't keep deep feelings closed down forever. I don't want to wake up when I'm her age and find my life is empty."

Hope's role as spiritual initiator is reinforced by others in the film equally committed to facilitating Marion's self-confrontation. Marion's sister-in-law (Frances Conroy) surprises her by asserting that Marion's brother hates her

both for her worldly success and for her lifelong condescension to his professional failures. "You're such a perceptive woman," Lynn tells her, "how can you not understand his feelings?" At a party, Marion and her husband, Ken (Ian Holm), listen to the boozily uninhibited revelations of another couple (Blythe Danner and Bruce Jay Friedman) concerning their sexual couplings on their living room floor, the conversation spurring Marion to wonder if there is any passion left in her marriage, or in her life. This worry is exacerbated by her recurrent memories of Larry Lewis (Gene Hackman), a novelist who attempted to dissuade her from marrying Ken so that she might marry him instead. Her insistence on honoring her previous commitment prompted Larry to accuse her of deserving Ken, because she is as smug, self-important, and passionless as he is. (Larry's indictment, while largely rejected by Marion because it is sparked by passion, is the one which cuts deepest, requiring that Marion earn his benediction if her crisis—like the film's plot—is to achieve resolution.) Trailing Hope through the streets one evening, Marion loses her but encounters a friend from college, Claire (Sandy Dennis), who drunkenly confesses her resentment of Marion for having alienated the affections of a man Claire loved while they were undergraduates at Bryn Mawr. Marion's stepdaughter (Martha Plimpton) has real affection for her, but Marion is depressed upon overhearing the girl tell her boyfriend that her stepmother "is a little judgmental—she stands above people and evaluates them." When Marion dreams about her first husband's rage at her decision to abort their child—all she cared about, he contends, was "your career, your life of the mind"—her encounter with the "dark side" of her personality is complete.

Another Woman was criticized by some reviewers as being excessively formulaic in structure, the highly traditional self-confrontation, reversal-and-recognition narrative being underlined by Marion's quotation of the final lines of Rilke's "Archaic Torso of Apollo": "For here, there is no place that does not see you: you must change your life."[4] When compared with the aleatorily postmodernist psychic indirections of *Celebrity,* what's most striking about *Another Woman* is how insistent this film is upon the capacity of the individual to use her head and heart to conceptualize, comprehend, and change her life. Philosophy professor Marion Post has no appetite whatsoever for self-scrutiny, but she is compelled nonetheless by the world around her to undertake a process of self-confrontation which the denouement reveals to be—at least in her assessment of it—efficacious. As a result of her psychic quest, Marion divorces her unfaithful husband, reconciles with her brother, and learns that her alter ego, as if validating Marion's own recovery, has terminated her psychoanalytic treatment, Hope effectively disappearing from Marion's life. Neither she nor Marion has reason any longer to feel as Hope did when Marion overheard her for the first time: "I couldn't tell who I really was."

Marion's ultimate reward for her personal journey is a literary confirmation that she is indeed a creature of passion. Reading Larry Lewis's latest novel, she discovers a passage about a character, Helinka, whom Marion dreams Lewis claimed to have modeled on her.[5] "Her kiss was full of desire," Lewis wrote, "and I knew I couldn't share that feeling with anyone else. And then a wall went up, and just as quickly I was screened out, but it was too late because I now knew that she was capable of intense passion, if she would one day allow herself to feel." What we watch in *Another Woman* are the days—and the psychic progress they adumbrate—that culminate in Marion's allowing herself to feel. She affirms the efficacy of her journey in the movie's closing lines: "I closed [Lewis's] book, and felt the strange mixture of wistfulness and hope. And I wondered whether a memory is something you had, or something you'd lost. For the first time in a long time, I felt at peace." The reiteration of the word in Marion's final monologue seems to validate her mood of psychic resolution: the woman who couldn't feel is very emphatically *feeling* "the wistfulness and hope" of Lewis's depiction and *feeling* at peace as her journey of self-confrontation ends.

Among the conflicting reviewers' responses to *Another Woman*—which ranged from its being described as "the most significant achievement of [Allen's] career" to "*Another Woman* is the weakest movie of his career"[6]—can be found no doubts expressed about the sincerity of its resolution. For all the evidence the film offers of Marion's emotional growth and development, there remains something teasingly ambiguous about the medium through which she achieves the reward—Joseph Campbell would say "boon"—of her journey. Marion's on-screen quest is inaugurated by her assertion that writing a book "requires that I cut myself off from everything but my work." If that act of self-seclusion is her symptom manifestation #1, resolving it through her reading of another book seems problematical, or at least potentially ironic. Richard A. Blake suggests that Marion's novelistic consolation reflects the notion that "for some people—and [Allen] would include himself in this category—the vicarious experience of passion through the arts may be a way to salvation, or even happiness."/ Perhaps so, but it's difficult not to wonder whether Allen isn't having some ironic fun at the expense of his bookish protagonist by having her be so desirous of redemption that she never doubts that a novelistic portrait reputedly inspired by her is anything less than incontrovertible evidence of a living human being's passion. Those unsympathetic with the character, in fact, might argue that Marion is so inhibited that the only affirmation of passion she could ever completely credit would be one she experienced in the pages of a novel. Larry's novel may have supplied her with the confirmation she sought of her passionate nature, in other words, or the peace she achieves may be a classic instance of desire generating fulfillment, of art confused for life.

In Marion, Allen is confronting once again the coldness in himself that he embodied dramatically through Eve in *Interiors* and Lane in *September,* and that he would revisit more comically in Harry Block, who writes a story about "a boy who can't love" whom Harry admits is himself. As we've seen, Allen's biographers have documented how incompletely Allen has resolved the penchant toward isolation he acknowledged in explaining, "I'm not social. I don't get an enormous amount of input from the world. I wish I could, but I can't."[8] By asserting that Marion is one of his characters with whom he most closely identifies,[9] Allen was affirming how thoroughly she constitutes the comic Woody Allen protagonist's flip side; consequently, we perhaps shouldn't expect his protagonists to be much more successful in reversing their emotional frigidities. Gena Rowland's performance, poignantly imbued with Sven Nykvist's textured, *Autumn Sonata*-invoking autumnal cinematography, makes us care about the outcome of Marion's self-confrontation in *Another Woman.* If the destination of her psychic journey seems a little too literary to pass as the validation of the capacity for passion she perceives it to be, the movie nonetheless affirms the spiritual significance of her trip and the capacity of human beings to use their heads—and hearts—to understand, learn, and grow through self-confrontation.

Celebrity denies practically all of that.

Lee Simon's descent into midlife crisis is provoked by a far more culturally prototypical and trivial source than is Marion's: a high school reunion. Seeing his classmates aged, balding, and bloated (one girl he dated has now "turned into her mother" and another, whose breasts he once fondled, is six feet under) inspires in Lee highly predictable—and predictably articulated— anxieties about mortality and the time that has passed without his ever living life fully. Echoing Marion's favorite Rilke poem as though filtered through "The Love Song of J. Alfred Prufrock," John Donne, and some self-help bromides, Lee unburdens himself to a psychoanalyst at the reunion: "I've got to change my life before it's too late. I just turned forty—I don't want to wake up at fifty and find I measured out my life with coffee spoons. . . . I don't know what the truth is anymore, I don't know. . . . One minute you're in the lunchroom at Glenwood High, and you fucking blink and you're forty and you blink and you can see movies on a senior citizens' pass. Ask not for whom the bell tolls, or to put it more accurately, ask not for whom the toilet flushes."

Whereas Marion is coolly analytical about her condition, approaching it intellectually as if it were more than a usually wrenching stimulus for philosophical contemplation, Lee is all over the place about his crisis, stammering and stuttering as he haplessly tries to articulate his plight and boomeranging from one woman to another in desperate pursuit of the only solution he (like most of Allen's male protagonists) can imagine to mortality anxieties. "Every curve of your body," Lee tells the supermodel (Charlize Theron[10]) with whom he has a brief, frustrating liaison, "fulfills its promise. If the universe has any meaning, I'm looking at it." The inefficacy of Lee's solution to his psychic extremity is summarized in his assurance to her, "For you, I'd be willing to come down with terminal cancer." Expecting carnality to provide salvation from death is like believing that smoking is an effective defense against emphysema.

Lee's parodically paradigmatic midlife crisis inspires him to divorce his wife of sixteen years, Robin (Judy Davis), and the narrative of *Celebrity* alternates between tracing their divergent paths as single adults. Robin stumbles upon a television producer (Joe Mantegna) who fervently courts her while transforming his inamorata into talk show celebrity. So accustomed is Robin to things working out badly in life that she's utterly unprepared for what a Paul Simon song characterized as "something so right"—romance without liabilities, love without deficits—that she intentionally subverts the relationship, fleeing her own wedding ceremony. Her fiancé reasserts his perfection by forgiving her this act of faithlessness, and by the movie's final scene Robin and Tony have married. Meeting her ex-husband at the premiere of a movie, the shooting of which opens *Celebrity,* Robin explains, "You know, it's luck, Lee. When it comes to love, it's luck." Her explanation echoes numerous Allen assertions that his own success has been completely a matter of luck,[11] and in both their cases the assurances constitute half-truths. The woman Robin once was—a high school teacher who, somewhat improbably, seems to have taught nothing but Chaucer—would be, as Lee reminds her, horrified by the media groupie she's become, someone who gushingly interviews celebrities in posh eateries and unself-consciously tosses off words despised by English teachers like "marvelous." As she and Tony arrive at the premiere, an *Entertainment Tonight* clone breathlessly welcomes the attendees, confirming Robin's happy existential trifecta for the nation's viewers to savor and envy: "Congratulations on your show, your marriage, your pregnancy." By Lee's standards, Robin has sold herself out to popular culture, but even he has to admit that she's happier this way. Her marriage parallels that of Fay and Larry in *Deconstructing Harry,* which validates Larry's assertion, "I can make her happier" than can Harry, who "puts his life into [his] art" rather than into his life. More significantly, Robin hasn't committed the mistake which redeems Harry's life and which renders Lee so desolate in the film's denouement: confounding art and life.

Lee's first serious relationship following his divorce culminates in Bonnie (Famke Janssen), a Random House editor, moving in with him. But on the night they are celebrating sharing their digs, Lee reencounters an actress (Winona Ryder) who all but wears a sign around her neck identifying her as a kamikaze woman. Lee is drawn to her attractions, of course, but her primary allure consists in his conviction that he created her. "I was wary of you," he tells her in explaining why he didn't follow up on their initial meeting, "because I knew that you triggered some real feelings in me. So once again I fucked up, but I'm going to rectify things by not getting in any deeper [with Bonnie]—so what are you doing tomorrow?"

"Wow," she responds to his perfervid confession, "is that you or your new novel?"

It's the latter.

"I *know* you," he asserts, "I've written about you twice. Twice you were the obscure object of desire in the books I've written."

She admonishes him not to be misled, insisting, "You didn't make me up," but he'll have none of that. "Why wouldn't I know where you live?" he asks her. "You were Steffie in my first book, Louise in my second, and now you're Nola." The character thereafter identified as Nola has already warned him that "every guy I meet thinks he's gonna be the one to make me faithful," and the viewer isn't surprised to find at the end of the movie that Lee isn't that guy, either.

In a movie which so often seems like *Manhattan* with a migraine, Lee has made the same mistake that Isaac does in "always thinking [he'll] be the one to make 'em act different" (*Manhattan,* p. 262). *Celebrity*'s protagonist imitates Isaac's error in choosing the sexy instability of Mary Wilke over the loyal, sane affection of Tracy by dumping Bonnie for Nola, an error Emmet Ray will replicate in *Sweet and Lowdown.*

In the nearly Calvinist moral economy of *Celebrity,* Lee's punishment for pursuing his novels' plots in the streets of Manhattan thoroughly fits the crime. Shortly before Bonnie moves in with him, Lee has completed a novel, a book which he earlier proclaimed "contains every aspiration, every authentic feeling I've had, every idea." As movers carry Bonnie's possessions into his apartment, Lee tells her that he's found someone else and asks that they terminate their one night's cohabitation. Outraged by his incredible inconstancy, Bonnie grabs the only copy of Lee's novel, fleeing with the manuscript to the docks across from Lee's apartment.[12] Boarding a departing tourist ship bearing the name Garden State, she scatters his "every aspiration, every authentic feeling I've had" to the winds, forcing Lee to satisfy himself with the real life Nola now that the fictional one who prefigured her has been dispersed upon the sea. Watching its pages swirl around the retreating ship, Lee has surely fallen from his garden state.

We never learn how literarily satisfying was Lee's novelistic depiction of Nola; we watch without surprise as the actual Nola proves thoroughly unsatisfying to Lee, the relationship collapsing a few months after it begins. And so Lee attends the premiere of the movie he watched Nicole Oliver (Melanie Griffith) shooting in the opening of *Celebrity*, where his depression is deepened by his encounter with his made-over, newly minted celebrity ex-wife. Inside the theater, the guests watch *The Liquidator,* which opens with Nicole running through an urban landscape as skywriting above her head communicates her condition: "HELP." The image of these letters recalls the instructions Nicole's director gave her while shooting the scene to assist her understanding of her character—instructions which provide a perfect gloss for Lee's circumstances as he watches *The Liquidator's* premiere. "You see the skywriting," the director (Greg Mottola) prompts Nicole, "you realize that everything has gone wrong, and you can't believe it because you thought you had it all figured out, but everything's chaos now. So what I really want you to project is despair. What I want to feel from you is the whole human condition." Even more eloquent testimony of the human condition as it is filtered through Lee's despair is the four-letter word sketched against the skies, "HELP," on which *Celebrity* closes. It's thoroughly appropriate that a man whose downfall eventuated from his confounding of art and life would have his condition perfectly summarized by a director instructing an actress on how to play her role; even his unarticulated cry for "HELP" is intertextually mediated, nothing more than a shot in somebody else's movie.

Given the shallowness of his impulses and the drubbing his literary commitments take, Lee's best moment in *Celebrity* happens in the first five minutes. Nicole Oliver tells him that she won't betray her husband by letting Lee penetrate her sexually, but adds, "what I do from the neck up—that's a different story." Nothing that happens to him in the next ninety-three minutes surpasses Nicole's fellatio. The structuring dirty joke at the heart of this relentlessly sleazy satire is revealed when Robin—who has paid a prostitute to instruct her in effective methods of oral sex—is asked by the celebrity interviewer at the premiere to what she attributes her triple success: "using my head," she explains. (Using her head earns Marion Post a perhaps ironic redemption; the best Lee and Robin are capable of is being given and giving head.) A blow job initiates Lee's downfall and facilitates Robin's rise to happiness and celebrity, and few viewers are likely to long remember either the loser or winner in this incessantly sour and soulless comedy. (Harry Block's sister claims that Harry has staked everything on physics and pussy; Lee doesn't even believe in physics.) The contrasting fates of *Celebrity*'s alternating protagonists seem to dramatize one amoral lesson: serious literary aspirations betray Lee into despair and solitude, while the glitzy pop culture world gains Robin a husband, a career, and a child. Robin's prosperity may exemplify nothing other than luck, but it also suggests that teaching literature is as self-defeating as confusing real people with the creations of the writerly imagination. Allen must have been tempted to insert the sound of a toilet flushing as "HELP" fades to black and *Celebrity* ends.

Woody Allen's most cynical film condemns the human capacity for blurring art and life, while providing absolutely no positive alternative to riding the superficial values of media culture as far as they will take you. "My book," Lee grandly informs an editor in the film, "is about a country gone astray— it's all show business, everything's show business." It's one of the dreary truths of *Celebrity* how thoroughly Lee Simon is implicated in his own cultural condemnation.

Roger Ebert's review of the film suggests that *Celebrity* doesn't completely rise above the corruptions of the world it depicts, Ebert contending that "the screenplay isn't as sharp as the movie's visuals. As the movie careens from one of Simon's quarries to the next, Allen pauses on most scenes only long enough to extract the joke, and the film begins to seem as desperately promiscuous as its hero."[13] That Woody Allen lined up the largest celebrity cast since *Around the World in Eighty Days* to produce this bleakly ironic anatomization of the pervasiveness of show business in America is perhaps *Celebrity*'s darkest element; that he resisted the temptation to declare himself completely above all the corruptions to which celebrity culture is subject is perhaps provisionally redemptive. But that remains a very long way from "For the first time in a long time, I felt at peace." As Allen's films have consistently demonstrated, even a fictionally inspired illusion of peace is preferable to the bleak truth of human corruptibility.

20

Allen and His Audience

Sweet and Lowdown

LINDA CHRISTIE: Do you realize we're in a room that holds some of
the highest achievements of Western Civilization?
ALLAN FELIX: There's no girls.

—Metropolitan Museum of Art scene in *Play It Again, Sam*

No element of Woody Allen's filmmaking career has been more markedly
Modernist than his aesthete's principled inattentiveness to the issue of audience. Allen's interviews proliferate with genial disavowals of accountability to
his audience, with affirmations of his greater commitment to craft than to
effect. Responding to the charge that his movies embody anti-Semitic attitudes, Allen characteristically sidestepped the concern by invoking the imperatives of art over audience sensibilities: "I've . . . had an enormous amount
of criticism from Jewish groups who feel that I've been very harsh or denigrat-
ing or critical. So there's a lot of sensitivity always on these matters. But the
only thing I try to let guide me is the authenticity of the scene."[1]

The authenticity of the scenes in *Stardust Memories* led critics as astute
as Pauline Kael to conflate Sandy Bates's subjectively distorted perception of
his audience with Allen's attitude toward his, provoking Allen to acknowledge
that "Some people came away [from *Stardust Memories*] saying I had contempt for my audience. This was not true. I never had contempt for my audience; if I had contempt for my audience, I'd be too smart to put it in the
picture. I'd grouse about it at home. I've always felt that the audience was at
least equal to me or more. I've always tried to play *up* to the audience."[2] The
Pirandellian interfusings of real life and filmicly constructed reality pervading
Stardust Memories and the fiction/autobiography conflations of *Deconstructing
Harry* are testament enough to Allen's willingness to challenge his audience's
assumptions about the distinguishability of actuality and illusion. That Allen
has, however, often experienced substantially greater ambivalence toward viewers than his "playing *up* to the audience" assertion acknowledges is a central
point of Adam Gopnik's *New Yorker* essay on Allen, "The Outsider." "It was a
complicated dance," Gopnik contended, one we've often glimpsed in these
pages: "On the one hand, [Allen] was reaching toward the audience and its
experience. On the other, he was working hard to set his values off from theirs."[3]

Allen's effort to distance his values from those of the audience is summarized by his comment to Tom Shales in an *Esquire* interview that "the best film I ever did, really, was *Stardust Memories*," the proof of whose superiority was "It was my least popular film. That may automatically mean it was my best film."[4] This peevish attitude toward his American audience has more recently been translated into the complaint, which Allen has articulated in interviews and enacted through Barbara Kopple's *Wild Man Blues* documentary, that—like Dixieland jazz—he and his films are more appreciated and loved in Europe than they are in their country of origin.

Typically, when Allen has fretted publicly about the effect of his movies on the audience, his ruminations carry an undercurrent of condescension. "Sometimes," he told Anthony DeCurtis, rehearsing Sandy Bates's central dilemma, "I've had the thought that to try to make films that say something, I'm not doing my fellow man a service. I would be better off abandoning asking the audience to try and to come to grips with certain issues because these issues finally always lead you to a dead end. They're *never* going to be solvable. We all have a terrible, fierce burden to carry, and the person who really does something nice is the guy who writes a pretty song or plays a pretty piece of music or makes a film that diverts."[5] The same slightly patronizing disposition is noticeable in Allen's invocation of the difference between artist and audience: "The vision of the audience is never as deep as the vision of the artist involved. They are always willing to settle for less than you want for yourself."[6] Accordingly, when Allen discusses films he considers unsuccessful (*Manhattan Murder Mystery*, for instance), it is himself that he feels his want of ambition has betrayed more than the audience, whose disappointment doesn't trouble him much: "So they'll pay their six dollars and it'll stink and they'll go home. It's not the end of the world."[7]

This is not to suggest that for Allen all fault lies on the audience's side of the screen. In the Stig Bjorkman interviews, Allen conceded that "to me, artists frequently are selfish. They need time alone, they need discipline, and they need sometimes to behave with people in ways that are important for them but are not really very nice for other people."[8] Consequently, the artist as Allen conceives of her/him must ultimately ignore the audience: "And then I started to think, that the less I know what people think of my work, the better off I am. I should just keep my nose to the grindstone and do the films I want to do. And put them out there. If people like them—great! It does not mean that I'm a genius, just because some newspaper writer says, 'This is a work of genius!' And it doesn't mean I'm an idiot if he says I'm an idiot. Just forget about what people say! I told the studio, 'Don't call me on the phone and tell me who's coming and how many people. I don't care.'"[9]

In *Broadway Danny Rose*, Danny confesses to Tina his disbelief in God, and then adds, "but I'm guilty over it." In *Sweet and Lowdown*, Allen dramatizes his Modernist's disdain for his audience; the playing out of the film narrative's central allegory affirms the fact that he's guilty over it.

Emmet Ray (Sean Penn) is, by his own reckoning, the world's second greatest jazz guitarist, a musician so utterly devoted to his art that he faints when the world's greatest jazz guitarist—Django Reinhardt—materializes. As an artist, Emmet is closer to Sheldon Flender, the *Bullets Over Broadway* proponent of the notion that "the artist creates his own moral universe," and to Harry Block, whose ex-wife characterizes him as a "pill-popping, alcoholic, beaver-banging excuse for a father," than he is to Eve of *Interiors,* for whom art and morality converge in a chilling, lifeless existential stasis. Among his character flaws, Emmet boasts pimping, kleptomania, egotism, obsessive gambling, alcoholism, murderous intentions toward garbage dump rats, and complete unreliability both as a professional musician and as an erotic partner.[10] As for Harry Block, so for Emmet Ray: all weaknesses are redeemed—perhaps even validated—by the fact that he's an artist. "I can't settle down here, I can't," he tells Ann (Molly Price), a lover he's about to discard, "I gotta be free. I'm an artist."[11]

When she complains that Emmet (like Eve in *Interiors,* like Marion in *Another Woman,* and Harry Block, too) keeps his "feelings all locked up and can't feel anything for anybody else," Emmet responds, "I love 'em [women]. It's just I don't need 'em. I guess that's just how it is when you're a true artist."

Allen, clearly, was not breaking any new ground in *Sweet and Lowdown,* a film whose title seems to invoke both the modesty of its intentions and the bleakness of its dying fall resolution. The juxtaposition of life and art throughout the movie recalls most clearly Harry Block's debate with Larry in *Deconstructing Harry,* in which Harry's demon tells him, "You put your life into your art; I put mine into my life." Because Harry's "no good at life," he's "only interested in fiction," and consequently Fay loves Harry's work but is in love with Larry, sentencing Allen's narcissist novelist to a life of art rather than of life. Harry's inspiration for writing a novel about a character "who can't function in life but only in art" provides an indecisively upbeat ending for *Deconstructing Harry,* the protagonist reprising Zelig's redemptive trick of transforming himself in such a way that, as Saul Bellow glosses the feat, "it was his very disorder that made a hero of him" (*Zelig,* p. 126). Allen revisits and reverses that resolution in *Sweet and Lowdown,* largely through allegorizing Emmet's dedication to art as the very attitude that alienates him from the audience which holds out his best hope for salvation. If Harry Blocks's life is saved by his art, Emmet Ray's seems to get sacrificed to his.

A criticism that Emmet repeatedly suffers in *Sweet and Lowdown* is that his feelings are so "locked up" that the unemotionality adversely affects his playing. "I've been trying to analyze what separates your playing from Django's," Blanche (Uma Thurman) tells him in the last stages of their marriage, "and I say that it's that his feelings are richer, he's not afraid to suffer in front of anybody. He doesn't hold his feelings in check." Sean Penn plays Emmet as a man whose face is constantly fixed in a derisive smirk, and whose voice is a gravelly, affectless croak. Upon meeting Emmet, Blanche comments, "not only are you vain and egotistical, but you have genuine crudeness"—a crudeness which seems the complete antithesis of the stunning music he generates from a guitar modeled on the one Django's brother, Joseph Reinhardt, played in the Hot Club of France. The disparity between substance and surface which Emmet embodies is probably best conveyed in the scene in which he performs lead accompaniment behind a jazz diva doing "All of Me" for a Hollywood short of the kind in which Louis Armstrong, Billie Holiday, and Lena Horne appeared in the 1930s. Intent upon catching the eye of Hollywood studios in hopes of becoming a star, Emmet produces dazzlingly beautiful riffs which just escape being nullified by his outrageously goony mugging for the cameras.

The music Emmet—jazz guitarist Harold Alden, in fact[12]—creates justifies his repeated insistence that "I'm an artist, a truly great artist," but every attempt the other characters make to discover in him a human being commensurate with the artist comes up empty. Seeking to illuminate the mystery of artistic creativity, Blanche asks him, "What do you feel when you're playing? What are your real feelings?" to which Emmet, after brief reflection, replies, "That I'm underpaid." Emmet epitomizes once again the skepticism about the superiority of art and artists we have tracked through Allen's oeuvre; *Sweet and Lowdown* allows Allen to revisit the notion introduced in *Bullets Over Broadway* that artistic creativity and human savagery have identical sources by paralleling Emmet's explanation of his musical gift with the explanation a hit man uses to account for his aptitude for rubbing out his boss's enemies: their genius "came naturally." When the hood (Anthony La Paglia) with whom Blanche has begun an affair asks her who is the better lover, she responds, "Emmet has a violent side, but it all turns to passion in his music. With you," she tells Al Torrio, "it's like I'm looking into the heart of darkness. Emmet is an artist, and because he's an artist, he needs no one. I mean, even in making love, he seems to exist in a world of his own."

What provisionally redeems this artist whose favorite recreation is shooting garbage dump rats and watching freight trains, briefly drawing him out of the "world of his own," is the same thing that saves Leonard Zelig: "the love of a good woman." Emmet initially wants nothing to do with Hattie (Samantha Morton), one of two women whom he and his drummer pick up on a day off. When he discovers that she doesn't speak, has suffered a deprived childhood, and is mentally limited, he dismisses Hattie as "a goddamned mute orphan halfwit," imagining that he's being sympathetic in asking if she lost her voice because somebody dropped her on her head. He softens toward her considerably when his playing of "I'm Forever Blowing Bubbles" utterly transfixes

Hattie, his music affecting her in a way that—despite his assertion that "I let my feelings come out in my music"—it never really does him. Because of the intensity of her response to his playing and the safety her voicelessness offers him, Emmet opens up to her as he does to no one else in the film, telling her of his father's abusive treatment of him, of his feeling that his mother's singing was "the most beautiful thing I ever heard." Henceforth Hattie accompanies Emmet to every performance, her face miming inestimable joy as she happily devours whatever dessert the restaurant he's playing in offers as gustatory complement to her pleasure in listening to his music. ("Hattie's so full of stuff: How can I convey all that she's thinking?" Samantha Morton wondered in preparing to play Hattie. "Learning lines is the easiest thing in the world. This was the hardest part I've ever played."[13]) Morton's Academy Award–nominated performance is among Allen's films' most luminescent cinematic achievements, one that is by no means minimized by *Sweet and Lowdown*'s construction of Hattie as a thoroughly allegorical figure.

A few reviewers of *Sweet and Lowdown* interpreted Hattie's muteness as symptomatic of misogynistic attitudes in Allen, contending that he—like Emmet—values her primarily for her passivity and inarticulateness.[14] A less ideological reading of the film construes Hattie instead as an embodiment of the audience to which Emmet is so Modernistically indifferent. Viewed in these terms, Hattie's incapacity to talk reflects that audience's parallel want of self-expression; her rapaciousness (both appetitive and sexual) invokes the audience's infinite hungers, while her abject devotion to Emmet images up the audience's dependency on artists to translate their most inchoate impulses into beauty.[15] (Like Joey of *Interiors,* Hattie is utterly lacking in artistic capacity; unlike Joey, who suffers her inexpressiveness as a terrible debility, Hattie is thoroughly content to let Emmet's guitar music be the voice she doesn't have.) Emmet anticipates the link that the film subsequently forges between Hattie and the artist's audience when he warns Ann, "I enjoy the company of women— I love 'em. It's just I don't need 'em. I guess that's just how it is if you're a true artist." For Emmet, as for Allen, a "true artist" is focused on aesthetic creation—on achieving "the authenticity of the scene"—rather than audience reception or the feelings of others. Consequently, Emmet perceives women throughout the movie as a threat to his artist's autonomy, cautioning them— much as Harry Block admonishes Fay in *Deconstructing Harry*—against falling in love with him since his art must always come first. Because Hattie so clearly comes to love the artist through loving his art, Emmet is unusually drawn to her, justifying his attraction by offering a slighting view (approximating Allen's own) of her and the audience of which she is a member and symbol: "You don't have to be bright," he assures her after inviting Hattie to hear him play, "music's for everybody, the smart or the dumb."

Modernist aesthetics repeatedly insist on the shabbiness of life-as-it-is, of the intolerableness of existence unimbued by art's elevating, clarifying redemptions, and so the film's embodiment of the unleavened audience must not only be figuratively and literally dumb, but must also lack any hint of sublimity or glamour. Appropriately, then, Hattie is a laundress. Desperately seeking to remedy the lack of glamour in the woman with whom he is spending more and more time, Emmet takes Hattie shopping for outfits he hopes will complement his own extravagant sartorial tastes, but for all the stylishness of the flapper garb he buys her, Hattie continues to look like the laundress she was when he met her. Her face alone, in the moments of pure ecstasy Emmet's music instills in her, lifts her beyond the pedestrian circumstances of which she is product and victim into an almost extrahuman prettiness, recalling Cecilia's hapless dependency on movies to elevate her life out of the Depression's desperate woes in *The Purple Rose of Cairo.* Troubled by the incompatibility of Hattie to his self-image and aspirations, Emmet banishes her from a performance when a wealthy sybaritic dowager seduces him with a stick of "tea"; the upshot of this betrayal of Emmet's ideal audience is that he wakes up in Stroudsburg, Pennsylvania, three days later, his dereliction having cost him his gig. His more final rejection of Hattie/his audience will figuratively cost him his life.

Chastened by this experience validating his career's dependency upon Hattie, Emmet grudgingly agrees to take her with him and drummer Billy Shields (Brian Markinson) to Hollywood for the shooting of the "All of Me" short. An amateur talent contest in rural Midwest America they discover en route to California allows Allen to substantiate the movie's identification of Hattie with the artist's audience. The other contestants competing for the cash prize are 1930s U.S. heartland versions of Danny Rose's acts: they do bird calls, play saws and spoons, or earnestly warble nineteenth-century faux operatic numbers, all of which amuses professional musician Emmet no end. These people belong in the audience, his smirking attention implies, and Hattie grows increasingly anxious at the blatant condescension he radiates toward these performing rubes with whom she clearly identifies. When his turn comes to perform, Emmet takes the stage, introducing himself as a birdseed salesman, and proceeds to play a dazzling rendition of "12th Street Rag" calculated to blow the room away. The audience is slow to respond to Emmet's virtuoso performance, their subsequent applause acknowledging his ability while their withholding of the prize money reflects how little they can appreciate his jazz stylings. As the scene shifts to the three travelers eating sandwiches next to Emmet's car on the roadside that evening, Shields expresses relief that Emmet's act didn't get them tarred and feathered. "The next time you're gonna hustle somebody," he admonishes Emmet, "don't play so great."

Emmet complains in self-defense, "I can't remember the tunes if I play badly."

Emmet's elitist incapacity to accommodate his art to his audience's limitations is amusingly rehearsed here, an attitude which Allen owned up to in an interview contemporaneous with the movie's release.[16] More significant is Hattie's anger both at the scam and Emmet's attitude toward the contest audience. He wonders if Django ever "hustled any suckers" as he has just tried to do, and when Hattie's face collapses in a resentful pout at his characterization, he tells Shields, "Look at her—she's frownin'—she doesn't like it. Well, they deserved it—they were jerks." Guiltily aware that he's implicitly attacked Hattie, Emmet briefly softens, explaining to Shields, "She's too good-hearted, a genuinely sweet person. I like that—I respect it." He won't, of course, emulate Hattie's nature, because "It won't get you anywhere in life." For Hattie, Emmet's music is precious for its honesty and sincerity; using that music to sucker what Emmet characterizes as "jerks" is a betrayal of everything she values in his art and in him. He makes light of her irritation, obliviously proceeding to recount to Shields a dream he's had about "being discovered in Hollywood as a major star" while they're filming the "All of Me" short. His egotism and self-isolation are precisely what will prevent him from becoming "a major star" in either jazz or Hollywood, the roadside scene prefiguring the inevitability of the Emmet/Hattie breakup by dramatizing the irreconcilable differences between their perceptions of his art, manifested most clearly in his Modernist's repudiation of art's accountability to other human beings, to the audience. The scene closes with Emmet reprising his tendency to parabolize his audience as women threatening him with entanglement: "You gotta keep your guard up," he warns Shields, "[if] you don't, the pretty ones get their worms into you, and then it's over, you're done. Particularly if you're an artist. I've seen too many guys crying in their beer. Me, I'm gonna be a star." (As if intuiting that this desire excludes rather than depends on her, Hattie stormily frowns.) In subsequent scenes, having rejected Hattie, Emmet lets a pretty one get her worms into him, he never becomes a star, and he ends up crying in his beer at a roadside joint before decimating the instrument he blames for having failed to win him the stardom he craved.

The "pretty one" is Blanche, a Chicago socialite beauty who dresses as flamboyantly as Emmet does and who has artistic aspirations of her own as a writer. Emmet is deep into his relationship with her before we learn why Hattie has vanished from the film. (The movie noticeably loses a level of intensity with Hattie's disappearance, replicating the emotional impoverishment that Emmet experiences as a consequence of discarding his link to human emotionality in the name of artistic freedom.) Emmet tells Blanche that one night he just took off, leaving Hattie five hundred dollars to remember him by. He doesn't explain that it was the word "love" written in her "chicken scratch" on a birthday card which precipitated his flight: having read Hattie's card, he rushes off to the bathroom to be sick. Blanche sizes up Emmet immediately, recognizing that their relationship is predicated on the fact that "any woman would be second to his music. He wouldn't miss me any more than the woman he abruptly left. He can only feel pain for his music—such is the ego of genius." The best that Emmet can manage in providing Blanche with a rationale for abandoning "the woman he abruptly left" is "I needed more than Hattie." Nonetheless, he calls out Hattie's name in his sleep one night, and when Blanche informs him of his sleeptalking the following morning, he asks her to marry him in a transparent attempt to deny the powerful hold Hattie continues to exert upon him. In marrying Blanche, Emmet is re-enacting Isaac Davis's error in *Manhattan* of favoring sophistication and erotically enticing instability over innocence and genuine sweetness, prompting jazz critic Nat Hentoff (one of a chorus of jazz enthusiast narrators serially projecting the movie's Emmet Ray yarns) to apostrophize, "There was always something unreal about it. Talk about a doomed relationship!"

Within weeks of their marriage, Emmet grows impatient with Blanche's incessant interrogations of the sources of his art and creativity. She defends her curiosity by explaining, "I'm trying to analyze your feelings so I can write about them." "Look," he responds, "I'm your husband. I'm not some goddamned book idea." Her perception of him as "a goddamned book idea" more than an erotic partner apparently persuades Blanche that she needs more than Emmet, sparking her affair with Torrio the gangster, which effectively ends her marriage to Emmet. For his part, Emmet comes to see that, in addition to trading in genuineness for self-consciousness, his replacement of Hattie with Blanche meant exchanging a sincere, responsive audience for a prying and invasive music critic. Blanche exaggerates the value and significance of Emmet's art in precisely the ways that Allen believes film and literary critics do in explicating his movies: she/they/we make too much of art, seeking answers to unanswerable questions like Blanche's: "The sound, the beat, the ideas—where do they come from?" Allen's Emmetesque response might be that they come from the pencil with which he writes the first drafts of screenplays on yellow legal pads. Hattie—like the ideal audience of Allen movies, who watch and then go home and quietly digest—never asks any of these questions: for her, Emmet's art is what it is—a simple and uncomplicated source of human pleasure. For her, his music is like New Orleans jazz as Allen defines it in *Wild Man Blues:* "There's nothing between you and the pure playing—there's no cerebral element at all." Hattie's face is an infallible critic of such music: it registers whether the music works or not.

Blanche's infidelity inspires Emmet to write a song, "Unfaithful Woman," which the movie's various jazz enthusiast narrators—Allen, Douglas McGrath (Allen's co-writer on *Bullets Over Broadway*), Hentoff, and Ben Duncan— agree is a milestone of his career, and which Emmet himself designates "a classic." The lesson implicit in the success of "Unfaithful Woman"—that art and life *are* related, that Ann was right in claiming that if he let his feelings out in real life, his music would be greater—is apparently not completely lost on Emmet. Providing a coda for the movie, jazz historian A.J. Pickman (David Okrent) affirms that Emmet's last recordings were his best: "he never played more beautifully, more movingly. Something just seemed to open up in him, and it was amazing because he really was as good as Django." It isn't the betrayal by Blanche that generates the enrichment of his art to which the aptly named Pickman refers, of course, but the fact that when Emmet returns to Hattie's New Jersey boardwalk laundry in an attempt to win her back, Hattie— in a wonderfully terse, bittersweet scene realized brilliantly by cinematographer Zhao Fei—informs him via her "chinaman" penmanship that she's married and has become a mother. Penn's nuanced portrayal of Emmet's need to conceal the magnitude of his disappointment in this scene constitutes rebuttal enough to those critics who claim Allen's films are lacking in effectively evoked emotion; the drunken bender Emmet goes on that night confirms the point.

Hattie's terminal removal from his life does not in itself nullify Emmet's chances of experiencing satisfying artistic achievements, and the summations of his career by Pickman and Allen allow us to imagine the pleasure which he might have derived from no longer having to declare himself second best to "this gypsy guitarist in France." But their judgments also make clear that Emmet never appealed to more than a small audience of jazz aficionados, the banishment of Hattie having sentenced him to being the favorite of a very select cult following. Pickman's celebration of Emmet's deepened artistic capacity is preceded by a darker admission: "I have no idea what happened to Emmet Ray. He just sort of disappeared, I guess." Allowing himself the last word, Allen echoes Pickman: "And then [Emmet] just seemed to fade away. I have no idea. Some people said he went to Europe, and some people feel he may have stopped playing altogether. But we do have, fortunately, those final recordings, and they're great—they're really beautiful."

In one of American literature's most celebrated dying fall endings, F. Scott Fitzgerald had the demoralized Dick Diver disappear into the small towns of rural New York, the narrator of *Tender Is the Night* a little archly concluding that, "in any case, he is almost certainly in that part of the country, in one town or another."[17] In *Sweet and Lowdown*, Emmet Ray vanishes into his recordings, his music usurping his life. Despite the fact that, as Stephanie Zacharek suggests, "jazz lore is loaded with alternate endings, reckless embellishments and outright fabrications,"[18] what neither Pickman nor Allen questions is the disappearance of Emmet Ray. The "dying fall" coda of his life seems to be gospel, the musician having apparently evaporated completely into his music. Whereas the comedian narrators of *Broadway Danny Rose* are content to let Danny recede into their felicitous myth of his reconciliation with Tina, *Sweet and Lowdown*'s similarly fablelike narrative ends on a distinctly more downbeat note, one generated by Emmet's complete failure to reconcile art and life.

The movie's closing dramatization of that failure depicts Emmet drunk and belligerent in a bar with his latest chorus girl, Ellie (Gretchen Mol), whom he unceremoniously drags off to a railroad crossing to watch the freight trains thunder past. He removes his instrument from its case in a drunken attempt to prove to Ellie that he can make the guitar sound like a train, but then starts into "Sweet Sue," which segues into "I'm Forever Blowing Bubbles"—the song whose performance won Hattie's heart. Because Ellie emblematizes the audience's bad side (she can't appreciate his playing because she needs to go to the bathroom), she is utterly oblivious to his performance, prompting him to verbally attack her, telling her to walk home: "Get out of here—leave me alone! I don't need anybody!" he moans before smashing his guitar against a light pole and pitifully wailing, "I made a mistake! I made a mistake!" But Ellie has already left the railway crossing, and consequently Emmet has unlocked his feelings too late for anyone to hear them—except on records.

Allen's closing encomia to the beauty of the recordings Emmet left behind for enthusiasts to treasure notwithstanding, the viewer understands those recordings to be the reapings of sorrow, the artistic harvest of "I made a mistake!" The mistake is believing that art can be quarantined from life; the mistake is failing to appreciate that the entanglements Emmet spends his life avoiding are in less self-isolated artists provocations to the greatest art, that the "terrible things that happen to people in love" inspire some of the world's most compelling artworks. By terminally separating himself from the audience's affections in repudiating Hattie, Emmet leaves himself with nothing but the cold—and merely temporary—comfort supplied by Blanche's critical interrogations of his art and the dubious solace of his cult following. Emmet's failure to restore himself in Hattie's love compels him to cap his career through rehearsing the lessons of hurt on records, his sincere sorrow and overwhelming sense of loss prompting him to produce the best music of his life. A very central point of this movie, however, is how completely Emmet's life has been eviscerated through its all-consuming devotion to art. The cost of "those final recordings" of Emmet's which Allen characterizes as "great—they're really beautiful" is that they usurped any life he had left.

By his own account, Woody Allen has never allowed his art to usurp his life. "I think that the thing I've had going for me is good focus," he told Harland and Peters. "Films are not my top priority. I want to have dinner with my friends at a restaurant, I want to eat a leisurely lunch and not rush through it. I want to come home at six o'clock at night and not ten o'clock. If the choice was doing another angle on a shot or something and going home so I could watch the Knicks on television, I'd go home and not do the shot. So often in the last twenty years, I do everything one shot. People said this is a style, but it's not a style, it's just laziness. I just don't have the patience. I'm bored with the scene after one time." His equivocal dedication to art isn't all that distinguishes Allen from his musician protagonist: "I always considered myself a very nice, sweet person, and not an artist. Not a dedicated artist at all. Sean Penn's character was a nasty, egotistical braggart, an insensitive person, who is quite a fabulous guitar player. Maybe not the best in the world, but quite great. I've never thought that about myself."[19]

Arguably, Allen's trademark denial of his protagonist as self-portraiture underestimates the coldness factor which unites him with Emmet while affirming the magnitude of the primary difference distinguishing them: Emmet sacrifices his life to his art, whereas Allen willingly sacrifices his art to leisurely meals with friends and Knicks games. In his review of Marion Meade's 1999 Allen biography, Michael Wood characterizes *Sweet and Lowdown* as "the movie where, perhaps for the first time, Allen gets the guilt of his central male character fully in focus, without allowing him to whimper, or slipping him a few excuses for his behavior."[20] Emmet's guilt at subordinating life—his lovers/his audience—to his art generates a full-blown dramatic epiphany in *Sweet and Lowdown*, one that provokes him to bawl, "I made a mistake!" to a deserted railway crossing. Emmet's mistake of over-valuing art is not one Allen is wont to make, clearly, and it is not unreasonable to read *Sweet and Lowdown*'s Emmet Ray fable as containing an implicit justification for Allen's equivocal commitment to his own cinematic art. If, as Blanche asserts, "even in making love,

[Emmet] seems to exist in a world of his own," his dedication to his art inhibiting his ability to make contact with his sexual partner, Emmet's creator seems to have devoted himself so deliberately to the world of his everyday life as to practically ensure that his art will never submerge his existence nor approach the intensity of self-confrontation which spawns Emmet's devastating epiphany. Subordinating one's art to the imperatives of maintaining a pleasant life can be, of course, an alternative means of "hold[ing] his feelings in check."

Janet Maslin's *New York Times* review of *Sweet and Lowdown* may have been obliquely addressing Allen's hedged aesthetic commitments in suggesting that his tone in the movie "is too genial, despite the character's obvious dark side, to allow Emmet much weight,"[21] and thus she judged the film "light." Perhaps so, but for an artist endlessly skeptical about the premises of and promises that have been made for art throughout a century's over-valuation, *Sweet and Lowdown* may constitute the perfect compromise between Allen's artistic ambition and personal impatience; it may strike the perfect balance equalizing Allen's cinematic aspiration, one-shot boredom, and individual modesty. For the purposes of this now-concluded study of Allen's films, the crowning irony of his career may be that this light, genial, lovely film more effectively and movingly epitomizes Allen's profoundly conflicted dedication to art than many of his more celebrated and serious movies. In its lowdown, one-shot, art-mistrusting way, in other words, *Sweet and Lowdown* may become Allen's "Unfaithful Woman"—one of the "classics" which will ultimately prove its artist to be, if not "as good as Django Reinhardt," at least "quite great." Should Allen achieve such a reputation, it will be a product not only of the very real substantiality of his individual films; it will be testimony as well to the distinctly postmodern ambivalence toward art that his filmmaking career has been unflaggingly dedicated to exploring, enacting, and projecting on movie screens.

Notes

1. That Old Black Magic: Woody Allen's Ambivalent Artistry

1. John Lahr, "The Imperfectionist," *The New Yorker,* December 5, 1996, p. 82.

2. "People tend to think [movies like *Husbands and Wives*] reflect my life in some way," Allen told the *Philadelphia Inquirer,* "But basically, they don't reflect my life." *Philadelphia Inquirer,* Sunday, August 22, 1993, p. G8.

3. Woody Allen, *Deconstructing Harry* (Fine Line Features, 1997).

4. John Baxter quotes Allen's acknowledgment that Roth was a model for Harry in *Woody Allen: A Biography* (London: Harper Collins, 1998), p. 436.

5. Carver's story (collected in *Where I'm Calling From: New and Selected Stories*) depicts a writer not unlike Carver being attacked by his ex-wife for using the unhappiness of their marriage as material for fiction. The existence of the story called "Intimacy" in Carver's story collection dramatically and cruelly validates the justice of the wife's charge of literary exploitation.

6. Woody Allen, *Stardust Memories,* in *Four Films of Woody Allen* (New York: Random House, 1982), p. 283.

7. Woody Allen, *Manhattan, Four Films of Woody Allen,* p. 259.

8. Woody Allen, *Annie Hall, Four Films of Woody Allen,* p. 4.

9. Frederick Exley, *A Fan's Notes* (New York: Harper & Row, 1968), p. 361.

10. Woody Allen, *Alice* (Orion Pictures, 1990).

11. Woody Allen, *Hannah and Her Sisters* (New York: Vintage Books, 1987), p. 150.

12. Woody Allen, *Shadows and Fog* (Orion Pictures, 1992*)*.

13. Woody Allen, *Play It Again, Sam* (Paramount Home Video, 1980).

14. Woody Allen, *Broadway Danny Rose,* in *Three Films of Woody Allen* (New York: Random House, 1987), p. 254.

15. Woody Allen, *Mighty Aphrodite* (Miramax Films, 1995).

16. "Here I am just fighting for a laugh and trying to do a scene," Allen said about critical responses to *Love and Death,* "and they're discussing it like it was genuinely Dostoevski." Lee Guthrie, *Woody Allen: A Biography* (New York: Drake Publishers, Inc.), p. 143.

17. Woody Allen, "Remembering Needleman," in *Side Effects* (New York: Ballantine Books, 1981), p. 6.

18. Allen, "My Apology," in *Side Effects,* p. 53.

19. Martin Ritt, *The Front,* screenplay by Walter Bernstein (Columbia Pictures, 1976).

20. Woody Allen, *Manhattan,* p. 197.

21. Stephen J. Whitfield, "Laughter in the Dark: Notes on American-Jewish Humor," in Sanford Pinsker, ed., *Critical Essays on Philip Roth* (Boston: G.K. Hall, 1982), p. 196.

22. Of the critical works published on Allen's films, Annette Wernblad's *Brooklyn is Not Expanding: Woody Allen's Comic Universe* (Rutherford, N.J.: Fairleigh Dickinson University Press, 1992) is the most firmly and consistently grounded in the traditions of Jewish American and Yiddish humor.

23. Eric Lax, *Woody Allen: A Biography* (New York: Alfred A. Knopf, 1991), pp. 197–98.

24. Amidst the unremittingly Kafkaesque bleakness of *Shadows and Fog,* Kleinman encounters his former fiancée (Julie Kavner), who still begrudges the fact that he couldn't be found on their wedding day because he was fornicating with her sister in a closet; amidst the bitter cycle of betrayals and joyless recouplings which is *Husbands and Wives,* Sally (Judy Davis) terrifies her hypercivilized, opera-loving date (Timothy Jerome) by screaming at her ex-husband (Sydney Pollock) on the date's telephone and then responding to his telling her that he

has gotten them tickets for this evening's performance of *Don Giovanni*, "Fucking Don Juans—they should cut his fucking dick off."

25. Stig Bjorkman, *Woody Allen on Woody Allen* (New York: Grove Press, 1993), p. 235.

26. Allen, *Broadway Danny Rose*, p. 175.

27. Mark Shechner, "Jewish Writers," in *Harvard Guide to Contemporary American Writing* (Cambridge, Mass: Harvard University Press, 1979), p. 239.

28. Julian Fox, *Woody: Movies from Manhattan* (Woodstock, New York: Overlook Press, 1996), p. 278.

29. Guthrie, p. 138.

30. Woody Allen, "Through a Life Darkly" (review of Ingmar Bergman's *The Magic Lantern*), *The New York Times Book Review*, September 18, 1988, pp. 30–31.

31. William E. Geist, "The *Rolling Stone* Interview: Woody Allen," p. 213.

32. Among the longest serving of Allen's senior production staff are Jack Rollins and Charles Joffe, executive producers; Robert Greenhut, producer; Gordon Willis, Carlo Di Palma and Sven Nykvist, cinematography; Susan E. Morse, editor; Juliet Taylor, casting; Mel Bourne and Santo Loquasto, production design, Jeffrey Kurland, costume design; Kay Chapin, script supervisor, Jimmy Sabat, sound engineer, and Dick Hyman, musical direction.

33. Bjorkman, pp. 77, 96.

34. Bjorkman, p. 127.

35. Geist, p. 213.

36. Guthrie, p. 144.

2. Strictly the Movies: *Play it Again, Sam*

1. Lax, *Woody Allen: A Biography*, pp. 26–27.

2. Jay Martin's discussion of *Zelig* in the context of his treatment of the postmodern annulment of the self effectively foregrounds this aspect of Allen's film. *Who Am I This Time?* (New York: W.W. Norton, 1993), pp. 88–90.

3. Although *Play It Again, Sam* isn't technically a Woody Allen film—it was directed by Herbert Ross—two facts argue for treating it as if it were: Allen wrote both the original play and the screenplay based on it, and Ross's cinematic style anticipates Allen's largely transparent use of filmic conventions. Ross, Allen said, "had seen the play and wanted to retain in the movie that which worked in the play; he wasn't looking for radical changes." Fox, *Woody: Movies from Manhattan*, p. 59.

4. Maurice Yacowar points up one of the film's central emblems of Felix's misordered psychic realities. When he first images up his ex-wife, "Felix takes a spatula and scrapes two fried eggs back from his plate into the frying pan. He seems to be living backwards. Indeed, he is, inasmuch as he regresses into fantasies and attempts to model his life after art, instead of taking art as an illumination of life." *Loser Take All: The Comic Art of Woody Allen* (New York: Frederick Ungar, 1979), p. 58.

5. In *Radio Days*, the narrator's Aunt Bea displays a similar tendency toward holding potential mates to "too high a standard," though she seems to be finding the men she dates insufficient not in relation to movie stars but as compared to the relationships evoked in popular songs.

6. In *Everyone Says I Love You*, Allen's Joe Berlin character, sans tails, gets to play the Astaire part in a *pas de deux* with Goldie Hawn on the Seine, the scene effectively poised on the borderline between champagne comedy sentimentality and parody.

7. Douglas Brode, *The Films of Woody Allen* (New York: Citadel Press, 1992), p. 256.

8. Lee Guthrie, *Woody Allen*, pp. 80–81.

9. Fox, p. 63.

10. Woody Allen, "My Secret Life with Bogart," *Life*, March 21, 1969, p. 66.

11. Fox, p. 63.

12. Guthrie, p. 92.

13. Tim Carroll, *Woody and His Women* (London: Warner Books, 1994), p. 92.

3. Getting Serious: The Antimimetic Emblems of *Annie Hall*

1. Judging *Love and Death* "one of [Allen's] best films," Douglas Brode perceives the film's central tension as its dramatization of the conflict in Allen between "the expert popular entertainer" and the "closet-intellectual existentialist who would, in *Interiors*, loudly come out" (*The Films of Woody Allen*, p. 135). Only through the benefit of a retrospective view of the evolution of Allen's career would a viewer be likely to discern in the prevailing caricature of *Love and Death* a serious concern with existentialism or Russian literature.

2. *Annie Hall*, p. 6.

3. *Play It Again, Sam* (Paramount Home Video, 1980).

4. Woody Allen, *Bullets Over Broadway* (Miramax Pictures, 1995).

5. Woody Allen, "Through a Life Darkly" (review of *The Magic Lantern*), *The New York Times Book Review*, September 18, 1988, p. 29.

6. Peter Cowie, *BFI Film Classics: Annie Hall* (London: British Film Institute, 1996), p. 46.

7. Annette Wernblad, *Brooklyn is Not Expanding*, p. 69.

8. This scene closely resembles Donald Barthelme's short story, "Me and Miss Mandible," in which the 35-year-old narrator is returned to fifth grade as an adult, ostensibly because of the failure of his initial education to give him "confidence in [his] ability to take the right steps and to obtain correct answers" (*Come Back, Dr. Caligari* [New York: Little, Brown, 1964], p. 110).

9. Graham McCann, *Woody Allen: New Yorker* (Cambridge, England: Polity Press, 1990), p. 198.

10. Were Brooks to have made a film like *Manhattan*—which he wouldn't have—he might have had his characters getting mugged and doing pratfalls in garbage-strewn streets to the tunes of George Gershwin; Allen presents the disparity between the ideal mental reality of New York City embodied in Gershwin standards and the corrupt hearts of New Yorkers through constant dramatic juxtaposition.

11. Compare the markedly divergent view of Mary P. Nichols, whose *Reconstructing Woody: Art, Love and Life in the Films of Woody Allen* (Lanham, Maryland: Rowman & Littlefield, 1998) discovers in Allen's films a consistent affirmation of art. Playing off the scene in which Annie's need to smoke grass before lovemaking prompts her soul to leave her body and begin drawing, Nichols asserts, "Allen's art captures the spirit. He is a better drawer. He draws human beings whole—thinking, loving, desiring, even if their objects are in part elusive because they too are capable of thinking, loving, and desiring. The illusory wholeness from grass that Annie seeks gives way to the more elusive wholeness of life that Allen's art intimates" (p. 44).

12. A similar scene, which Allen filmed but rejected, had Alvy in Times Square wondering what to do about Annie's move to L.A. He looks up at the *New York Times* headlines scrolling across the Allied Chemical Building, which reads, "What are you doing, Alvy? Go to California. It's okay. She loves you." "Viewing the scene in dailies," Eric Lax explained, "Woody hated it so much he went to the nearest reservoir and threw the reels in." Quoted in Julian Fox, *Woody: Movies from Manhattan*, p. 96. Allen returns to this joke in "Oedipus Wrecks," Sheldon Millstein's mother's garrulous appearance in the skies of New York ensuring that everyone in the city streets knows his most personal conflicts and problems.

13. Ralph Rosenblum and Robert Karen, *When the Shooting Stops . . . the Cutting Begins* (New York: Penguin Books, 1979), p. 283.

14. Never one to let a good joke go to waste, Allen has Harry Block descending into Hell in an elevator in *Deconstructing Harry* as the intercom system informs him which sinners have been consigned to which levels of Hell.

15. The deletion of this surreal scene left behind a truncated echo: in the released film, Alvy and his second wife, Robin (Janet Margolin), attend a party of prestigious writers and publishers, Alvy irritating Robin by fleeing the living room literary chitchat and finding a bedroom in which to watch a Knicks' game on television.

16. Rosenblum and Karen, pp. 279–80.

17. Bjorkman, *Woody Allen on Woody Allen*, p. 37.

18. Ralph Rosenblum's account of the process of skit deletion by which *Annie Hall* came into being (in a chapter tendentiously titled "Annie Hall: It Wasn't the Film He Set Out to Make") attributes more of the script's metamorphosis to his efforts as editor than it does to Allen's intention to make a deeper movie, but it is nonetheless clear that Allen agreed, at times reluctantly, to the deletion of "all that surrealistic stuff" he and/or Brickman had written. Rosenblum and Karen, pp. 273–90.

19. Even here, Alvy's selective memory is at work, inflecting the montage. Instead of kissing him immediately after opening the box containing the negligee as the montage depicts the scene, Annie had turned to him and said, "This [the negligee] is for you!" The kiss is his reward for the watch she opened next.

20. Rosenblum, film editor on Allen's movies through *Interiors*, discusses the endings Allen scripted or shot for *Bananas, Take the Money and Run,* and *Sleeper,* which bear little relation to the theatrical release endings, explaining that the experience of reconfiguring the endings of these films during production inspired Allen to omit completely a conclusion to the *Annie Hall* script, writing on the last page "Ending to be shot." Rosenblum and Karen, p. 262. Allen's "God (A Play)," in *Without Feathers,* dramatizes the problems of WRITER and ACTOR in devising an ending for the play they're in.

21. Nancy Pogel, *Woody Allen* (Boston: Twayne Publishers, 1987), p. 149. Mark Siegal reads *Stardust Memories* as a parody of *8½* in "Ozymandias Melancholia: The Nature of Parody in Woody Allen's *Stardust Memories,*" *Literature/Film Quarterly* 13, 2 (1985), pp. 76–83.

22. Guthrie, *Woody Allen,* p. 144.

4. Art and Idealization: I'll Fake *Manhattan*

Epigraph quoted in Anthony DeCurtis, "The *Rolling Stone* Interview: Woody Allen." *Rolling Stone,* September 16, 1993, p. 50.

1. John Irving, *The World According to Garp* (New York: Dutton, 1978), p. 328.

2. In their gender-focused study of *Manhattan,* Terry L. Allison and Renee R. Curry contend that the film's early dramatization of a mature and remarkably expressive relationship between males ultimately dwindles to a contest for the female—Mary—between Yale and Isaac best characterized by Isaac's question to Yale, "What are you, six years old?" "Frame Breaking and Code Breaking in Woody Allen's Relationship Films," in Renee R. Curry, ed., *Perspectives on Woody Allen* (New York: G.K. Hall, 1996), p. 127.

3. Pauline Kael, Allen's most sagacious and probing reviewer and far from his most sympathetic critic, objected to the ethical antinomy at the heart of *Manhattan:* Allen, she argued, "contrasted [Mary's, Yale's and Isaac's] lack of faith with the trusting, understanding heart of a loyal child. . . . What man in his forties but Woody Allen could pass off a predilection for teenagers as a quest for true values?" *For Keeps* (New York: E.P. Dutton, 1994), p. 868.

4. The same basic disjunction between interior human corruption and musical/aesthetic wholeness is epitomized by Hannah's parents in *Hannah and Her Sisters*. In private, they wrangle bitterly with each other, he charging her with drunkenness and infidelity, she accusing him of failing to support the family and of being a non-person; in public, the solidity of their union is dramatized at parties by the romantic standards they jointly perform at the piano together such as "You Are Too Beautiful" and "Bewitched, Bothered and Bewildered," the contents of the songs bearing no resemblance to the deeply conflicted emotional realities of their marriage.

5. Schickel, "Woody Allen Comes of Age," *Time*, April 30, 1979, p. 65.

6. "From now on Lady, I insist/ For me no other girls exist"; "Embrace me, my irreplaceable you"; "I'm a little lamb who's lost in the wood/ I know I could always be good to someone who'll watch over me," *The Great Songs of George Gershwin* (Secaucus, N.J.: Warner Brothers Publications, n.d.), pp. 95, 164, 137.

7. Allen confirmed to Stig Bjorkman that Isaac's view that "people should mate for life like pigeons and Catholics" is close to his own: "that is what everybody tries to achieve, a deep, lasting relationship with a single other person" (p. 110).

8. "The original idea for the picture," Allen told Silvio Bizio, actually "evolved from the music. I was listening to a record album of overtures from famous George Gershwin shows, and I thought, 'This would be a beautiful thing to make a movie in black-and-white, you know, and make a romantic movie.'" Quoted in Julian Fox, *Woody: Movies from Manhattan*, p. 109. The plots of *Radio Days* and *Everyone Says I Love You* are similarly soundtrack-influenced. In both films, Allen accommodated narrative to the inclusion—even performance—of songs he recalled from his childhood.

9. Stanley Elkin, *The Living End* (New York: Dutton, 1979), p. 92.

10. Sam B. Girgus, *The Films of Woody Allen* (Cambridge: Cambridge University Press, 1993), p. 45.

11. Tom Shales summarized the significance of Alvy's forthright vulnerability: "Woody Allen as much as any other public male made it all right to be anxious and nervous and scared, particularly about sexual performance, and still be masculine." "Woody Allen: The First 50 Years," *Esquire*, April, 1987, p. 95.

12. Richard Freadman suggests that Alvy, like other Allen protagonists, is actually exploited by his love and then rejected. "If the man's aura of painful vulnerability and enchanting idiosyncrasy has a certain sexual magnetism, these features seem to harbor a kind of built-in affective obsolescence which virtually guarantees that, having 'loved' him, the Beloved will ultimately become restless for precisely what 'Woody' lacks: virility, confidence, good humor, and a certain prepossessing swagger of conventionality." Mary's rejection of Isaac in favor of Yale follows the same pattern Freadman explicates. "Love Among the Stereotypes, or Why Woody's Women Leave," in Avvner Ziv and Anat Zajdman, eds., *Semites and Stereotypes: Characteristics of Jewish Humor* (Westport, Connecticut: Greenwood Press, 1993), p. 110.

13. That such a notion was on Allen's mind in scripting the film is suggested by a line he and Marshall Brickman wrote for Mary Wilke: "Don't you guys see that [the 'silence of God' in Bergman's films] is the dignifying of one's own psychological and sexual hangups by attaching them to these grandiose philosophical issues?" (*Manhattan*, pp. 194–95).

14. In *Play It Again, Sam* Alan Felix explains that "I can't drink—my body will not tolerate alcohol," which poses a dilemma since his Bogart projection has counseled him that heartbreak "is nothing a little bourbon and water won't fix." The first sign that Harry Block of *Deconstructing Harry* is an unsympathetic character is the fact that he so ostentatiously brandishes a bottle of booze in the first scene in which he appears.

15. Were there any doubt that Joey is the only heroic character in *Interiors*, it's dispelled

by the fact that she passes Isaac's test of courage by diving into the ocean in an attempt to save her mother from drowning in the film's dramatic climax.

16. One of the critical cruxes of *Manhattan* arises from the belated introduction of the issue of Isaac Davis's moralism, what Yale refers to as his tendency to be "self-righteous" and to "think you're God" by holding others to impossible moral standards. Those reviewers and critics who have accepted what is basically Isaac's self-serving perception of himself neglect to notice the considerable inconsistencies in his behavior in the film. When Yale confesses his adulterous relationship with Mary, Isaac never rebukes him for it, and his own casual relationship with seventeen-year-old Tracy, as Kael suggests, doesn't exemplify moral probity. Although Isaac does wait until Yale and Mary have parted to begin actively pursuing her, explaining that he would "never in a million years" betray his friend, the fact that his involvement with Mary is well along before he breaks off with Tracy makes him a highly dubious nominee for saint among narcissist sinners. Isaac's complete reversal, after Mary has left him for Yale, of his earlier enthusiastic advocacy of Tracy's attending London's Academy of Music and Dramatic Arts in London reflects a similarly situational and self-serving ethic. "Woody could have made a safer picture, like *Annie Hall*," Michael Murphy, who played Yale Pollock, said. "This film is a lot tougher, harder-edged. And it was a bold step for Woody not to be a hero" (p. 65). Quoted in Richard Schickel, "Woody Allen Comes of Age," p. 65.

17. Those critics who failed to notice that development in the evolution of the Allen protagonist tended to overlook it as well in *Stardust Memories* and *Crimes and Misdemeanors*, two other films in which the familiar and likable Allen mannerisms deceived viewers into feeling a sympathy for Sandy Bates and Clifford Stern greater than their screenwriter seems to feel.

18. Mary's egotistical comment on her own attractiveness provides an important corrective to Isaac's worship of feminine beauty: "Uh, you'll never believe this, but I never thought I was pretty. Oh, what is pretty anyway? I mean, I hate being pretty. It's all so subjective anyway" (p. 208).

19. Yale's objection to Isaac that "you just can't live the way you live. It's all too perfect," suggests that Allen was imbuing Isaac with the tendencies toward self-righteousness and insularity which are Eve's chief characteristics in *Interiors*. Nothing in Isaac's character supports Yale's description.

20. Fox, p. 108. .

21. Fox, p. 114.

22. Lax, p. 276.

23. Fox, p. 110. It's difficult not to read as a parable expressing Allen's conviction of beauty's mutability the fact that, sixteen years after *Manhattan*, Allen cast Mariel Hemingway in *Deconstructing Harry* not as "the most beautiful woman the world has seen," but as a self-righteous mother endlessly harassing Harry about his fatherly responsibilities to his son.

24. Bjorkman, p. 108.

25. Diane Jacobs was the first of Allen's critics to compare the close-up of Isaac's face closing the film to the final close-up of the little tramp in *City Lights* (which Allen has designated "Chaplin's best—and probably anybody's best—comedy" [Guthrie, *Woody Allen: A Biography*, p. 123]). That these two directors of primarily comic films use close-ups so sparingly is perhaps one reason that the two scenes invite comparison. The closing shot of *City Lights* focuses on the tramp's nervously smiling face as he desperately awaits the flower girl's reaction to his revelation that it was he and not, as she believed, a rich man who financed the operation which restored her sight. In both films, the audience must interpret the facial expression of the protagonist to move from a feeling of irresolution to a sense of closure, though the disparity between Charlie's look of intensely desperate hopefulness and Isaac's smirk of ironic resignation is so great as to seem to epitomize the trajectory of American innocence over the half century separating the production of the two films.

5. Strictly the Movies II: How *Radio Days* Generated Nights at the Movies

1. The jokes which comprised his routine were what Allen referred to as "verbal cartoons": "They have a surreal, fantastic quality to them," Eric Lax argued, "but even so they are somehow believable, when Woody describes them, as events that could happen, if only to him; his jokes work so well because he delivers them as if they were problems in his life." Lax, p. 129.

2. Lax, p. 159.

3. One collection of Allen's stand-up routines from the 1960s is *Woody Allen: Standup Comic,* Casablanca Records, 1978, which includes three of the jokes Alvy Singer tells. A more recent anthology is *Woody Allen: Standup Comic, 1964–68* (Rhino Records, 1999). The monologue Allen drew from for *Annie Hall* is reproduced in Linda Sunshine, *The Illustrated Woody Allen Reader* (New York: Alfred A. Knopf, 1993), pp. 9–11.

4. Recall Allen's comment, cited in the *Annie Hall* chapter, that the original draft of the script "was originally a picture about me exclusively, not about a relationship. It was about me, my life, my thoughts, my ideas, my background, and the relationship was one major part of it." Rosenblum and Karen, p. 283.

5. Tim Carroll, *Woody and His Women* (London: Warner Books, 1994), p. 311. One of the explanations offered for Leonard Zelig's eccentric psychological behavior is a brain tumor, but it's the doctor who hypothesizes this diagnosis, not Zelig, who dies from one.

6. Carroll, pp. 168–69.

7. Fox, p. 111.

8. Fox, p. 102.

9. Lax, p. 179.

10. The link between *Annie Hall* and *Manhattan Murder Mystery* is by no means mere appearance. The murder mystery plot of the latter film, Allen has admitted, was originally an element of the original *Annie Hall* script. Bjorkman, p. 225.

11. Lax, p. 179.

12. Carroll, p. 137.

13. Allen's description of Bates quoted in Lax, p. 273.

14. One of Allen's habits which doesn't fit at all with the personalities of his protagonists (except, perhaps, in its obsessiveness) is his preparation for elevator rides, his need to have a problem to work through on the elevator so that the time expired during the ride won't be wasted. John Lahr, "The Imperfectionist," *The New Yorker,* December 9, 1996, p. 82.

15. Lax, p. 28.

16. Carroll, p. 137.

17. Woody Allen, *Radio Days* (Orion Pictures, 1987).

18. Richard Schickel, *Time,* February 2, 1987, p. 73.

19. Allen provides a more extensive catalogue of elements of his childhood which he gave the protagonist of *Radio* Days in Bjorkman, p. 158.

20. Bjorkman, p. 162.

21. The film's ambivalence about its autobiographical roots seems signaled by its very deliberate omission of the name "Joe." The one point where the use of his name seems unavoidable, his Aunt Bea tells his mother, "We're going to take your son to the city with us."

22. Thierry de Navacelle, *Woody Allen on Location* (New York: William Morrow, 1987), passim.

23. At $16 million, *Radio Days* was Allen's most expensive production before *Bullets Over Broadway,* the estimated negative cost of which was $20 million (Fox, pp. 226, 269).

24. In Eric Lax's biography, Allen recalled a similar experience of the power of radio— one that he and Dick Cavett experienced during a visit to Los Angeles in the early 1960s. "As

they passed by [Jack Benny's house] they imagined Benny and his wife, Mary Livingston, and Eddie Anderson, who played Rochester, putting together the night's show," Lax explained. "They knew that wasn't really happening, but years of listening to the show on the radio had given them a mental picture of Beverly Hills and the Benny household that in many ways was more real than what they were seeing" (p. 178).

25. Woody Allen, *Radio Days* (Hollywood: Hollywood Scripts, n.d.), p. 9.

26. In the early script, the failed Polly Phelps rescue was clearly intended as a thematic counterpoint to the original opening radio broadcast, subsequently deleted, in which a magician named Tonino successfully escapes from a milk can submerged off the Jersey Coast, the contrast dramatizing the disparity between radio as a repository of entertainment spectacle and grim news. In the released film, the Phelps episode constitutes a reversal of the new opening: whereas a burglary attempt at the Needlemans' apartment turns into a windfall through the intervention of radio when the thieves identify correctly the three songs being played on *Guess that Tune*, radio's presence is powerless to transform the Polly Phelps drama into felicity. As David Edelstein suggested in a review of the film, radio "can bind the nation together . . . but cannot conquer death." *The Village Voice*, February 3, 1987, p. 53.

27. Allen informed Bjorkman (pp. 168–69) that he remembered the broadcast of an incident resembling Polly Phelps's death in the film, though he was a teenager, not Polly's age— eight—when he listened to it.

28. Woody Allen, *Crimes and Misdemeanors* (Orion Pictures, 1989).

29. Richard Combs, (review of *Radio Days*), *Monthly Film Bulletin,* July, 1987, p. 212.

30. Even here, however, the possibility of betrayal lurks: this image from *The Philadelphia Story* constitutes a false consummation, no "big finish" at all, since Hepburn in the film's conclusion is romantically united not with Stewart but with Cary Grant.

31. A bleaker construing of radio's affect on the family seems to be manifested through Little Joe's cousin Ruthie (Joy Newman), whose sole character trait is that she constantly listens in on the Waldbaums' party line. Vicarious eavesdropping on others' realities as compensation for a want of a life of one's own would be a cynic's summation of the family's dependency on radio.

32. Julian Fox (p. 180) points out that an earlier cinematographic conception of the film distinguished more categorically between Rockaway home and radio worlds: it was Allen's original intention to make the warm colors of the family scenes consistently contrast with the coldly art deco aura of the radio studio scenes.

33. Woody Allen, *The Purple Rose of Cairo,* in *Three Films of Woody Allen* (New York: Vintage Books, 1987), p. 395.

6. Life Stand Still Here: *Interiors* Dialogue

1. Bjorkman, p. 120.

2. The psychoanalytically minded might argue that Sachs's affirmation of *Duck Soup* involves more than a love of funny movies. Allen has repeatedly associated his family—toward whom he has expressed ambivalent feelings—with the Marx Brothers, explaining that in his home, "relatives were always running in and out of rooms. It was like living in a Marx Brothers movie." "I'm obsessed by the fact that my mother genuinely resembles Groucho Marx," he suggested elsewhere, and in *Take the Money and Run,* he seems to be making the same association in having Virgil's parents, who are ashamed of their son's life of crime, disguise themselves in Groucho masks for their interview. Tim Carroll, *Woody and His Women* (London: Warner Books, 1994), pp. 14, 20. Allen's response to meeting Groucho, Eric Lax suggests, was "He seemed like one of my Jewish uncles" (p. 171).

3. Lee Guthrie, *Woody Allen: A Biography,* p. 171.

4. Virginia Woolf, *To the Lighthouse* (New York: Harcourt Brace Jovanovich, 1955), p. 241.

5. Wallace Stevens, "The Idea of Order at Key West," in *The Collected Poems of Wallace Stevens* (New York: Alfred A. Knopf, 1954), p. 129.

6. Quoted in John Updike, "The Heaven of an Old Home" (review of *Souvenirs and Prophecies: The Young Wallace Stevens*, by Holly Stevens), in *Hugging the Shore* (New York: Alfred A. Knopf, 1983), p. 610.

7. Woody Allen, *Another Woman* (Orion Pictures, 1988).

8. Marion "discovers more truth about herself in novels, plays and poetry than from people," Richard A. Blake argued. "Art bears more meaning for her than life, and more than the German Idealism she has immersed herself in for so many years." *Woody Allen: Sacred and Profane* (Lanham, Maryland: Scarecrow Press, 1995), p. 162.

9. Woody Allen, *Bullets Over Broadway* (Miramax Films, 1995).

10. That Frederick, the quintessential Modernist-artist-in-withdrawal, is played by Max Von Sydow, an actor best known in America for his roles in Bergman's films, reinforces a point pervading this chapter: that, in Allen's mind, the ambition to create serious art and the Modernist inflation of the aesthetic are inextricably linked with Ingmar Bergman.

11. Bjorkman, p. 242.

12. Quoted in Maurice Yacowar, *Loser Take All*, p. 183.

13. Michiko Kakutani, "Woody Allen: The Art of Humor I," *The Paris Review*, 136 (Fall, 1996), p. 216.

14. Lax, p. 373.

15. Woody Allen, "Through a Life Darkly" (review of Ingmar Bergman's *The Magic Lantern*), *The New York Times Book Review*, September 18, 1988, p. 30.

16. F. Scott Fitzgerald, "The Ice Palace," in *Babylon Revisited and Other Stories* (New York: Charles Scribner's Sons, 1960), p. 14.

17. Lax, p. 342.

18. In the final appearance of the window motif which takes place at the celebration following the wedding, Pearl, dancing with Arthur, waves at Joey who stands on the other side of a door of glass panes, seeming to be on the outside of a window looking in. One of the working titles of *Interiors*, Allen acknowledged, was *Windows* (Bjorkman, p. 96).

19. Another implicitly parental link between Joey and Pearl is suggested by the fact that Pearl's son supports himself selling paintings on velvet of clowns.

20. Jack Kroll criticized Allen for creating in *Interiors* "a blatantly simple cleavage between 'art' and 'life'" in the two women ("The Inner Woody" [rev. of *Interiors*], *Newsweek*, August 7, 1978, p. 83). Nancy Pogel's chapter on the film offers a particularly careful analysis of the ways in which the three daughters' interrelationships with each other and with these mother figures throw nuancing crosslights upon the film's dominant allegory. *Woody Allen* (Boston: Twayne Publishers, 1987), pp. 99–116.

21. David Edelstein, rev. of *Radio Days* in *The Village Voice*, February 3, 1987, p. 53.

22. Lax, p. 179.

23. Diane Jacobs argues persuasively that Joey's comment, "I felt compelled to write these thoughts down. They seemed very powerful to me," reflects her realization that her interior life has value for her without its being communicated to a wider audience through art.   . . . *but we need the eggs: The Magic of Woody Allen* (New York: St, Martin's Press, 1982), p. 126.

24. Bjorkman, p. 99.

25. See Alan Wilde, *Horizons of Assent: Modernism, Postmodernism and the Ironic Imagination* (Baltimore: Johns Hopkins University Press, 1981), pp. 46–47.

26. Jacobs, p. 126.

27. The omission of these elements of Pearl's character undermines for me Mary P.

Nichols' *Reconstructing Woody* argument that Pearl is an unambiguously positive figure in the movie, solely "a force that foils the self-contained interiors that constitute the life of [the family] members and that isolate them from the world" (p. 63).

28. Allen's explanation of the *Love and Death* use of the *Persona* image: "Sure, we just used anything we wanted to in those days. We took Russian books and Swedish films and French films and Kafka and French existentialists. Whatever gave us an amusing time, we used." Bjorkman, p. 74. The content of the image in *Persona* to which Allen's closing scene clearly alludes seems, in fact, utterly unrelated to anything going on at the end of *Interiors*: the three sisters of Allen's film are in no sense psychically intersecting with one another as Sister Alma and Lisabeth Vogler are in the pivotal *Persona* image.

29. Pauline Kael, "Fear of Movies," in *For Keeps: Thirty Years in the Movies* (New York: E.P. Dutton, 1994), p. 786.

30. Bjorkman, p. 210.

31. Bjorkman, p. 80.

7. In the Stardust of a Song: *Stardust Memories*

1. Frank Rich, "An Interview with Woody," *Time*, April 30, 1979, p. 69.

2. Carlos Baker, ed., *The Selected Prose and Poetry of Percy Bysshe Shelley* (New York: Modern Library, 1951), p. 375.

3. If challenged to defend my critical insistence upon linking *Annie Hall* and *Stardust Memories*, I'd cite Allen's comment about the deliberate subjectivity of both films: "The one film I finally got into the mind completely was *Stardust Memories*. That was all taking place in the mind, so anything could happen. But in *Annie Hall* I was trying this for the first time." Bjorkman, p. 88.

4. Kakutani, "The Art of Humor," p. 203.

5. Lax, p. 285.

6. In subsequent scenes in Bates's apartment, the wall similarly reflects the protagonist's mental state. A happy period with Dorrie is projected through the image of a grinning Groucho Marx embracing a lady friend; a more stressful episode of their relationship in which Dorrie accuses him of being interested in her teenage cousin getting epitomized by fragmentary newspaper headlines, "Against Mom" and "Incest Between Fathers and. . . ."

7. Bjorkman, p. 124.

8. Pauline Kael's annihilating review of the film, which assumed that Bates is "the most undisguised of [Allen's] dodgy mock-autobiographical fantasies," includes judgments such as "Woody Allen has often been cruel to himself in physical terms—now he's doing it to his fans," and "Allen sees his public as Jews trying to shove him down into the Jewish clowns' club . . . he's angry with the public, with us—as if we were forcing him to embody the Jewish joke, the loser, the deprived outsider forever" (*For Keeps* [New York: E.P. Dutton, 1994], pp. 863, 864, 866).

9. Jacobs, p. 147; Lax, p. 276.

10. Bjorkman, p. 123.

11. Tennessee Williams, *The Glass Menagerie* (New York: New Directions, 1966), p. 3.

12. One minor mystery of Allen's films concerns the intertextual references to Nat Bernstein. In *Stardust Memories*, his sudden death seems to have precipitated Bates's spiritual crisis; in *Radio Days* he is similarly no more than a name, about whom Tess, Little Joe's mother, asks the question, "What was wrong with Nat Bernstein?" Aunt Bea's answer is that Bernstein was not a serious suitor for her because he wore white socks with a tuxedo.

13. McCann, p. 209.

14. Many of *Stardust Memories*' reviewers—Pauline Kael primary among them—inter-

preted its ending as being consistent with what they perceived as the movie's overall attack on the filmgoing audience, its unflattering depiction of Sandy Bates's most dedicated admirers and most sympathetic critics having proven very easy to translate into Allen's onslaught against *his* audience. My *Radio Days* chapter attempted to address the persistent problem of viewers' and critics'—and, sometimes, Allen's own—confusion of Allen with his protagonists. *Stardust Memories* hardly presents a Frank Capraesque affirmation of the American film audience, certainly, but what Bates stares at before walking out of the theater is not filmgoers but the screen on which his film appeared, and Allen clearly devotes more energy in his movie to signaling the confused artistic impulses underlying Bates's film than he does to establishing its audience's deficiencies. The failure of Bates's happy ending to have the cheering affect on the audience he assumedly intends it to have says as much about Bates and the limits of cinematic art as it does about the audience's responsive inadequacies, the lapse in communication having sources on both sides of the screen. It's the relationship between Bates and the film that is his self-projection which interests Allen in this movie far more than satirizing his fans, I would argue; dramatizing the difference between Bates's ending and his own constitutes a primary motivation for Allen's having made the film.

15. Nancy Pogel reads the last half hour or so of *Stardust Memories* as offering a number of alternative endings: Bates's declaration of his refusal to marry Isobel, his murder, his proposal of marriage on the train, etc. *Woody Allen,* pp. 146–49.

16. Pauline Kael's review of *Sleeper* constituted the annunciation of the arrival of a major comic filmmaker, her essay generously and sympathetically celebrating Allen's comedic gifts while defining, with striking prescience, the obstacles of temperament and disposition which could interfere with his achieving the comedic heights she projected for him. "The running war between the tame and the surreal," she wrote in 1973, "—between Woody Allen the frightened nice guy trying to keep the peace and Woody Allen the wiseacre whose subversive fantasies keep jumping out of his mouth—has been the source of the comedy in his films. Messy, tasteless, and crazily uneven (as the best talking comedies have often been), the last two pictures he directed—*Bananas* and *Everything You Always Wanted to Know About Sex*—had wild highs that suggested an erratic comic genius." The major threat to the fulfillment of his promise, Kael suggested, was that "he overvalues normality" (*For Keeps,* p. 535). That Allen gradually turned away from the "loose, manic highs" of those films was a primary cause of Kael's increasing captiousness toward his films, *Sleeper* itself already prefiguring what would become Allen's career trajectory in that "it doesn't unhinge us, we never feel our reason is being shredded." The Kael reviews of Allen films which followed this one regularly decry their abandonment of the early films' "vulgar vibrancy," their rambunctiousness, playfulness, raucousness, their "hostility . . . and freak lyricism," their "organic untidiness" and general air of deliberate comedic subversion. When she wrote in her take-no-prisoners review of *Stardust Memories,* "From the tone of this film, you would think that vulgarians were putting guns to Woody Allen's head and forcing him to make comedies," the judgment carried its own tonality of personal betrayal, one never completely absent from Kael's subsequent reviews of his films.

17. Again Mary P. Nichols and I draw diametrically opposed conclusions: "I agree that Allen's films address these modern—or postmodern—positions," she argued. "But Allen's films do not celebrate this lack of moral or intellectual coherence or give birth to myriad and contradictory interpretations that cannot be resolved." *Reconstructing Woody,* p. xiii.

18. Quoted in McCann, p. 208.

19. Frederico Fellini, *8½.*

20. The identification of this suddenly ambiguous figure with Allen is probably obviated by a trivial fact Lax records: Allen's "unwillingness to have his vision interfered with extends to not wearing sunglasses because of the alterations they make in color and light" (p. 233).

21. A seminal difference between Mary P. Nichols' *Reconstructing Woody* perception of Allen's view of art and mine is that she insists upon a distinction between Allen's art and that of his characters. Nichols maintains that neither Bates nor Cliff of *Crimes and Misdemeanors* is the artist Allen is, the disparity containing for her the difference between the art Allen satirizes and the more substantial art he creates and thus affirms. Although I'd agree that the quality of Allen's work is greater than that of his artist protagonists, I'm not at all convinced that the dubious attitude toward the artistic enterprise dramatized in his films and voiced by his protagonists is completely ironized in such a way as to elevate Allen's own work above the critique. Nichols contends that Allen's art transcends its own critique of art in the same way, say, that Joyce's *Portrait* transcends the art of the young artist it depicts; my dissenting argument is that, because of his very real dubiety about the claims of aesthetic transformation, Allen's art consistently accuses and indicts itself.

8. Woody's Mild Jewish Rose: *Broadway Danny Rose*

1. The contrast between the highly sympathetic depiction of the world of Jewish-American comedy and the much more negative vision of Hollywood in Allen's next film, *The Purple Rose of Cairo*, isn't surprising, given Allen's career choices, but it is nonetheless instructive. The Hollywood film within *Purple Rose* presents nothing but illusions belied by the actions and characters of the actors who appear in the movie, but which the hopeless economic straits of the audience compel them desperately to embrace; the comedians are aware of and sensitive to their audience, enjoying each other at the Carnegie Deli as if they *are* that audience.

2. Woody Allen, *Broadway Danny Rose*, in *Three Films of Woody Allen* (New York: Vintage Books, 1987), p. 255.

3. Jonathan Baumbach, "The Comedians" (review of *Broadway Danny Rose*), *Commonweal*, March 23, 1984, p. 182.

4. Another small consonance between beginnings and endings in the Danny Rose fable: when Danny arrives at Tina's apartment to meet her for the first time, she's talking to Lou on the telephone; when she arrives at Danny's apartment on Thanksgiving to make up with him, he's talking on the telephone.

5. John Pym, review of *Broadway Danny Rose*, *Sight and Sound*, Autumn, 1984, p. 300.

6. Baumbach, p. 182.

7. The comedians are not the only ones being nostalgic in *Broadway Danny Rose*. Weinstein's Majestic Bungalow Colony, a Catskills resort where Danny is pictured pumping his acts, is where Allen's performing career had its start, the sixteen-year-old Allan Konigsberg having performed magic tricks there. Recent Allen biographies have also established that the Danny Rose character was inspired in part by Harvey Meltzer, the agent Allen had before signing on with Charles Joffe and Jack Rollins. Meltzer is said to have used phrases similar to Danny's signature expression, "Might I interject a concept at this juncture?" Fox, p. 151.

8. Vincent Canby, "'Danny Rose': Runyonesque, But Pure Woody Allen" (review of *Broadway Danny Rose*), *The New York Times*, January 29, 1984, II, 13, p. 1.

9. Gilbert Adair, review of *Broadway Danny Rose*, *Monthly Film Bulletin*, September, 1984, p. 272.

10. David Denby, review of *Broadway Danny Rose*, *New York*, February 6, 1984, p. 64.

11. The union of Danny and Tina would also confirm the prediction of Tina's favorite fortune-teller, Angelina, that Tina would marry a Jew. That confirmation might be said to balance somewhat the film's dramatization of Danny's ethic so clearly triumphing over her cultural beliefs. That Tina's culture is largely reduced to "fortune-tellers and meat hooks" is admittedly one of the film's less pleasing comic strategies.

12. Allen's decision to have the comedians portray themselves rather than providing them with fictional identities creates a minor fact/fiction tension in the film, reversing the juxtaposition of the fictional Leonard Zelig with actual documentary footage, which was the central rhetorical ploy of *Zelig,* his previous film.

13. Andrew Sarris, review of *Broadway Danny Rose, Village Voice,* February 7, 1984, p. 47.

14. Daphne Merkin, "Comedy on Three Levels," (review of *Broadway Danny Rose*), *New Leader,* March 5, 1984, p. 19.

15. Joseph Gelmis, review of *Broadway Danny Rose, Newsday,* January 27, 1984, II, p. 3.

16. Jack Kroll, "Woody's Bow to Broadway" (review of *Broadway Danny Rose), Newsweek* January 30, 1984, p. 69.

17. William K. Zinsser, "Bright New Comic Clowns Toward Success," *Saturday Evening Post,* September 21, 1963, p. 26.

18. Maurice Yacowar, *Loser Take All: The Comic Art of Woody Allen* (New York: Frederick Unger Inc., 1979), p. 21.

19. In a very grumpy review of the film, Pauline Kael suggests, "Although Woody Allen knows how repulsive Lou Canova's act is, Danny Rose doesn't. He isn't permitted to have either taste or consciousness" (*State of the Art* [New York: E.P. Dutton, 1985], p. 124). Whether Allen's film is as insistent upon the repulsiveness of Canova's act as Kael is highly questionable—Nick Apollo Forte's performances in the film apparently differ little from the stage show he once regularly performed. The value system of *Broadway Danny Rose* is the showbiz ethic of the Carnegie comics and cruise ship lounges and Joe Franklin's *Memory Lane* television show, and much of the viewer's pleasure in the playing out of the film's fable is her/his immersion in that frankly and unapologetically vulgar realm in which singers perform medleys of "crooners who are now deceased." Consequently, "taste or consciousness" are expressly not what this film is about, except in that Danny has too much of either to sacrifice human beings to the showbiz winner-take-all worship of success. The question Kael might have posed to herself before dismissing the premises of *Broadway Danny Rose* was the one with which she closed her review of *Another Woman:* "How can you embrace life and leave out all the good vulgar trashiness?" (*Movie Love* [New York: E.P. Dutton], 1991, p. 16).

20. Woody Allen, *Zelig, Three Films of Woody Allen,* p. 126.

21. Yacowar, p. 215.

9. The Fine Art of Living Well: *Hannah and Her Sisters*

1. Woody Allen, *Hannah and Her Sisters* (New York: Vintage Books, 1987), pp. 96, 97–98.

2. Bjorkman, p. 157.

3. Allen's original, preferred ending, he told Anthony DeCurtis, focused upon Elliot rather than Mickey and Holly. Lee had married again, and Elliot had reunited with Hannah, but he remains in love with Lee, the film never resolving his erotic conflict between sisters. "Woody Allen, The *Rolling Stone* Interview," p. 49.

4. Mickey's and Holly's image in the mirror provides a visual antithesis to an earlier scene in which a mirror figures prominently: Mickey's botched suicide attempt results in his blasting the glass out of a mirror in his apartment.

5. The clown in *Shadows and Fog* does repudiate his career as a circus artist in order to be a father to the abandoned child he and Irmy have found, but his commitment is counterpoised with Kleinman's culminating dedication of his life to assisting in the creation of Irmstedt's illusions.

6. Mia Farrow, *What Falls Away* (New York: Doubleday, 1997), pp. 195, 227.

7. Walter Isaacson, "The Heart Wants What It Wants" (interview with Woody Allen), *Time Magazine,* August 31, 1992, p. 59.

8. Quoted in Phoebe Hoban, "Everything You Always Wanted to Know about Woody and Mia (But Were Afraid to Ask)," *New York*, September 21, 1992, p. 39.

9. Quoted in Tim Carroll, *Woody and His Women*, p. 244.

10. *What Falls Away*, p. 239.

11. *What Falls Away*, p. 228.

12. *What Falls Away*, p. 283.

13. Kristi Groteke with Marjorie Rosen, *Mia and Woody: Love and Betrayal* (New York: Carroll and Graf, 1994), p. 68.

14. William Geist's 1987 *Rolling Stone* interview illustrates Allen's relative equanimity at the time, Allen attributing his good mood in part to the relationship with Farrow (p. 214).

15. With the exception of the Depression-wracked *The Purple Rose of Cairo*, Allen's films concentrate on characters for whom having sufficient money to live is not a problem. Sandy Bates's comments to Daisy on this issue seem to reflect Allen's own preferences in writing screenplays: "But what happens if you're living in a more, you know, uh, more affluent society. And you're lucky enough not to have to worry about that. Let's say you're surviving. . . . So, then your problems become, can I fall in love, or why can't I fall in love, and why do I age and die, and what meaning can my life possibly have?" (*Stardust Memories*, p. 351).

16. Douglas Brode points out the further parallel between *Interiors* and *Hannah and Her Sisters* of the three central sisters: Renata/Hannah, the successful artist whose achievements overshadow and intimidate her sisters; Joey/Holly, who desires to create but lacks the requisite talent, and Flyn/Lee, whose physical beauty is her primary artistic accomplishment. *The Films of Woody Allen*, p. 244.

17. The fact that the minuscule role of Frederick is played by Max Von Sydow, an actor so closely identified with Ingmar Bergman, suggests how little Bergmanian brooding is permitted to infect *Hannah and Her Sisters*, ostensibly one of Allen's sunniest serious films.

18. Holly's first play is stitched together from what Lee has told her of Hannah and Elliot's marital problems, and constitutes an act of revenge upon her more accomplished sister; the second script which she reads to Mickey allows her to avenge herself against April (Carrie Fisher), who took architect David away from her. Mickey's unwillingness to criticize the draft says more about his romantic designs on Holly than about the virtues of her play.

19. "Intriguingly," Brode argues, "Allen's own character Mickey appears to belong to another film from the rest of the characters, who are tightly knitted together. Other than the fact that he was once married to Hannah, he seems to be functioning in an alternative universe" (p. 247).

20. *What Falls Away*, p. 226.

21. *What Falls Away*, p. 234.

22. *Crimes and Misdemeanors* is the other "novel-on-film." Lax, p. 274.

23. The original screenplay contained only the opening Thanksgiving celebration. After substantial shooting had been completed, Allen added the Thanksgiving two years later, and then the intervening holiday in which Hannah proclaims "it's so dark tonight," Elliot's affirmation of love for her precipitating the film's alteration of direction from atomization toward union and resolution. Geist, "The *Rolling Stone* Interview: Woody Allen," p. 214.

24. Allen wasn't referring specifically to *Hannah and Her Sisters* when he told Bjorkman that filmmakers "create a world that [they] would like to live in. You like the people you create. You like what they wear, where they live, and it gives you a chance for some months to live in that world. And those people move to beautiful music, and you're in that world" (p. 51). Nonetheless, this description evokes few scenes of his as compellingly as Hannah's first Thanksgiving—until, that is, he began shooting the still more idealized world of *Everyone Says I Love You*.

25. Whereas Hannah's professional life is presented as unexceptionally successful, her

career apparently encountering no conflicts between the institutions of the theater and her desire to express herself artistically on the stage, Mickey's show's ratings are down, its reviews are "terrible," the sponsor is consequently hostile, and the writers are bitter about Standards and Practices' suppression of their sketches, the resultant tensions prompting him (like *Manhattan*'s Isaac Davis) to repudiate television and quit his job.

26. Saul Bellow, *Herzog* (New York: Viking Press, 1964), pp. 92–93.

27. Evidence that Allen has some such cultural polarization in mind in scripting the television production scene, aligning Mickey and the show with Jewish cultural concerns, is provided by the fact that the evening's show includes a skit in which Christianity's most celebrated symbol, the Pope, is characterized as a child molester. Another sketch deals with the Palestine Liberation Organization, and when things get too much for him, Mickey looks to the ceiling and invokes the classic Old Testament formulation of divine injustice, echoing Job's question of "Why me, Lord?" (pp. 30–31). That his assistant is portrayed by Julie Kavner, who would, in Allen's "Oedipus Wrecks" segment of *New York Stories,* play the first Jewish character with whom an Allen protagonist becomes romantically involved since Carol Kane and Janet Margolin portrayed Alvy Singer's first two wives in *Annie Hall,* arguably reinforces the elements of Jewish American culture pervading this scene in *Hannah.*

28. Pauline Kael was the most committed of Allen's critics to finding the WASP/Jewish antinomy at the center of his work. In her review of *Another Woman,* she argued, "You can see in his comedies that he associates messy emotions with Jewishness and foolishness and laughter, but he wants to escape all that and be a 'serious' dignified artist, so he sets his dramas in an austere Gentile world. And then what is the protagonist's tight-nostrilled anguish about? Being repressed. Being a perfectionist. Not being emotional enough. That was the interior-decorator mother's soul-sickness in *Interiors,* and it's Marion's soul-sickness here. Woody Allen is caught in his own Catch-22: his protagonist's problem is not being Jewish." *Movie Love* (New York: E.P. Dutton, 1991), p. 15. Kael's assumption that Woody Allen couldn't recognize this cultural tension in himself as thoroughly as she did and use it as the dramatic basis for film narratives is this chapter's primary argument with Kael's position.

29. Elliot's final comment on the affair, "Everything that happened between us seems more and more hazy" (p. 176), might be read as Allen's attempt to minimize its future affect on Elliot and Hannah's marriage by suggesting the relationship is coming to seem to him like a dream.

30. Bjorkman, p. 55. Elsewhere, Allen called "the romanticized view of Mia" in *Hannah and Her Sisters* "the hardest thing we've done. There was so much ambivalence to the character, her goodness, her too-goodness, her niceness to her sisters but her feeling superior to them. In order to be successful, the character had to move in and out of all those feelings throughout the picture." Sam Rubin and Richard Taylor, *Mia: Flowerchild, Madonna, Muse* (New York: St. Martin's Press, 1989), p. 118.

31. Farrow suggested that the inspiration for the three sisters element of the film was her family, and her mother, Maureen O'Sullivan, concurred. Fox, p. 164.

32. Quoted in Carroll, *Woody and His Women,* p. 237.

33. Farrow's description of a Las Vegas morning with Frank Sinatra exemplifies her tendency to depict her life as being determined by the decisions of others or of forces beyond her control: "By what series of decisions, I wondered, was I here, now, in Las Vegas, in this golf cart, at five in the morning, with a man wearing a shoe box driving full speed toward death by plate glass? Should I have done something differently? No, I decided as we raced toward the window; there was nothing to be done differently, not then or now. All the occurrences of our common time, tender or troubled, were linked as surely as the beads on a rosary" (p. 110).

34. *What Falls Away,* p. 226.

35. *Mia and Woody,* p. 186.

36. Groteke and Rosen, p. 68.

37. Mickey's suicide attempt and his subsequent affirmation of "being part of the experience" of living may owe something to Henrik's comic attempt at self-destruction in Bergman's *Smiles of a Summer Night.* Henrik tries to hang himself, but the rope slips off its tether, the action tripping a bed to appear from the wall. Henrik decides that if the world is sinful, he wants to sin, too, and there in the bed is the perfect occasion for sin—his father's kept woman, Anne.

38. Allen's odd association of the Konigsberg family with the Marx Brothers seems to give even his *Duck Soup* epiphany an eccentric element of familial affirmation.

39. Brode, p. 246.

40. Allison and Curry interpret Lee's complaint that the quarrel between Hannah and Holly is making her dizzy as halting the self-consciously intrusive, circling camera's movements. "Allen thus allows his women characters to demonstrate seeming insight into and power over the ways in which perception by external mechanisms—such as cameras or patriarchal manipulations—distorts women's relationships with each other" (p. 131). Their argument that the title characters of the film are consistently framed by male perceptions seems to me completely persuasive.

10. If You Want a Hollywood Ending: *Crimes and Misdemeanors*

1. In recognition of the film's moral seriousness, the *New York Times* invited three theologically inclined professors to respond to the ethical issues raised by *Crimes and Misdemeanors:* James Nuecterlein saw it as epitomizing the fate of contemporary intellectuals who seek to believe but fail to achieve belief; Rabbi Eugene Borowitz argued that the film's depiction of Rabbi Ben "uniquely displays the truth of faith, at least my Jewish faith"; while Mary Erler read the ending as demonstrating that "not only do moral questions not have answers, even asking them is pointless." "Woody Allen Counts the Wages of Sin," October 15, 1979, Section III, pp. 15, 20, 22.

2. After seeing the first rough cut of the movie, Allen saw the disparity between the two plots—Judah's crime and Cliff's misdemeanor—as a failure of balance. "In comparison to Judah's story," he told Sandy Morse in a conference recorded by Eric Lax, "I'm not getting big enough things happening [with Cliff and Halley]." My critical contention is that, in the final version, that disparity becomes very much what *Crimes and Misdemeanors* is about. My pretensions to penetrating Allen's ultimate intentions in the film notwithstanding, Lax's extended recording of Allen's debate with Sandy Morse over the narrative *of Crimes and Misdemeanors* (pp. 362–66) provides an excellent corrective, supplementing Ralph Rosenblum's essay and Navacelle's *Woody on Location,* to any notion that Woody Allen's scripts arrive in the form of full-bodied, coherent, thematically consistent plots requiring no revision.

3. Although in both name and biographical details Louis Levy resembles Primo Levi, author of *Survival at Auschwitz, The Drowned and the Saved,* and other works describing his experience in the Nazi Holocaust, Allen insists that his *Crimes and Misdemeanors* philosopher wasn't modeled on Levi but derives from the murdered professor plot originally included in the *Annie Hall* script. Fox, pp. 204–5.

4. The two plots of *Crimes and Misdemeanors* remain separate until the meeting of Judah and Cliff in the film's concluding scene, but Allen's screenplay carefully establishes links between the Cliff and Judah plots: one of the threats Dolores makes to Judah in hopes of forcing him to leave Miriam for her is that if they're not together, "I don't know what I'll do, Judah—I'll jump out the window, I swear."

5. There is significant evidence in the film that Halley is another character deluded by love, that she too is choosing "the wrong person" in her engagement to Lester. She loved her first husband "at first sight," but, by her own admission, she "should have looked again," her comment suggesting that she's prone to error in love relations. The film's characterization of Lester never fully contradicts Cliff's negative perception of him as an egotist who exploits others by appealing to their fascination with his wealth and success, which is Cliff's explanation for Halley's agreeing to marry him. Although she tells Cliff that she's "professionally ambitious," in both love relationships Halley has allowed romance to take precedence over her professional aspirations, abandoning her legal career following her first marriage, going to London to produce films and apparently spending much of her time there securing a fiancé instead.

6. Using Allen's review of Ingmar Bergman's autobiography, *The Magic Lantern*, for context, Sam B. Girgus persuasively argues that the vision/blindness motifs of the film find subtextual reinforcement in the film's Bergmanesque attempt to make visible "the soul's landscape." "'The eyes of God,' a phrase from *Crimes and Misdemeanors*," Girgus explains, "describes precisely how [Allen] wants the camera and his filmmaking to look within and bring out that world for art." *The Films of Woody Allen*, p. 116.

7. One of the moral issues glossed over by this film so focused upon ethics, Pauline Kael argued, is the consequence of Judah's decision for its victim. "We aren't asked to have any feeling for [Dolores]," Kael asserted; "We see the situation strictly in terms of her threats to break up [Judah's] marriage and expose his financial manipulations. . . . The film's emphasis is confusing: the spectator has more anxiety about the doctor's possibly revealing his crime to the authorities than about what he does to her." *Movie Love*, pp. 199, 203.

8. Ironically, Allen considered ending *Crimes and Misdemeanors* with a scene from a Hollywood movie—an Esther Williams film, or *Yankee Doodle Dandy*, or *It's a Wonderful Life*—as a way of dramatizing that, despite his rejection by Halley, Cliff is getting on with his life. Lax, p. 362.

9. David Denby judged *Crimes and Misdemeanors* as "Allen's most ambitious and completely organized film yet" (*New York*, October 29, 1983, p. 124); Mike McGrady said, "Woody is Woody, and he has done it once again—provoked, excited, amused, entertained, and made one of the year's best movies" (*Newsday*, October 13, 1989, Part III, p. 3); Jack Kroll described the film as "one of his most affecting movies and perhaps his most disquieting portrait of the urban psyche-scape" (*Newsweek*, October 16, 1989, p. 67); for Richard Schickel, the film's mood swings "stir us from our comfortable stupor and vivify a true, moral, always acute and often hilarious meditation on the psychological economy of the Reagan years" (*Time*, October 16, 1989, p. 82); J. Hoberman saw the film as "a smart, absorbing, inventive movie, with startling intimations of greatness. Woody Allen hasn't simply caught up to his ambition, in some ways he has run past it" (*Village Voice*, October 17, 1989, p. 87).

10. Consistent with her *Reconstructing Woody* project, Mary P. Nichols argues that Judah's closing monologue contains manifestations of lingering guilt, proof that he's deluding himself in declaring himself "home free." In support of her moral ameliorist reading of Allen's films, Nichols cites Sander Lee's argument that Judah's need to disburden himself to others of his "murder story with a very strange twist" will ultimately lead to his arrest for murder. Nichols, pp. 158–59, 239.

11. It's worth noticing that the contemporary Manhattan of *Crimes and Misdemeanors* is not the "expressionistic New York," the idealized city of *Manhattan, Manhattan Murder Mystery*, or *Everyone Says I Love You*. Sven Nykvist's camera visualizes it as a dark, if relatively clean, urban assemblage of apartments, never for a moment pausing to offer a composed image of the cityscape.

12. Wendy's indictment of her husband sounds very much like Sandy Bates's indictment

of his "stupid little films" in *Stardust Memories,* the two movies dramatizing a dismissive attitude toward comedy which gets reversed in the earlier work but not in *Crimes and Misdemeanors.*

13. William Butler Yeats, "The Second Coming," *Selected Poems and Two Plays of William Butler Yeats,* M.L. Rosenthal, ed. (New York: Collier Books, 1962), p. 91.

14. Blake, *Woody Allen: Sacred and Profane,* pp. 183–84.

15. Girgus, p. 124.

16. In his characterization of Cliff, "Woody Allen is tweaking his own highmindedness," Pauline Kael argued, "yet he also appears to be revealing himself more nakedly than in his other movies. He appears to be saying, 'This is who I am'" (*Movie Love,* p. 202). David Denby described Cliff as "a witty man yet also one of the bitterest studies of failure ever put on film" (p. 124).

17. Lester's popularity with the public epitomizes an attitude Allen has consistently expressed about popular reaction to his own films. "The best film I ever did, really," he told Tom Shales, "was *Stardust Memories.* It was my least popular film. That may automatically mean it was my best film." Tom Shales, "Woody Allen: The First 50 Years," *Esquire,* April, 1987, p. 95.

11. Everyone Loves Her/His Illusions: *The Purple Rose of Cairo* and *Shadows and Fog*

Epigraph quoted in *The Purple Rose of Cairo,* p. 373.

1. Michiko Kakutani, "Woody Allen: The Art of Humor," p. 221.

2. Allen got stalled in writing the screenplay of *The Purple Rose of Cairo,* the solution being the introduction of Gil Shepherd, the actor who plays Baxter, into the plot. Bjorkman, p. 148.

3. Sam B. Girgus sees the movie characters' fate as partaking of the film's concern with freedom of choice: "Allen's way of resolving the extended joke about the escaped character dramatizes the deeper point regarding the moral dimension of narrative that must include responsibility for endings. Unable to participate in the writing of their own stories, the characters are fated to either slavery or destruction." *The Films of Woody Allen,* p. 86.

4. Monk's incessant crapshooting with his friends suggests that he is seeking remedy for his condition through the very cause of that condition—gambling with money in a game of chance which will ultimately wipe out all of the players.

5. Lax, p. 27.

6. Graham McCann's description of Cecilia's habitual posture staring up at movie screens very effectively summarizes her character: "Cecilia's face seems to have become fixed in this position, gazing up at people and things: she lives in a state of suspense engendered by an obsession with other people's stories. Her days are spent waiting—for her husband to assault her, for her employer to fire her, for Ginger to dance with Fred." *Woody Allen: New Yorker,* p. 214.

7. Christopher Ames, *Movies About the Movies* (Lexington: The University Press of Kentucky, 1997), pp. 116, 119.

8. Arnold Preussner, "Woody Allen's *The Purple Rose of Cairo* and the Genres of Comedy," *Literature/Film Quarterly* 16, 1 (1988), p. 42.

9. I'm not alone among Allen critics in conferring such ultimate status on *Purple Rose:* Richard Schickel described it as "one of the best movies about movies ever made" (*Time,* March 4, 1985, p. 85), while Ralph Tutt argued that, whereas *Crimes and Misdemeanors* readily acknowledges its indebtedness to other films, *Purple Rose* "transcends homage and genre. It gives us a bona fide auteur working independently in the seriocomic mode most congenial to his talent" ("Truth, Beauty and Travesty: Woody Allen's Well Wrought Urn," *Literature/Film Quarterly,* 16, 1 [1988], p. 108). In conversations for Lax's biography, Allen affirmed that he considered *Purple Rose* "the best film he's made" (p. 371).

10. Bjorkman, p. 210.

11. The "final solution" implications of *Shadows and Fog* and its allusions to *Night and Fog* are explored in detail in Mashey Bernstein's "'My Worst Fears Realized': Woody Allen and the Holocaust," *Perspectives on Woody Allen,* ed. Renee R. Curry (New York: G.K. Hall & Company, 1996), pp. 218–36.

12. At a time when so much of American film could be characterized by the title of the Jim Carrey film *Dumb and Dumber,* it seems particularly anomalous to see sophisticated reviewers carping with Allen's evocation of Kafka, Brecht, German Expressionist film techniques, and similar references to the history of film and ideas in *Shadows and Fog* and his other films. Seldom did the negative reviews of *Shadows* suggest *why* the movie's numerous allusions to film and literature were false or ineffective; David Denby's *New York* description of *Shadows and Fog* as, "in art-world jargon, postmodernist pastiche" ("Fogged In" [review of *Shadows and Fog*], March 30, 1992, p. 58) typified the accusation-constitutes-indictment mentality of reviews written by the movie's detractors. Allen's films have proven particularly susceptible to the sort of review which manifests little interest in evaluating the movie responsibly or illuminating its concerns for readers but perceives it instead as an occasion for self-indulgent displays of the reviewer's verbal cleverness. Richard Schickel's *Time* review was much more explanatorily helpful: "*Shadows and Fog* is most obviously an exercise in style, a beautifully made tribute to the expressionist cinema of 1920s Germany. It's all here: a homicidal maniac stalking the menacing night streets of a nameless, timeless city; a circus and a brothel populated by fringe figures who, naturally, are less hypocritical socially and sexually than the police, the church and the bourgeoisie; a score that features the music of Kurt Weill; lighting and a camera that pay homage to the whole Weimar school of cinematography" (March 23, 1992, p. 65).

13. The only human activity unaffected by the presence of death is—not surprisingly, given a Woody Allen film—sex. "There's only one thing men will brave murder for," one of the prostitutes argues, "the little furry animal between our legs." That the brothel is aligned with the art-allegorizing circus is suggested by the response of one of the prostitutes to Irmy's assertion that she is a sword swallower in the circus: "A sword swallower? That's my specialty too."

14. Woody Allen, "Death (A Play)," in *Without Feathers* (New York: Ballantine Books, 1983), p. 106. Perhaps because the release of the film made it seem a less effective first draft of *Shadows and Fog,* "Death (A Play)," like "God (A Play)," isn't included in *The Complete Prose of Woody Allen,* which otherwise reprints the complete contents of *Without Feathers, Side Effects,* and *Getting Even.*

15. *The Purple Rose of Cairo* and *Shadows and Fog* both offer a real world middle ground between the polar opposites of reality and fantasy: a brothel. The kindly whores of *Purple Rose,* unaware that they're encountering a fantasy projection in Tom Baxter, offer him all sorts of fantasy gratifications free of charge. The prostitutes of Felice's Place in *Shadows and Fog* are even more self-conscious about their roles as facilitators of male fantasy. Dory (Jodie Foster) comments on the disparity between worlds: "They look so innocent and dignified when they walk in here . . . and then the things they want you to *do!*" The brothel madam, Felice (Lily Tomlin) offers a parable of a man who likes to be ridden by a naked woman as she digs her spurs into his sides, and who achieves a "marriage made in heaven" when he finds a woman who enjoys riding him. The brothel clearly is a place where reality and fantasy effectively converge. The prostitutes' forthrightness about sexual realities contrasts with the *legerdemain* and prevarication of the townsmen, while partaking of the circus's gratification of fantasy, thus accounting for Allen's characterization of the film's emotive dynamic: "The thing that tied it all together was that there was the shadows and fog going through the night all the time. And then there was the occasional respite in the brothel. An occasional warm respite indoors" (Bjorkman, p. 235).

16. Quoted in Frank Gado, *The Passion of Ingmar Bergman* [Durham, North Carolina: Duke University Press, 1986], p. 239.) Bergman's influence on *Shadows and Fog* is less obvious

than that of German Expressionist film, and yet the preoccupation of Bergman's *The Magician* with the absolute disparity between human magic tricks and the Christian miracle of resurrection seems to be echoed in the failure of Irmstedt's magic to capture the killer/arrest the process of death.

17. Given the negativity of Allen's characterization of Paul early in the film, his comment to Stig Bjorkman about clowns is illuminating: "I never liked clowns—unlike Fellini. And this may be because what we get in the United States is radically different from European clowns. I've never enjoyed clowns." Bjorkman, p. 5.

18. Woody Allen, *Husbands and Wives* (Columbia TriStar Home Video, 1992).

19. Allen's concurrence with Kleinman's judgment that the inevitability of death prevents anything good from happening pervades his work. "There is no other fear of significant consequence," he told Stig Bjorkman, as the fear of death. "All other fears, all other problems, one can deal with. Loneliness, lack of love, lack of talent, lack of money, everything can be dealt with. In some way, there are ways to cope. You have friends that can help you, you have doctors that can help you. But perishing is what it's all about" (Bjorkman, p. 106).

20. Michael Kerbel's *Cineaste* essay, "The Redemptive Power of Art," suggests that, "Unlike the ending of *Deconstructing Harry*, this conclusion [of *S&F*] proclaims both the power and the evanescence of our artistic creations." In addressing *Harry*, I will argue that that film is no less ambivalent in its claims about art than is *Shadows and Fog*.

12. Poetic License, Bullshit: *Bullets Over Broadway*

1. Allen characterized that film style in describing the first Bergman film he saw as a teenager, his description anticipating the *mise en scene* he would attempt to create in *Shadows and Fog:* "I never knew who directed the film, nor did I care, nor was I sensitive at that age to the power of the work itself—the irony, the tensions, the German Expressionist style with its poetic black-and-white photography and its erotic sadomasochistic undertones." "Through a Life Darkly," p. 29.

2. Fox, p. 243.

3. The Doctor in *Shadows and Fog* makes a similar argument conjoining artistic and destructive tendencies: "Sometimes certain impulses that inspire an insane man to murder inspire others to highly creative ends." In *Sweet and Lowdown* the same point is made through the paralleling of Emmet Ray's musical gift to a gangster's gift for killing.

4. Although Shayne's debt to these playwrights is expressed largely through his own melodramatic excesses, Allen is clearly locating the fault in Shayne and not in his models. Allen is, he told Eric Lax, "a product intellectually, artistically and emotionally—and for better or worse—of that group of sort of New York playwrights. . . . Theirs was the era of the well-made play, three- or two-act plays with a certain old-fashioned construction. It permeates my work in one way or another. . . . I would have been, I think, very happy and functioning well in the 1920s and '30s with [Anderson, George S. Kaufman, Odets, O'Neill and Robert Sherwood]." Lax, p. 241.

5. At least some of Cheech's aesthetic derives from Allen's directorial practice. According to Farrow, he would say to an actor, "I don't believe a word of it. . . . Human beings don't talk that way." *What Falls Away*, p. 203.

6. Lionel Trilling, "Reality in America," in *The Liberal Imagination* (New York: Charles Scribner's Sons, 1976), pp. 3–4.

7. Trilling, p. 13.

8. At the end of *Shadows and Fog*, Irmy and Paul leave the circus just as Kleinman is joining it; by the close of *Husbands and Wives*, Sally and Jack have reconciled after announcing

their separation in the film's opening scene to Gabe and Judy, who have divorced by the movie's final scene; Carol is initially the character obsessed with the murder in *Manhattan Murder Mystery*, but by the end, her husband Larry's preoccupation with it has surpassed hers; Linda Ash doesn't know that Larry Weinrib has adopted her child when they meet for the first time in *Mighty Aphrodite*, and he's unaware that he has fathered the child with her at their final meeting.

9. Woody Allen and Douglas McGrath, *Bullets Over Broadway* (Studio City, Hollywood: Hollywood Scripts, n.d.), p. 111.

10. Allen and McGrath, p. 109.

11. It is one of the real oddities of this film in which plagiarism is a central theme that *Bullets Over Broadway* so often echoes another film with which Allen was associated which also dealt with ghostwriting—*The Front*. The "artist or the man" issue is found there; Florence (Andrea Marcovicci) admits to "having made this kind of mistake before, confusing the artist with the man," as is the title notion, and Howard Prince (Allen) pretends to be the author of work by blacklisted writers and criticizing their scripts when they don't live up to the standards "his" previous efforts have established.

12. In both *Crimes and Misdemeanors* and *Bullets Over Broadway*, artistic idealism is embodied in characters with insufficient strength of character or integrity to withstand the real world's capacity for undermining that stance. Cliff's wife speaks disparagingly about her husband's documentaries with their implicit "fantasies about changing the world": "he's a man who thinks he can change the world. He makes these films, and in the end they come to nothing." Shayne believes it is the "theater's duty . . . to transform men's souls," but *Bullets* makes clear that it is the thoroughly corrupt world of the theater which is most in need of transformation.

13. Peter Rainer tentatively posited a connection between Cheech's murderously aesthete stance and Allen's initial reaction to the Mia Farrow imbroglio: "It's possible—though not very productive—to interpret the movie as Allen's apologia for his above-it-all stance during the early stages of his famous troubles" (*Los Angeles Times Calendar*, October 21, 1994, p. 1). Andrew Sarris was more categorical: "*Bullets Over Broadway* is as close as he'll get to saying 'I'm sorry.'" Allen has now wrested poetry from "pain and guilt . . . regret and remorse" (quoted in Georgia Brown, "Biting Bullets" (review of *Bullets Over Broadway*), *Village Voice*, October 18, 1994, p. 54).

14. Lax, p. 277.

13. Let's Just Live It: Woody Allen in the 1990s

1. Fox, p. 246.

2. *Celebrity* eclipsed both films, costing more than $20 million.

3. A variation on these embodiments of pragmatism is the "Woody's pal" character played by Tony Roberts in *Annie Hall*, *Stardust Memories*, and *Midsummer Night's Sex Comedy*, and by Michael Murphy in *Manhattan*. This character contrasts with the Allen protagonist in his more forthright devotion to materialism and his greater sexual libertinism. Whereas the pragmatists make the Allen protagonist doubt his idealistic impulses, the Roberts/Murphy character makes him regret his own inhibitions as well as inspiring a measure of envy for his pal's prosperity.

4. Harry Block, a less sympathetic Allen protagonist, also looks to the skies for confirmation of the real: "I'm strictly, you know, quarks and particles and black holes," Harry explains, "all the rest is junk to me."

5. Mashey Bernstein, "'My Worst Fears Realized': Woody Allen and the Holocaust," in *Perspectives on Woody Allen*, ed. Rene Curry (New York: G.K. Hall, 1996), p. 223.

6. Woody Allen, "Random Reflections of a Second-Rate Mind," *Tikkun: A Bimonthly Jewish Critique of Politics, Culture and Society* (July, 1991), reprinted in Joyce Carol Oates, ed., *Best American Essays 1991* (New York: Ticknor and Fields, 1992), p. 8.

7. Lax, p. 373.

8. John Lahr, "The Imperfectionist," *The New Yorker,* December 9, 1996, p. 74.

9. Lax, p. 285.

10. Lax, p. 293.

11. Wilde, *Horizons of Assent,* p. 15.

12. DeCurtis, p. 50.

13. Graham McCann makes a similar argument in slightly different terms: "The aesthetic wholeness Allen finds in a work by Fellini or Renoir is no more or less likely than the aesthetic wholeness people find in, say, *Hannah and Her Sisters.* For all his talk of wanting to make a 'masterpiece,' Allen does not yet possess the self-confidence to acknowledge (even to himself) the fine things in his work. His romantic notion of greatness belittles his own achievements." *Woody Allen: New Yorker,* p. 169.

14. Bjorkman, p. 156.

15. Allen's impulse to end films with scenes from other films (*Duck Soup* in *Hannah, The Lady from Shanghai* in *Manhattan Murder Mystery,* and his early intention to close *Crimes and Misdemeanors* with a film clip) seems a filmmakers' version of this desperate need: if you can't arrive at your own resolution, offer the representation of one from another movie. *Celebrity* closes with Lee Simon (Kenneth Branagh) watching a film in which a word skywritten by an airplane summarizes his condition: "HELP."

16. Quoted in Alexander Nehamas, *Nietzsche: Life as Literature* (Cambridge: Harvard Univ. Press, 1985), p. 44.

17. DeCurtis, p. 50.

18. Cynthia Ozick, "Saul Bellow's Broadway," in *Fame & Folly* (New York: Alfred A. Knopf, 1996), p. 182.

14. Because It's Real Difficult in Life: *Husbands and Wives*

1. Walter Isaacson, "The Heart Wants What It Wants" (interview with Woody Allen), *Time Magazine,* August 31, 1992, p. 61.

2. David Denby, review of *Husbands and Wives, New York,* September 21, 1992, p. 60.

3. John Baxter sees both *Midsummer Night's Sex Comedy* and *Zelig* (which were shot almost simultaneously) as films whose good spirits reflect the emotional buoyancy of the Allen/ Farrow coupling. *Woody Allen: A Biography,* pp. 308–9.

4. *Deconstructing Harry,* which shares some of *Husbands and Wives'* aura of emotional demoralization translated into cinematic technique, interrupts Allen's typical uniformity of opening title presentation by cutting in jarringly repetitive images of Lucy arriving at Harry's apartment building, the alternation prefiguring the film's constant destabilizing shifts from Harry's life to scenes from his fiction.

5. These qualities have attracted other filmmakers and screenwriters as well as audiences: movies written or directed by Marshall Brickman, Albert Brooks, Nora Ephron, Spike Lee, Ron Howard, Rob Reiner, and Kenneth Branagh (particularly in *Peter's Friends* and *A Midwinter's Tale*) clearly reflect the influence of Allen's scripts and scene composition.

6. Kenneth Turan's review of *Husbands and Wives* described the film as a "reverse mirror-image" of *Hannah and Her Sisters. Los Angeles Times Calendar,* September 18, 1992, p. 1.

7. Bjorkman, p. 244, 255.

8. "What is This Thing Called Love?" with its attendant, heartfelt questions—"Just

who can solve its mystery? Why should it make a fool of me?"—provides the opening and closing musical theme of *Husbands and Wives,* but the title of one of Rain's short stories epitomizes much more precisely the film's antiromantic, anti-aesthetic, bluntly erotic, and completely demoralized conclusion: "Oral Sex in the Age of Deconstruction."

9. Bjorkman, p. 112.

10. Fox, p. 230.

11. David Ansen's review of *Husbands and Wives* characterized it as "Allen's most uninhibited film in years," one displaying no sign of the "compulsive tidiness" of the director's recent films. *Newsweek,* September 21, 1992, p. 76.

12. Isaacson, *Time Magazine,* p. 61.

13. Only in the opening and closing title sequences and in party scenes where a pianist is performing is *Husbands and Wives* provided with a musical soundtrack. The *Interiors*-like absence of music is a highly significant omission, its lack implicitly verifying how important a role songs in other Allen films play in structuring scenes and informing the construction of characters.

14. Jack Mathews' description of Gabe's encounter with one of Rain's "midlife crisis set" conquests perfectly captures the erotic distortions and dislocations of *Husbands and Wives:* "There's a hilarious scene where Gabe and Rain are accosted on a street by Rain's agitated ex-lover (Ron Rifkin), the sixtysomething psychoanalyst who fell in love with her while trying to help her overcome her fetish for older men." Review of *Husbands and Wives, Newsday,* September 18, 1992, Part II, p. 67.

15. It's difficult not to see the shadow of the solitary exits of the little tramp in Chaplin's films in the scenes in Allen's films in which the protagonist he portrays is abandoned by those he's trusted. Danny Rose's walking in the rain after Lou Canova dumps him as his manager is one such highly melodramatic image; another is Gabe's walking through a downpour after renouncing his incipient affair with Rain and realizing he no longer has Judy to go home to.

16. Because it is itself about Isak Borg's attempt to estimate the value of his life, Bergman's *Wild Strawberries* is a perfect film for Gabe to cite in attempting to affirm the value of his marriage.

17. In Ann Beattie's story, "Snow," the narrator, looking back disconsolately on a terminated affair, offers a similar argument: "Who expects small things to survive when even the largest get lost?" she asks. "People forget years and remember moments. Seconds and symbols are left to sum things up." "Snow," in *Where You'll Find Me* (New York: Linden Press/Simon & Schuster, 1986), p. 25.

18. Woody Allen, *Deconstructing Harry,* Fine Line Films, 1998.

19. Maureen Dowd, "Auteur as Spin Doctor," The *New York Times,* Sunday, October 1, 1995, Section D, p. 13.

20. The identification of Gabe's work with Allen's is reinforced by Rain's mother's comment about her and her husband's affection for Gabe's work: "We're tremendous fans of yours—we wish you'd still write those sad funny stories of yours."

21. Allen's protagonist's first name also seems to reinforce the identification with Philip Roth, since the protagonist of one of Roth's best-known novels, *Letting Go,* is Gabe Wallach.

22. Lahr, p. 82.

23. Baxter, p. 335.

24. Ibid., p. 292.

25. In *What Falls Away,* Farrow describes the relief from the Soon-Yi scandal her being offered a part in a movie soon to begin shooting in Ireland promised: "When I couldn't sleep, I went into the nursery to watch the children safe in slumber.

"Malignant specters of the dark night moved into familiar positions. Hounds tugged on taught leather lines, howling horrible. While the children slept, I dreamed of Ireland, awaking in gentle light: gray stone walls hemming the damp fields, sheep across the stretch of the Wicklow mountains and the glowering hills of Connemara; apples in the branches near Inistioge; oars dip the sea at Ballyhack; the blue-eyed daughters of Ballyknocken trudge to school" (p. 321).

26. Allen described the intensification of his relationship with Soon-Yi Farrow Previn in similar terms. "But you fell in love with her?" Walter Isaacson asked. "Yes, yes," Allen responded. "My flair for drama. What can I say?" Isaacson, p. 60.

27. Fox, p. 230.

28. Terence Rafferty's predominantly critical review of *Husbands and Wives* sees this convergence of life and art in the film as its primary liability. "What keeps you absorbed in 'Husbands and Wives' isn't the power of Woody Allen's art, and what you feel when it's over isn't the aesthetic pleasure of heightened understanding" ("Getting Old" [a review of *Husbands and Wives*], *The New Yorker,* September 21, 1992, p. 104.) I don't disagree with that judgment, although I'm arguing that the film embodies a quite deliberate skepticism about the capacity of artworks to generate "the aesthetic pleasure of heightened understanding."

29. Woody Allen, *Mighty Aphrodite,* Miramax Films, 1995.

15. Rear Condo: *Manhattan Murder Mystery*

1. Woody Allen, *September* (Orion Pictures, 1987). A major goad of the querulousness that Pauline Kael's reviews regularly expressed toward Allen's films is contained in Lloyd's speech. "Of course [the universe is] morally neutral," she objected in reviewing *September,* "Can't Allen accept that and move on?" (*Hooked* [New York: E.P. Dutton, 1989], p. 427.) Kael could never forgive Allen's films for repeatedly confronting what he considers to be the irresolvable existential bind which is humanity's spiritual heritage and which she perceives as the truth of being in the world and thus only the existential precondition of dramatic narrative, not its source. "It's a funny thing about Woody Allen," she suggested in reviewing *Hannah and Her Sisters,* "the characters he plays learn to accept life and get on with it, but then he starts a new picture and his character is back at square one" (*Hooked,* p. 114).

2. Bjorkman, p. 245.

3. Lahr, "The Imperfectionist," p. 71. Allen has Treva Marx (Julie Kavner), the disillusioned psychic in "Oedipus Wrecks," articulate the pessimistic view of the idea that something beyond the senses exists: "I always have hopes; I always think that there's more to the world than meets your eye—hidden meanings, spiritual mysteries. Nothing ever works, ever." What works, the chapter of *New York Stories* suggests, is romantic love, the one spiritual mystery Allen's 1990s movies consistently, if somewhat ambivalently, affirm.

4. Lahr, p. 79.

5. As we saw in the early draft of *Bullets Over Broadway,* Allen, like many artists working in dramatic narrative, signals his uncertainty about the effective communication of his purposes in films by overexplicating them. Toward the end of *Alice,* Dr. Yang very forthrightly explains what the viewer has clearly grasped about the change which has transpired in the title character in the course of the film: "I think Mrs. Tate has better idea of who she is than before she came to Dr. Yang. Who her friends are, who is husband, lover, sister, mother . . . what are her innermost feelings. May not know all answers, but has a better idea, no?" Woody Allen, *Alice* (Orion Pictures, 1990). Allen's preferred ending had Alice undergoing an even greater transformation, the protagonist flying to India as she does in the released film, but remaining there to work with Mother Teresa. Anthony DeCurtis, "Woody Allen: The *Rolling Stone* Interview," p. 49.

6. In contrast, the Dorrie/"Stardust" scene in *Stardust Memories* requires no special effects and retains much of its magic even after the viewer realizes it's not a beautiful memory but Sandy Bates's cinematic rendering of one.

7. Although Carlo Di Palma used a handheld camera in photographing *Manhattan Murder Mystery*, its presence is far less visually pronounced and jarring than it is in *Husbands and Wives*, reflecting the greater formal containment of the later film.

8. Philip Kemp, review of *Manhattan Murder Mystery, Sound and Sense*, Vol. 2, No. 2 (February, 1994), p. 46.

9. Carroll, *Woody and His Women*, p. 299; Bjorkman, p. 257.

10. "Play It Again, Woody," *Newsweek*, August 30, 1993, p. 53.

11. DeCurtis, p. 46.

12. Lax, p. 285.

13. DeCurtis, p. 46.

14. "Through an accident of casting," David Denby contended in his review of *Murder Mystery*, "the film has become an unintended sequel to *Annie Hall*. What if Annie had stayed in New York and married Alvy Singer? Well, it's twenty years later, they've raised a son, and Annie still doesn't know what to do with herself." Review of *Manhattan Murder Mystery*, *New York*, August 23, 1993. p. 57.

15. Bjorkman, p. 255.

16. *Wild Man Blues* (Orion Pictures, 1998).

17. Bjorkman, p. 192. Corroborating Allen's judgment, Richard Schickel asserted, "Ambition is an essential goad to [Allen's] sensibility. It pushes him toward the rueful resonances of those previous Brickman collaborations and toward the magical transformations of reality in *The Purple Rose of Cairo* and *Radio Days*." "Just Funny Isn't Enough" (review of *Manhattan Murder Mystery*), *Time*, August 23, 1993, p. 67.

18. Bjorkman, p. 51.

19. Trivializing issues for the sake of comedy is the most resonant critique Rain makes of Gabe Roth's novel manuscript in *Husbands and Wives*.

20. Girgus, p. 98.

21. As Larry confronts House outside his theater, the soundtrack, as if commenting on the source of Larry's newly discovered courage, plays Coleman Hawkins's "Out of Nowhere."

22. "The Outsider," *The New Yorker*, October 23, 1993, p. 93.

23. That wealth Manhattan-style is a source of real excitement for Allen is confirmed by his telling John Lahr that he "still gets a thrill" when he sees "those families take their kids to those private schools and their chauffeurs pulling up, and see the guys in tuxedos and the women coming down, and the doormen getting them cabs" (p. 82). *Alice* is more pervaded by evidence of this "thrill" than any other Allen film until *Everyone Says I Love You*, though, significantly, Alice has delivered her children from such luxuries by the film's end.

24. The level of Allen's idealization of that era is reflected in his comment in an interview that "My guess is that in the Twenties and Thirties there was probably nothing to equal Manhattan ever in the history of the world." William E. Geist, "The *Rolling Stone* Interview: Woody Allen," p. 216.

25. Kael, *Hooked*, p. 116.

26. James M. Welsh commented on similarities between *Rear Window* and Allen's film in his review of *Manhattan Murder Mystery*, *Films in Review*, November/December 1993, p. 413; Mary Nichols briefly discusses the link in *Reconstructing Woody*, p. 177.

27. Bjorkman, p. 256.

28. Alfred Hitchcock, *Rear Window* (Universal, 1954).

29. Rich, p. 69. In discussing *Manhattan Murder Mystery* with Stig Bjorkman, Allen alludes to a Bob Hope film, *The Great Lover*, as being similarly a "very broad comedy but also a murder mystery" (p.257).

30. Mary P. Nichols offers an effectively detailed argument that *Manhattan Murder Mystery* dramatizes Carol and Larry's education in the proper balance between art and life: Larry learns

that mysteries are part of life, not just movies, and Carol realizes that life needn't imitate romantic films to be meaningful (p. 175).

16. That Voodoo That You Do So Well: *Mighty Aphrodite*

1. Baxter, p. 418.

2. Woody Allen, *Mighty Aphrodite* (Miramax Films, 1996).

3. Nick James, review of *Mighty Aphrodite, Sound and Sense,* April, 1996, p. 49.

4. Bernhard Zimmerman, *Greek Tragedy: An Introduction,* trans. Thomas Marier (Baltimore: Johns Hopkins University Press, 1991), p. 24.

5. Bernard Knox, *Oedipus at Thebes: Sophocles' Tragic Hero and His Time* (New York: W.W. Norton, 1971), pp. 171–79.

6. Quoted in Knox, p. 47.

7. Lenny's intervention in Linda Ash's fate reprises the Pygmalion theme observable in Allan Felix's relationship with Linda Christie in *Play It Again, Sam,* in Alvy Singer's transformation of Annie Hall into a self-confident performer, and in Isaac Davis's coaching of Tracy in the ways of sophisticated adulthood in *Manhattan.* The theme emerges again in Harry Block's relationship with Fay Sexton in *Deconstructing Harry:* "It was Henry Higgins and Eliza Doolittle," she admits.

8. Nichols, *Reconstructing Woody,* p. 204.

9. Mia Farrow's memoir indicates that Allen's repudiation of genetics in *Mighty Aphrodite* is not merely a literary conceit. She recalls his responding to a visit to his parents' apartment, "Can you believe I came from these people?" (*What Falls Away,* p. 237).

10. David Denby, "Woe Unto Woody" (review of *Mighty Aphrodite*), *New York,* October 30, 1995, p.109.

11. Carroll, *Woody and His Women,* p. 280.

12. Denby's review of the *Mighty Aphrodite* used the film's repudiation of the chorus's bleak imperatives as an occasion to deliver a pointed lecture: "Woody Allen may want to believe that he can safely ignore his conscience, that some of his wilder flights into foolishness with adopted children are perfectly okay. In *Mighty Aphrodite,* he's not dramatizing an obsession: he's in the grip of one—but the roots of it are obscure and unproductive, and the movie, despite its clever frame, remains an uneasy experience" (p. 109).

13. A feminist objection to *Mighty Aphrodite* would argue that in "changing Linda's life," Lenny is actually bringing her in from the social outlands into containment within masculine-defined structures of family and marriage.

14. Nichols (*Reconstructing Woody,* p. 209) suggests that the helicopter's appearance may indicate that Zeus actually answers the prayers left on his answering machine, a reading at odds with my interpretation of the Greek pantheon in the film as pure projections of Lenny's psychic life.

15. The reviews generally debated the effectiveness of the buoyancy of *Mighty Aphrodite,* ranging from Brian Johnson's judgment that "in the film one of America's great directors finally gives in to all the fans who kept asking him to stop with the art and be a comedian again. He gets the laughs, but they have a hollow ring" (*Maclean's,* October 20, 1995, p. 27) to Janet Maslin's comment that "even when it becomes unmistakably lightweight, *Mighty Aphrodite* remains witty, agile, and handsomely made" (*New York Times,* October 27, 1995, C, p. 1) to Anthony Lane's view that "When the picture does work—most often in the scenes between Allen and Sorvino—you find yourself sighing with relief at its lightness of heart" (*The New Yorker,* October 30, 1995, p. 113).

16. Allen discussed his fondness for Jimmy Cannon columns and his childhood desire to be a sportswriter with sportswriter Ira Berkow of *The New York Times.* "From Defense to Offense" *The New York Times,* November 2, 1995, C, 1.

17. Helena Bonham-Carter, who didn't find working with Allen gratifying, objected to the unmotivated reversal Amanda undergoes at the end of the movie, wondering "Whose fantasy am I in here?" (Baxter, p. 423). Clearly, her role was the victim of two circumstances in addition to expedient plotting: Mira Sorvino's overwhelming presence in her Oscar-winning performance, and the fact that Bonham-Carter was in the unenviable position of being the first actress in two decades to play the romantic lead in a Woody Allen film featuring neither Mia Farrow or Diane Keaton.

18. James, p. 49; Stanley Kauffman similarly found the gag getting "heavier and heavier" until culminating in the chorus's singing and dancing, which he characterized as "borscht belt shtick in excelsis." "Return of a Trouble" (review of *Mighty Aphrodite*), *New Republic*, November 27, 1995, p. 29.

19. Quoted in Fox, *Woody: Movies from Manhattan*, p. 254.

20. Julian Fox's description, p. 254.

21. Anthony Lane expressed similar admiration for Sorvino's overpowering of the scene: "As you would expect, Allen crams the scene with aghast twitches and breathy comeback, but for once we don't even look at his side of the frame; Sorvino is too much fun to miss. . . . Sorvino's control of the movie is almost embarrassing; she makes everyone else look listless and indifferent to life." "Scarlet Women" (review of *Mighty Aphrodite*), *The New Yorker*, p. 113.

17. And What a Perfect Plot: *Everyone Says I Love You* and *Zelig*

1. Gado, *The Passion of Ingmar Bergman*, p. 183.

2. John Baxter suggests two sources for the egalitarian musicale that is *Everyone Says I Love You* are Jacques Demy's *La Parapluies de Cherbourg* and *Les Demoiselles de Rochefort*. *Woody Allen: A Biography,* p. 427.

3. David Denby, "Amateur Hour" (review of *Everyone Says I Love You*), *New York*, December 9, 1996, p. 72.

4. Quoted in Sarah Blacher Cohen, "Jewish Literary Comediennes," in *Comic Relief: Humor in Contemporary American Literature,* ed. Sarah Blacher Cohen (Urbana: University of Illinois Press, 1978), p. 185.

5. Woody Allen, *Everyone Says I Love You* (Miramax Films, 1996).

6. In her memoir, Mia Farrow suggests that her meditations on the strangeness of living on top of other people in apartments and the presence of a therapist in the apartment next door to hers inspired Allen to evolve the eavesdropping plot used in *Another Woman. What Falls Away,* p. 245.

7. It's possible that, were Von a more substantial character, viewers might have objected more to the film's endorsement of the invasion of her privacy which facilitates these comic moments; as they stand, these scenes constitute Allen's mapping of the difference between soulmates constructed in comedy as opposed to the darker convergences of *doppelgangers* in the dramatic narrative of *Another Woman.*

8. Von's rejection of Joe repeats a pattern in Allen's films which Richard Freadman noted in *Play It Again, Sam:* Allan Felix has "helped Linda to achieve a stage of maturation that signals his own emotional dispensability . . . symbolically and sadly, the volatile Jew has enriched the Gentile world to a point where it no longer needs him. Linda leaves and returns to Dick." "Love Among the Stereotypes, or Why Woody's Women Leave," p. 114.

9. Woody Allen, *Play It Again, Sam* (Paramount Pictures, 1972).

10. Richard Schickel, "They Sorta Got Rhythm" (review of *Everyone Says I Love You*), *Time*, December 9, 1996, p. 82.

11. Pauline Kael, "Charmer" (review of *The Purple Rose of Cairo*) in *State of the Art* (New York, E.P. Dutton, 1985), p. 337.

12. Perhaps it is the equivocal mood of the dance scene that accounts for reviewers' remarkably polarized responses to this moment and to the film's success at romantically transporting the viewer. For Denby, the actors' want of musical comedy skills means that "there's no exhilaration, no release" for the audience; Lisa Schwarzbaum perceived the film as "melancholia disguised as a romantic fantasia" such that "this celebration of love and good fortune doesn't seem very festive at all" ("Woody Sings!" *Entertainment Weekly,* December 20, 1996, p. 70). Stanley Kauffmann, perhaps the world's least enthusiastic Woody Allen moviegoer since John Simon retired, found the song and dance of the film "sometimes frenetic, sometimes poignant, always enjoyable" (*The New Republic,* November 11, 1996, p. 40); David Ansen suggested that "Hawn's flying through the air feels more theoretical than exhilarating" (*Newsweek,* December 9, 1996, p. 58); Peter Travers described that scene as "a trick done with wires, but Allen's warm touch transforms it into romantic sorcery. At captivating moments like this, *Everyone Says I Love You* proves the musical can still cut it as sublime entertainment" (*Rolling Stone,* February 20, 1997, p. 74).

13. Michael Hirschorn, "Woody Sings!" *New York,* September 9, 1996, p. 53.

14. Todd McCarthy, "Tin Pan Allen" (review of *Everyone Says I Love You*), *Premiere,* January, 1997, p. 46.

15. Hirschorn, p. 50.

16. John Lahr, "The Imperfectionist," p. 70.

17. Janet Maslin, "When Everyone Sings, Just for the Joy of It," *The New York Times,* Friday, December 6, 1996, III, p. 1.

18. Woody Allen, "Zelig," in *Three Films of Woody Allen* (New York: Vintage Books, 1987), p. 76.

19. Irwin Yalom's novel, *When Nietzsche Wept* (New York: Basic Books, 1992), uses the same dynamic: in order to coerce Friedrich Nietzsche into confronting his despair, Joseph Breuer convinces him that it is the psychologist's own despair that their sessions are seeking to remedy.

20. Jay Martin's *Who Am I This Time?: Uncovering the Fictive Personality* (New York: W.W. Norton, 1988) addresses at length the contemporary psychological phenomenon of fabricated selves as they have been manifested in literature, film and American culture; the work briefly discusses Allen's *Zelig* (pp. 88–90).

21. Daniel Green, "The Comedian's Dilemma," *Literature/Film Quarterly,* Fall, 1991, p. 74.

22. Bellow has Arthur Sammler provide a rationale for Zelig-like behavior, one accompanied by a moralism incompatible with Allen's depiction of the human chameleon, who imitates in order to be liked and to gain acceptance by others. "Better, thought Sammler, to accept the inevitability of imitation and then imitate good things. The ancients had this right. Greatness without models? Inconceivable. One could not be the thing itself—Reality. One must be satisfied with the symbols. Make it the object of imitation to seek and release the high qualities. Make peace, therefore, with intermediacy and representation. Otherwise, the individual must be the failure he now sees and knows himself to be." *Mr. Sammler's Planet* (New York: Viking Press, 1970), p. 149.

23. Lahr, p, 82.

24. Jacobs, p. 146.

25. John Updike, "More Love in the Western World" (review of *Love Declared* by Denis de Rougemont), in Assorted Prose (New York: Knopf, 1965), p. 299.

18. How We Choose to Distort It: *Deconstructing Harry*

Epigraph quoted in McCann, *Woody Allen: New Yorker,* p. 209.

1. William E. Geist, "The *Rolling Stone* Interview: Woody Allen," p. 211.

2. Bjorkman, p. 103.

3. Even in this one-liner of a short story plot Allen reasserts the *Zelig* moral: Harvey's transformation of himself into Mandel Birnbaum results in self-erasure.

4. Harry's characters, although more broadly comic, anticipate the loathsome cultural caricatures of Allen's 1999 film, *Celebrity,* a movie whose unrelenting bitterness might be interpreted as the necessary culmination of Allen's having written his protagonist out of the romantic closure of *Everyone Says I Love You* and his satire of art-as-redemption in *Deconstructing Harry.*

5. Lest Allen be taken as exaggerating the magnitude of public condemnations of artists like Harry in the movie, consider Samuel H. Dresner's description of Allen and the Jewish viewers who have admired his films: "Allen has contributed mightily to the whole perverse pursuit to the depths of human infamy. . . . The silence of Jews to Allen's attack on their most prized possession, family morality, his celebration of their death through intermarriage, and his demeaning of those with religious commitment is a betrayal both of the Jewish faith and of the Jewish people. In failing to repudiate the perverse behavior advocated by Allen in his writings and his films, his Jewish audience has forsaken fundamental Jewish values: the sanctity of marriage and the significance of the family." "Woody Allen and the Jews," *Midstream,* December, 1992, p. 23, rpt in *Perspectives on Woody Allen,* p. 197.

6. The majority of the 1990s Allen films which depict the Allen protagonist as being in some sense attenuated or withdrawn from life end in rebirths: Larry (*Murder Mystery*) and Lenny (*Mighty Aphrodite*) spark regenerations of their marriages, and David Shayne (*Bullets*) rejects the theater in favor of marriage and family. The darkest of the decade's films, *Husbands and Wives,* and the sunniest, *Everyone Says I Love You,* leave the Allen protagonist unattached and dismal, as do *Celebrity* and *Sweet and Lowdown.*

7. David Ansen noted the influence of *Wild Strawberries* on *Deconstructing Harry* in his review of Christmas 1997 releases. "Season of the Grinch" (review of *Deconstructing Harry*), *Newsweek,* December 22, 1997, p. 85.

8. Harry's two enthusiasms converge in a conversation he has with Cookie Williams, an African-American prostitute. "You know what a black hole is?" he asks her; "Yeah," she replies, "that's how I make my living."

9. Borg's revisitings of his past in Bergman's film precisely anticipate Allen's favorite mode of flashback: in the work of both filmmakers, the character remembering the event is physically present in it, sometimes—as in Borg's meeting with his fiancée, Sara, or Judah's appearance at his father's seder in *Crimes and Misdemeanors*—being able to converse with those occupying the memory.

10. The script's consciousness of its own art/life duplicities is signaled not only through the blurring of Harry's stories and his experiences, but also in his assurance to Fay that "You fell in love with my work—that's a different thing . . . But this is not a book. We're not characters in a fictional thing."

11. The prospect of "growing up" is particularly threatening to Harry because doing so probably means sacrificing what he values most in the world: his attractiveness to women. "Because of my immaturity," he tells a friend, "I have a boyish quality which works for me [with women]."

12. The incessant "whining" of Allen's protagonists which Woodyphobes often cite as a primary objection to his movies is precisely this kind of unrelenting narcissistic self-affirmation: it's the individual self's unyielding, insistent demand that exterior reality respond to its endless demands of "I want," and constitutes his strongest link to the Jewish American literary tradition. Compare the declaration of Stanley Elkin's Push the Bully: "I didn't make myself. I probably can't save myself, but maybe that's the only need I don't have. I taste my lack and that's how I win—by having nothing to lose. It's not good enough. I want and I want and I will die

wanting. . . ." "A Poetics for Bullies" in *Criers & Kibitzers, Kibitzers & Criers* (New York: Random House, 1966), p. 216.

13. Harry's elevator journey into Hell is, like the plot of *Manhattan Murder Mystery*, a vestige of the original Allen/Brickman *Annie Hall* script, including a reprise of the department store-like annunciation of its circles as he descends. *Annie Hall* script: "layer five: organized crime, fascist dictators, and people who don't appreciate oral sex" (Rosenblum and Karen, p. 280); *Deconstructing Harry:* "Floor six: right wing extremists, serial killers, lawyers who appear on television."

14. Frank Gado finds the same Oedipal tension underlying *Wild Strawberries*, quoting Bergman's acknowledgment of his hatred for his father. "Only after overcoming [that hatred]," Bergman argued, "could I, without forcing myself to, talk with him and see that he was a poor old man whom I could take pity on and feel sympathy for." Gado, *The Passion of Ingmar Bergman*, p. 224.

15. "Anhedonia" may have been scrapped as the title of *Annie Hall*, but the condition is seldom absent from the psychological makeups of Allen's protagonists. "For a guy who makes a lot of funny movies," Daisy tells Sandy Bates, "You're kind if depressive, you know?" (*Stardust Memories*, p. 351).

16. *The Purple Rose of Cairo*, p. 440.

17. Allen's choice of a song to soundtrack this scene is truly inspired: as the incipiently unblocked Harry walks in to the celebration, an orchestra is playing "[If They Asked Me] I Could Write a Book."

18. Adam Gopnik's excellent essay on Allen, "The Outsider," makes much of Allen's adoption of Modernist canons: "Just when the *Partisan Review* hierarchy of values, which placed high modernism above all other modes and traditions, was disappearing for good, Woody chose to become the last apostle. He went serious" (p. 90). As I've tried to indicate in these pages, the Woody Allen films I'm delineating often present Modernist aesthetic values as possible sources of affirmation, only to—as in *Deconstructing Harry*—register serious concluding reservations about their validity.

19. John Barth, "Lost in the Funhouse," in *Lost In the Funhouse: Fiction for Print, Tape, Live Voice* (New York: Doubleday, 1968), p. 97.

20. Allen's dissent from the idea that producing children alters this basic human condition is implied in Harry's neglecting to mention that, in addition to a hooker and corpse, he's brought his son to his old school.

21. Lahr, "The Imperfectionist," p. 74.

22. John Updike, "Van Loves Ada, Ada Loves Van," in *Picked-Up Pieces* (New York: Alfred A. Knopf, 1975), p. 202.

23. Barbara Kopple, director, *Wild Man Blues* (Fine Line Films, 1997).

19. From the Neck Up: *Another Woman* and *Celebrity*

1. "An Interview with Woody," p. 67.

2. Allen described the intensification of his relationship with Soon-Yi Farrow Previn in similar terms. "But you fell in love with her?" Walter Isaacson asked. "Yes, yes," Allen responded. "My flair for drama. What can I say?" Isaacson, p. 60.

3. As the *Everyone Says I Love You* chapter suggests, the overhearing of psychoanalytic sessions is a central plot element in both *Another Woman*, in which it functions dramatically, and *Everyone Says I Love You*, where the device serves the comic purposes of Joe Berlin's psychically invasive courtship of Von.

4. Pauline Kael: "The movie is so lucidly constructed it's like a diagram of all the

characters' relationships to each other" (*The New Yorker,* October 31, 1988, p. 81). In his interview with Michiko Kakutani, Allen defended such plots in acknowledging his debt to drama and the novel. "I love the classic narrative form in a play. I love it in the novel. I don't enjoy novels that aren't basically clear stories. . . . when I watch Chekhov or O'Neill, where it's men and women in human, classic crises—that I like." "The Art of Humor," p. 207.

5. At the end of the film, Marion suggests that Lewis's character Helinka is "rumored to be" based on her. This revision may reflect Allen's signal that Marion hasn't merely dreamed the connection between herself and Helinka. And yet, the fact that Marion reads the scene as a reproduction of her and Lewis's most romantic moment together may suggest how badly she wants this work of fiction to confirm her passionate nature.

6. Tim Pulleine, *Monthly Film Bulletin,* August, 1989, p. 232, lauded the movie; David Sterritt, *Christian Science Monitor,* October 17, 1988, p. 23, slammed it.

7. Richard A. Blake, (review of *Another Woman*), *America* 159 (December 17, 1988), p. 517.

8. Lax, p. 179.

9. Ibid., p. 28.

10. The soundtrack song repeatedly elicited by Charlize Theron's appearances is Billie Holiday's "Did I Remember," whose refrain—"did I remember to tell you I adore you?"—takes on an aura of Hollywood insincerity when associated with this quintessential media creation. Lest the viewer miss the fact in Allen's assessment of this character, he has the supermodel—like Sam in *Husbands and Wives* babbling mindlessly about the zodiac—express an interest in horoscopes.

11. "You see, I was lucky," Allen told William Geist. "I was lucky in that I had a talent to be amusing. If I didn't have that talent, I'd have been in great peril. You can only be independent that way if you luck out. But you can't count on it." Geist, p. 218.

12. Providing his writer/protagonists with personal computers would have cost Allen central elements of two plots: the single copy of a novel manuscript figures in both *Husbands and Wives* (Rain leaves Gabe's novel in a taxi) and in *Celebrity.* Harry Block is depicted in the last scene of *Deconstructing Harry* pounding away at a portable typewriter, his reliance on early twentieth-century technology replicating his creator's preferences.

13. Roger Ebert, review of *Celebrity, Chicago Sun-Times,* November 11, 1998.

20. Allen and His Audience: *Sweet and Lowdown*

1. Bjorkman, p. 47.

2. Shales, "Woody: The First Fifty Years," p. 90. Twenty years of Allen's objections to the confusion of Sandy Bates with himself notwithstanding, the critical tendency to read Woody through Sandy survives. In *The Unruly Life of Woody Allen* (New York: Scribner, 2000), a biography published too late to contribute to this study, Marion Meade speculated, "As for his feelings about us [the audience], the question appeared to be curiously answered in *Stardust Memories,* in which he painted his affectionate fans as ghouls. That didn't mean we abandoned him. Instead, we automatically struggled to understand the wretchedness which drove him" (p. 18).

3. Gopnik, "The Outsider," p. 91.

4. Shales, p. 90.

5. DeCurtis, "The *Rolling Stone* Interview: Woody Allen," p. 50.

6. Lax, pp. 370–71.

7. Shales, p. 94.

8. Bjorkman, p. 103.

9. Ibid., p. 96.

10. Allen has obviously enjoyed the mildly masochistic process of self-scurrilization which

has generated post-scandal protagonists Harry Block, Lee Simon in *Celebrity*, and Emmet Ray, these characters representing a manifest improvement over the bland condo dwellers Allen scripted and portrayed in *Manhattan Murder Mystery* and *Mighty Aphrodite* in what some interpreted as an attempt on Allen's part to recuperate his public image. In "Scuzzballs Like Us," Jonathan Romney offers a less positive estimation of *Deconstructing Harry*'s protagonist, which Romney describes as being "as close to dammit to being *explicitly* the dark side of Woody" (*Sight and Sound*, April 1999, p. 12).

11. Woody Allen, *Sweet and Lowdown*, Sony Pictures Classics, 1999.

12. Jazz guitarist Howard Alden contributed to Penn's creation of Emmet not only through performing "I'm Forever Blowing Bubbles," "I'll See You in My Dreams," and the other 1930s standards which constitute Emmet's early repertoire, but also by coaching Penn in reproducing the fingerings of a master guitarist so that he might offer a passable imitation of a musician capable of Reinhardtlike fretboard virtuosity. Alden is accompanied by Bucky Pizzarelli, rhythm guitar, Kelly Friesen, bass, Ken Peplowski, clarinet, and Ted Sommer, drums. The film's music was conducted and arranged by Dick Hyman, who provided Allen's films with original songs and updated renditions of American popular standards from *Zelig* forward.

13. Elizabeth Gleick, "Her Silence Is Golden," *Time*, December 6, 1999.

14. Amy Taubin ("Sean Penn's High Wire Act: Wisconsin Gothic," *The Village Voice*, December 1–7, 1999, p. 89) argues that "Though [Samantha] Morton never cloys, Allen's misogyny vis-à-vis this character is so blatant that it almost defies mention." Lisa Schwarzbaum (*EW* Online, December 3, 1999) makes her review an occasion for sending Soon-Yi Allen a warning: "And may I repeat, the woman Ray loves truest is an enthralled MUTE who's as simply satisfied as an adopted child, demanding nothing more than a sandwich and a shred of attention? Soon-Yi, honey, Morton carries off the premise because she's capable of wordless eloquence, but for pity's sake, don't let your husband get away with all that jazz."

15. Stephanie Zacharek's *Salon* review of the *Sweet and Lowdown* (December 3, 1999) similarly identified Hattie with the artist's audience: "She's a metaphor for the idea that even for the most brilliant musician, it's the listener who completes the equation."

16. "I would never do anything to curry favor with the audience. When I put out a film, if you asked me, I would say I much prefer that people like it, and that they laugh at it and enjoy it. If they don't, they don't, but I'm certainly not going to change the film or do anything to make them like it. Or reject an idea because I know up front it's too dark or inaccessible or something. But I always prefer them to like it between the two choices." Pamela Harland and Jenny Peters, "The Sweet and Lowdown from Woody Allen on his New Film . . . ," *if* magazine 10.3 (December 23, 1999).

17. F. Scott Fitzgerald, *Tender is the Night* (New York: Charles Scribner's Sons, 1934), p. 315.

18. *Salon*, n.p.

19. Harland and Peters, n.p.

20. Michael Wood, "A Kind of Slither" (review of *The Unruly Life of Woody Allen* by Marion Meade), *London Review of Books*, 27 April 2000, p. 3.

21. "'Sweet and Lowdown': Jazz, Out of the Shadows and Into the Spotlight," *New York Times*, December 3, 1999.

Bibliography

Adair, Gilbert. Review of *Broadway Danny Rose*. *Monthly Film Bulletin* (September, 1984), p. 272.

Allen, Woody. *Alice*. Orion Pictures, 1990.

———. *Annie Hall*. United Artists, 1977.

———. *Another Woman*. Orion Pictures, 1988.

———. "Attention Geniuses: Cash Only." *The New Yorker* (February 21 and 28, 2000), pp. 148–52.

———. *Broadway Danny Rose*. Orion Pictures, 1984.

———. *Bullets Over Broadway*. Miramax, 1995.

———. *Celebrity*. Miramax, 1998.

———. *Crimes and Misdemeanors*. Orion Pictures, 1989.

———. *Deconstructing Harry*. Fine Line Features, 1997.

———. *Everyone Says I Love You*. Miramax Films, 1996.

———. *Four Films of Woody Allen*. New York: Random House, 1982.

———. *Getting Even*. New York: Vintage Books. 1978.

———. *Hannah and Her Sisters*. New York: Vintage Books, 1987.

———. *Husbands and Wives*. Columbia TriStar, 1992.

———. *Interiors*. MGM Home Video, 1978.

———. *Midsummer Night's Sex Comedy, A*. Warner Home Video, 1982.

———. *Mighty Aphrodite*. Miramax Films, 1995.

———. "My Secret Life with Bogart." *Life* (March 21, 1969), pp. 64–67.

———. "Oedipus Wrecks." *New York Stories*. Touchstone Home Video, 1989.

———. *Play It Again, Sam*. Paramount Home Video, 1980.

———. *The Purple Rose of Cairo*. Orion Pictures, 1985.

———. *Radio Days*. Orion Pictures, 1987.

———. *Radio Days*. Studio City, Hollywood: Hollywood Scripts, n.d.

———. "Random Reflections of a Second-Rate Mind." *Tikkun: A Bimonthly Jewish Critique of Politics, Culture and Society* (January/February 1990), pp. 13–15, 71–72.

———. *September*. Orion Pictures, 1987.

———. *Shadows and Fog*. Orion Pictures, 1992.

———. *Side Effects*. New York: Ballantine Books, 1981.

———. *Sweet and Lowdown*. Sony Pictures Classics, 1999.

———. *Three Films of Woody Allen*. New York: Random House, 1987.

———. "Through a Life Darkly." *The New York Times Book Review* (September 18, 1988), pp. 1, 29–30, 34.

———. *Without Feathers*. New York: Ballantine Books, 1983.

———. *Woody Allen: Standup Comic*. Casablanca Records, 1978.

———. *Zelig*. Orion Pictures, 1983.

Allen, Woody and Douglas McGrath. *Bullets Over Broadway*. Studio City, Hollywood: Hollywood Scripts, n.d.

Allison, Terry L. and Renee R. Curry. "Frame Breaking and Code Breaking in Woody Allen's Relationship Films." *Perspectives on Woody Allen,* ed. Renee R. Curry. New York: G.K. Hall, 1996, pp. 121–36.

Ames, Christopher. *Movies About the Movies*. Lexington: The University Press of Kentucky, 1997.

Ansen, David. "Dancing Chic to Chic" (review of *Everyone Says I Love You*). *Newsweek* (December 9, 1996), p. 82.

————. "Woody: The Movie" (review of *Husbands and Wives*). *Newsweek* (September 21, 1992), p. 76.

————. "Season of the Grinch." *Newsweek* (December 22, 1997), p. 85.

Barth, John. "Lost in the Funhouse." *Lost in the Funhouse: Fiction for Print, Tape, Live Voice.* New York: Doubleday, 1968.

Barthelme, Donald. *Come Back, Dr. Caligari.* New York: Little, Brown, 1964.

Baxter, John. *Woody Allen: A Biography.* London: Harper Collins, 1998.

Baumbach, Jonathan. "The Comedians." *Commonweal* (March 23, 1984), pp. 182–83.

Beattie, Ann. "Snow." *Where You'll Find Me.* New York: Linden Press/Simon & Schuster, 1986.

Bellow, Saul. *Herzog.* New York: Viking Press, 1964.

————. *Mr. Sammler's Planet.* New York: Viking Press, 1970.

Benayoun, Robert. *The Films of Woody Allen.* Translated by Alexander Walker. New York: Harmony Books, 1985.

Berkow, Ira. "From Defense to Offense." *The New York Times* (November 2, 1995), C, p. 1.

Bernstein, Mashey. "My Worst Fears Realized: Woody Allen and the Holocaust." *Perspectives on Woody Allen,* ed. Renee R. Curry. New York: G.K. Hall & Company, 1996, pp. 218–36.

Bernstein, Walter. *The Front.* Columbia Pictures, 1976.

Bjorkman, Stig. *Woody Allen on Woody Allen.* New York: Grove Press, 1993.

Blake, Richard A. *Woody Allen: Sacred and Profane.* Lanham, Maryland: Scarecrow Press, 1995.

Brode, Douglas. *The Films of Woody Allen.* New York: Citadel Press, 1992.

Brown, Georgia, "Biting Bullets" (review of *Bullets Over Broadway*). *The Village Voice* (October 18, 1994), p. 54.

Canby, Vincent. "'Danny Rose': Runyonesque, But Pure Woody Allen" (review of *Broadway Danny Rose*). *The New York Times* (January 29, 1984), II, 13, 1.

Carroll, Tim. *Woody and His Women.* London: Warner Books, 1994.

Carver, Raymond. *Where I'm Calling From: New and Selected Stories.* New York: Atlantic Monthly Press, 1988.

Cohen, Sarah Blacher. "Jewish Literary Comediennes." *Comic Relief: Humor in Contemporary American Literature.* Urbana: University of Illinois Press, 1978, pp. 172–86.

Combs, Richard. Review of *Radio Days. Monthly Film Bulletin* (July, 1987), p. 212.

Cowie, Peter. *BFI Film Classics: Annie Hall.* London: British Film Institute, 1996.

De Curtis, Anthony. "The *Rolling Stone* Interview: Woody Allen." *Rolling Stone* (September 16, 1993), pp. 45–50, 78–82.

De Navacelle, Thierry. *Woody Allen on Location.* New York: William Morrow, 1987.

Denby, David. "Amateur Hour" (review of *Everyone Says I Love You*). *New York* (December 9, 1996), p. 72.

————. "Fogged In" (review of *Husbands and Wives*). *New York* (March 30, 1992), p. 60.

————. "Guy and Doll" (review of *Broadway Danny Rose*). *New York* (February 6, 1984), p. 64.

————. "Beyond Good and Evil" (review of *Crimes and Misdemeanors*). *New York* (October 29, 1989), p. 124.

————. "Imitation of Life" (review of *Husbands and Wives*). *New York* (September 21, 1992), p. 60.

————. "Rear Hallway" (review of *Manhattan Murder Mystery*). *New York* (August 23, 1993), p. 57.

————. "Woe Unto Woody" (review of *Mighty Aphrodite*). *New York* (October 30, 1995), pp. 108, 136.

Didion, Joan, "Letter from Los Angeles" (review of *Annie Hall, Interiors,* and *Manhattan*). *New York Review of Books* (August 16, 1979), p. 18.

Dowd, Maureen. "Auteur as Spin Doctor." *The New York Times* (Sunday, October 1, 1995), D, p. 13.

———. "The Five Women of *Hannah and Her Sisters*." *New York Times,* January 2, 1986, II, pp. 1, 23.

Dowell, Pat. "Woody's Effort to Reconstruct Himself." *Cineaste* XXIII, 3 (1998), pp. 35–36.

Dresner, Samuel H. "Woody Allen and the Jews." *Perspectives on Woody Allen,* ed. Renee R. Curry. New York: G.K. Hall & Company, 1996, pp. 188–97.

Dresser, David and Lester D. Friedman. *American Jewish Filmmakers: Trends and Traditions.* Urbana: University of Illinois Press, 1993.

Ebert, Roger. Review of *Celebrity. Chicago Sun-Times* (November 11, 1998).

Edelstein, David. "Easy Listening" (review of *Radio Days). The Village Voice* (February 3, 1987), p. 53.

Elkin, Stanley. "A Poetics for Bullies." *Criers & Kibitzers, Kibitzers & Criers.* New York: Random House, 1966.

———. *The Living End.* New York: Dutton, 1979.

Exley, Frederick. *A Fan's Notes.* New York: Harper & Row, 1968.

Farrow, Mia. *What Falls Away.* New York: Doubleday, 1997.

Feldstein, Richard. "Displaced Female Representation in Woody Allen's Cinema." *Discontented Discourses: Feminism/Textual Intervention/Psychoanalysis,* ed. Marleen S. Barr and Richard Feldstein. Urbana: University of Illinois Press, 1989, pp. 68–83.

Fitzgerald, F. Scott. *Tender Is the Night.* New York: Scribner's, 1934.

———. "The Ice Palace." *Babylon Revisited and Other Stories.* New York: Charles Scribner's Sons, 1960.

Fox, Julian. *Woody: Movies from Manhattan.* Woodstock, New York: Overlook Press, 1996.

Freadman, Richard. "Love Among the Stereotypes, or Why Woody's Women Leave." *Semites and Stereotypes: Characteristics of Jewish Humor,* ed. Avvner Ziv and Anat Zajdman. Westport, Connecticut: Greenwood Press, 1993, pp. 107–20.

Gado, Frank. *The Passion of Ingmar Bergman.* Durham, North Carolina: Duke University Press, 1986.

Geist, William E. "Interview with Woody Allen." *Rolling Stone Interviews: The 1980s,* ed. Sid Holt. New York: St. Martin's Press, 1989.

Gelmis, Joseph. Review of *Broadway Danny Rose. Newsday* (January 27, 1984), II, p. 3.

Girgus, Sam B. *The Films of Woody Allen.* Cambridge: Cambridge University Press, 1993.

———. "Philip Roth and Woody Allen: Freud and the Humor of the Repressed." *Semites and Stereotypes: Characteristics of Jewish Humor,* ed. Avner Ziv and Anat Zajdman. Westport, Connecticut: Greenwood Press, 1993, pp. 121–30.

Gittelson, Natalie. "The Maturing of Woody Allen." *The New York Times Magazine* (April 22, 1979), pp. 30–32, 102–5.

Gleick, Elizabeth. "Her Silence Is Golden." *Time* (December 6, 1999).

Gopnik, Adam. "The Outsider." *The New Yorker* (October 23, 1993), pp. 87–93.

Green, Daniel. "The Comedian's Dilemma." *Literature/Film Quarterly* (Fall, 1991), pp. 71–76.

Groteke, Kristi with Marjorie Rosen. *Mia and Woody: Love and Betrayal.* New York: Carroll and Graf, 1994.

Guthrie, Lee. *Woody Allen: A Biography.* New York: Drake Publishers, 1978.

Harland, Pamela, and Jenny Peters. "The *Sweet and Lowdown* from Woody Allen on His New Film . . ." *if* magazine 10.3 (December 23, 1999).

Hirsch, Foster. *Love, Sex, Death, and the Meaning of Life: Woody Allen's Comedy.* New York: McGraw-Hill, 1981.

Hirschorn, Michael. "Woody Sings" (review of *Everyone Says I Love You). New York* (September 9, 1996), pp. 49–53.

Hoban, Phoebe. "Everything You Always Wanted to Know About Woody and Mia (But Were Afraid to Ask)." *New York* (September 21, 1992), pp. 32–41.

Hoberman, J. "Just Desserts" (review of *Crimes and Misdemeanors*). *The Village Voice* (October 17, 1989), p. 87.

Irving, John. *The World According to Garp*. New York: Dutton, 1978.

Isaacson, Walter. "The Heart Wants What It Wants." *Time* (August 31, 1992), pp. 59–61.

Jacobs, Diane. *. . . but we need the eggs: The Magic of Woody Allen*. New York: St. Martin's Press, 1982.

James, Nick. Review of *Mighty Aphrodite*. *Sight and Sound* (April, 1996), pp. 48–49.

Johnson, Brian. "Constant Cravings" (review of *Mighty Aphrodite*). *Maclean's* (October 20, 1995), p. 27.

Kael, Pauline. *Hooked*. New York: E. Dutton, 1989.

———. *For Keeps*. New York: E. Dutton, 1994.

———. *Movie Love*. New York: E. Dutton, 1991.

———. *State of the Art*. New York: E. Dutton, 1985.

Kakutani, Michiko. "Woody Allen: The Art of Humor I." *The Paris Review* 136 (Fall, 1996), pp. 200–22.

Kauffman, Stanley. "The Food of Love" (review of *Everyone Says I Love You*). *The New Republic* (November 11, 1996), p. 40.

———. "Return of a Trouble" (review of *Manhattan Murder Mystery*). *New Republic* (November 27, 1995), p. 30.

Kemp, Philip. Review of *Manhattan Murder Mystery*. *Sight and Sound* 2 (February 2, 1994), p. 51.

Kerbel, Michael. "The Redemptive Power of Art." *Cineaste* XXIII, 3 (1998), pp. 36–37.

Koppel, Barbara. *Wild Man Blues*. Fine Line Features, 1997.

Knox, Bernard. *Oedipus at Thebes: Sophocles' Tragic Hero and His Time*. New York: W.W. Norton, 1971.

Kroll, Jack. "The Inner Woody." *Newsweek* (August 7, 1983), p. 72.

———. "Comedy 50, Tragedy 50" (review of *Crimes and Misdemeanors*). *Newsweek* (October 16, 1989), p. 67.

———. "Woody's Bow to Broadway" (review of *Broadway Danny Rose*). *Newsweek* (January 30, 1984), p. 69.

Lahr, John. "The Imperfectionist." *The New Yorker* (December 9, 1996), pp. 68–83.

Lane, Anthony. "Scarlet Women" (review of *Mighty Aphrodite*). *The New Yorker* (October 30, 1995), pp. 112–13.

Lax, Eric. *Woody Allen: A Biography*. New York: Alfred A. Knopf, 1991.

McCann, Graham. *Woody Allen: New Yorker*. Cambridge, England: Polity Press, 1990.

McCarthy, Todd. "Tin Pan Allen" (review of *Everyone Says I Love You*). *Premiere* (January, 1997), p. 46.

McGrady, Mike. "Getting Away with Murder, Woody Allen Style" (review of *Crimes and Misdemeanors*). *Newsday* (October 13, 1989), III, p. 3.

Martin, Jay. *Who Am I This Time?* New York: W.W. Norton, 1988.

Maslin, Janet. "A Greek Chorus Warns, But Does Allen Take Heed?" (review of *Mighty Aphrodite*). *The New York Times* (October 27, 1995), C, p. 1.

———. "*Sweet and Lowdown*: Jazz Out of the Shadows and into the Spotlight." *New York Times*, December 3, 1999.

———. "When Everyone Sings, Just for the Joy of It" (review of *Everyone Says I Love You*). *The New York Times* (December 6, 1996), III, p. 1.

Mast, Gerald. "Woody Allen: The Neurotic Jew as American Clown," in *Jewish Wry: Essays on Jewish Humor*, ed. Sarah Blacher Cohen. Detroit: Wayne State University Press, 1987, pp. 125–40.

Mathews, Jack. "Too True, Too True" (review of *Husbands and Wives*). *Newsday* (September 18, 1992), II, p. 67.

Meade, Marion. *The Unruly Life of Woody Allen*. New York: Scribner's, 2000.

Merkin, Daphne. "Comedy on Three Levels" (review of *Broadway Danny Rose*). *New Leader* (March 5, 1984), pp. 19–20.

Nehamas, Alexander. *Nietzsche: Life as Literature*. Cambridge: Harvard Univ. Press, 1985.

Nichols, Mary P. *Reconstructing Woody: Art, Love and Life in the Films of Woody Allen*. Lanham, Maryland: Rowman & Littlefield, 1998.

Nuecterlein, James, Eugene Borowitz and Mary Erler. "Woody Allen Counts the Wages of Sin." *The New York Times* (October 15, 1979), III, pp. 15, 20, 22.

Ozick, Cynthia. "Saul Bellow's Broadway." *Fame and Folly*. New York: Alfred A. Knopf, 1996.

Pally, Marcia. "The Cinema as Secular Religion." *Cineaste* XXIII, 3 (1998), pp. 32–33.

Pogel, Nancy. *Woody Allen*. Boston: Twayne Publishers, 1987.

Preussner, Arnold. "Woody Allen's *The Purple Rose of Cairo* and the Genres of Comedy." *Literature/Film Quarterly* 16, 1 (1988), pp. 39–43.

Pym, John. Review of *Broadway Danny Rose*. *Sight and Sound* (Autumn, 1984), 300.

Quart, Leonard. "Woody Allen's Reflexive Critics." *Cineaste* XXIII, 3 (1998), pp. 34–35.

Rafferty, Terrence. "Getting Old" (review of *Husbands and Wives*). *The New Yorker* (September 21, 1992), pp. 102–5.

Rainer, Peter. "There's an Art to Allen's Shots at 'Broadway'" (review of *Bullets Over Broadway*). *Los Angeles Times* (October 21, 1994), F, pp. 1.

Rapping, Elayne. "A Feminist's Love/Hate Relationship with Woody." *Cineaste* XXIII, 3 (1998), pp. 37–38.

Rich, Frank. "An Interview with Woody." *Time* (April 30, 1979), pp. 67–69.

Romney, Jonathan. "Scuzzballs Like Us." *Sight and Sound* (April, 1999), 12–14.

Rosenblum, Ralph and Robert Karen. *When the Shooting Stops . . . the Cutting Begins*. New York: Penguin Books, 1979.

Rubin, Sam and Richard Taylor. *Mia: Flowerchild, Madonna, Muse*. New York: St. Martin's Press, 1989.

Sarris, Andrew. Review of *Broadway Danny Rose*. *The Village Voice* (February 7, 1984), p. 47.

Schickel, Richard. "Postscript to the '80s" (review of *Crimes and Misdemeanors*). *Time* (October 16, 1989), p. 82.

———. "Just Funny Isn't Enough" (review of *Manhattan Murder Mystery)* *Time* (August 23, 1993), p. 67.

———. "Now Playing at the Jewel" (review of *Purple Rose of Cairo*). *Time* (March 4, 1985), p. 78.

———. "Dream Machine" (review of *Radio Days*). *Time* (February 2, 1987), p. 73.

———. "Return to Weimar" (review of *Shadows and Fog*). *Time* (March 23, 1992), p. 65.

———. "They Sorta Got Rhythm" (review of *Everyone Says I Love You*). *Time* (December 9, 1996), p. 81.

———. "The Wages of Fame" (review of *Celebrity*). *Time* (November 16, 1998).

———. "Woody Allen Comes of Age." *Time* (April 30, 1979), pp. 62–65.

Schneller, Johanna. "Woody Allen." *US* 229 (February 1997), pp. 46–50, 114.

Schwarzbaum, Lisa. Review of *Sweet and Lowdown*. *EW Online* (December 3, 1999).

———. "Woody Sings!" (review of *Everyone Says I Love You*). *Entertainment Weekly* (December 20, 1996), p. 74.

Shales, Tom. "Woody Allen: The First 50 Years." *Esquire* (April, 1987), p. 88–95.

Shechner, Mark. "Jewish Writers." *Harvard Guide to Contemporary American Writing*. Cambridge, Massachusetts: Harvard University Press, 1979, pp. 191–239.

———. "Woody Allen and the Failure of the Therapeutic." *From Hester Street to Hollywood,* ed. Sarah Blacher Cohen. Bloomington: Indiana University Press, 1983, pp. 231–44.

Shelley, Percy Bysshe. *The Selected Prose and Poetry of Percy Bysshe Shelley,* ed. Carlos Baker. New York: Modern Library, 1951.

Siegal, Mark. "Ozymandias Melancholia: The Nature of Parody in Woody Allen's *Stardust Memories.*" *Literature/Film Quarterly* 13, 2 (1985), pp. 76–83,

Sinyard, Neil. *The Films of Woody Allen.* New York: Exeter Books, 1987.

Stevens, Wallace. "The Idea of Order at Key West." *The Collected Poems of Wallace Stevens.* New York: Alfred K. Knopf, 1954.

Steuer, Joseph. "Woody Allen: A Celebrity in Spite of Himself." *Indie* (September/October 1998), pp. 14–15, 38–39.

Sunshine, Linda. *The Illustrated Woody Allen Reader.* New York: Knopf, 1993.

Taubin, Amy. "Sean Penn's High Wire Act" (review of *Sweet and Lowdown*). *The Village Voice* (December 1–7, 1999), 89.

Travers, Peter. "Everything Old is New Again" (review of *Everyone Says I Love You*). *Rolling Stone* (February 20, 1997), p. 96.

Trilling, Lionel. "Reality in America." *The Liberal Imagination.* New York: Charles Scribner's Sons, 1976.

Turan, Kenneth. "Beyond the Gossip, Now the Movie" (review of *Husbands and Wives*). *Los Angeles Times* (September 18, 1992), F, p. 1.

Tutt, Ralph. "Truth, Beauty and Travesty": Woody Allen's Well-Wrought Urn." *Literature/Film Quarterly* 19/2 (1991), pp. 104–8.

Updike, John. "More Love in the Western World" (review of *Love Declaired* by Denis de Rougemont). *Assorted Prose.* New York: Knopf, 1965.

———. "Van Loves Ada, Ada Loves Van." *Picked-Up Pieces.* New York: Alfred A. Knopf, 1975, pp. 199–210.

Welsh, James M. Review of *Manhattan Murder Mystery. Films in Review* (November/December, 1993), p. 413.

Wernblad, Annette. *Brooklyn Is Not Expanding: Woody Allen's Comic Universe.* Rutherford, New Jersey: Fairleigh Dickinson University Press, 1992.

Wilde, Alan. *Horizons of Assent: Modernism, Postmodernism and the Ironic Imagination.* Baltimore: Johns Hopkins Univ. Press, 1981.

Whitfield, Stephen J. "Laughter in the Dark: Notes on American-Jewish Humor." *Critical Essays on Philip Roth,* ed. Sanford Pinsker. Boston: G.K. Hall, 1982.

Williams, Tennessee. *The Glass Menagerie.* New York: New Directions, 1966.

Wood, Michael. "A Kind of Slither" (review of *The Unruly Life of Woody Allen* by Marion Meade). *London Review of Books* (27 April 2000), 3.

Woolf, Virginia. *To the Lighthouse.* New York: Harcourt Brace Jovanovich, 1955.

Yacowar, Maurice. *Loser Take All: The Comic Art of Woody Allen.* New York: Frederic Unger, 1979.

Yalom, Irwin. *When Nietzsche Wept.* New York: Basic Books, 1992.

Yeats, William Butler. "The Second Coming." *Selected Poems and Two Plays of William Butler Yeats,* ed. M.L. Rosenthal. New York: Collier Books, 1962.

Zacharek, Stephanie. Review of *Sweet and Lowdown. Salon* (December 3, 1999).

Zimmerman, Bernhard. *Greek Tragedy: An Introduction,* trans. Thomas Marier. Baltimore: Johns Hopkins University Press, 1991.

Zinsser, William K. "Bright New Comic Clowns Toward Success." *Saturday Evening Post* (September 21, 1963), pp. 26–27.

Index